Jean-Luc Godard's Political Filmmaking

Irmgard Emmelhainz

Jean-Luc Godard's Political Filmmaking

palgrave
macmillan

Irmgard Emmelhainz
Independent scholar
Mexico City, Mexico

ISBN 978-3-319-72094-4   ISBN 978-3-319-72095-1 (eBook)
https://doi.org/10.1007/978-3-319-72095-1

Library of Congress Control Number: 2018939752

© The Editor(s) (if applicable) and The Author(s) 2019
This work is subject to copyright. All rights are solely and exclusively licensed by the Publisher, whether the whole or part of the material is concerned, specifically the rights of translation, reprinting, reuse of illustrations, recitation, broadcasting, reproduction on microfilms or in any other physical way, and transmission or information storage and retrieval, electronic adaptation, computer software, or by similar or dissimilar methodology now known or hereafter developed.
The use of general descriptive names, registered names, trademarks, service marks, etc. in this publication does not imply, even in the absence of a specific statement, that such names are exempt from the relevant protective laws and regulations and therefore free for general use.
The publisher, the authors and the editors are safe to assume that the advice and information in this book are believed to be true and accurate at the date of publication. Neither the publisher nor the authors or the editors give a warranty, express or implied, with respect to the material contained herein or for any errors or omissions that may have been made. The publisher remains neutral with regard to jurisdictional claims in published maps and institutional affiliations.

Cover design by Jenny Vong

This Palgrave Macmillan imprint is published by the registered company Springer Nature Switzerland AG.
The registered company address is: Gewerbestrasse 11, 6330 Cham, Switzerland

Acknowledgments

Earlier versions of some chapters or parts of chapters, which I have fully updated and in most cases substantially developed and expanded, were originally published in the following: "From Thirdworldism to Empire: Jean-Luc Godard and the Palestine Question," *Third Text*, Vol. 23, no 5, 2009, pp. 659–656; "Between Objective Engagement and Objective Cinema: Jean-Luc Godard's 'militant filmmaking' (1967–1974)," *e-flux journal* no. 34, April 2012; and *e-flux journal*, no. 35, May 2012); "Jean-Luc Godard: To Liberate Things from the Name We have Imposed on Them (*Film*…) to Announce Dissonances Parting from a Note in Common (*Socialisme*)," in *A Companion to Jean-Luc Godard*, ed. Tom Conley and Jeff Kline (Oxford: Wiley-Blackwell, 2014); "Trademark Images and Perception: Godard, Deleuze and Montage", *Nierika, Revista de estudios de arte*, Vol. 5, May 2014, "Conditions of Visuality Under the Anthropocene," *e-flux journal* no. 63, March 2015; "Self-Destruction as Insubmission Or How to Lift the Earth Above All That is Dying?" *e-flux journal* no. 87, December 2017; "Militant Cinema: from Third Worldism to Neoliberal Sensible Politics," *Furia umana* no. 33, 2018.

I am indebted to Alejandra Barrera, Jeroen Verbeeck, David Faroult, Will Straw, Edward Smith, Pedro Reyes and Michael Witt, for helping me gain access to material that was key for completing this book and difficult to access from Mexico City. To Gretchen Bakke for her help in putting together the book project. To Rebecca Comay, Peter Fitting and John Ricco at the University of Toronto, who inspired and enriched it in many different ways. I thank at the end of this journey those who made it more bearable, exciting and supported it unwaveringly. In Toronto, Eshrat and

Jeevan Erfanian, Bruce Parsons, Rosa Macip, Romi Mikulinski, Etienne Turpin, Alessandra Renzi, Christine Shaw, John Greyson and B. H. Yael. From Mexico, Miguel Ventura, Silvia Gruner, Fausto Esparza, Pilar Reyes, Helga Kaiser, Iliana Padilla, Ana Paola Frías, Jimena Acosta, Karen Cordero Reimann and Stephen Vollmer. Elsewhere: Shay de Grandis, Margaret Schlubach-Rueping, Maria José Bruña, Mélanie Potevin, Thierry de Duve, Nora Adwan, Kiffah Fanni, Mikki Kratsman, Haggai Matar, Matan Kaminer, Katie Miranda, Khadijeh Habashneh, Mustapha Abu Ali, Majd Abdel Hamid and Sally Abu Bakr. Nathalie Khankhan, Romi Mikulinski and Etienne Turpin read the earliest drafts of this work and contributed to it with invaluable feedback. Tom Williams' brilliant insights and editorial comments shed light not only on earlier versions but on the project as a whole. Finally, to Layla García and Lizzy Cancino, who are there for me every day.

Contents

1 **Introduction**   1
   Representation and Its Crisis   10
   Representativity and Authorship   15
   Conditions of Visuality/Les Signes Parmi Nous   20
   Bibliography   29

2 **Who Speaks *Here*? Jean-Luc Godard's 'Militant Filmmaking' (1967–74)**   31
   Jean-Luc Godard's Avant-Garde   31
   Art, Realism, Spectacle: Aragon and Debord   37
   Committed Positions: André Breton and Jean-Paul Sartre   40
   Maoism and the Dziga Vertov Group   49
   Materialist Filmmaking and Materialist Fictions   55
   Realism, Materialist Filmmaking and Materialist Fictions   62
   The Capture of Speech and Le Vent d'Est   67
   Guernica *and* Ici et Ailleurs, *1974*   74
   Bibliography   81

3 ***Elsewhere*: Dialogue of Points of View: Jean-Luc Godard and *Tiersmondisme***   87
   The Third World in European Eyes   87
   Godard's Tiersmondisme   92

Radical Tourism and the Palestinian Revolution: Jusqu'à la
Victoire 96
From Jusqu'à la Victoire *to* Ici et Ailleurs 100
Sonimage and Anxiety of Blindness 104
*Sonimage, the Carnation Revolution and the Newly Independent
Mozambique* 111
*Comment Changer d'Image/Montrer une Image du
Changement?* 116
Bibliography 122

4 **Technique and Montage: Saying, Seeing and Showing
the Invisible** 127
Materialist Filmmaking and Spectacle 127
Toward New Forms of the Political 131
*How to See and to Provide A Means to See? Cinematic Voice and
the Regime of Enunciation* 135
Technique and Video: An Epistemology of Seeing 140
Brand Images 142
Perception, History and Montage 152
Appropriation, Stoppage, Défilé 161
Passion *and* Le Rapport Darty: *Materialist Filmmaking,* Encore 168
Bibliography 173

5 **Representing the Unrepresentable: Restitution, Archive,
Memory** 177
Witness-Images, Alienated Subjectivities and Restitution 177
*Representation and the Shoah: Forbidden Images, Forbidden
Montage, Forbidden Testimony* 183
*The Wars of Annihilation/Memory and Resistance Against War
and the Reign of Fear* 198
The Image Has Been Covered by Text 208
From Speaking in the Name of Others to a Simple Conversation 218
Shot/Reverse-Shot 225
Annihilation, the "Pure Past" and Phaedra 227
The Memory of the Film 234
Apology of the Vanquished for their Loss 238
Our Music 242
Bibliography 246

6 **Conditions of Visuality and Materialist Film at the Turn of the Twenty-First Century** 253
  Dialectical Materialist Film-making in Film Socialisme 259
  The Exhaustion of the Imaginary 264
  Sensible Memory in Film Socialisme 269
  Nos Humanités 272
  Adieu au Langage *or Film as Metaphor* 281
  Bibliography 291

7 **Conclusion: The Legacy of Militant Filmmaking or How to Rise Above Everything That Is Dying?** 295
  Bibliography 306

Index 309

CHAPTER 1

Introduction

Nothing happens in tragedies today … The curtain is drawn, both poets and audience have left – there are no cedars or processions, no olive branches to greet those coming in by boat, weary from nosebleed and the lightness of the final act, as if passing from one fate to another, a fate written beyond the text, a woman of Greece playing the part of a woman of Troy, as easily white as black, neither broken nor exalted, and no one asks: "What will happen in the morning?" "What comes after this Homeric pause?"
… as if this were a lovely dream in which prisoners of war are relieved by fairness of their long, immediate night, as if they now say: "We mend our wounds with salt," "We live near our memory," "We shall try out an ordinary death," "We wait for resurrection, here, in its home in the chapter that comes after the last …"
Mahmoud Darwish. (Excerpt from "No Flag Flutters in the Wind," from his collection *Now as you Awaken*, translated from the Arabic by Omnia Amin and Rick London (Pacifica: Big Bridge Press, 2006))

L'esprit emprunte à la matière les perceptions d'où il tire sa nourriture, et les lui rend sous forme de mouvement, où il a imprimé sa liberté.

Henri Bergson[1]

---

[1] "Spirit borrows from matter the perceptions on which it feeds, and restores them to matter in the form of movement which it has imprinted with its own freedom." This is the last sentence of Henri Bergson's *Matière et mémoire. Essai sur la relation du corps à l'esprit* (1939). Available at http://classiques.uqac.ca/classiques/bergson_henri/matiere_et_memoire/matiere_et_memoire.pdf. English translation: *Matter and Memory* (New York: Dover Publications, 2004), p. 332.

Vladimir Lenin predicted that the background of the twentieth century would be wars and revolutions and thus the world's common denominator would be violence.[2] Taking Lenin's statement further, and in historical materialist terms, Hannah Arendt argued in 1969 that revolutionary violence had brought history to a standstill worldwide as opposed to accelerating historical progress toward its completion. "The Revolution" had been Western Modernity's hegemonic referent and discourse within Leftist intellectual culture. As a discursive container, "Revolution" became retroactively the fatal harbinger of terror and totalitarianism. With the increased prevalence of this casual arithmetic (Revolution + Realization = Totalitarianism), the enthusiasm for any potential human emancipation or redemptive change waned,[3] or became its own cause for suspicion. Despite attempts to ideologize, depoliticize and aestheticize, and accusations of Eurocentrism, conservatism and classicism, Jean-Luc Godard's work follows the educated, liberal and positivist tradition of radical Western leftist intellectuals engaged with proclaiming and helping to advance the Modernizing potential of the Revolution. Godard's films are inscribed in a long-standing reflection of a complex meditation and are a rewarding exploration of the contradictions embedded in the relationship between ethics and politics and the artist's ability or responsibility to represent or to be involved in historical or contemporary political events. These interrogations translate into matters of visibility and technique, how to render present the absent or give presence to those who lack a voice, in the relationship between action or intervention and *poiesis*. In order to pursue this, Godard encompasses in his work Dziga Vertov's factography, Bertolt Brecht's pedagogy, Jean-Paul Sartre's engagement, Maoist direct action, Guy Debord's iconoclasm, the post-structuralist demise of representation, militant film, the emancipatory potential of the media as counter-information, self-representation and the post-colonial native informant, an inquiry into the capacity of images to bear witness or to give testimony, the irrepresentable, the sacredness of the image and the problem of the hyperreal versus more dialectical approaches dealing with the privileged position of the observer/reporter/artist-ethnographer. Most importantly, his *oeuvre* must be inscribed within the tradition of materialist aesthetics and his films described as "dialectical materialist films." Materialism is a

---

[2] Hannah Arendt, *On Violence* (New York: Harcourt, 1970), 3.
[3] See Martin Jay, "Mourning a Metaphor: The Revolution is Over," *Parallax* 9:2 (April 2003), pp. 17–20.

method to produce objective knowledge through the cognition of this objective whole, describing it in *action*, focusing on the relationships of production. Moreover, materialism seeks to render the world visible by producing *reflections* or *consciousness* of the relationships of production by means of the dialectic between essence and appearance, thereby producing objective knowledge of the world. Rooted in debates in the late 1960s about engaged filmmaking and partly inspired by Godard's own work, Jean-Paul Fargier defines political films neither as ideological nor as undoing ideology, but as achieving a non-ideological status by realizing a form of theoretical practice.[4] Non-ideological films are truly political precisely because they are conscious of the materials they are based on, they are not confused with political practice, and in them aesthetic-ideological specificity is elevated to a stage of knowledge that transforms the subjective element and thus contributes to social change.[5]

In *Le Gai savoir* (1969) Godard establishes the foundations of his materialist filmmaking. In the film, two students, Patricia Lumumba and Émile Rousseau, meet in a television studio for seven days to investigate techniques and strategies to shatter representation and implement a new visual regime. The first year, the plan is to collect sounds and images; the second year, to critique, reduce, decompose and substitute them. In the third, they give themselves the task of building alternatives. All activities converge in Godard's own filmmaking program, which is based on a radical questioning of the signifying and representational logic of filmmaking and an epistemological inquiry in tune with key structuralist and post-structuralist works like Louis Althusser's *Pour Marx* (1965), Jacques Derrida's *Of Grammatology* (1967), Michel Foucault's *Archeology of Knowledge* (1969), Roland Barthes' *Éléments de semiologie* (1964) or Julia Kristeva's *Séméiôtiké* (1969). It could be said that the tasks Patricia and Émile give themselves of speaking, listening and seeing as a way to move from *savoir* (impersonal, objective knowledge) to *connaissance* (subjective or personal knowledge),[6] were the methods followed for decades by Godard both alone and together with his long-term partner and collabo-

---

[4] Jean-Paul Fargier, "Hacia el relato rojo: Notas sobre un nuevo modo de producción del cine" in Jean-Louis Comolli, et al. *Mayo Francés: La cámara opaca: El debate cine e ideología*, compilador Emiliano Jelicé (Buenos Aires: El Cuenco de Plata, 2016).

[5] Emiliano Jelicé, Jean-Louis Comolli, et al. *Mayo Francés: La cámara opaca: El debate cine e ideología*, comp. Emiliano Jelicé (Buenos Aires: El Cuenco de Plata, 2016), p. 22.

[6] See Kaja Silverman and Harun Farocki, *Speaking About Godard* (New York and London: New York University Press, 1998).

rator, Anne-Marie Miéville. In the little-known films from the Dziga Vertov Group (DVG) period that Godard made in collaboration and/or in dialogue with Jean-Pierre Gorin and Jean-Henri Roger, Paul Bourron, Isabel Pons, Raphaël Sorin, Nathalie Biard and D.A. Pennebaker—from *One Plus One/Sympathy for the Devil* (1968), *One A.M.* (1968), *British Sounds/See You at Mao* (1969), *Pravda* (1969), *Le Vent d'Est* (1970), *Luttes en Italie* (1970), *Vladimir et Rosa* (1971) to *Tout va bien* and *Letter to Jane* (both 1972)—they take further the theoretical explorations Godard began in *Le Gai savoir* on the relationship between text and image, words and sounds in the context of the crisis of aesthetic representation (voice, image, text). In the DVG films, the crisis of representation is explored explicitly in terms of the political processes of the ordeals experienced by militants in the context of the effervescence of May 1968 and the demise of Marxism-Leninism epitomized in *Tout va bien* (1972) and of *Tiermondisme* (or Third Worldism) in *Ici et ailleurs* (1976).

A film about the Palestinian Revolution, *Ici et ailleurs* (originally titled *Jusqu'à la victoire*) was made in collaboration with Jean-Pierre Gorin and Armand Marco and co-edited with Anne-Marie Miéville within the context of their Sonimage project. Critics such as Raymond Bellour and Colin MacCabe see in this film a radical break in Godard's *oeuvre* at the level of his political commitment and aesthetic engagement, as they see a qualitative and quantitative change between the Marxist-Leninist period and the Sonimage one. This break is usually described as the quandary of an intellectual, who, realizing the limitations of his previous position of "erroneous engagement," enacted a "turn" that would prevent such a "mistake" from occurring again. Along similar lines, film historian Junji Hori notes a passage in Godard's work moving from an active Third Worldism to a melancholic reflection about Europe's destiny and its complexities.[7] I, however, along with Michael Witt, see coherence in Godard's work with regards to his militant practice. Moreover, recent scholarship on Godard by Georges Didi-Huberman, James S. Williams, and Stoffel Debuysere has given *Ici et ailleurs* its justly deserved place not only as a key work in Godard's *oeuvre*, but also in the history of militant filmmaking and its relevance to contemporary debates that address a range of issues, including commitment and political art, the legacy of radical filmmaking, the

---

[7] Junji Hori, "La Géopolitique de l'image dans les *Histoire(s) du cinéma* de Jean-Luc Godard," available at http://www.desk.c.u-tokyo.ac.jp/download/es_3_Hori.pdf

Image in times of the regime of the visual, and the controversy about Godard's take on the representation of the Israeli–Palestinian conflict and the Shoah. *Ici et ailleurs* marks qualitative changes in Godard's political engagement insofar as they respond to the actuality and to the shifting historical conditions that have brought changes to the form of political action. Therefore, against the idea that Godard "retreated" from his political engagement or that he "retrenched back to Europe" (his position had always been self-reflexively Eurocentric) one can argue that the historical conditions for engagement changed and Godard's work along with them. The impasse of the Left regarding Marxist engagement was spelled out by Merleau-Ponty: the militant could, on the one hand, accept the factual reality that allows for effective militantism and engaged practice, and on the other, seek refuge in a quiet philosophical state in which the principles of Marxism could be maintained (i.e., at the level of the "imaginary" proletariat).[8] The choice here is between an objective long-term engagement and a subjective immediate intervention—both overseeing the "bastard reality." Godard took up neither of Merleau-Ponty's options, insisting on a practice of theoretical filmmaking engaging with material reality. The two television series that followed *Ici et ailleurs*, produced in collaboration with Miéville—*Six fois deux: Sur et sous la communication* (1976) and *France/tour/détour/deux/enfants* (1978–79), as well as their video-film *Numéro deux* (1976)—deal with a kind of "familial politics," exploring the private sphere in relationship to the pervasiveness of television at home. After the end of the Leftist period, Godard continued to explore the contradictions between the political and the aesthetic, by constructing the confrontation of the subjects and the objects of history and the actuality, exploring further the European historical, philosophical and aesthetic imaginary. Moreover, Godard would experiment with a relationship between aesthetics and the political as exclusive of each other but crossing paths in *Passion* (1982) and in *Nouvelle vague* (1990), in which we see signs not of the notion of a Marxist class struggle but of class antagonism.[9]

---

[8] Merleau-Ponty, cited by Rossana Rossanda, "Les Intellectuels Révolutionnaires et l'Union Soviétique," *Les Temps modernes* no. 332 (March 1974), p. 1537.

[9] Yosefa Loshitzky argues that "Godard's former subscription to the Marxist utopia of a classless society has been replaced by a belief in the Christian utopia of the 'Kingdom of Heaven' promised by Jesus to his poor followers...In Godard's new semi-religious vision, the world of money is the world of materialism and the world of nature is the world of spiritualism." I disagree with Loshitzky on the grounds of the necessity to avoid turning religion into an episteme. This argument, however, would be worth exploring more in terms of Godard's

Another example is Godard's *Allemagne année 90 neuf zéro* (1991), in which he outlines the change of the world politically, economically, cinematically and historically in the aftermath of the fall of the Berlin Wall. In that regard, we could trace a series of transitions in Godard's work coherent with historic-political changes from an anti-capitalist politics grounded in class relations and relationships of production, to an ethics of restitution in *Histoire(s) du cinéma*, to a kind of dialectical materialism strongly critiquing humanitarianism grounded in Homeric history whose (post- or pre-political) subjects are established either as victors and vanquished in *Notre musique* (2004) (but with a genesis in *Je vous salue, Sarajevo* (1993) and *For Ever Mozart* (1996)), to a search for the means to revive the paradigm of the French resistance against the Nazi occupation as a means to resist forms of power at the turn of a Dantesque twenty-first century (*Éloge de l'amour*, 2001; *Film Socialisme*, 2010). In this regard, Godard's version of history resonates with Lenin's prediction and Arendt's assessment, as he sees the twenty-first century as inheriting the failed revolutions of the twentieth century translated into ethnic wars. In this context, Godard's Eurocentric cartography addresses the contemporary "realist" politics of Neoliberal Empire, positing the world as engaged in a total, righteous, permanent war of "all against all."[10] In Godard, righteous cultural (and actual) wars stand against a "sky red with explosions" inhabited by restored ruins, still in flames, purporting the false unity of a culturalized past as the condition of possibility of a present of "co-existence" codified by the culture and memory industries, which in the 1990s, in a Frankfurt School vein, becomes the target of his critique.

Therefore, in this book I situate Godard's work *as an aesthetico-political project* according to historical changes in the past 50 years: from the "politics of representation" and its crisis in the 1960s (as explored in the DVG films), to the "politics of visibility" and counter-information in the 1970s, which he posits as "audiovisual journalism" in his Sonimage videos, to an exploration of the new modes of subjectivation by capitalism and self-representation in the 1980s (the Marithé-François Girbaud videos (1987), *Le Rapport Darty* (1989)), to his critique of the culture and memory industries (*Je vous salue, Sarajevo, Éloge de l'amour, Notre musique*), to the ethics of speaking truth to power and humanitarianism (*Je vous salue,*

---

rhetorical (secular) shift to Icon theory in terms of montage and to some religious motifs that have appeared in his films since *La Chinoise* (1967). See Yosefa Loshitzky, *The Radical Faces of Godard and Bertolucci* (Detroit: Wayne State University Press, 1995), pp. 97–98.

[10] See: Seyla Benhabib, "The Legitimacy of the Human Rights," *Daedalus*, vol. 137, No. 3, (Summer 2008).

Sarajevo, Notre musique, The Old Place (2001)), to his controversial juxtaposition of the Shoah and the Nakba (*Ici et ailleurs, Histoire(s) du cinéma, Notre musique*) and his plea to restitute the verb to the dead bodies, to the post-political call for the redistribution of the sensible and to peripheral languages (*Vrai faux passeport* and *Voyage(s) en utopie, Film Socialisme* and *Adieu au langage* (2014)), to his engagement with three-dimensional (3D) technology as a way to reverse the "loss of historical depth" brought by the technology itself (*Les Trois désastres* (2013), *Adieu au langage*). These concerns relate to Godard's long-standing explorations of how to retrieve a genuine Image from the imagery circulating in Spectacle, the mass media, the cultural industry: the sensible regime.[11]

In a 1967 interview he gave in front of students at Nanterre University on the outskirts of Paris, Godard declared that cinema under the yoke of capitalism is aberrant; that is why he gave himself the task of fighting against capitalism in cinema, attacking first "imperialist film" and the "mass media" in the 1970s, and the "culture industry" since the 1990s.[12] In this context, he has claimed to be "the Jew of cinema." This statement is a paraphrase of Adorno's declaration in *Minima Moralia*: "German words of foreign derivation are the Jews of language."[13] We can read Godard's utterance as central to his ongoing effort to construct a marginal position within the hegemonic historical discourse of Judeo-Christian Europe, a self-proclaimed position of an insider of Cinema analyzing it from the position of an outsider—his current production company with Miéville is called *Périphéria*.

---

[11] "The sensible regime," is a conceptualization by Jacques Rancière in *The Future of the Image*; sensible, in this context, is what is apprehended by the senses, and sensible regime refers to how roles and modes of participation are allotted in the social world according to how things are made visible and invisible, sayable and unsayable, audible and inaudible by forms of power. Debatably, Rancière's concept is an elaboration of Godard's *les signes parmi nous* (the signs amongst us), which is the title of Chapter 4(b) of the *Histoires du cinéma* and appears subsequently in his films. *Les signes parmi nous* is cinema and audiovisual history, both of which are regimes of visibility determined by context and epoch. Franco Berardi (Bifo), has coined the term "the infosphere," inspired by Teilhard de Chardin's concept of the *noosphere*, which is a transcendental site where all of the knowledge of humanity is deposited. For Berardi, informational overstimulation in our era supersedes our capacity to consciously process it and criticize it, leading to the disembodiment and de-erotization of language. As a consequence, communication no longer guarantees the exchange of meaning. When I refer to "the sensible regime" I am taking all these nuances of the term into account.

[12] Interview between J-L Godard and M. Cournot, "Quelques evidentes incertitudes," *Revue d'esthétique* (Janvier-mars, 1967), pp. 115–122.

[13] Theodor Adorno, *Minima Moralia: Reflections from Damaged Life* (Verso, 2005) p. 110.

History ("mon histoire, l'histoire du cinéma, raconter une histoire ou pas")[14] is a pivotal concern. Godard's history is Eurocentric and privileges World War II. Godard was 15 when the extermination of European Jewry unfolded in silence: "On disait, qu'on n'avait rien vu, rien entendu…je me suis rendu compte beaucoup plus tard…qu'est-ce qui c'est passé, tout ça; en regrettant souvent qu'ils n'ont jamais fait des films de 40 au 45."[15] In another interview, he stated: "Alors c'est ici qu'on peut dire que là où le cinéma s'est pris les pieds dans lui-même, c'est que cette obligation de voir, il n'a pas su, n'a pas voulu, il n'a pas pu, il ne l'a pas fait au moment du nazisme."[16] Godard hints here at his idea that the history of cinema is that of a missed rendezvous with the history of its century during World War II. By this Godard does not mean that cinema was incapable of filming the extermination camps but that cinema was unable to *see* and to *provide a means of seeing* (donner à voir) what was going on. In a project of restitution and resurrection, Godard constructs a history in *Histoire(s) du cinéma* (1988–98) of films providing a "forewarning" of the extermination; they include *Faust* (1926), *Die Nibelungen* (1924), *La Règle du Jeu* (1939), *The Great Dictator* (1940), *Das Cabinet des Dr. Caligari* (1920) and *Nosferatu* (1922).[17]

[14] "My history, the history of cinema, whether to tell a story or not." Godard in an interview with Olivier Bombarda and Julien Welter for *Cahiers du Cinéma* on November 2007. http://www.cahiersducinema.com/article1424.html

[15] "It used to be said that no-one had seen anything, heard anything … it wasn't until much later that I started to comprehend all that had happened … regretting often that there hadn't been any film-making between 1940 and 1945." Ibid.

One of the axioms of the *Histoire(s) du cinéma* is that during World War II too few films addressed the topic of the Holocaust; mostly, they were the exception, and generally came too late. Godard also denounces the lack of films about the Resistance and thus cinema's capitulation in the face of key historical events. The consequences were the shutting of the documentary eye, and the dehumanization of the concentration and extermination camps, which led to the severance of the link between man and the world. This is why cinematic renewal can only take place in montage, and why Godard set himself a double task in this film: first, to denounce cinema for not having filmed the extermination camps, and second, by means of the juxtaposition of images from Western visual culture (including documentary images of the camps), to render temporarily visible the horrors of the Shoah.

[16] "Thus, it is at this point that we could say that cinema stumbled, because its obligation is to see. And at the time of Nazism it did not know how to or want to." Youssef Ishaghpour in dialogue with Godard, *Archéologie du cinéma et mémoire du siècle* (Tours: Farrago, 2000), p. 73.

[17] Debatably, Godard's reading of cinema before and during World War II is aligned with Siegfried Kracauer's psychological reading of German film between 1918 and 1933 in which he argues that films were addressed to the middle class, influencing mass behavior and shaping public opinion, creating "deep psychological dispositions predominant in Germany…

The "missed rendezvous" between cinema and history concerns the *fictional* objects constructed by the confrontation between poetics and temporalities in his monumental *Histoire(s) du cinéma* (1988–98).[18]

Akin to Walter Benjamin, Godard conceives the past as an infinite gallery of images that we can interrogate, render eloquent and charge with meaning. These images are deposited in our memory. The filmmaker, as an archivist or a collector, gathers the fragments of the past in order to save it, recomposing it by means of asymmetrical juxtapositions that, rather than rewriting history, ask questions. His method is the Benjaminian-Reverdian juxtaposition of two images and/or sounds potentially evoking an unthought third. The potential of seeing happens in montage, by juxtaposing two "good" images. As he expounds pedagogically in his 2006 film *Vrai faux (Passeport pour le réel)*, "good" images bear with them a "passport" that allows them to "reach the border to the real." The "real" in cinema is the "false" reproduction that we come to believe in. In Godard's theory, cinema neither seeks truth nor stands as proof of something other than the Image itself, which is at the border between two images—sounds, texts, figures—in montage. It may be that sometimes two "bad" images (e.g., low density images, stereotypes, shield-images) do not make up a third. Thus to juxtapose two "good" images is to make two different scales co-exist, to associate two textures, to confront two points of view as through the montage technique of the shot/reverse-shot. The purpose of these operations is to disturb our visual habits and that is how they provoke the unthought: alternative visions of the past and the present. For Godard "une bonne image vient d'un long cheminement" (a good image has made a long journey) and it is a combination of Brunschvicg's "trinity," composed of Montaigne's "I doubt," Descartes' "I know" and Pascal's "I believe."[19] The Image is reached through self-

---

which influenced the course of events during that time and which will have to be reckoned with in the post-Hitler era." (Kracauer, p. 10) Examples include Caligari's idolization of power, insane authority and state omnipotence or *Die Niebelungen* as the triumph of the ornamental over the human and as the patterns of the film appropriated by Nazi pageantry; or *Kuhle Wampe*, a film in which young athletes glorify collective life (Kracauer, p. 20). See Siegfried Kracauer, *From Caligari to Hitler: A Psychological History of the German Film* (Princeton: The University Press, 1947).

[18] Jacques Rancière, in the interview with Marie-Aude Baronian and Mireille Rosello in 2007, available at http://www.artandresearch.org.uk/v2n1/jrinterview.html#_ftn5. See also Rancière's *La Fable cinématographique* (Paris: Seuil, 2001), p. 217.

[19] He is quoting Léon Brunschvicg's *Descartes et Pascal: Lecteurs de Montaigne* (Neuchâtel: Balconnière, 1942). For Brunschvicg, the three authors share the concern with taking the

reflexivity and machinic epistemology; for Godard (as for Dziga Vertov), making images is not "taking images" (*une prise de vue*), but a way of considering the camera as an epistemological tool that can "capture" something that is neither visible nor audible that can be complexified by montage. Doubt in the image is the ambivalence woven in between the thing, text, and image; belief in the image is the search for man's destiny and place in the world in the Modern situation of the shattering of the link between man and the world, rooted in a desire to see.

REPRESENTATION AND ITS CRISIS

For Martin Heidegger, Modernity is the era of representation and, as such, it is characterized by presenting a point of view that draws a certain relationship between the masses, the individual and power. In the political realm, representation implies that the state or political parties deal with individuals who are "represented" in the universal sphere, marking a gap between their empirical particularity and their legal universality. In aesthetics, representation is a description, an image that stands for something in the world to make present what is absent; the presentness, is however, always incomplete and only temporarily present with the aid of speech. Yet representation, in fact, operates through its own restraint because it presupposes a totality and can thus become a totalitarian form of control and of representation.[20] In aesthetics, fascist representation means that meaning is reified, reflexivity and criticality eliminated along with relationality, ambiguity, even beauty; appearances become a series of minor variations derived from the same source. In spite of the potential claims for totality and the colonizing dangers of representation, the relationship between political engagement and aesthetics as the problem of representation, following Fredric Jameson, "must be perpetuated as a throbbing pain that won't go away, rather than as an X-ray plate."[21] From this we can infer that

---

question of man away from a formal discipline (epistemology, empiricism) in order to address issues concerning man's place in the world and destiny. "I doubt, I know, I believe" expresses fundamental attitudes of thought and denounces the mediation of metaphysics, evidencing a relationship to Christian theology and French thought. Godard cited Brunschvicg in "Jean-Luc Godard—Elias Sanbar," *Politis*, January 16, 2005, available online: http://www.politis.fr/article1213.html

[20] Jacques Rancière, *The Future of the Image* (London and New York: Verso, 2006), p. 133.

[21] Fredric Jameson, *The Geopolitical Aesthetic: Cinema and Space in the World System* (Bloomington: Indiana University Press, 1992), p. 164.

representation should be taken not as a formal device, but as a tortuous mechanism that is a given, necessary to account for the act of mediation by way of translation, intercession, negotiation, which are the means that are inherent to conveying a world, a point of view.

The totalizing aspect of representation was underscored by post-structuralism and by the May 1968 movement, bringing aesthetico-political representation into crisis. Making a homology between knowledge, language and politics, students and workers in May 1968 contested their authority as regimes of representation[22] by asking: "Who speaks and acts, for whom and how?" This question can be traced back to Lenin's inquiry, "What is to be done?" which assigned intellectuals the role of anticipating or theorizing the coming emancipation of the proletariat. Having inherited the Leninist model of engagement, intellectuals associated with the French Communist Party assumed the roles of *compagnons de route* (fellow travelers) and of representing the consciousness of the people. Along with professors and labor union delegations, intellectuals' scholarly theories, and the representativeness of language, students and workers rendered party representatives suspicious as totalizing enterprises. In political terms, the call during May 1968 for self-organization and direct intervention did away with representation by breaking away from organizing around the fixed signifiers of the Party and of class struggle. Activists dismissed the Party and organized around specific struggles in *groupuscules*, emphasizing direct action and the capture of speech. At the same time, students and workers brought knowledge and common sense to their limit by breaking down language to demonstrate its paucity and inability to account for reality. This was manifested through stammering, nonsensical speech, and by a refusal to speak. Speaking in the name of others was deemed unworthy and anyone and everyone was encouraged to speak in their name, all in an attempt at non-mediated expression, exercising direct democracy. In tune with political struggles, post-structuralist philosophers laid out an intellectual project to undo representation, in Western metaphysics (and thus art and literature) by bringing difference to the core of representation, separating signifier from signified and text from voice. Godard joined the battle against representation, transubstantiating the class struggle into the image/sound struggle by way of the aphorism:

---

[22] Michel De Certeau, "The Power of Speech," *The Capture of Speech and Other Political Writings*, trans. Tom Conley (Minneapolis and London: The University of Minnesota Press, 1997), p. 26.

"Le son c'est le délégué syndical de l'oeil."[23] He furthermore highlights in his films the fact that the condition for representation is language: as he also posits in *Le Gai savoir*, in every image "someone speaks." That is, speech is part of what is made seen and thus representation depends on speech in order to render it visible. If the essential function of speech is to make seen and to arrange the visible, it does so by fusing two operations, a substitution (which places "before our eyes" that which is remote in space and time) and an exhibition (which makes visible what is hidden from sight—*ça montre*). Speech thus makes visible by referring, summoning the absent and calling forth the hidden.

Because the danger of fascism is always present in representation, Godard's radical representation includes a practice of self-reflexivity. For instance, in his "documentary" about the Black Panthers, in collaboration with D.A. Pennebaker,[24] *One American Movie* or *One A.M.* (1968), Godard interviews—or rather records, as he is visibly intimidated by the leader and hardly dares to address him—Eldridge Cleaver giving his views about the black struggle. Later on in the movie, Cleaver's recorded speech is replayed and repeated by a white actor in various contexts: at a school, on the streets of New York, in a classroom full of black teenagers and while dressed up as a Native American. The film highlights the mutations Cleaver's speech undergoes as it is spoken through a white body in various contexts. By using an array of strategies for cinematic reflexivity, Godard seeks to make the viewer aware of how the film's representation of the Black Panthers' struggle is contingent upon Godard's and Pennebaker's white, male gazes. Placing self-reflexivity at the core of the movie enables the filmmaker to express solidarity with the black struggle. The need for self-reflexivity in political and aesthetic representation in order to avoid fascism (or reified representation as an embodiment of power) is linked to the double bind that constitutes Modernism: as Godard's film seeks to pedagogically show, in representation something always needs to be exposed or represented, and yet the desire to expose or represent is colo-

---

[23] "Sound is the union delegate of the eye." From the script of *Le Gai savoir* (1969).

[24] *One A.M.* (or *One American Movie*) is the title of an unfinished film by Godard shot in the United States in 1968 in collaboration with D.A. Pennebaker and Richard Leacock, and produced by the Public Broadcast Laboratory, a forerunner of the Public Broadcasting Service (PBS). After shooting, Godard left with Jean-Pierre Gorin to travel in the United States and thus Pennebaker edited it alone and in their absence, titling it *One P.M.* or *One Parallel Movie* (or *One Pennebaker Movie*).

nizing. At the same time, concealing and failing to represent or speak on behalf of others is no less colonizing.

Godard's take on aesthetico-political representation in cinema has drawn not only on the way that post-structuralist thought brought representation (or representative thinking) into crisis, but also on interpretations of Marx and realism in the 1960s. For Godard, an image produced photographically "n'est pas le réel d'une réflexion mais la réflexion du ce réel."[25] Aligned with Brecht's critique of Lukács, Godard's filmic materialism entails that there is a gap between reality and its cinematic reflection, which is, according to apparatus theory, rendered opaque by the cinematic apparatus. Through the scientific practice of filming and montage, it becomes possible to pierce through the ideology of the apparatus and arrive at the real—which is self-knowledge: "I try to see." In a word play between reflection in the materialist sense and *réflexion* (which in French also connotes "thought process"), he has stated, "Je réfléchis des réflexions,"[26] calling attention to his conception of the camera as an epistemological tool and of montage as a site for thought: "*Réfléchir*, pas renvoyer une image." Furthermore, for Godard "capturing" an image (*prise de vue*) is, to use Barthes' expression, "mortal", although the recording of reality can capture something that is neither visible nor audible otherwise. For Godard, that which is captured can be restituted and resurrected by way of montage and projection. That is why, for him, "Le cinéma, c'est vingt-quatre fois la vérité par seconde."[27]

The technical component of the cinematic apparatus consists of the projection of a succession of photographic images in a roll of film. A curious aspect of human visual perception is that the retina retains a memory of the previous photogram, and that is why in the projection we see the illusion of cinematic continuity. For Godard, this visual memory is tied to language because we narrativize the film *after-image*. Furthermore, there is, again adapting Barthes, something deadly about sight, insofar as forgetting is immanent within actualization by way of the language of visual memory—this is where the potential of the new is lodged. Godard's call to resist giving up the essential is not a denigration of vision, but an acknowledgment of the limits of the visible. The "essential" is the belief in

---

[25] "...does not deal with the reality of a reflection; rather, it is a reflection of what is real". The sentence was written on a wall in the flat where *La Chinoise* (1967) was filmed.
[26] In *Le Petit soldat* (1963) and *JLG/JLG, autoportrait de décembre* (1994).
[27] "Cinema is reality twenty-four times per second."

images, which can only be sustained in dissimilitude because things in images are substantially foreign to the things themselves. This further implies, following the logic of the icon, that the image is instituted in the gap between the visible and the subject of the gaze, as this gap is made visible by the voice.[28] The "essential" is the possibility of "incarnation," a promise of corporeality: the becoming verb, word, of the voice and of speech, and the body is the threshold for containing the verb. Therefore, for Godard cinema is a privileged site for the interplay between language and the image; it is "des formes qui cheminent vers la parole."[29]

A formulation that may prove more effective to describe representation in aesthetics and politics is "sensible." The sensible is the juxtaposition of the "form of the visible" and the "form of the utterable" that creates a diagram or figure made out of discursive and visible formations. This means that the visible and the expressible define two different regimes that are irreducible to each other, as incommensurable strata that cross over, regulating the "visible" through technologies of observation and procedures of expression. Here, visibility and utterability are not the product of sight and speech, but what can be rendered as intelligible and knowable in a society during a given epoch.[30] In this regard, everything can be represented for Godard, and he has drawn distinctions between the "unrepresentable," the "invisible," and the "inexpressible." For instance, in *Soft and Hard* (1985), a short collaboration with Miéville, the latter states that images of tenderness between a couple are inexpressible, and that the relationship can be viewed only from the outside, following the analogy of the shell of an egg that allows us to see the surface but not what is happening inside. The unrepresentable in icon theory is God's face, and incarnation is its image. For Godard, the unrepresentable is "No movement, no depth, no artifice: the sacred."[31] The sacred is linked to the redemptive aspect of his project of giving images back the verb by way of montage, as we will see. Thus, in his films he summons images to appear before the viewer, delivering sensibilities ("les signes parmi nous" [the signs amongst us]), as opposed to rendering or making visible. "Making visible" pre-supposes concealment; absence and invisibility as the opposite of

---

[28] Marie-José Mondzain, *L'image peut-elle tuer?* (Bayard, 2015), p. 19.

[29] "Forms moving towards speech." From the voiceover of *Histoire(s) du cinéma*, chapter 3a (1998).

[30] D.N. Rodowick, *Reading the Figural or Philosophy After the New Media* (Durham: Duke University Press, 2001), pp. 54–56.

[31] Delivered by Godard in his lecture in *Notre musique*.

visibility. For Godard, to deliver sensibilities is to offer the possibility of *seeing*. According to the logic of the icon to which Godard subscribes secularly, the invisible is not the negative of the visible, but the ambivalence of the material apparition of an immateriality, an ambivalence that is sustained by the voice. Exploring the image's relationship to the visible, that is, how it appears within the apparatus and how it addresses the viewer, he experiments with technique, form and a pedagogical mode of address—imbued by anxiety of blindness (see page 23, below) and the desire to see. To deliver sensibilities, Godard invokes allegories, performing the acts of naming, showing, juxtaposing, and citing. His methods are the Kino-eye, appropriation and stratigraphy. For him, cinema is not "une pensée qui forme," but "très exactement une forme qui pense"[32]—that is the power of montage.

Representativity and Authorship

The opening scene of *Le Petit soldat* (1963) begins with the statement in the voice-over: "Pour moi le temps de l'action a passé, j'ai vieilli. Le temps de la réflexion commence."[33] The film is about the existentialist dilemmas of Bruno Forestier (Michel Subor), a militant who arrives in Geneva from France and receives orders to murder a radio commentator as an action in support of Algerian independence. He falls in love with an aspiring actress, Veronika Dreyer (Anna Karina) and changes his mind about carrying out the mission; activists with the FLN (Front de Libération Nationale, the Algerian independence movement) kidnap and torture him. The film deals with France's dirty war and torture of those who were involved and sympathized with the FLN, as well as the dilemmas of Modern man in a post-war society. The character embodies Jean-Paul Sartre's existentialist quandary of what choice, freedom and responsibility are in relation to political engagement. In the film, for the first time, appear Godardian tropes and aphorisms such as "Le cinéma, c'est vingt-quatre fois la vérité par seconde," the history of painting, classical music, the question of what an image is, newspaper clips and an engagement with philosophy and literature, that would come to characterize his work and research. In a wall in Forestier's apartment there are

---

[32] "...a thought that forms", "quite exactly, a form that thinks." From the voiceover of 3a in *Histoire(s) du cinéma* (1998).

[33] "For me, the time of action has passed. I've grown older. It's now time to reflect."

images and references to World War II, the Spanish Civil War, Brigitte Bardot, a Soviet tank and André Malraux's *La Condition humaine* (1933), which are juxtaposed and serve to show his ideological confusion.[34] In a way, Forestier is Godard's alter-ego undergoing existentialist predicaments. He embodies a contradiction grounded in his desire for Veronika, which compels him to flee with her, and being governed by duty, which is the same quandary experienced by the Communist characters in *La Condition humaine*. The parallel that is drawn between the torture routinely practised by the French in Algeria and Nazi criminality, moreover, expresses Godard's early interest in the construction of historical memory to understand the present that can potentially be linked to a paradigm of resistance to actual forms of power.

In *Le Petit soldat*, as in most of his films, the characters are historical figures in the materialist sense that they are born out of a reality: they are social types in struggle, conveying objective meaning in the total context of the materialist worldview of class struggle (i.e., "Maoist Student," "Third Worldist Filmmaker," "Worker," "Oligarch," "Poet," etc.).[35] These figures are constructed and deconstructed over and over again, as they come to be traversed by the forces of the historical moment and of capital. For instance, *Éloge de l'amour* (2001) tells "not the history of Eglantine, but the moment of history traversing Eglantine," as we hear in the film. How that history is told is a matter of the technical conjunction of politics and aesthetics. Other characters stand for the filmmaker's alter ego to express autobiographical quandaries or philosophical concerns. In this regard, it can be argued that one of Godard's main concerns is *representativity*—his own, and that of his characters. In order to explore representativity self-reflexively, he has posited himself in his films as Maoist, self-repentant Maoist, self-flagellating failed filmmaker, machine, idiot, "individual", blank screen (and thus literally medium), "JLG," historian, dialectical-materialist filmmaker, professor, gardener, etc. This constitutes a diversification of authorial voice in line with the demise proclaimed in May 1968 of the notion of *auteur* and experiments with reconfiguring the authorial voice in relationship to political discourse in literature, art and cinema as *écriture*.

---

[34] Philip Watts, "Godard's Wars," in *A Companion to Jean-Luc Godard*, Tom Conley and T. Jefferson Kline, eds. (Oxford: Wiley Blackwell, 2015), p. 197.
[35] Georg Lukács, "Realism in the Balance" (1938) trans. Rodney Livingstone, *Aesthetics and Politics*, ed. Ernst Bloch (London and New York: Verso, 1987), p. 33.

In "The Death of the Author" (1968), an essay that moves between literary enunciation and political engagement, Roland Barthes distinguished three realms of speech: artistic enunciation (artist/writer), engaged activism (intellectual) *and* pedagogical project (professor). These are intrinsically linked to each other: the professor is on the side of speech, the artist/writer is the "operator", the creator of form on the side of *écriture*, and the intellectual is in between the two, printing and publishing his speech. For Barthes, when the *professor speaks*, there is an intrinsic connection between voice and mind, and thus with the voice's signifier; when the intellectual writes, there is also a production of the signifier through writers' or intellectuals' operative symbolization through conventions of written words or artworks. What is being produced is something signified, an absent subject, not the truth of a voice or of authorial identity. For Barthes, *writing* (*écriture*) is a site in which the subject is absent, his/her identity is lost, and writing has as its sole function the practice of the symbol. *Écriture* is a hand that loses its voice and thus its origin; writing begins when the author enters his/her own death. For Barthes, therefore, writing implies death and destruction insofar as enunciation is an empty process, writing is a gesture of inscription and not of expression. Barthes' solution to the problem of political engagement and literary enunciation was embodied in the figure of the *scripteur*, "situated halfway between the party member and the writer, deriving an ideal image of the committed man and the idea that a written work is an act."[36] Foucault's critique of Barthes' concept of *écriture* opposes the notion of the "death" of the author. For Barthes, it is a matter of the separation between speech and appearance—the author "disappears" into his/her text, as opposed to dying for a signifying voice. For Foucault, the relationship between text and author lies in the manner in which the text points to the "figure" of the author, which is outside of it and antecedes it: this "figure" is an appearance, as opposed to an absence or effacement. Foucault critiques the notion of "death" of the author because, in his view, this idea transposes the empirical characteristics of the author into a transcendental anonymity, creating enigmatic excess and the *a priori* neutralization of the voice. What is important for Foucault is to draw a distinction between writing and expression (as self-expression), as for him, writing refers only to itself, to its own unfolded exteriority, effac-

---

[36] Roland Barthes, "Écrivains, Intellectuels, Professeurs," *Tel Quel* no. 47 (Fall 1971), p. 3, and "The Death of the Author" (1968), in *Image, Music, Text* (New York: Hill and Wang, 2003) 142–146. See also Derrida's *Of Grammatology*, p. 11.

ing the writing subject's individual characteristics and canceling out the signs of his/her particular individuality. Foucault insists that the author has disappeared, and even the author's name is the manifestation and appearance of a certain set of discursivities indicating the status of this discourse within a society and culture. Thus, Foucault considers the subject as a variable and complex function of discourse.[37]

Godard was aware of these debates and experimented with different models of authorship and thus forms of representativity. Serge Daney explains Godard's use of cinematic voice and authorship, based on his practice of authorial divestiture by repeating the already-said-by-others as a kind of ventriloquism. For him, Godardian voice-overs from his 1960s and 1970s films are like lectures (Barthes' professor); in his account, in Godard's films, the filmmakers become professors repeating their lesson and reiterating word by word that which others have said. For Daney, Godard's appropriation of citations, slogans, posters, jokes, histories and newspaper headlines, is a questionable anti-archaeological procedure. This is because Godard takes word by word that which others have said with the purpose of avoiding establishing his own regime of enunciation.[38] Daney thus locates the weight of Godard's authorship in montage, because:

> A l'obscénité d'apparaître comme auteur (et bénéficiaire de la plus-value filmique), il a préféré celle qu'il y avait à se mettre en scène dans l'acte même de la rétention.[39]

Debatably, Godard not only repeats a given discourse, but he seeks another discourse, enunciation, image or sound that will bring the two into creative contradiction: montage includes voice, and both constitute enunciation.

According to Daney, Godard's archaeological method turns him into an empty place, a blank screen through which images and sounds coexist, neutralize, recognize, designate, and struggle with each other. Furthering Daney's argument about Godard's discursive site as a blank screen through

---

[37] Michel Foucault, "Qu'est-ce qu'un auteur?" (1970), in *Écrits Complets*, vol. II (Paris: Gallimard), 821. Translated by Donald F. Bouchard and Sherry Simon, "The Author Function," available online at http://foucault.info/documents/foucault.authorFunction.en.html

[38] Serge Daney, "Le thérrorisé (pédagogie godardienne)," p. 33.

[39] "To the obscenity of appearing as *auteur* (and beneficiary of the greatest filmic surplus value), he has preferred to stage himself in the very act of memorization." Serge Daney, "Le thérrorisé (pédagogie godardienne)", *Cahiers du Cinéma*, nos. 262–263 (1976), special issue of five essays on *Numéro Deux* by Godard, p. 37.

which others' quotations pass, Kaja Silverman uses a phenomenological and psychoanalytical model to explain it. She argues that Godard's is a project of authorial divestiture that implies an infinite staging of authorial suicide, rendering him a receiver. In her view, the first time Godard committed suicide as an author was in *Weekend* (1967), by consigning the film in his opening title sequence to "the scrap heap." From then on, Godard's research into authorial divestiture consisted of incessantly staging his own authorial death by ceding responsibility to quotation. In Silverman's account, Godard is something like Veronica's veil, the total embodiment of a blank screen, a "pure receiver" with a double function: the surface onto which perceptual phenomena project themselves and the wall from which such phenomena bounce back toward the spectators. In Silverman's model of reception/deliverance *techne* and *poiesis* are inextricable, the former defined as "making appear," the latter as "bringing into presence" or "unveiling." In Silverman's Heideggerian reading, Godard, in his double being as receptacle and reflector, *offers* his own authorial death so that the world can appear. For Silverman, Godard's alleged attempt to receive Being and to display what comes to him from the world, becomes a pure act of giving.[40] This notion of authorship follows a model that implies that all expression realized in a medium must disappear in the fully realized expression; once the medium—the author—disappears, it "gives to see." The world Godard "gives to see" is given from the point of view of the historian/historiographer interweaving the history of the twentieth century, his own biography, the history of cinema, art and the visual and history as it has been recorded by reproducible images. Godard thus makes history by bringing together disparate phenomena as the basis for the creation of poetico-historical images.[41] As Georges Didi-Huberman recently put it, through formal interventions, Godard puts forth propositions about the future by means of an immense constellation of "quoted pasts" destined to open our eyes to the historical world his images are interwoven with. In Godard, citation is an act of language that transforms the quotation while depersonalizing speech, creating a distance while producing effects of signification.[42] Godard summons images, sounds and texts,

---

[40] Kaja Silverman, "The Author as Receiver," *October* no. 96 (Spring 2001), pp. 17–34, and Silverman's interview with Gareth James, in *I Said I Love. That is the Promise: The TVideo Politics of Jean-Luc Godard* (Berlin: oe + b Books, 2003).

[41] Michael Witt, *Jean-Luc Godard, Cinema Historian* (Bloomington and Indianapolis: Indiana University Press, 2013), p. 11.

[42] See: Georges Didi-Huberman, *Passés cités par JLG: L'œil de l'histoire, 5* (Paris: Minuit, 2015), pp. 15–19.

according to Didi-Huberman, based on a dialectic of a simultaneous double gesture that states *vois, là* (see, there), which implies orienting the gaze, proposing relationships and *voilà*, a gesture that supposes artistic freedom: take it or leave it. For Didi-Huberman, this dialectic delivers a contradictory effect and a centrifugal play of associations, sometimes susceptible to contradictory or irreverent effects.[43] By this Didi-Huberman means that Godard's efforts to *show things otherwise* suggest a clear political line which is not always aligned with political correctness and is clearly and unwaveringly anti-imperialist, anti-capitalist and anti-occupation. Regarding the last, for Godard, as we will see, the frame for political and aesthetic struggle since the defeat of the revolutions of the 1960s and 1970s, and in the present, is that of *occupation*, of which the Nazi occupation of France is the model translating to the occupation of everyday life, history, memory and culture by the pervasiveness of capitalism, for instance.

Conditions of Visuality/ *Les Signes Parmi Nous*

For Godard in the late 1960s, a critique of Spectacle following Debord's indictment of the "totalitarianism of the mass media" was untimely because such critique is predicated upon the notion of the need for fixed forms of political representation, appealing to the utopia of social authenticity as well as burdening images with the weight of "truth" and therefore with the apparent desires of the collectivity. The question of Spectacle, as having come to mediate social relationships imbued with capital, is for Godard not a problem of the "truth" of images, or their relationship or non-relationship to the "original," but the fact that they make concrete a concept ("sign value") according to which reality becomes a system of signs. According to Baudrillard, this means that in Late Capitalism, even the most ordinary things have become signs, and all the signs lead to another sign creating chains of signs, decoding and recoding one another. What is at stake here are, on the one hand, the forms of the intelligibility of the visible that we have in common when reality comes to be perceived as a system of signs. The transformation of things into signs is evidently one of the principles of cinema, and for Godard this implies "the submission of cinema to the narrative." On the other hand, the relationship to alterity as in this system,

---

[43] Ibid., p. 46.

"On produit et on consomme notre image avec celle de l'autre."[44] As in *Adieu au langage* Godard posits digital media as having destroyed language and face-to-face communication. In *Soft and Hard* Godard explains that the mass media have disturbed the relationship to alterity through the logic of projection in psychoanalysis to explain the constitution of the subject, which in his view has been substituted by Television: "With cinema, one projects oneself on the screen, while television projects itself upon the spectator." And yet, the image itself includes the possibility of restituting a link to the other as "Une image [photographique] est un regard, sur un autre regard présenté à un troisième regard, déjà représenté par l'appareil."[45] Godard repeats his formula in *JLG par JLG* (1993) as the "law of stereo": "l'un est dans l'autre et l'autre est dans l'un,"[46] a triangle which constitutes a projection. The image is thus for Godard a relationship between I and the other—a third—and in many of his films he transubstantiates couples' dilemmas into larger socio-political and historical ordeals. In *Tout va bien*, the problems of a couple of militants, played by Yves Montand and Jane Fonda, are transubstantiated into class struggle as a strike; *Nouvelle vague* (1991) is a film about a couple whose asymmetrical relationships are parallel to those between the upcoming financial oligarchy and the working class; and in *Adieu au langage*, the couple's problems with communication are restored by Roxy the dog. Godard and Miéville further insist on the "being two" of images—in *Notre musique* (2004), as we will see, this "being two" of images is translated into the shot/reverse-shot logic in montage. "To be two" means not only juxtaposing two images to deliver a third, but as we have seen, in the sense of *Le Gai savoir* and the way in which Godard and Miéville had been working in their Sonimage films, as being two to see, to discuss, to speak images.

One of the aspects of Godard's work, which is often overlooked, is his contribution to and reflections on what is known as *Tiermondisme*, a form of political engagement in France in the 1960s and 1970s that implied solidarity with revolutionary subjects seeking self-determination by way of decolonization and national liberation movements. Disinterested emphatic intellectuals, cultural producers and journalists engaged with Third World

---

[44] "We produce and consume our image with that of the other," from the voiceover in *Ici et ailleurs*.

[45] "An image is a gaze upon another gaze presented to a third gaze, already represented by the apparatus," from the voiceover in *Ici et ailleurs*.

[46] "The one is in the other as the other is in the one"

struggles on the basis of a common political ideology side by side with a new historical figure that embodied a political agent in a decolonizing struggle seeking self-determination. Godard created self-reflexive films under this genre of political filmmaking, having traveled to Cuba, the United States, Canada, London, Czechoslovakia and Italy, as well as to Palestine and Mozambique. His trips to Vietnam and Portugal were imaginary.

When the revolutions failed or became totalitarian dictatorships, a new form of emancipation of the people of the Third World was grounded, leading to the substitution of politics for a new ethics of intervention. *Tiermondisme* (Thirdworldism) had been a universal cause, giving a name to a political wrong. For the first time, the "wretched of the earth" emerged for a specific historic period as a new figuration of "the people" in the political sense: the colonized were discursively transformed into the political figures of the Algerian immigrant worker, the Chinese barefoot doctor, the revolutionary from elsewhere.[47] Yet, a new "ethical" humanism (or humanitarianism), substituted revolutionary enthusiasm and political sympathy with pity and moral indignation, transforming them into political emotions within the discourse of "pure actuality" and emergency. This led to new figures of alterity in the 1980s and 1990s, the "suffering other" that needs to be rescued, and to the post-colonial "subaltern" demanding restitution, pre-supposing that visibility within a multicultural social tissue would follow emancipation. The urgency of the state of exception elsewhere prompted morally interested observers to bring the precariousness of life to the fore in the most direct and realistic way possible, leading to an explosion of visibilities of "wounded subjectivities" demanding to be rescued or recognized. Documentary form is the privileged genre to carry out the ethico-political imperative to bear witness and to speak truth to power, because of its capability to convey "reality effects" that signify immediacy and urgency. Moreover, the domain of rights as "non-discourse" tends to efface the distinction between the documentarist's position as external observer. Victims and witnesses speak the language of singular counter-memory, testimony or confession, denouncing oppression, injustice and dispossession. The problem is that presence is imposed as immediacy at the expense of speech, rendering the speaking subject and the subject of speech indistinguishable, amalgamating *voice* and *face* as well as document *and* subject of speech. This is linked to

[47] Kristin Ross, *May '68 and its Afterlives* (Chicago: University of Chicago Press), 2002, p. 11.

images' burden of conveying knowledge (or information) and their interexchangeability with the kind of knowledge that can be acquired from empirical experience. For Godard representation becomes a matter of regulating the *distance* to what is seen and heard, as we will see, while he tracks all these changes in the *figuring* of others and their political struggles as well as those in the foreign intellectual engaged in them, most notably in *Notre musique*, which also conveys Godard's critique of the "humanitarianist turn."

Thus in Godard's films, not only the link to the other is at stake, but the link between humans and the world (*De l'origine du XXIème siècle*, 2000). After contesting pragmatic perception through montage in his films, the problem became for Godard the fact that the world had become unbearable: as it ceased to be a place in which humans act, humans had become onlookers of its unbearability. For Godard this is linked to the fact that the concentration camps bring into question the notion of "humanity" as prescribed by the Enlightenment. And because this is intolerable, the world ceased to be able to produce meaning or to think itself. The intolerable is not, in Paola Marrati's reading of Deleuze, serious injustice (the banality of evil), but the permanent state of everyday banality. The way out is "[t]o believe, not in a different world, but in a link between man and the world, in love or life, to believe in this as an impossible, the unthinkable, which nonetheless cannot but be thought."[48] Godard's battle against the excess of "realistic" visibilities, the violence of exposure, how the subject, in being the subject of an image, has been captured by apparatuses of power and is grounded in his efforts to resacralize the image to re-enchant the world in a battle against the disappearance of meaning, history and the destiny of man. The link in the world and to the other can be re-established by seeing, which is for Godard a pragmatic act that begins with the declaration: *Je vois* (I see) blindly; sight is enabled by means and in the process of montage. *Ici et ailleurs* belongs to the genre of the "vidéo-essai," which means: I try to see (*Video* in latin means "I see"). As for Rimbaud, the act of seeing for Godard is conditioned by a disarray of the senses, by a shock of thought.

Chapter 2 begins with an exploration of Godard's "militant filmmaking" in the context of the intellectual history of May 1968 and the debates

---

[48] Paola Marrati, "The Catholicism of Cinema: Gilles Deleuze on Image and Belief," *Religion and Media*, ed. Hent de Vries and Samuel Weber (Stanford: The University Press, 2001), p. 238.

around political filmmaking in France. The chapter centers on the period known as his "Marxist-Leninist Years" (1967–74) and is oriented around the question that was asked by both students and workers in May 1968: "Who speaks and acts, from where, for whom and how?" This question brought about a crisis of aesthetico-political representation and is the lens through which I analyze Godard's films of this period, which were made within the frame of the Dziga Vertov Group (the collective formed with Jean-Pierre Gorin in 1969). I propose that in their experiments with image and sound juxtapositions, the DVG stage over and over again the crisis of representation while they experiment with the ideologemes of the Left. I also examine their use of Maoist techniques, such as the logic of contradictions, self-critique or positing the sound/image struggle as analogous to the class struggle. Two final questions that persist in the DVG's films and that are asked in an array of experimental forms relate first to the representability of the political struggle and indignation, and second, the authority of the voice of the filmmaker as the harbinger of political change.

Chapter 3 is focused on Godard's militant filmmaking in relationship to *Tiermondisme* (Thirdworldism). In 1969 Godard and Gorin visited Palestinian training and refugee camps to make a film sponsored by the Palestinian Liberation Organization. In this chapter, I consider this film—originally titled *Jusqu'à la victoire*—in the context of the visits of Western intellectuals and artists to Third World countries undergoing revolutionary or decolonizing political processes. I then posit anxiety of blindness, or the fear of blind naïve identification with the struggle, as the key issue that Godard grappled with as he finished *Ici et ailleurs*. In order to sustain this claim, I compare *Ici et ailleurs* to Michelangelo Antonioni's *The Passenger* (1975) and *Chung kuo - Cina* (1972).

Once Marxism-Leninism was rejected as the frame of progressive politicized filmmaking and international solidarity relationships, Godard moved on, in collaboration with Anne-Marie Miéville, to experiment with mass media and information as the potential yet problematic means of bringing about socio-political change. They were mainly interested in furthering an "epistemology of seeing," influenced by Dziga Vertov, calling their practice "journalism of the audiovisual". I explore this in Chapter 4, including an analysis of Godard's experimentation with the video-apparatus in *Ici et ailleurs* to describe his notion of "videographic machinic expression," which he developed in the context of the change from the paradigm of Spectacle to that of Flows of Information. In parallel, Godard developed his concept of "images de marque," or brand images, images from the mass media that become part of history and that need to be deconstructed, which he sought to do through the method of additive montage in the film. During the "winter years" (from the late 1970s and on through the 1980s), the working class began to slowly disappear from the political arena in Europe. Bearing this in mind, in this chapter I devote a section to comparing *Numéro deux* and *Passion*, where Godard portrays—among other things—the ordeals of the working class and of women while exploring the former's incipient political disappearance. During these years, Godard is careful not to resort to either counter-culture or to cynicism; instead of adapting previous positions to the present, he tries to resituate them in the context of the failure and falling myths and political models of the twentieth century.

Taking this into account, I further develop the idea that Godard's juxtaposition in *Passion* of classical paintings with an array of contemporary figures, such as a circus acrobat, a film director, a factory worker, a café owner, etc., as well as a variety of urban settings (a hotel, a factory, suburban housing) is the basis for further experiments in his series of commercial short films commissioned by fashion designers Marithé Bachellerie and François Girbaud. In them, Godard shows classical portraits alongside everyday street images of Paris, ordinary people and the models hired to wear Girbaud jeans. Godard ponders—as he does in *Ici et ailleurs*—what is the *in-between* of these images and the text in the voice-over? This research is taken further in *Le Rapport Darty*, where he explores the new forms of semiocapitalist exploitation: filming Darty's workers in action, he and Miéville analyze the incipient form of "affective labor" based on communication and personal interrelations; while they deconstruct (literally and textually) the then ubiquitous consumerist experience, they maintain their search for the figure that will lead history forward. Finally, I take up Christa Blümlinger's discussion of the cinematic apparatus of the "défilé" as used by Godard in *Ici et ailleurs* and one of the Girbaud shorts, *On s'est tous défilé* (1988), which is an exploration of the becoming image of the *figurants*. In *Le Rapport Darty* as in *On s'est tous défilé*, Godard experiments with the reduction of figures to semiotic matter and their disjunction from the background; the image of the figure of history to come is to be seen in the gap between stasis and movement, slowing down and *video-mélange*.

Chapter 5 begins with positing the aesthetico-political problem of the figure of the victim as witness and proceeds, in the first part, with an analysis of Godard's controversial filmic debate and interviews with Claude

Lanzmann (in Godard's *Histoire(s) du cinéma* in which he responds to Lanzmann's *Shoah*) on the matter of the representability of horror, catastrophe and trauma. When Georges Didi-Huberman stated that Auschwitz had been rendered unimaginable, he was referring, amongst other things, to the polarity and polemic around the ethics and aesthetics of the representability of the Shoah triggered by Godard's *Histoire(s) du cinéma* (released in 1998). In this film, Godard set himself a double task: first, to denounce cinema for not having filmed the extermination camps, and second, by means of the juxtaposition of images from Western visual culture (including documentary images of the camps), to render temporarily visible the horrors of the Shoah. Critiquing Godard for statements he made about the existence of archival footage of the Shoah and about the possibility of filming the event, I analyze the stakes in French psychoanalyst Gérard Wajcman's claims that the Shoah is unrepresentable not as a matter of choice or interdiction, but because "it is *impossible* to see." I further elucidate Wacjman's position with regards to Claude Lanzmann's, for whom the very existence of the extermination camps implies a forbidden representation. For the filmmaker "there is nothing to see," because what the Holocaust shows is that "there is no image." These injunctions mean that the horror of the event exceeds any image seeking to transmit it. Any attempts to represent it would be grotesque, and images trying to convey the horror would domesticate the event, create a distance or provide consolation. Bearing these issues in mind, this chapter focuses on the Godard/Lanzmann debate under the light of *Bilderverbot* (the Biblical interdiction on representation) as well as on Godard's controversial juxtaposition of the Shoah and the Nakba, the Jewish and the Palestinian catastrophes, for which Godard has been accused of anti-semitism.

The second part of Chapter 5 is devoted to *Notre musique*, starting with a description of Godard's Dantesque version of the twenty-first century, a vision foreshadowed by his short video-films of the 1990s: *De l'origine du XXIème siècle/ The Origin of the 21st Century* (2000) and *Je vous salue, Sarajevo* (1993). I further devote a few pages to describe the characters in *Notre musique*, a combination of "real" and "imaginary" figures that intersect in Purgatory. In the following section I address the question of the relationship between text and image in the film, which is inextricable from Godard's method of montage of the shot/reverse-shot. I then discuss how Sarajevo and the Balkans War became the paradigm of intervention elsewhere in the 1990s, elucidating Godard's clear ambivalence toward "humanitarian solidarity" with war victims and survivors. This is linked to the filmmaker's critique of the "humanitarian intellectual" and helps explain why he decided to go to Sarajevo after it had been "reconciled," to think about the Israeli–Palestinian conflict. Here I draw a comparison between Roberto Rossellini's *Germania Anno Zero* (1948) in which he situated a story of survival documenting the ruins of Berlin, and Godard's decision to come to Sarajevo after "reconstruction" and "reconciliation." A further section is devoted to Godard's critique of the "commemoration industry" through the role that the reconstruction of the Vijećnica Library and the Mostar Bridge play in the film. In the following section, I discuss how Godard engages with the work of Elias Sanbar and Mahmoud Darwish, and makes a plea beyond "speaking in the name of others" to "simple conversations" bestowing the potential of salvation to the "vanquished." I conclude with Godard's apology on behalf of the text, as "it has been covered by images," while he vouches for a secular resacralization of the image. By way of the logic of the icon, he problematizes the current obsession with visualization, which has reduced images into standardized objects equated to empirical knowledge.

Chapter 6 is centered on Godard's dialectical materialist filmmaking for the twenty-first century. As I argue, Godard's most recent feature length films—*Vrai faux passeport* (2006), *Film Socialisme* (2010), *Le Pont des soupirs* (2014), *Les Trois désastres* (2013) and *Adieu au langage* (2014)—as well as his 2006 exhibition at the Centre Georges Pompidou, *Voyage(s) en utopie*, take up his decade-long explorations of the relationship between the contemporary and history, aesthetics and politics, image and text, sound and language, the ontology of the image and its status with regard to the legacy of Modernism. By analyzing and comparing these films, I articulate the coherence between Godard's original and more recent explorations of representability, irrepresentability and representation that can be thought of as an array of experiments with montage. For instance, *Voyage(s) en utopie* is an experiment in 3D translated into the exhibition format of the museum installation in which Godard plays with various supports of the image to (re)visit the utopian aspects of his work in dialogue with contemporary art and mass media creating a kind of archive of rescued utopias. In *Vrai faux passeport*, Godard takes up the pedagogy of the image that he began to develop in *Le Gai savoir* and the DVG films, which becomes an exercise of judging images as "good" or "bad" in dialogue with Serge Daney's notion that not any image makes an image. *Film Socialisme* encompasses images, sounds, histories and characters that resonate with each other and deliver an image of the past—the betrayed potential of the concept and idea of Socialism—that affords actualization in the present. A recurrent aphorism in Godard's movies, "L'image viendra au temps de la résurrection" [The image will come at the time of resurrection], attests in *Film Socialisme* to Godard's faith in the redemptive potential of the Image that will come by invoking images of resistance, revolution and revolt that persist in the collective imaginary. In *Adieu au langage*, Godard reintroduces the logic of the shot/reverse-shot he explores in *Notre musique* by positing it as a tension of opposite points within a single frame filmed with 3D technology. This tension within the frame becomes an allegory of the crisis of communication brought about by the dictatorship of digital media. Both *Film Socialisme* and *Adieu au langage* address the failure of humanities to define the human. His most recent film begins and ends with a classic protest song, Alfredo Bandelli's "La violenza" (1968). I conclude that like *Film Socialisme*, *Adieu au langage* is a call to arms; if the former foresaw the massive 2011–12 worldly mobilizations, *Adieu* is the novelty announced by the scream of the newborn and the bark of Roxy the dog, which we hear at the end of the movie. In both films what is to come—a political project and new forms of mediation and enunciation—is yet to be invented.

In Chapter 7 I conclude with an analysis of the legacy of Godard's militant filmmaking in the 1960s and 1970s. Before the impending need to visibilize the intolerable brought about by permanent war everywhere, recent films and art projects have revisited militant filmmaking. The legacy of Godard's political filmmaking, however, is very far removed from his post-1970s materialist filmmaking and manifests today in a problematic niche in cultural production termed *sensible politics*. Godard's materialist filmmaking is a constant search for figures that bear a concrete relationship to history and to possibilities for resistance by revealing historical consciousness. The legacy of Godard's militant filmmaking can be described as: first, questioning Modernity as expressed in the definition of the "human" by the humanities and of "alterity" by Western universalism; second, Godard shows that the modern promise of an enlightened humanism is bankrupt, as exemplified by SS guards who listen to Beethoven while they perform their duties; third, he makes a plea in the name of fiction in an attempt to restitute the link between man and the world and an ongoing call to resist the current manifestations of capitalist occupation.

BIBLIOGRAPHY

Adorno, Theodor W. *Minima Moralia* (London: Verso, 2004)
Arendt, Hannah. *On Violence* (1969) (New York: Harcourt, 1970)
Barthes, Roland. "Écrivains, Intellectuels, Professeurs," *Tel Quel*, no. 47 (Fall 1971)
Barthes, Roland. "The Death of the Author" (1968), *Image, Music, Text* (New York: Hill and Wang, 2003)
Derrida, Jacques. *Of Grammatology* (Baltimore: Johns Hopkins University Press, 1998)
Benhabib, Seyla. "The Legitimacy of the Human Rights," *Daedalus*, vol. 137, No. 3 (Summer 2008)
Bergson, Henri. *Matière et mémoire. Essai sur la relation du corps à l'esprit* (1939). Available at: http://classiques.uqac.ca/classiques/bergson_henri/matiere_et_memoire/matiere_et_memoire.pdf. English translation: *Matter and Memory*, (New York: Dover Publications, 2004)
Daney, Serge. "Le thérrorisé (pédagogie godardienne)", *Cahiers du Cinéma*, nos. 262–263 (1976), special issue of five essays on *Numéro Deux*
De Certeau, Michel. "The Power of Speech," *The Capture of Speech and Other Political Writings*, trans. Tom Conley (Minneapolis and London: The University of Minnesota Press, 1997)
Didi-Huberman, Georges. *Passées cités par JLG: L'œil de l'histoire, 5* (Paris: Minuit, 2015)
Farocki, Harun and Silverman, Kaja. *Speaking About Godard* (New York and London: New York University Press, 1998)
Foucault, Michel. "Qu'est-ce qu'un auteur?" (1970), *Écrits Complets*, vol. II (Paris: Gallimard), p. 821. Translated by Donald F. Bouchard and Sherry Simon, "The Author Function." Available at: http://foucault.info/documents/foucault.authorFunction.en.html
Foucault, Michel. *The Order of Things: An Archeaology of the Human Sciences* (New York and London: Vintage, 1994).
Godard, Jean-Luc. "Jean-Luc Godard—Elias Sanbar," *Politis*, January 16, 2005. Available at: http://www.politis.fr/article1213.html
Godard, Jean-Luc. Interview with M. Cournot, "Quelques evidentes incertitudes," *Revue d'esthétique* (Janvier-mars, 1967), pp. 115–122.
Godard, Jean-Luc. Interview with Olivier Bombarda and Julien Welter for *Cahiers du Cinéma*, November 2007. Available at: http://www.cahiersducinema.com/article1424.html
Hori, Junji. "La Géopolitique de l'image dans les *Histoire(s) du cinéma* de Jean-Luc Godard," available at: http://www.desk.c.u-tokyo.ac.jp/download/es_3_Hori.pdf

Ishaghpour, Youssef. Dialogue with Godard, *Archéologie du cinéma et mémoire du siècle* (Tours: Farrago, 2000)
Jameson, Fredric. *The Geopolitical Aesthetic: Cinema and Space in the World System* (Bloomington: Indiana University Press, 1992)
Jay, Martin. "Mourning a Metaphor: The Revolution is Over," *Parallax* 9:2 (April 2003), pp. 17–20.
Jelicé, Emiliano and Comoli, Jean-Louis. *Mayo Francés: La cámara opaca: El debate cine e ideología*, comp. Emiliano Jelicé (Buenos Aires: El Cuenco de Plata, 2016)
Kracauer, Siegfried. *From Caligari to Hitler: A Psychological History of the German Film* (Princeton: The University Press, 1947).
Loshitzky, Yosefa. *The Radical Faces of Godard and Bertolucci* (Detroit: Wayne State University Press, 1995)
Lukács, Georg. "Realism in the Balance" (1938) trans. Rodney Livingstone, *Aesthetics and Politics*, ed. Ernst Bloch (London and New York: Verso, 1987)
Marrati, Paola. "The Catholicism of Cinema: Gilles Deleuze on Image and Belief," *Religion and Media*, ed. Hent de Vries and Samuel Weber (Stanford: The University Press, 2001)
Mondzain, Marie-José. *L'image peut-elle tuer?* (Paris: Bayard, 2010)
Rancière, Jacques. Interview with Marie-Aude Baronian and Mireille Rosello in 2007. Available at: http://www.artandresearch.org.uk/v2n1/jrinterview.html#_ftn5
Rancière, Jacques. *La Fable cinématographique* (Paris: Seuil, 2001)
Rancière, Jacques. *The Future of the Image* (London and New York: Verso, 2006)
Rodowick, D.N. *Reading the Figural or Philosophy After the New Media* (Durham: Duke University Press, 2001)
Ross, Kristin. *May '68 and its Afterlives* (Chicago: The University Press, 2002)
Rossanda, Rossana. "Les Intellectuels Révolutionnaires et l'Union Soviétique," *Les Temps Modernes*, no. 332 (March 1974)
Silverman, Kaja. "The Author as Receiver," *October*, no. 96 (Spring 2001), pp. 17–34.
Silverman, Kaja. Interview with Gareth James, in *I Said I Love. That is the Promise: The TVideo Politics of Jean-Luc Godard* (Berlin: oe + b Books, 2003)
Watts, Philip. "Godard's Wars," in *A Companion to Jean-Luc Godard*, Tom Conley and T. Jefferson Kline, eds. (Oxford: Wiley Blackwell, 2015)
Witt, Michael. *Jean-Luc Godard, Cinema Historian* (Bloomington and Indianapolis: Indiana University Press, 2013)

CHAPTER 2

Who Speaks *Here?* Jean-Luc Godard's 'Militant Filmmaking' (1967–74)

JEAN-LUC GODARD'S AVANT-GARDE

It is often argued that between 1967 and 1974 Jean-Luc Godard was operating under a misguided assessment of the social and political situation and producing the equivalent of "terrorism" in filmmaking, on the one hand, by subverting the formal operations of narrative film and, on the other, by being biased toward an ideological political engagement.[1] Godard's films of this period, however, are more than partisan political statements or formal experimentations countering narrative filmic form. The filmmaker's response to the intense political climate during what he would retrospectively call his "Leftist trip" years was based on a filmic-theoretical praxis in a Marxist-Leninist vein through which he explored the function of both art and intellectuals and their relationship to empirical reality. Godard examined these in three arenas: politically, aesthetically and semiotically, within the realm of moving depiction. His work between 1967 and 1974 includes the production of collective works within the Dziga Vertov Group (DVG) until its dissolution in 1972 and culminates

---

[1] See Serge Daney's "Le thérrorisé (pédagogie godardienne)," *Cahiers du Cinéma*, nos. 262–263 (January 1976), 32–39; Colin MacCabe, *Godard: Images, Sounds, Politics* (London: British Film Institute/Macmillan, 1980); Raymond Bellour, *L'entre-images: photo, cinéma, vidéo* (Paris: La Différence, 2002); and Peter Wollen, "Godard and Counter Cinema: *Le Vent d'Est*," in *Readings and Writings: Semiotic Counter-Strategies* (London: Verso, 1982), pp. 79–91.

© The Author(s) 2019
I. Emmelhainz, *Jean-Luc Godard's Political Filmmaking*,
https://doi.org/10.1007/978-3-319-72095-1_2

in his collaboration with Anne-Marie Miéville within the framework of Sonimage, a new production company founded in 1973 as a project of "journalism of the audiovisual."

Godard's Leftist trip period could be explicated by bracketing it with two references to artistic practices loyal to a cause or committed positions: opening with a reference Godard makes to André Breton in *Camera Eye*, his contribution to the collectively made film, *Loin du Vietnam*, of 1967, and closing with the appearance of Picasso's *Guernica* in his and Miéville's film made during the course of 1970–74 and released in 1976, *Ici et ailleurs* (*Here and Elsewhere*). When he is citing Breton, on the one hand, Godard is (mis)attributing to him an engaged position aligned with the French Communist Party (Parti Communiste Français, PCF) that implies the instrumentalization of art in the name of a political cause, what we will call "objective denunciation." With his reference to *Guernica*, on the other hand, Godard enters into a conversation with Jean-Paul Sartre's debate with Theodor W. Adorno about the alleged effectiveness of images or the superiority of words for transmitting political messages, and with Sartre's theories on political engagement and aesthetic autonomy. In dialogue with these aesthetico-political positions, Godard carved out his own by opposing "objective denunciation" to Sartre's incommensurable split between "artistic enunciation" and "active political engagement." Godard synthesized the three positions, exploring the contradiction between the practice of "filmmaker" and "militant." He also created a revolutionary imaginary in which Dziga Vertov and Bertolt Brecht are the pioneers, Breton is a deviation, Guy Debord's *Society of the Spectacle* becomes a shared paradigm, Sartre will become his *bête noire*, and philosophers such as Michel Foucault, Julia Kristeva and Gilles Deleuze are his *compagnons de route* (fellow travelers).[2] We must consider, however, that Godard's revolutionary constellation cannot be reduced to these literary references. For example, in *La Chinoise* (1967), Godard establishes the

---

[2] According to Stefan Kristensen, Godard's thought is nourished by an array of thinkers, writers, painters, scientists, philosophers and political scientists and thus we must situate cinema in relationship to the activity of thinking. His point of departure is Maurice Merleau-Ponty, Gilles Deleuze and Félix Guattari. For Kristensen, Godard's point of departure is Maurice Merleau-Ponty but he also suggests to avoid indexing any of Godard's films to such currents of thought, or to divide his work into "philosophical periods" according to authors that would correspond to the readings that marked certain films. I agree with Kirstensen that the questions he has posed in his films since the 1960s, in dialogue with certain thinkers, are always enriched and transformed in later works. See: Stefan Kristensen, *Jean-Luc Godard Philosophe* (Lausanne: L'Âge d'Homme, 2014).

genealogy of his politicized aesthetics, parting from European intellectual history by classifying literary authors, philosophers and artists as either "reactionary" or "revolutionary."

The French literary references to Breton and Sartre are inseparable from the history and tradition of the French avant-garde, which should be considered in the light of the intellectuals' relationship to the PCF. Modeled after Lenin's vanguardist party, intellectuals had a pivotal role in the PCF between the end of World War II and 1965 in producing and conveying political knowledge for the proletariat. As described in *What Is To Be Done?* Lenin's Party functioned as the vanguard of the proletariat, a highly centralized body organized around a core of intellectuals or "professional revolutionaries," leading the social democratic revolution by producing and conveying political knowledge to the proletariat.[3] This ideological avant-garde operated in the realm of opinion and Leftist commonsense, putting art or aesthetics at the service of a political or an ethical cause—resulting in the socialist realism genre—taking for granted the artist's position as the *porte parole* of humanity. Such an avant-garde posits a transitive relationship between art and politics, that is, a causal relationship between the two, even the instrumentalization of art in the name of Leftist political ideology.

Because it was the main referent for political engagement, committed French avant-garde artists, intellectuals and writers had to take a position *vis-à-vis* the PCF and its dogmatic, aesthetic, socialist-realist tendencies. For example, Althusser and Aragon were members, Breton was a dissident and Sartre was a distanced "fellow traveler" and the "party's consciousness." As a dissident, Breton claimed to be a communist while demarcating his artistic practice from the PCF's preference for socialist realism, lamenting their "bad taste."[4] The heyday of the PCF as a point of reference for intellectuals coincided with the high point of Structuralism, when political discourse and the ethics of intellectuals were influenced by Marxism, psychoanalysis and linguistics. At this moment, "the signifier" (the author, the intellectual, the phallus, the father) was treated with the

---

[3] See *What Is To Be Done?*, printable edition produced by Chris Russell for the Marxist Internet Archive, available at www.marxists.org, p. 46.

[4] In André Breton, *Manifestes du Surréalisme*, édition complète (Paris: France Loisirs, 1962), p. 248.

greatest respect.[5] In the 1960s, intellectuals had a status as the consciousness of the party and thus, of society; however, the intellectual, along with the author, the signifier, the phallus, the father and the party were contested as figures of authority and sources of truth. With Marxism-Leninism, for the first time it became possible for radical militants and intellectuals to conceive revolutionary work outside and independently of the PCF.[6] To subscribe to Maoism was a way of taking a position against the Communist Party in accord with the Sino-Soviet split, but disconnected from the dark outcome of the Cultural Revolution. Aside from trying to break away from the model of the vanguardist intellectual, the Maoists "established" themselves in factories working alongside the workers, rejecting the interiority of discourse in favor of the exteriority of practice, believing in the creative potential of the workers, and giving preference to direct, unmediated intervention. Maoist students and workers contested engaged intellectuals', artists' and delegates' representativity, accusing them of being aligned with bourgeois interests. Their legitimacy as disinterested agents who could speak critically in the name of universal values in order to accompany the emancipation of humanity by means of announcing or advancing the Revolution was brought into question. Furthermore, Maoism had declared war against the despotic regime of the signifier, the *figure from above who speaks truths*, a struggle crystallized around the question of representation and representativity in the following interrogation: *Who speaks and acts, from where, for whom and how?* Equating the production of knowledge with power, the question *Who speaks?* interrogates representativity, and it was addressed to union delegates, intellectuals, professors, writers and artists. The question *From where?* means: from which regime of enunciation or from which hegemonic or minoritarian discursive position is the voice speaking? *For whom?* interrogates representability: in the name of whose interests or what community? *How?* is a practical question regarding the relationship between theory and practice, form and content, an issue that stems ultimately from the materialist quest for knowledge and a scientific-pedagogical endeavor. Walter Benjamin's critique of Lenin's professional intellectual was influential in this context. For Benjamin, when engaged intellectuals attempt to integrate themselves with

---

[5] See Michel Foucault's preface to Deleuze and Guattari's *Anti-Oedipus*, trans. Brian Massumi (Minneapolis: University of Minnesota Press, 1983), p. xiii.

[6] Fredric Jameson, "Periodizing the Sixties" *Social Text* no. 9/10 (Spring-summer 1984), p. 182.

the proletarian forces, they come to be placed in a stratum in between classes. As a consequence, they ignore *their own position in the process of production*, falling into the trap of *logocracy*.[7] Benjamin calls "logocracy" an already made activist position in which the intellectual fails to acknowledge his/her own role or position in the process of production, and a system in which words are the ruling power. In order to avoid this trap, Maoists decided to dismiss discourse and to take action, working alongside workers, focusing their energy on the transformation and liberation of the forms and instruments of production, geared at autonomy in management and in representation.

Godard's dialogue with the crisis of representativity and his response to the intense political climate in and around May 1968 were articulated in a strategy based on a theoretical praxis in a Marxist-Leninist line. He explored the contradictions inherent in the question of the artist's "function" and his/her relationship to empirical reality. During the events of May 1968 Godard was involved in the collective production of *ciné-tracts*, a form of filmic tract conceived by Dziga Vertov in the 1920s. Moreover, Godard's Marxist-Leninist vanguard was predicated upon a relationship to art of the past in a movement of reclamation, contradiction and disavowal. His strategy consisted of repeating, testing and incorporating different historical and contemporary avant-garde strategies (Maoism, militant and materialist filmmaking, Brechtian theater, etc.) in a self-referential rhetoric, pointing out the avant-garde's contradictions and ideological pitfalls. Arguably, the logic under which Godard was operating was not that of the avant-garde but of the *war of position*,[8] a strategic rather than an ideological stand. This form of differentiation included the avant-garde's negativity embedded in the Surrealist and Situationist positions, which operated under an anarchic

---

[7] See Walter Benjamin, "The Author as Producer," *New Left Review* 1, no. 62 (July–August 1970), pp. 83–96.

[8] Godard's radical *avant-garde position* somehow resembles—at least metaphorically—Antonio Gramsci's *war of position*, a combination of strategy and tactics, as opposed to a frontal attack like the vanguardist position. The war of position is a stage in the struggle that takes place behind the trenches, a battle against ideology. The war of position, thus, does not take place in armed struggle but in the political plane; for example, Gandhi's passive resistance. See Antonio Gramsci, "State and Civil Society," *Selections from the Prison Notebooks*, edited and trans. Quentin Hoare and Geoffrey Nowell Smith (New York: International Publishers, 1971), 296–298, and Chantal Mouffe, "Hegemony and Ideology in Gramsci," *Gramsci and Marxist Theory*, ed. Mouffe (London: Routledge & Kegan Paul, 1979), pp. 195–198.

logic that posited one pole against the other, for example, freedom against oppression. This form of negativity is predicated upon a synthesis that takes place at the point of the destruction of the enemy, for example, "the bourgeoisie." For his part, Godard's was a form of radical negativity influenced by the Maoist double negativity or logic of contradictions. Rejecting the reconciliation of opposites by annihilation of one of the members of the dialectic, Maoist contradiction can be described as some kind of non-dialectical, eternal struggle of opposites, starting from a principal contradiction to which sets of other contradictions are subordinated. Maoist contradiction is thus a self-revolutionizing logic that, instead of reaching a higher order, advances from qualitative (data) to quantitative (knowledge) through leaps forward and self-critique. Maoist contradiction could be posited as an endlessly repeated negation. In trying to keep the Revolution alive by avoiding temporary stabilization or restorations of the old order, the problem is that this form of non-dialectical struggle leads to a "bad infinity." In order to avoid the "bad infinity" of Maoist contradiction, Godard would experiment, as we will see in Chapter 4, with different montage techniques while always parting from one main contradiction—class struggle, for instance—that bifurcates into further contradictions, following Maoist logic, as we will see below.[9]

Godard's avant-garde was nominal, insofar as it transformed proper names, cries, battles and avant-garde positions into concepts and slogans, fictionalizing the "class struggle" and documenting political actuality. Furthermore, his contradictory avowal and critique of the history and tradition of political Modernism is at the crossroads of the post-structuralist epistemological shift of the separation of the referent from the signifier and the signified, which pointed at the crisis of representation precisely embedded in the theoretical and practical ideologemes of the Left: instrumentality, realism, reflexivity, didacticism and historiography.[10] Therefore, Godard engaged with the French avant-garde as a genealogical tradition

---

[9] In *Passées cités par JLG: L'Oeil de l'histoire*, 5 (Paris: Éditions de Minuit, 2015), Georges Didi-Huberman also notes the Maoist influence in Godard's montage as a dialectic of contradictions parting from the analysis of a "concrete situation" (pp. 51, 52).

[10] Following Fredric Jameson in "Periodizing the Sixties," p. 186. The Leftist ideologemes I mention are part of materialist theoretical practice that was derived from certain readings and practices of Marxism in the 1960s.

inherited transversally.[11] Such genealogical inheritance was deconstructed and modulated in his work as a series of contradictions according to the new problems that Marxism could no longer account for, such as the unprecedented educated middle class of consumers or art's relationship to the explosion of the media and information. The Marxist *Weltanschauung* was radically questioned through the crisis of representativity brought by Maoist practice's insistence on specifying struggles by way of subjectivation, seeking recognition and equality as opposed to universalizing the workers' struggle. In this manner, Maoist practice changed classical political action, which had been predicated upon space and position, embodied in the national or class struggle, with the goal of taking over power. The Marxist problem of changing people's "consciousness" evolved toward a critique of the political, economic and institutional regimes that produced truth and discourses (Althusser's ideological state apparatus) that needed to be contested. In other words, Marxist struggle against ideology through science is displaced toward resistance against the production and propagation of "truth" and "knowledge" by those in power.[12] As we will see below, Godard was also in dialogue in his work with an emerging filmic genre that was put at the service of the working class as counter-information, as a form of intervention or mobilization against capitalism and imperialism. Known as "militant cinema," its stakes, positions and outreach were debated and redefined (in part by Godard's work) in collective films and texts in journals like *Positif, Cahiers du Cinéma, Cinéma Écran, La Révue du cinéma, Image et son* and *Cinéthique*.

Art, Realism, Spectacle: Aragon and Debord

Aside from Maoism and militant filmmaking, there are more elements to be considered in order to account for Godard's vanguardist war of position. During the events of May 1968, Parisian university walls served as

---

[11] As opposed to vertically. Sartre's relationship to the Gauche Prolétarienne exemplifies this transversality: he was something like the "great uncle" of the Maoists—*la mascotte*, as Deleuze put it. As we will see, Sartre's iconic figure of political engagement took over the role that the PCF had occupied before; intellectuals, writers and artists needed to take a position regarding Sartre's engaged position.

[12] Michel Foucault, "La fonction politique de l'intellectuel," *Politique Hebdo*, 29 (November–December 1976), 31–33, reprinted in *Dits et écrits*, volume III (1976–1979). (Paris: Gallimard, 1994), pp. 113–114.

anonymous sites for expression: a graffiti at the Sorbonne read, "L'art est mort. Godard n'y pourra rien."[13] This statement contains three conundrums: the first one is the death of art understood as the failure of modern art's political project. By this I mean the general disenchantment with modern art's utopian project of announcing, accompanying or contributing to the Revolution. The second conundrum is, as we have seen, the Maoist contestation of intellectuals' representativity. The third conundrum is the sublimation of the fate of art into a(n impotent) proper name. By 1968, "Godard" had come to stand for cinema and as the heir to the tradition of modern art. In a text from 1965, Louis Aragon affirms: "C'est que l'art d'aujourd'hui c'est Jean-Luc Godard."[14] Aragon saw Godard's work as the contemporary realization of great art of the past and compared *Pierrot le fou* (1965) to Delacroix's *La Mort de Sardanapale* (1827). For Aragon, who championed socialist realism and who was an ardent member of the PCF, Godard was in 1965 "what we have become."[15] In contrast, the graffiti at the Sorbonne, "L'art est mort. Godard n'y pourra rien," bears the anarchic and iconoclastic spirit of the Situationist International, recalling an acerbic text written in 1966 by Guy Debord in which he rebuffs Aragon's conviction that Godard was the "inspired leader of modern art."[16] For Debord, Godard *and* modern art had been outmoded immediately by the May 1968 movement. In his view, Godard was a "spectacular manufacturer of a superficial, pseudo-critical art rummaged out of the trashcans of the past."[17] With an anarchist standpoint toward tradition and images—evident in his monument to iconoclasm, the 1952

---

[13] "Art is dead. Godard will not be able to save it." Julien Besançon, *Les murs ont la parole: Journal mural Mai 68 Sorbonne Odéon Nanterre etc....*, (Paris: Tchou, 2007), p. 42.

[14] "The art of today is Jean-Luc Godard." Jacques Aumont would further Aragon's conviction by equating modern art to *cinema* (as the most advanced art form of the twentieth century and thus Modernism) as its proper name: "Godard." See Jacques Aumont, "The Medium" (New York: MoMA, 1992).

[15] Louis Aragon, "Qu-est ce que l'art, Jean-Luc Godard?" *Les Lettres Françaises* no. 1096 (September 9–15, 1965). Available online at: http://tapin.free.fr/godard/aragon.html. Date consulted: February 1, 2007. We can see how Aragon would read *Pierrot le fou* and *Une femme mariée* as socialist realist films.

[16] There was another graffiti at the Sorbonne that recalls Situationist animosity toward Godard: "Jean-Luc Godard est le plus con des suisses pro-chinois." [Godard is the biggest pro-Chinese Swiss asshole.] Julien Besançon, *Les murs ont la parole*.

[17] Guy Debord, "The Role of Godard" (1966), in *Situationist International Anthology*, ed. Ken Knabb (Berkeley: The Bureau of Public Secrets, 1989), pp. 175–76.

film *Hurlements en faveur de Sade*—Debord's avant-garde implies a double negativity predicated upon a historical understanding of the avant-garde's project as the negation of art that ultimately finds accommodation within the institution of art and therefore requires it to be negated again. Debord's battlefield is Spectacle, a stage in capitalism in which everything has become its own simulacral inversed image (in the negative Platonic sense): "Tout ce qui était directement vécu s'est éloigné dans une représentation."[18] The conditions for Spectacle are the democratization of signs and an unprecedentedly literate society that produces and consumes its own desires through images. Debord's double negation would result in anti-art: a utopian space beyond labor and leisure in which the masses could be liberated from the oppression of the tyranny of blinding Spectacle. Debord's avant-garde negates both Dada's institutionalization and Surrealism's reverent desacralizations; in them, the logic of destruction served as an ideological weapon against the field of bourgeois culture.[19] Debord's avant-garde is predicated upon the abolition of art as the realization of art aimed at making that aesthetic production transcend the realm of Spectacle. For Debord, Spectacle invades everything and allows for the totalitarian administration of the conditions of existence and thus the purpose of his negativity is self-emancipation from the material bases of Spectacle's inversion of truth.[20] The methods to overcome the tyranny of Spectacle are *détournement*, psycho-geography and unitary urbanism, which are aimed at inciting new situations and new behaviors.

In sum, Godard and Debord would come to hold two contradictory positions regarding the production and consumption of images for and by an unprecedented highly literate middle class. In this regard, there is a clear shift from the main issue that the Russian vanguardists faced in the 1920s: that of addressing an illiterate public made up of peasants in the process of becoming proletarians. How was their art thus going to put itself into the service of the masses? And how would it deal with the Russian art of the past? Differently, Godard and Debord shared the problem of addressing an unprecedentedly literate society made up of middle

---

[18] "Everything that was directly lived has drifted away in its own representation." *La Société du Spectacle* (1967) (Paris: Gallimard, 1996), p. 9. Available in English at http://www.marxists.org/reference/archive/debord/society.htm

[19] Tom McDonough, *"The Beautiful Language of My Century": Reinventing the Language of Contestation in Postwar France, 1945–1968* (Cambridge, MA: MIT Press, 2007), p. 103.

[20] Guy Debord, *La Société du Spectacle*, p. 176.

class consumers. In contrast with Debord's iconoclastic stand, Godard's iconophile project in the late 1960s is inextricably linked to the question of representation posed as a materialist quest for scientific knowledge; such knowledge would be laid out for the viewer to decrypt as a kind of pedagogic visual literacy. Godard tackled further the double burden of bearing a proper name that stood for the failed project of aesthetico-political modernism ("L'art est mort. Godard n'y pourra rien") and against being the forced heir of the "realist" avant-garde embedded in Aragon's phrase: "C'est que l'art d'aujourd'hui c'est Jean-Luc Godard." Godard, therefore, eschews the discursive position that Aragon conferred on him, the proper name of modern art in the 1960s, by repeating modern art's aesthetico-political project in order to critique it through self-critique.

COMMITTED POSITIONS: ANDRÉ BRETON AND JEAN-PAUL SARTRE

As I mentioned above, Godard's Leftist period can be bracketed with two references that claim different committed positions: Breton and Sartre. First, he claimed an avant-garde position that he (maliciously or mistakenly?) misattributed to André Breton in *Camera Eye*, his contribution to the collectively directed film from 1967, *Loin du Vietnam*. The second committed declaration is a scene from *Ici et ailleurs* that crystallizes the conundrum of the Left around May 1968, in which we see a reproduction of Picasso's *Guernica*, presumably bearing upon Godard's relation to Sartre. We should recall that *Guernica* was condemned by Sartre in 1960 and championed by Adorno in 1966; the image's status as both an icon for militant struggles and a kitsch object, unlikely to be hanging on a wall in a working-class family home, renders its presence in the scene quite ambiguous in the diegesis.[21] The painting's role in this scene from *Ici et*

---

[21] The symbolic power that *Guernica* has acquired throughout the twentieth century was highlighted by its being covered up in the UN headquarters at the end of January 2003 when a Security Council meeting was held discussing the impending war in Iraq. The reproduction of *Guernica* was covered in order to impede the production of photographs of the Security Council with the image in the background. The collective Retort begins its book *Afflicted Powers* with a reflection on the meaning of this event crystallized in the photograph of Donald Rumsfeld in front of the UN's reproduction of *Guernica* as a way into the question of Spectacle after September 11th. See Retort, *Afflicted Powers: Capital and Spectacle in a New Age of War* (London and New York: Verso, 2005), p. 16.

ailleurs poses the question, "Who speaks and acts, from where, for whom and how?" *vis-à-vis* the relationship between art and politics, and the new role of intellectuals in relation to the encroaching obsolescence of the Marxist vanguard. The scene takes place in a working-class family's home, in a room where *Guernica* hangs on the wall and in which a little girl is doing her homework. Off-screen we hear the woman asking her husband, "T'as trouvé?", and he answers, "Non, je suis arrivé trop tard."[22] The father goes into the room to greet the girl, who in turn, asks him: "Tu m'expliques papa? Je ne comprends pas!!" He answers while walking out: "Non, je n'ai pas le temps, on verra ça plus tard."[23] The scene ends with the girl's sigh of frustration. In this scene Godard and Miéville stage the putting out of work of political representation, aligning it with the crisis of patriarchy and militancy. The father can neither work nor help, like the union delegate or the intellectual. Explaining and helping to understand—which are tasks for intellectuals, militants and fathers—are deferred and put out of work. In this scene, Godard and Miéville draw an analogy between patriarchal responsibility and the revolutionary's responsibility to mobilize at home. Instead of answering the call to act, the revolutionary postpones action indefinitely: "I don't have time, we'll see later."

In *Camera Eye*, Godard's contribution to the collective film *Loin du Vietnam*, we see the image of the filmmaker standing behind his camera on a Paris rooftop interspersed with images from everyday life in Vietnam: children at school, peasants harvesting rice, village scenes. In the voice-over, Godard states that the images of Vietnam that we are seeing are similar to those that he would have filmed if the authorities had granted him a visa. He declares that his engaged position of "the long revolutionary wait and of objective and declarative enunciation" is after André Breton. This is the *attendiste* position, held by the PCF, and it is malicious that Godard attributes it to Breton because, as mentioned above, it is well known that he had distanced himself from the PCF. This position implies that the artist, while waiting for the revolution, speaks out ceaselessly to convey indignation in the name of just causes. In *Camera Eye*, Godard calls for the imperative to listen and transmit a scream of horror against injustice, denouncing the barbarity of humanity. "Where do

---

[22] "Did you find (a job)?" "No, I arrived too late."
[23] "Can you explain it to me dad? I don't understand!!" "No, I don't have time now, we'll see later."

you speak from?" is the question he seems to be answering when he states that he, as a French filmmaker, is aware that art cannot change the world but *what he can do, as a filmmaker in France*, is to articulate his rage and criticism to transmit a scream of indignation as often as he can. We further learn that this is the reason why Godard decided to mention the war in Vietnam in every single one of his films until it ended. And he did so, from *Vivre sa vie* (1962) until *Tout va bien* (1972). The position Godard takes in *Camera Eye* is, therefore, that of *objective denunciation*, which implies aesthetics' transitive relationship to politics insofar as art is put at the service of a critical function. The problem Godard and Breton had with this position is that it denies autonomy to the artistic field with regard to the ethical and political one. In a manifesto, *Pour un art révolutionnaire indépendant* (1938), Breton stated the following:

> True art, which is not content to play variations on ready-made models but rather insists on expressing the inner needs of man and of mankind in its time—true art is unable *not* to be revolutionary, *not* to aspire to a complete and radical reconstruction of society. This it must do, were it only to deliver intellectual creation from the chains which bind it, and to allow all mankind to raise itself to those heights which only isolated geniuses have achieved in the past. We recognize that only the social revolution can sweep clean the path for a new culture.[24]

For Breton, "true art" or advanced art can be led only by social revolution. Therefore, Breton's position implies a causal link between aesthetics and politics: if political freedom (through social revolution), then aesthetic liberation and vice versa. Thus, "true art" or advanced art is necessarily revolutionary, and it cannot be severed from having as its basis freedom and as its purpose the emancipation of humanity. The position of *objective denunciation*, in contrast, entails that aesthetic activity be intrinsically linked to political action as the means to achieve or announce the emancipation of humanity, denying autonomy to the aesthetic field. As we will see, in dialogue with both Breton and the PCF's militant positions, Godard complicated his own by also encompassing Jean-Paul Sartre's.

---

[24] André Breton, "Towards a Free Revolutionary Art," trans. Dwight MacDonald, in Charles Harrison and Paul Wood, eds. *Art in Theory, 1900–2000: An Anthology of Changing Ideas*, 2nd edition (Malden, MA: Blackwell Publishers, 2003), 533. Originally published in *Partisan Review* IV, no. 1 (Fall 1938), pp. 49–53.

Sartre believed that artists are not mandated by anyone and yet they are called to speak critically in the name of the emancipation of humanity. In that sense, objective denunciation is close "collective objectivity," which implies the exercise of one's freedom in order to act in the name of universal values. Sartre's position, however, implies a split between the "writer function" and the "intellectual function." In Sartre's view, a writer inhabits a fundamental contradiction. On the one hand, the artist/writer is creator and purports his/her *being-in-the-world* through language producing partial yet universalizing non-knowledge. The writer is also capable of producing practical knowledge, and does so not in his/her own work, but by operating in "lived reality" in the name of universal truth. What is at stake here for Sartre is the "utility" of works of art and the contradictory situation in which writers live in: the non-knowledge (knowledge that is not scientific or objective, *savoir* as opposed to *connaissance*) that the writer produces in his literary work, for the most part ends up serving the class in power and has limited reach toward the masses. That is why for Sartre the writer has two functions, the intellectual function and the writer function. While the writer is not mandated by anyone and therefore produces practical truths in the name of universality, the intellectual is able to reach out toward the masses to help lead their emancipation.[25] For Sartre the two activities were unbridgeable. In an interview in 1972, Godard explained his relationship to Sartre's engaged position:

> I participated with him [Sartre] in a few actions for [the journal] *La Cause du peuple*.[26] And after, I tried to establish a dialogue with him but it was impossible. I was trying to find out the relationship in his texts about the Russell Tribunal or about the Houillères, which were amazing texts, and his older or more recent studies about Flaubert and Mallarmé. He then tells you that there are two men in him. One who continues to write about Flaubert because he doesn't know what else to do, and another one who has thrown himself with all his soul into the struggle, by going to address the

---

[25] See Jean-Paul Sartre, Bernard Pingaud and Dionys Mascolo, *Du rôle de l'intellectuel dans le mouvement révolutionnaire* (Paris: Le terrain vague, 1971), and Sartre's three conferences from Kyoto, Japan from 1965 published in *Situations, VIII: Autour de 68* (Paris: Gallimard, 1972).

[26] *La Cause du people* along with *J'accuse* were journals directly linked to the Proletarian Left supported by Sartre (amongst other intellectuals) but dissolved due to internal conflicts in 1972.

workers at the Renault factory standing on top of a barrel. We don't deny either position. We simply think that as an intellectual radicalising himself, he should bridge both positions.[27]

While "Sartre-the-intellectual" fulfills the function of speaking out, the writer works subjectively with language. Clearly, Sartre drew a distinction between the writer and the intellectual functions in order to avoid a transitive relationship between politics and aesthetics. For Sartre *objective denunciation* must take place separately from the field of aesthetic production, in the domain of *engaged activism*. Literature (and art) is thus severed from a critical function. "Freedom" in the aesthetic and in the political domain is maintained not by a transitive link, but by a separation: art is autonomous non-knowledge and it may be subservient to the class in power and because of that, the conscious artist/writer is in the awkward position of being pushed forward to act politically in the empirical realm. Furthermore, for Sartre, a work of art or literature does not have to be measured regarding its "effectiveness" in the political or ethical realm because artworks *should not be* effective in the political realm. Taking Picasso's *Guernica* as an example, he famously stated: "Does anyone think that it won over a single heart to the Spanish cause?"[28] Further, Sartre's intellectual function involves a *dépassement radical* (radical overcoming) of the bourgeois condition of the writer function in order to become a "transcendental consciousness" and to bring truth to institutions that lacked it (as the Party's consciousness), as well as carrying philosophy to the streets (as the proletariat's fellow traveler).[29]

Godard grappled with Sartre's split between *engaged activism* and *artistic enunciation* in his text titled "Manifeste", published in 1970 in Fatah's journal in France, *El Fatah*: "En littérature et en art, lutter sur deux fronts. Le front politique et le front artistique, c'est l'étape actuelle, et il faut apprendre à résoudre les contradictions entre ces deux fronts."[30] Adopting Breton's

---

[27] Godard in the interview with Marlène Belilos, Michel Boujut, Jean-Claude Deschamps and Pierre-Henri Zoller, first published in *Politique Hebdo*, no. 26–27 (April 1972); reprinted in *Godard par Godard*, p. 374.

[28] *What is Literature?* trans. Bernard Frechtman (New York: Harper Colophon Books, 1965), p. 5. First published in France in 1947.

[29] See Pierre Bourdieu, "Sartre, l'invention de l'intellectuel total," *Libération*, 31 March 1983, pp. 20–21.

[30] Quote from *Manifeste* (1970): "In literature, as in art, to struggle on two fronts. The political front and the artistic front; it is the current stage, and we will need to learn to solve

and Sartre's avant-garde positions as contradicting attitudes and holding the two in suspension allowed Godard to point out the contradictions inherent in both models of the aesthetico-political avant-garde. This mirrored his own effort to problematize both the transitive relationship between politics and aesthetics purported by objective denunciation and the separation of artist and activist implying art's autonomy and therefore its severance from a critical function. As we have seen, Godard claimed that Sartre did not go far enough because, in his view, he should have attempted to reconcile the intellectual function with the writer function. Therefore, Godard experimented with bridging Sartre's split between *active engagement* and *artistic enunciation*, opposing it to *objective denunciation* and declaring that he had taken the position of "militant filmmaker." In this manner, Godard kept his filmmaking practice somehow separate from Sartre's "intellectual" function of active engagement, yet the two positions—militant *and* filmmaker—can be easily conjoined because in his Marxist-Leninist films he experiments constantly with the intransitivity between aesthetics and politics, weaving and then unravelling their relationship.

In his political sympathies, Godard gravitated toward the Proletarian Left Party (La Gauche Prolétarienne, a Maoist party active from 1969 to 1973), collaborating in actions around its journal *La Cause du peuple*. Godard also wrote five articles for the Maoist journal *J'accuse* and participated in the creation of the newspaper *Libération*.[31] When the DVG was officially formed in 1969, Godard reinvented his practice as a filmmaker. Godard began to make films collaboratively when he met Jean-Henri Roger in 1968, a member of the editing committee of the extreme Left journal *Action*. Godard was commissioned later on that year by Kestrel Films to film a portrait of England and thus he and Roger together made *British Sounds* in 1969. That same year, they worked together on *Pravda*.[32] From that moment on, Godard reinvented his practice as a filmmaker. His purpose was to rethink the notion of authorship, specifically *Cahiers du Cinéma*'s *auteur* theory, and to position himself *vis-à-vis*

---

the contradictions between the two fronts." Reprinted in *Jean-Luc Godard: Documents*, p. 138.

[31] For an account of Godard's involvement with the Leftist French press during the DVG period see Michael Witt, "Godard dans la presse d'extrême gauche" in *Jean-Luc Godard: Documents*, 165–177.

[32] For a detailed history of the Dziga Vertov Group see Antoine de Baecque, *Godard Biographie* (Paris: Grasset & Fasquelle, 2010), pp. 445–448.

other militant film collectives and their avant-garde agendas. In the summer of 1969, Godard began to shoot *Le Vent d'Est* based on an idea by Daniel Cohn-Bendit. Jean-Henri Roger, along with other militants who gravitated around him and Godard—Paul Bourron, Isabel Pons, Raphaël Sorin and Nathalie Biard, all of whom were friends of Jean-Pierre Gorin and with whom Godard met regularly since 1968—joined them in Rome for the shooting. They were all Maoists and Althusser, Eisenstein and Vertov were important to them. According to Antoine de Baecque, a small band was born then with the same objective: to make films differently and to hold discussions for hours. Officially, *Le Vent d'Est* marks the birth of the DVG.[33]

The group thought of itself as a cell (as a political group or *groupuscule*), but differently from other filmmaker collectives and Maoist groupuscules that were organized around concrete struggles (i.e., solidarity with female workers, with Chile or Vietnam, etc.), they adopted the banner of the filmmaker Dziga Vertov, seeking to situate their own praxis within the history of cinema.

Standing against the vanguardist logic that seeks to delineate a future emancipatory image of the world, the DVG movies show the political actuality; by describing their films as "materialist fictions," they took a position with regards to "realist" and "materialist" politicized cinema, as we will see below. Moreover, Godard's and Gorin's program adopted Vertov's affirmation that film is a secondary task to the revolution, a task that they had decided to make their principal activity.[34] Also, after Vertov they claimed that their aim was to see and show the world in the name of the revolution. Why Vertov? For the filmmakers, he was the inventor of film-tracts and "the only Bolshevik filmmaker" in opposition to the "bourgeois filmmaker" Sergei Eisenstein. This split within the Russian avant-garde is related to the fact that Eisenstein was said to have held an "idealist" as

---

[33] Antoine de Baecque, *Godard Biographie*, pp. 450–457.

[34] "Cinéma, tâche secondaire de la révolution pour nous actuellement en France; mais nous faisons notre activité principale de cette tâche secondaire." [Cinema is for us, in France, a secondary task to the revolution, but we make of this secondary task our principal activity.] *Manifeste* (1970) reprinted in *Jean-Luc Godard: Documents*, p. 138. Godard wrote: "There is no cinema above classes, no cinema above class struggle: also we know that the cinema is a secondary task and our program is very simple: to see and show the world in the name of the world proletarian revolution." Jean-Luc Godard, "Pratique révolutionnaire," *Cinéthique* nos. 9–10 (Fall 1971), p. 74.

opposed to "materialist" position in filmmaking, because he accepted images without exploring their validity and constructed them without being reflexive about their process of production. In contrast, Vertov's "materialist" position implied his concern with the constructive aspect of images. His concept of the Kino-Eye directed his preoccupation with drawing a distinction between the naked eye's and the camera's relationship to reality, ascribing to the camera the role of "seeing" the world. In other words, Vertov's Kino-Eye implies: "The possibility of making the invisible visible, the unclear clear, the hidden manifest, the disguised overt, the acted, non-acted: making falsehood into truth."[35] For Vertov, cinema was a factory of facts (*factography*), a form of visual thinking able to decode life "as it is." Godard and Gorin's repetition of Vertov's revolutionary paradigm in terms of image production transformed Vertov's practice; leaping into the French context some 40 years later, they modulated the Kino-Eye adapting it to the new "revolutionary" conditions. Beyond the old vanguardist logic influenced by dialectical materialism, the DVG's aim was not to supersede the history of cinema through its negation but to create it anew by repeating the old. None of their nine films are signed. Rather, they are vindicated *a posteriori* in places such as interviews or written documents.[36]

---

[35] Dziga Vertov, *Kino-Eye: The Writings of Dziga Vertov* (Berkeley: University of California Press, 1984), p. 88.

[36] Ambiguity attended the birth of the DVG; while *British Sounds* and *Pravda* were made by Godard in collaboration with Jean-Henri Roger and were retrospectively vindicated by the Group, *Le Vent d'Est* and *Luttes en Italie* (1970) were mostly made by Godard and Gorin. According to Baecque, *Vladimir et Rosa* (1971) is the only "true" film by the Group, as it is the result of the effective co-operation of the half a dozen people working on it. Armand Marco joined in as the *chef opérateur* in 1969 to supervise the shooting in Palestine for what would become *Ici et ailleurs* (1976). *Letter to Jane* (1972) was also made by Godard and Gorin and *Un film français* is a project that dates from 1968 written by Jean-Pierre Gorin and Nathalie Biard about France, "an experimental film about France's history, actuality, revolution and other political struggles." The film was never made and neither was *La Jeune Taupe*, written by Nathalie Biard and Raphaël Sorin in 1972, a "documentary fiction film" and portrait of a Leftist community and of an engaged woman. *L'ailleurs immédiat* was written collaboratively by Gorin, Sorin, Biard and Pons and their establishing of Tout Va Assez Bien Films company signaled the beginning of the rupture with Godard rendered definitive by Gorin's move to California in 1974. See: Antoine de Baecque, *Godard Biographie* (Paris: Grasset & Fasquelle, 2010), pp. 500–513. See also Faroult, "Never More Godard," *Jean-Luc*

I noted above that Godard implemented anarchic negativity toward the *institution* of cinema, but I argue that he reversed the logic of anarchy, in the sense that his aim was not to destroy film in order to begin *tabula rasa* to create the conditions for a new beginning from a blank screen. Rather, in Godard, the history of cinema makes up for a black screen from which the clichés need to be extracted by means of confrontational juxtapositions of sounds and images. Instead of aiming at cinema's ideal form, the DVG reinvented the rules of cinema by expanding them to the general regime of image production. In other words, revolutionizing the institution of cinema meant, on the one hand, making films that were considered as "non-cinema" or at the margins of cinema and, on the other, taking up a battle in all modes of image production techniques: film, painting, photography, journalism, television, advertisements, and hoping to expand its innovations into the realm of televisual production and technique. Television was for the group the place where it could create new relationships of production. It was a site that could offer the group a wide range of technological innovations, the possibility of creating new relationships between spectator and text, and the chance to exploit the pedagogical potential of television, which had been so far repressed in institutional television practice.[37] The DVG's films—*British Sounds* (1969), *Pravda* (1969), *Lotte in Italia/ Luttes en Italie* (1970), and *Vladimir et Rosa* (1971)—were co-produced by London Weekend Television, Munich Tele-Pool, the European Center for Radio-Film-Television and RAI, respectively.[38] In most cases, the producers refused to show the films. The DVG also critiqued the institution of cinema by staging Godard's "disappearance" as *auteur*. As he stated:"Abandonner la notion d'auteur, telle qu'elle était. C'est là qu'on voit la trahison, le révisionnisme intégral. La notion d'auteur est complètement réactionnaire."[39] Since 1968 he furthermore retreated to

---

Godard: Documents, 123 and Julia Lesage, "Godard and Gorin's Left Politics," *Jump Cut*, no. 23 (April 1983).

[37] Colin MacCabe, *Godard: Images, Sounds, Politics*, with Mick Eaton and Laura Mulvey (London: British Film Institute, 1980), p. 120.

[38] David Faroult, "The Dziga Vertov Group filmography," *Jean-Luc Godard: Documents*, pp. 132–133.

[39] "To abandon the notion of *auteur*, such as it was. We find it treacherous, sheer revisionism. The notion of *auteur* is completely reactionary." Statement by Godard in an interview with *Tribune socialiste* (23 January, 1969) quoted by Antoine de Baecque, p. 445.

the margins of the mainstream ways of production and distribution of films. Godard clarified his position as follows:

> There has never been revolutionary film within the System. There cannot be. There is the need to be at the margins, trying to profit from the contradictions inherent to the System in order to survive outside of the System. In this manner, we can profit from the System, attempting to radicalize it if it is reformist, like a student reformist: to radicalize it.[40]

In disappearing, Godard demonstrated that films and filmmakers exist only with a specific set of production relations. Godard's gesture is linked to two aspects of cinema that he criticizes reflexively: one, the financing of films, that is, the methods of production and distribution (what comes to mind is the opening sequence in *Tout va bien* in which we see Godard signing the checks that will pay for the production costs of the movie), and second, the notion of *auteur* which implies a certain way of organizing sounds and images in particular films.[41]

MAOISM AND THE DZIGA VERTOV GROUP

In ideological and general terms and in direct opposition to the revisionism of the PCF and of their faction, the CGT (Confédération générale du travail), the DVG's *political* line was Marxist-Leninist or Maoist.[42] As we have seen, the Maoists in France took a position against the PCF in accordance with the Sino-Soviet split but were effectively disengaged from the dark outcome of the Chinese Cultural Revolution and Chinese state-power interests. During the 1960s in general, intellectual militant practice impinged directly on advanced cultural practice and production. In this respect, militant filmic practice was very much in line with a "tradition" linking political parties and filmmakers. Militant practice in film entailed introducing the class struggle into the sphere of culture, just like the Formalists' and the *Proletkult*'s avant-garde strategies in Leninist Russia. In historical terms, the coming together of students' contestation with workers' struggle in May 1968 brought about new forms to engage with workers. Many of the members of the former Union des Jeunesses

---

[40] *Godard par Godard*, p. 334.
[41] Colin MacCabe, *Godard: Images, Sounds, Politics*, p. 18.
[42] See Gérard Leblanc, "Sur trois films du Groupe Dziga Vertov," *VH 101* no. 6 (September 1972), unpaginated.

Communistes Marxistes-Léninistes (UJC (ml)) were or had been Althusser's students. Amongst them were Jacques Rancière, Alain Badiou, André Glucksmann and Jean-Pierre Gorin. During the events of May and June, the UJC (ml) as a party decided not to participate in the strikes, provoking its breakdown. Some of the members mythically gathered in September 1968 to discuss the events, to study most notably Lenin's *What Is To Be Done?* They also created a Maoist "party," La Gauche Prolétarienne, and the journal *La Cause du peuple*, both of which were made illegal by Pompidou's régime.[43] Wanting to overcome the limitations of CGT delegates, the Maoists targeted their bureaucratic structure and denounced their inability to go beyond attempting to satisfy workers' bread-and-water demands. The Maoists also rejected the model of the Leninist vanguardist party and any kind of permanent organization with leadership functions. The bringing into crisis of the representability of professional intellectuals and mediators inspired them to seek direct communication and to listen to workers. They gave themselves the task of learning from workers as opposed to being at their side or in the front leading their struggle. Their goal was further to create anti-despotic and anti-hierarchical forms of organization, with the working class rendering their position immanent to the struggle.[44] They evidently aimed at going beyond old intellectual types, prioritizing people's speech as opposed to intellectual expertise or knowledge: "la parole des gens: que le pouvoir révolutionnaire se fixe comme prioritaire l'expression."[45] In the Maoist war against despotic power, they sought not to fight the power of the State in the singular, but to attack diffuse forms of power by diffusing speech. Creating operational models and drawing strategic and theoretical lessons from actions, they sought to bridge the gap between manual and intellectual labor, by working in the production plants right alongside workers, a practice known as *établissement*.[46] The Maoists also

---

[43] By 1972 many *gépistes* were in prison on political grounds. This drew attention to the deplorable state of French prisons, prompting the creation of the GIP or "Groupe d'information sur les prisons".

[44] Michèle Manceaux, *Les Maos en France* (Paris: Gallimard, 1972), 201. Cited by Belden Fields, *Trotskyism and Maoism: Theory and Practice in France and in the United States*, (Brooklyn: Autonomedia, 1988) p. 102.

[45] "People's speech: that the priority of revolutionary power is established as expression." Pierre Victor (pseudonym of Benny Lévy), *On a raison de se révolter* (Paris: Gallimard, 1974), p. 103.

[46] The practice of *établissement* was not new. In the mid-1930s, the thinker and activist Simone Weil experienced the assembly line by enlisting to work in a factory. See Simone Weil,

confronted the police at the factories and organized base committees and general assemblies. Other Maoist tactics included occupying plants, kidnapping bosses until they accepted the workers' demands, sabotage and resisting the paramilitary CRS when it attempted to take over the occupied plants, which garnered media attention.[47] A notable Maoist action was the confrontation with the police at the Renault factory in Flins in June 1969; violent confrontations reached a peak in February and March 1972 when Pierre Overney, a Maoist worker who had been fired, entered the gates of the factory and was shot by a security guard. Allegedly, 200,000 people (including Sartre and Foucault) attended Overney's funeral at Père Lachaise.[48]

In as far as Godard and Gorin's political line was Maoist,[49] they subscribed to Maoist materialism for filmmaking. Maoist materialism is a tool for understanding the development of something by observing the thing's relationships to other things. Mao designed this method because for him, in their process of development, complex things hold many contradictions. Maoist contradiction differs from dialectical materialism in that it posits change differently than sublation into a higher unit: Maoist contradiction implies quantitative changes and leaps into qualitative changes. Following the Maoist method, Godard and Gorin located a particular contradiction dominating a concrete situation and subordinated other contradictions pertaining to the situation to the principal one,[50] seen from various points of view. Their films *British Sounds, Pravda, Lotte in Italia/Luttes en Italie, Vladimir et Rosa* and *Jusqu'à la victoire* (among others) are thus concrete analyses of the political situations in Britain, Czechoslovakia, Italy, France and Palestine respectively.[51] For example, the main contradiction in *Lotte in*

Oppression and Liberty (1955), (London: Routledge, 2001) and *La Condition ouvrière* (Paris: Gallimard, 1951). See also Robert Linhart's *L'Établi* (Paris: Éditions de Minuit, 1978), where he narrates his experience in a factory and describes the dehumanizing conditions of Taylorist assembly lines.

[47] Belden Fields, *Trotskyism and Maoism*, p. 103.

[48] Ibid., pp. 101–130.

[49] For an extremely detailed account of the "political lines" followed by the DVG see Gérard Leblanc, "Sur trois films du groupe Dziga Vertov," *VH 101*, no. 6 (September 1972).

[50] See Mao Tse-Tung's "On Practice: On the Relation between Knowledge and Practice, between Knowing and Doing," and "On Contradiction," *On Practice and Contradiction* (London: Verso, 2007), 52–102; also available at www.marxists.org

[51] For detailed descriptions of the DVG films see Peter Wollen,"Godard and counter cinema: *Vent d'est*"; Julia Lesage, "*Tout va bien* and *Coup pour coup*: Radical French Cinema in Context," *Cineaste* 5, no. 3 (Summer 1972); David Faroult, "Never More Godard"; James

Italia—class struggle—branches out into the contradictions of the main character, a female, middle-class student, who is also an activist. Afterwards, Godard and Gorin built images according to the contradictions and proceeded to self-critique. The DVG's application of the Maoist method for filmmaking implied making "simple" images that would reflect a double process of cognition and codification by analyzing concrete situations applied to social practice. For instance, Godard made *La Chinoise* in 1967 about a Maoist groupuscule that, in a way, anticipates the events of May 1968 about the concrete situation in Paris. *Vladimir et Rosa* and *Tout va bien* also engage with the Parisian situation during the moment of fully fledged Maoist activism.[52] Bearing in mind that the DVG aimed at bridging form and content in its films without amalgamating them, we can describe them as concrete analyses of the political actuality seen through the lens of engaged theory and practice, aiming at defamiliarizing Maoist militant theory and practice. For example, the phenomenon of *établis dans des usines* (students working in factories to learn from workers) is explored in two of DVG's films: *Lotte in Italia* and *Vladimir et Rosa*. *Lotte in Italia* shows a militant student, Paola, dealing with the contradictions inherent in her subjectivity as conditioned by her objective modes of existence in Italy. In the film we learn about her experience of working in a factory and about her relationships with aspects of the ideological state apparatus, such as family, love, university and language.[53] *Vladimir et Rosa* is a taxonomy of French and American militant Leftist factions, transposed into a fictionalized account of the trial of the Chicago Seven situated in Paris. In *La Chinoise*, *Vladimir et Rosa* and *Lotte in Italia*, the characters are militants assembled in cells or groupuscules, dealing with the contradictions inherent in their militant practice. *Tout va bien* (1972) addresses Maoist activism four years after May 1968. Here, the activists are older and their engagement is in conflict with their

Roy MacBean's *Film and Revolution* (Bloomington: Indiana University Press, 1975); and Gérard Leblanc and David Faroult, *Mai 68 ou le cinéma en suspense* (Paris: Syllepse, 1998).

[52] For analytical descriptions and analyses see Peter Wollen, Julia Lesage, "Godard and Gorin's *Le Vent d'est*: Looking at a Film Politically," *Jump Cut*, no. 4 (November–December 1974), David Faroult, "Du Vertovisme du Groupe Dziga Vertov," *Jean-Luc Godard: Documents* (2006), James Roy MacBean, *Film and Revolution*, (Bloomington: Indiana University Press, 1975), Colin MacCabe, *Godard: Images, Sounds, Politics* (Bloomington: Indiana University Press, 1980), and Gérard Leblanc, "Sur trois films du groupe Dziga Vertov."

[53] According to David Faroult, *Lotte in Italia* is a *mise-en-scène* of Althusser's text "Idéologie et Appareil Idéologique d'Etat" [Ideology and ideological state apparatus], 1970, to which Godard had access through Gorin because it circulated clandestinely amongst his students before it was published.

adult life. To sum up, the application of the Maoist method for the acquisition of knowledge by the DVG implied making "simple" images that *reflect* a double process of cognition and codification, analyzing concrete situations applied to social practice: a pedagogical enterprise in a Brechtian vein that maintained the fiction that is necessary for artistic discourse in order to distance the group and the viewer from the ideological implications inherent to the concrete situations analyzed in the group's films. In his recent book on Godard, Georges Didi-Huberman also notes the influence of Mao's dialectic in Godard's work. According to Didi-Huberman, this dialectic is based on bifurcating contradictions parting from "concrete situations" in which "problems are situated as in a carpet," positing them "where contradictions are most acute." For Didi-Huberman, however, an image addresses us appearing as "a concrete analysis of a concrete situation" as it is embedded within the economy of montage which is fundamentally dialectic. I would argue, however, that for Godard the "concrete situation" is not an image in itself, but rather, a specific situation that he constructs with images delivering contradictory points of view. In Godard's films, concrete situations are: Czechoslovakia after the Soviet invasion in 1968 (*Pravda*); a Maoist student's everyday dilemmas in Italy (*Lotte in Italia*); the situation of the Black Panthers in the United States (*One A.M.*, 1968); the political and cultural situation in England (*Sympathy for the Devil*); and Germany after the fall of the Soviet Union and the communist bloc (*Allemagne année 90 neuf zéro*, 1991). And more recently, Sarajevo after the "reconciliation" (*Notre musique*, 2004) or Europe today as in *Film Socialisme* (2010). The dialectic is thus constructed, not only through an economy of montage joining images, texts and sounds in polysemic interplay, but in the construction itself of a concrete situation.[54] Further, the DVG films postulate the political actuality as a historicizing fiction, placing actuality beyond individual and collective events, turning "social types" (i.e., "workers") and historical figures (i.e., "third world revolutionaries") into the films' characters. Historical specification here becomes relevant because the DVG is describing history *in action*, positing critically Maoist militants as the actors of history rather than engaging with the universalizing discourse of "class struggle." In these films, Maoism is taken not as

[54] See: Georges Didi-Huberman, *Passées cités*, pp. 51–52.

an ideological basis but becomes the *method* for making images rather than the *code* of representation or the films' discourse; Godard and Gorin render Maoist practice literal by calling their films "materialist fictions."

Furthermore, the DVG built each one of its films following the method of Maoist self-critique. In an interview that took place during a visit of the DVG to the United States in 1970, the group described this method as the means that enabled it "to go one step forward."[55] Self-critique is a distancing, self-referential tool that it further used in order to condemn its films to failure and therefore to "rescue" them from being ideological accounts of the political actuality. For example, the DVG disavowed *Pravda* in a text handed out after the film had been shown, stating that it now saw the film as bourgeois, insofar as it had been shot via the means of "political tourism," and for being a superficial analysis of the current situation in Czechoslovakia. According to this text, neither the montage nor the shooting had been successful. I cite a passage from the handout from the Musée d'Art Moderne de Paris in February 1970, on the occasion of a projection of *Pravda*: "Tournage hâtif, opportuniste, petit-bourgeois. Tournage qui n'est pas du 'montage avant le montage' (Vertov). Montage qui n'est que du montage avant le montage, au lieu d'être du montage dans le montage… Des images encore fausses parce que produites dans le camp de l'idéologie impérialiste."[56] In an interview, Godard and Gorin self-critically stated about another one of their films: "We made the effort to finish it, and not to quit and say it is just garbage. But having made the psychological effort, we must also put a sign on it, to indicate that this is a garbage Marxist-Leninist movie, which is a good way of titling it. At least now we know what not to do anymore. We've visited a house in which we'll never go again. We thought it was a step forward but we realized [it was], how do you say, a jump into emptiness. It was a learning process. And the first thing we learned was that it was not done by group work, but by two individuals."[57] In another instance of self-critique, Gorin states

[55] Jean-Luc Godard, "Interview with Godard and Gorin (with Goodwin and Marcus)," in Michael Goodwin and Greil Marcus, *Double Feature: Movies and Politics* (Dutton, 1972), p. 36.

[56] "Hasty, opportunistic and *petit-bourgeois* shooting. This shooting is not 'montage before montage' (Vertov). Montage that is not montage before montage, instead of being montage within montage…False images because they were still produced from the viewpoint of imperialist ideology." Reprinted in *Godard par Godard*, 340.

[57] Kent E. Carroll, "Film and Revolution: Interview with the Dziga Vertov Group," *Evergreen Review* 14, no. 83 (October 1970), p. 54.

about *One A.M.*: "The principle was all wrong. We tried to produce some fiction out of a certain reality, but the problem was the reality itself. You can't do it like that." About *Sympathy for the Devil*, Godard states: "There are a lot of things in the movie that are not understandable, and the picture can be faulted for that because it was dealing with things in an absolute unclear way."[58]

Self-critique is different from synthetic critique or anarchic obliteration: Brecht's *V-effect*, for example, is another form of critique that refuses synthesis. Furthermore, for the group, "starting at zero," meant beginning with the Althusserian basics of "hearing and seeing," at the blank blackboard of non-knowledge. In a way, DVG's self-critique is a victory embedded in a defeat: it uses revolutionary practice, language, form and content nominally and methodologically in order to be able to disavow it. Self-criticism in the DVG's work functions as Maoist self-revolutionizing, which means not to overcome contradictions, but to create grounds for an arborescent proliferation of contradictions. Discursively, self-criticism is not only a correction of the program once the pitfalls become evident, but also, it is a tool for changing from one stage of development to another, in order to produce subjective knowledge (leaping forward).[59]

MATERIALIST FILMMAKING AND MATERIALIST FICTIONS

It could be argued that Godard and Gorin's *materialist fictions* are at the crossroads of Brechtian Realism, Althusserianism and materialist filmic practice. Realism stems from the historical materialist *Weltanschauung*, which presupposes an objective whole based on the relationships of production as the basis for history. Materialism is a method to produce objective knowledge through the cognition of this objective whole, describing it in *action*, focusing on the relationships of production. Moreover, materialism seeks to render the world visible producing *reflections* or *consciousness* of the relationships of production by means of the dialectic between essence and appearance, producing objective knowledge of the world. In literature, after Lukács, *realism* is the *reflection* of the objective reality constituted by a materialist worldview that, in line with a political party, functions like an ideological weapon. In Lukács'

---

[58] Both quotes are from *Double Feature*, pp. 10 and 20 respectively.
[59] Mao Tse-Tung, "On Contradiction," pp. 63–64.

formulation, realism perceives the overall significance of the phenomenon described, depicting *social types in struggle* that have objective meaning in the total context of the materialist worldview.[60] "Objectivity" implies here that the thing depicted exists *independently* from the subject that perceives it and thus, perception is the reality of the object.

Brecht's theoretical practice of producing self-knowledge, his mandate of technical innovation and of unveiling the truth inherent to power discourses, became influential within the French filmmaking context in the 1960s. For Brecht, a scientific-theoretical practice is crucial to be able to bring forth technical and formal innovations and address the proletariat. Brecht tackled the problem of realism seeking to transform the process of "knowing the world" into a form of aesthetic experience bound to the real, making the viewer see reality in a new way. Therefore, in Brecht, the concept of realism acquires cognitive as well as aesthetic and pedagogical status.[61] His aim was *to unmask the prevailing view of things*, which is the view of those who are in power, and to go beyond realism's premise of bringing the class struggle into narrative content.

Materialist filmmakers in France problematized the objectivity of filmic images, arguing that cinema's transparency is rendered opaque by the ideology of the cinematic apparatus. Whereas the object may exist independently from the subject, the cognition of the object is inevitably imbued with ideology and therefore it is not necessarily true to objective reality. That is why the true existence of an object can only be known transcending sensory cognition *through a scientific reflection*; in other words, true reality can only be apprised by piercing through its ideology-imbued reflection, verifying its "objectivity" by means of theoretical practice. In general, Leftist filmic practices from the mid-1960s to the late 1970s were characterized by filming social movements aimed at showing the "reality" from which the members of the movements sought to emancipate themselves. In the 1975 December issue of the journal *Écran*, Guy Hennebelle and Daniel Serceau defined militant cinema in the following manner:

---

[60] Georg Lukács, "Realism in the Balance" (1938) trans. Rodney Livingstone, *Aesthetics and Politics*, ed. Ernst Bloch (London and New York: Verso, 1987), p. 33.

[61] Fredric Jameson, "Reflections in Conclusion," *Aesthetics and Politics* (New York: NLB, 1979), p. 205.

Cinéma militant designates films that generally present the double characteristics of having been shot on a very small budget, in the margins of the commercial production system, and of having the goal of short-term political intervention or long-term ideological intervention.[62]

This "realist" militant cinema was put at the service of the working class and addressed an activist public. Around May 1968, filmmakers and workers gathered around collectives such as SLON (Société pour le lancement des oeuvres nouvelles), Les Groupes Medvedkine, Cinéastes révolutionnaires prolétariens, Cinéma Libre, Cinélutte, Dynadia, and Ligne Rouge. The DVG was one amongst them. Paul Douglas Grant has described its practice as generally seeking non-hierarchical forms of collectivization. The group also debated whether workers should be the ones holding the cameras and sought political forms of film distribution. Some militant filmmakers conceived film as popular education to disseminate communist ideas to the masses, others sought to contribute to elaborating a tactic for revolution by conducting a concrete analysis of national situations. They were all anti-capitalist, anti-revisionist and anti-imperialist.[63]

One main challenge of militant film was to break with traditional and bourgeois forms, and to contest the spectacular aspect of film, as well as its becoming the object of consumption, but without creating dogmatic films that would alienate the masses. Militant filmmakers also fought against the figure of the author and wanted to push the limits of what constituted filmmaking.[64] In sum, as a practice, militant cinema sought to overcome socialist realism in transforming it formally. This means that it attempted to demystify the process of cinematic production and the notion that the cinematographic image is a pure or objective register of reality, seeking to produce self-knowledge based on self-criticism.

Considering the discussions around militant film, the DVG claimed to produce *materialist fictions* that address the viewer didactically and in a Brechtian vein, and consider him or her as an active agent in the decodification of the movie.

---

[62] Guy Hennebelle and Daniel Serceau, *Écran* (Décembre 1975) quoted by Paul Douglas Grant, *Cinéma militant: Political Filmmaking & May 1968* (New York: Columbia University Press, 2016), p. 7.
[63] Grant, *Cinéma militant*, p. 36.
[64] Ibid.

In "realist" filmmaking (or militant films), content (social types in struggle) prevails over form. Examples of militant films based on a materialist cinematic practice include SLON'S *À bientôt, j'espère* (1967) or Marin Karmitz's *Coup pour coup* (1972). As a practice, *materialist cinema* sought formally to demystify the process of the film's own making, deconstructing the apparent "objectivity" (discourse) of the filmic apparatus by producing self-knowledge. The formula of materialist militant films is to film the reality of a concrete struggle and to introduce the mechanisms of cinematic self-reflexivity (i.e., a shot of the camera in front of a mirror filming itself).

The DVG's first written manifesto, "Premiers Sons Anglais," appeared in the film journal *Cinéthique*, no. 5 (September–October 1969). In it, the group began to outline its political praxis, which it articulated further in a text published in 1970 by the British film review *Afterimage* entitled "Quoi Faire?" Godard described the militant program of the DVG by underscoring a distinction between political films and films conceived politically, directly engaging in the debates about militant cinema in France. Political films correspond, in Godard's view, to a metaphysical conception of the world: these films *describe* situations, for example, the misery of the world, and are thus in accord with bourgeois ideology and operate under representational logic. In contrast, "films made politically" belong to the dialectical conception of the world which implies doing concrete analysis of concrete situations with the purpose of showing the world in struggle in order to transform it. Instead of making images of the world that are "too whole" in the name of a relative truth, making films politically entails studying the contradictions that exist between the relations of production and productive forces and producing scientific knowledge of the revolutionary struggles and their history. In sum, in line with militant filmmaking, the DVG insisted on a theoretical preoccupation with the relationships between world, image and representation.[65] Along with the impending need to account for the explosion of information and art becoming information, this led the group to create semiotic-visual experimentations, which became the basis of the pedagogy of the "blackboard films." In them, the DVG aimed at fabricating contradictory images that are not "too whole," but "just [*juste* in French]," by articulating disjunctions between "true" sounds put on top of "false" images. Its practice was based on a

---

[65] From the original manuscript, reproduced in *Jean-Luc Godard: Documents*, pp. 145–151.

"productivist" model. This means that the group sought to achieve autonomy in the means of production and distribution of its films.

Specifically, Godard problematized militant films, most notably in a letter addressed to Carole Roussopoulos in 1979, accusing her of "hiding herself" behind the images she filmed.[66] More concretely, the differences between a (realist or materialist) militant film and the DVG's materialist fictions become evident if we compare Karmitz's *La Cause du peuple* with *Tout va bien*, which came out the same year. Starring "real" female workers, *La Cause du peuple* is a documentary fiction of a factory strike in the North of France. Karmitz's film uses real workers and video as a tool for auto-critique: the video tape shot would be shown to actors who decided if they felt they had been adequately represented and who debated how the material could be improved. In an interview from 1970, Karmitz declared: "there are two possibilities in film: militant film and what I call the democratic front film. Militant films are in the form of a tract and are designed to attract an activist audience. The democratic front film is designed to unify all those who can be unified politically, whether they are militant or not... a film cannot be independent of political reality and political reality at the moment consists of militants who do their political work through a party or through mass organizations... a democratic front film is aimed at those mass organizations."[67] The issues raised by the film are predictable, as the narrative is centered on women's oppression in the familial and working environment. Godard and Gorin's *Tout va bien* is a remake of Karmitz's film. The film begins like the first one, with a strike where the workers have kidnapped the boss. Jane Fonda is a Leftist journalist who arrives at the factory to do an *enquête* (interview) about the strike, accompanied by her partner, Yves Montand. They end up being held hostages in the factory where Fonda is able to observe firsthand how the workers are oppressed by their working conditions. She and Montand literally "put themselves in the place of" the workers, as we see them in consecutive scenes making sausages and cutting beef in the factory. When the strike ends and they come out, they face the frustrating

---

[66] First printed in *Cahiers du Cinéma* no. 300, special issue by Godard (1979), reprinted along with a response from Roussopoulos in *Jean-Luc Godard: Documents*, pp. 298–299. Godard would make similar critiques in his films in the 1970s of photo-journalistic and documentary images, which have "objective" meaning for Godard in that "no-one speaks" in them, thereby hiding the point of view of the speaker.

[67] "Towards a Proletarian Cinema: An Interview with Marin Karmitz," *Cinéaste* Vol. IV, no. 2 (Fall 1970), pp. 20–25.

aspects of their contradictory lives: Fonda's story is refused by her boss, the couple enters a crisis, and Montand is unhappy because as a former militant filmmaker, he is now forced to make commercials to earn a living. *Tout va bien* ends with the staging of Pierre Overney's funeral, and of a ransacking of a supermarket by Maoists. A number of devices allude to the ideological condition of the filmic apparatus in *Tout va bien*, such as the legendary panning shot of the two-floored factory set, or the initial sequence of checks being signed to fund the production.

In discussions around materialist filmmaking, the Marxist notion of the "objective" whole of the historic-dialectical *Weltanschauung* was contested next to André Bazin's cinematic realist ontology. The critique of filmic "objectivity" was laid out in a 1969 debate between two influential film journals, *Cahiers du Cinéma* and *Cinéthique*, concerning the matter of realism, indexicality and cinematic reflexivity.[68] Bazin conceived photographic images as the impression of reality; that is, as the transference of reality onto its own reproduction. In Bazin's view, photographic image-production is an essentially objective, natural phenomenon, a genesis without mediation that attests to its own veracity. For Bazin, photographs are founded on the absence of man and thus they are essentially objective; this gives photographic images a power of credibility that painting does not have because it is "illusionistic." In addition, with photography, nature shows itself to the camera and, because of that, images are transparent windows on reality. Cinema, for Bazin, temporalizes the imprint of reality within the filmstrip. The credibility of cinematographic images is further achieved by means of montage, which should seek to unify the factors of the action in a single cinematographic plane in order to elicit our belief in them. In the famous debate, *Cahiers* accused Bazin of "phenomenological positivism" and "materialist mechanism," which considered photographic images as creations based on the absence of a human hand, and the camera as an unmediated source. Taking a classic avant-garde position, *Cinéthique* underlines the need for a cinema based on the transformation from "a neurotic ideological discourse to a scientific and revolutionary discourse" that could help the proletariat in its struggle for power. This transformation could be made possible by making a break (*coupure*, in Althusser's

---

[68] In 1969 Godard broke with *Cahiers*, for which he had written since the late 1950s, and joined *Cinéthique*, demanding that *Cahiers* take a position regarding *Cinéthique* and to elicit a political program. See the *Cahiers/Cinéthique* debate: *Cahiers du Cinéma*, nos. 216–17 (October–November 1969) and *Cinéthique* no. 5 (September–October 1969).

sense of a split between ideology and science) in the history of cinema between idealist and materialist films.[69] Based on practical theory, *Cinéthique* hoped to overcome cinema's ideological function by conceiving it as self-knowledge. By "rendering visible" its physical and social materiality, they further aimed at showing the ideological, political and economic functions proper to cinema. "Rendering visible" is the act of unveiling the apparatus by which the film accedes to a theoretical level, breaking away from film's verifiability as an "impression of reality."[70] *Cahiers* opposed this program because it believed that a cinematic theoretical practice is impossible and that theory is impotent in transforming the ideology inherent in film and science. In its view, there can only be "revolutionary critics," and this meant that it refused to prescribe a political program for cinema. It further established that the knowledge that a film can produce is of an epistemological order, and thus *not* scientific knowledge. *Cahiers* further critiqued *Cinéthique's* "false" opposition between materialist and idealist film; for it, *Cinéthique's* aim at transforming cinema into self-knowledge was futile because it did not modify cinema's ideological nature. In the view of *Cahiers*, the practice of "unveiling" the process of fabrication does not convey scientific or objective knowledge, but transforms film into its own discourse: "A camera filming itself is neither science, theory nor 'materialist cinema': reflection of a reflection, ideology mirrors itself." *Cahiers* situated its battleground elaborating a mode of critique that would make evident how certain films display ideological conformity to the system. It further set itself the task to do detailed critical work about the conditions of possibility of representation, analyzing how the mechanisms of representation are rendered innocent in cinema.[71]

To summarize, for the DVG and for *Cinéthique*, the critical function of cinema was to cut through ideology formally, rendering visible the techniques or the social relations of filmic production by means of cinematic reflexivity in order to produce self-knowledge. Godard starts with the presupposition that images and sounds belong to ideological discourses and thus his aim was to establish a program to test images and sounds in a way

---

[69] For a taxonomy of "ideological" and "materialist" filmmaking see Jean-Louis Comolli and Jean Narboni, "Cinéma/idéologie/critique," *Cahiers du Cinéma* no. 216 (October 1969).

[70] Jean-Paul Fargier, "La parenthèse et le détour," *Cinéthique* no. 5 (September–October 1969), p. 21.

[71] Jean Narboni and Jean-Louis Comolli, "Cinéma/idéologie/critique 2: D'une critique a son point critique," *Cahiers du Cinéma* no. 217 (November 1969), p. 9.

that would allow him to get beyond ideology. As we have seen, Godard presented his "theoretical practice" for the first time in *Le Gai savoir* (1969).[72] The method he laid out there claims to be scientific filmmaking, focused on a concern with the relationships between world, image, sound, discourse and representation.[73] This method is loosely based on Louis Althusser's own theoretical practice, which was aimed at demystifying Ideological State Apparatuses through the process of gathering heterogeneous information and experiences. In *Le Gai savoir*, the main characters Patricia Lumumba (Juliet Berto) and Émile Rousseau (Jean-Pierre Léaud) set themselves the tasks of first, gathering images and recording sounds in order to make experiments with them. Second, they criticize them by means of decomposition, reduction, substitution and recomposition of ensembles of images and sounds. Finally, they fabricate models of relationships between sounds and images, followed by an auto-critique. The three steps—gathering, criticizing, and building models—overlap most of the time. *Le Gai savoir* and the DVG's films further experimented with the recent epistemological shifts prompted by post-structuralist thought. Such shifts dealt with a new object that emerged from the contestation of the figure of truth and origin, which was paired up with ideological deconstruction: the *text* in Barthes' sense, which opened up meaning to the infinity of the signifier.[74] Post-structuralism implied further a fundamental reorganization (or revolution) of representation in favor of difference: the redistribution of the relationships between writing and speech, space and representation (subject and object), by way of theoretical practice. Godard would explore this redistribution and introduction of differential relationships between word, image and sound in the domain of cinema.

Realism, Materialist Filmmaking and Materialist Fictions

Departing from the materialist principles of *Cinéthique*, the DVG shares Bazin's anti-Platonism insofar as, for the latter, the photographic image is the transference of reality onto its own reproduction. The photograph's

---

[72] For an account of *Le Gai savoir* through the lens of post-structuralism see Kaja Silverman and Harun Farocki, *Speaking About Godard* (New York: The University Press, 1998).
[73] Arguably, *Le Gai savoir* inspired the position *Cinéthique* took in the 1969 debate with *Cahiers*.
[74] Roland Barthes, "From Work to Text" (1971) in *Textual Strategies: Perspectives in Poststructuralist Criticism,* ed. Josue V. Harari (Ithaca, New York: Cornell University Press, 1979), pp. 155–164.

origin is by contact, entailing a physical and material process of transference from reality to its reproduction. From this perspective, analogue images are transparent insofar as they verify their own origin, conferring thereby credibility. In a scene from *La Chinoise*, we see written on the wall in the background: "Il faut confronter des idées vagues avec des images claires."[75] This sentence evidences that for Godard, as for Bazin, images are not "pure" or "good" copies or originals but belong to a different domain than ideas or essences. Parting from the post-structuralist differentiation of Plato's subordination of false appearances (bad copies) to the realm of ideas (truth), for Godard, as for Bazin, an image's origin is the image itself. They diverge, however, in the role they bestow upon cinematic montage with regard to images' transparency. If, for Bazin, montage gives cinematic images verifiability, for the DVG montage is a means not only to shatter the verifiability of images and sounds, but a way to prompt our suspicion toward the ideology infused in them, because ideology renders them opaque as opposed to transparent. This means that, in addition to the post-structuralist splintering of Platonism, Godard takes a materialist position regarding the status of images as *reflections* of reality. When he states: "La photographie n'est pas le reflet du réel, elle est le réel de ce reflet,"[76] Godard puts forth an understanding of images as "opaque" mirrors subordinated to the "reality" of the mode of cognition proper to the filmic apparatus. Images are thus real reflections of themselves: they are material presences (as opposed to appearances) bearing the code of social practice. Godard's theory of the relationship between image and text is inextricable from montage, a relationship that he explores through Reverdy's, Breton's and Benjamin's notions of the image as that which emerges from the juxtaposition of two other images, as we will see further in Chapter 4.

The DVG's aphorism, "Pas des images justes, juste des images [not exact or fair images, but simple images]," is a rearticulation of Mao's theory of knowledge that asserts that "correct ideas" *come from social practice*. "Not [to make] correct images, but simple images" or "Not [to make] images that are fair, only [to make] images" implies differentiation in kind, "simple" as opposed to "correct"; the latter would imply a moral or ethical judgment, "good" or "true" as opposed to "bad" or "false." The contradiction

---

[75] Vague ideas should be confronted with clear images."

[76] "Photography is not a reflection of what is real, but the reality of that reflection". Jean-Luc Godard, "Premiers sons anglais," *Cinéthique* no. 5 (September–October 1969), reprinted in *Godard par Godard*, p. 338.

raised by the differential opposition between "simple" and "correct" images, as qualitative differentiation versus moral judgment, seeks to initiate a leap toward conceptual knowledge. This leap, according to Mao, happens in two stages: first, when sufficient perceptual knowledge is accumulated (from objective matter to subjective consciousness, from existence to ideas); second, the qualitative leap from consciousness back to matter, from ideas back to existence, in which all knowledge gained in the first step is applied to social practice. There is an extra third leap (auto-critique) that proves the correctness or incorrectness of the first leap in cognition and/or the measures formulated in the course of reflecting the objective external world. In Marxist-Leninist terms, therefore, cognition is the process of codification of *qualitative resemblances* and its application to practice, whose success can be measured by *quantitative equivalences*, or by its efficacy in its application to social practice.[77] The DVG's application of the Maoist method for the acquisition of knowledge implied making "simple" images that *reflect* a double process of cognition and codification, the analysis of concrete situations and its application to social practice: a pedagogical enterprise in a Brechtian vein that retained the fiction necessary for artistic discourse in order to distance the filmmakers (and the viewer) from the ideological implications inherent in concrete situations. Rather than communicating pre-existing ideas to a passively receptive audience, the DVG's films are semiotic machines for making viewers think actively about the world in a new way.[78]

According to Julia Lesage, Brecht's *Me-Ti* was a key influence on Godard and Gorin as a model to render current political events fictional.[79] *Me-Ti* is a collection of short anecdotes inspired by the ancient writings of Mo Tzu (Me-Ti in German), relating them to contemporary politics, Brecht's own life and the Russian Revolution. The entries in *Me-Ti* are didactic and whimsical and feature Chinese fictional characters that refer in code to Marx, Lenin, Engels, Stalin and so on. Differently from Socialist realist characters, which are indexes of a pre-existing social class with its specific ideological values and worldview, the DVG's characters, like

---

[77] See Mao Tse-Tung, "Where do Correct Ideas Come From?" (1957), in *On Practice and Contradiction: Slavoj Zizek presents Mao*, pp. 167–168.

[78] See Peter Wollen, *Signs and Meaning in the Cinema* (expanded edition), (London: BFI, 1998).

[79] See Julia Lesage, "Godard and Gorin's Left Politics: 1967–72," *Jump Cut*, no. 25 (April 1983).

Brecht's, are socio-historical figures that transcend individual and collective events. The DVG's characters could be understood as social categories, as "species" inscribed in social processes, rendered as narratives; the characters are further made up of agglutinations of codes that may or not correspond to the "species," that is, they embody contradictions. For example, the "feminist" character played by Anne Wiazemsky in *Vladimir et Rosa* is an MLF (Mouvement de Libération des Femmes) member whose emancipatory struggle is contradicted by her traditional relationship with her boyfriend. The DVG's films further postulate the political actuality as a historicizing fiction, placing actuality beyond individual and collective events, turning "social types," (e.g., "worker") into historical figures within a narrative, for example, "Third World revolutionary as a dysfunctional paternal figure" in *Ici et ailleurs*, or "Militant filmmaker facing the quandary of making a living" in *Tout va bien*. Historical specification becomes relevant here because the DVG films describe history *in action*, specifically, by conceptualizing French militantism as a historical phenomenon as opposed to engaging in a universalizing discourse of "class struggle"—like socialist realism.

A pivotal concern in Godard's work during the DVG years was to find new modes of expression (new images and new techniques) that would logically account for the Maoist bringing into crisis of mediation as representation. As a provisory conceptualization, I will argue that the DVG's films transform Marxist-Leninist "dogma" (content, theory) into Maoist "action" (form, practice). Therefore, Maoism becomes the *code* of representation and the *method* for making images—rendering Maoist practice literal, inscribing the signifier "Revolutionary class struggle" in the image.

By way of montage, the DVG systematically disjointed sound-image relationships, most of the time opposing one another through interpretative confrontations. From the DVG's point of view, sound's property of being the most powerful mediator of images, and images' quality of mediating or reflecting reality through the mechanism of representation, needed to be put out of work. As we have seen, the DVG's project included bridging the gap between (political) form and content. It tried to make this bridge by transubstantiating the militant problem of "class struggle" into the domain of sound/image relationships. Godard had already posited this in *Le Gai savoir* as Patricia Lumumba states: "Le son c'est le délégué syndical de l'oeil; il va de soi que l'image, elle est le bureau politique de l'oreille."[80] According to Godard, because sound coincides exactly with its index, it is inseparable from the referent, and that is why it is more powerful than image. In the films from the late 1960s, Godard thus explored the problem of sound taking over images and determining our reading of them. When Patricia states that sound is the delegate of the eye, she points to sound's ability to enforce an image by becoming its signifier. In her conceptualization of the problem, the image becomes a site for listening. The cinematic image is made problematic on two grounds: an image is not only representative of something, but is in turn represented by a sound that has been put "on top" of it. The task of montage is, therefore, to liberate images and allow them to speak for themselves, by means of bringing sounds and images together in such a manner that the juxtaposition would give leeway to interpretative confrontations, hindering images from becoming vehicles for specific messages. Put differently, sounds have the property of hindering images' intertextuality. In cinema, we do not *hear* an *image of a sound*, we hear a "sound-image" which is sound itself,[81] and thus, sounds *speak on behalf of images*. For Patricia Lumumba, if sounds are true, then when images are adequate to reality, they are false.

This means that for Godard, images are true only when they fail to represent us. The main lesson to be drawn from *Le Gai savoir* is therefore that neither images nor sounds present a true mirror of reality. In the DVG films, Godard continues to explore the relationship between sound-image transposed to class struggle. Sound (as voice, as discourse) is laid out in *Ici et ailleurs* as being "too loud":

> Prendre le pouvoir est possible quand l'image // au même temps qu'elle renforce un son en se présentant à sa place // quand l'image à son tour elle est représentée par un autre son // comme un ouvrier se fait représenter par son syndicat // et que cette organisation traduit ça par des mots d'ordre // qu'en les appellent elle les retourne à l'ouvrier comme mots d'ordre.[82]

---

[80] "Sound is the union delegate of the eye; it goes without saying that the image is the political front desk of the ear." From the script of *Le Gai savoir: Mot-à-mot d'un film encore trop réviso* (Paris: Union Ecrivains, 1969), unpaginated.

[81] Jean Baudry quoted in Kaja Silverman, *Acoustic Mirror: The Female Voice in Psychoanalysis and Cinema* (Bloomington: Indiana University Press, 1988), p. 4.

[82] "Taking power is possible when the image // at the same time that it reinforces a sound by presenting itself in the place of a sound // when the image in return lets itself be represented by another sound // like a worker letting himself be represented by his union //

The Capture of Speech and *Le Vent d'Est*

In May 1968, the position of the speaker as a producer of knowledge and as representative of truths was contested. The limits of knowledge or commonsense were put to work by demonstrating language's paucity and its inadequacy to account for reality. Therefore, the Maoists attempted to create instances of direct communication and to produce egalitarian spaces to speak in one's own name. In that sense, May 1968 symbolized emancipation from the despotism of the minority in power and the capture of speech by the majority stammering, blabbering, refusing to speak and so on.[83] Thus, the utopia of May 1968 materialized as a society completely transparent to itself by means of the direct exchange of free direct speech (without mediation) in the "General Assembly." The French government's repressive response to Maoist activism[84] and the unconscious taking hostage of the momentary "liberation" of speech by the Maoists, however, turned their voices into despotic sound and into *logorrhea*, both of which the DVG explored in its work along with the limits of the "General Assembly." Logorrhea is a moment of "bad parrhesia" or inadequate free speech (passion-action, noise), defined as verbal activity that reflects uncritically anything that comes from someone's mind. For his part, Philippe Gavi described the limitations of the "General Assembly" in the following terms:

> On ne discute jamais dans une assemblée générale. Tous les gens repartent frustrés en disant 'ce n'est pas possible'. Pire, certaines organisations, comme l'AJS ont pour triste habitude de s'accrocher au micro et de faire voter la motion quand ils ne restent plus qu'eux dans la salle. Au contraire, la vraie discussion apporte à chacun. Comment peut-elle devenir un moyen de lutte, une pratique politique?[85]

and the union translates this fact (of representation) // into slogans which are in turn applied and given back to the worker as order-words."

[83] Michel de Certeau, *The Capture of Speech and Other Political Writings* (Minneapolis and London: The University of Minnesota Press, 1997).

[84] For an account of the repressive measures taken by Raymond Marcellin, the French Minister of the Interior, between 1968 and 1973, see Jean-Pierre Le Goff, *Mai 68, l'héritage impossible* (Paris: La Découverte, 1998).

[85] "We never have discussions during a general assembly. Everybody leaves frustrated saying 'it's not possible.' Worse, in certain organizations like the AJS [Alliance des Jeunes pour le Socialisme] they have the sad habit of hanging onto the mike to ask people to vote for a motion when it's only them who are left in the room. On the contrary, true discussion con-

Insofar as the "liberation of speech" evidenced the paradox of democracy—everyone is free to speak and yet only a minority speaks and acts in the name of the majority—a new interrogation emerged: who can utter what needs to be heard and from what regime of enunciation?[86] In their films, Godard and Gorin were critical of Maoist "fellow travelers."[87] While they acknowledged that Maoists had contributed to political practice with radically new elements, they held that the Maoist contestation of the intellectuals' role in the revolution had not gone far enough.[88] As we have seen, for the Maoists, intellectuals, instead of speaking in their name, were supposed to put themselves humbly at the service of the working class, communicate directly with the workers and be "re-educated" by them. According to DVG, however, Maoist intellectuals denied their privileged position only in appearance. In the end, they concluded that workers do expect that intellectuals tell them things, as opposed to the radical practice of intellectuals refusing to speak to them or on their behalf from above. Another of the DVG's critiques of the relationship between Maoists and workers was the fact that the former belong to the realm of non-productive labor, and the latter to productive labor. In order to bridge that difference, Maoists used the interview or the *enquête*, with the purpose of placing the project under the direction and control of collective labor by workers, who discussed and elaborated together a text, sentence by sentence. The *enquête* thus serves the political role of *regrouping* workers around a project, the

cerns everyone. How can discussion become a means of struggle, a political practice?" In *On a raison de se révolter*, p. 280.

[86] See Tom Conley's "Afterword" to de Certeau's *The Capture of Speech and Other Political Writings*, p. 183.

[87] Following Christophe Bourseiller, who stated that the Proletarian Left used the generic terms of "democrats" or "fellow travelers" to designate the intellectuals who gravitated around the party. They included Sartre (who assumed the editorship of the Maoist journal *La Cause du Peuple*), de Beauvoir, Karmitz, Katia Kaupp, Mariella Righini, Alexandre Astruc, Agnès Varda, and Gérard Fromanger. Bourseiller, *Les Maoïstes: La Folle histoire des Gardes-Rouges français* (Paris: Points, 2008), pp. 152, 198.

[88] Jean-Pierre Gorin stated: "Le gauchisme, en tant que pratique politique, a apporté des éléments radicalement nouveaux, mais en ce qui concerne les intellectuels, ce qu'il propose est une solution de type révisionniste réadaptée aux exigences d'une lutte et d'une pratique anti-révisionniste." [Leftism as a political practice has brought in radically new elements, but in what concerns intellectuals, what they propose is a kind of revisionist solution that is re-adapted to the demands of a struggle and a practice that are in principle anti-revisionist.] Interview with Marlène Belilos, Michel Boujut, Jean-Claude Deschamps and Pierre-Henri Zoller, *Politique Hebdo* nos. 26, 27 (April 1972), reprinted in *Godard par Godard*, 374.

production of the text acting as a unifying force that initiates or sustains the process of self-formation of the group, reinforcing its consciousness of its own existence as a group, and breaking down the hierarchy between manual and intellectual work and the activist's directing position.[89] Still, for Godard and Gorin, the method of *enquête* fails to obliterate the main source of difference between workers and Maoists, which is the question of salary. In a public discussion, when someone justified and praised militant practice on the basis that it was non-salaried work (the rhetoric of *self-sacrifice* pervaded amongst Maoists),[90] Godard furiously responded:

> Mais ce n'est pas vrai, ces gens ne travaillent pas avec salaire. Excuses-moi c'est un discours fasciste, même pas fasciste, un discours d'esclave du fascisme—c'est pire que tout. Tu vas interviewer des gens et t'a pas de salaire? Et tu vas interviewer un mec dont le seul problème c'est d'en avoir un? Et tu n'en as pas? Qu'est-ce que tu vas lui dire pauvre pomme? RIEN!!![91]

The problem was that Maoist activists did not have the means to bridge their differences with workers in order to communicate directly with them. Arguably, the two groups spoke different languages (salaried, productive work as opposed to non-salaried and non-productive labor) and could not understand each other simply because they operated in different realms of production: factory labor and education or activism.

In *Le Vent d'Est* (1970), Godard and Gorin reflect upon the problem of "liberated speech" that confronted militants and militant filmmakers in the aftermath of May and June 1968 in Italy. The film was scripted by Daniel Cohn-Bendit, directed by Jean-Luc Godard and starred Gian Maria

---

[89] See Ross, *May '68 and its Afterlives* (The University Press, Chicago, 2002), pp. 110–111.

[90] See the 1973 discussion on sacrifice and militantism between Philippe Gavi, Pierre Victor and Jean-Paul Sartre in Victor, *On a raison de se révolter*, pp. 178–198.

[91] "But it's not true that these people work without receiving a salary. Excuse me, but this is a fascist discourse; in fact, it goes beyond fascism. This is the discourse of a slave of fascism, which is as bad as anything. You go off to interview people and you do not earn a salary out of it? And you interview a guy whose sole problem is to find a job that pays him one, and you do not have a salary? What are you going to discuss with the poor chap? Nothing!" From unpublished material transmitted on June 22, 1976. Source: the archives of the Phonothèque, l'Institut National de l'Audiovisuel, Paris. For the television series he made with Miéville, *Six fois deux: sur et sous la communication* (1976), they interviewed a number of people, including a mathematician, a painter, a prostitute, a peasant, a photo-journalist and a young man. For Godard, the interview is work, and he makes it a point to have remunerated his interviewees the equivalent of an hour of work.

Volonté (Italy's box-office favorite at the time).[92] Young militants, intellectuals and actors also participated in making this "Italian Western about the May '68 French events."[93] The film brings together two discursive realms, provoking a kind of clash of codes: the discourses, voices, speeches, and sounds of May 1968 are superimposed on images of Western filmmaking. In other words, the *form of the content* or genre is the Western and the *form of expression* (or code) is class struggle. There are three scenes in the film that are particularly relevant to the question of Maoist "liberation speech": (1) the chronicle of a strike in which we hear "lying" and "stammering" voices; (2) the delegate sequence, in which workers and the delegate are shown speaking different languages—the delegate is thus a *traduttore, traditore* (translator, traitor), and mediation is inevitably mistranslation; and (3) the General Assembly, in which Godard and Gorin reflect on the moment of frenzied speech, logorrhea and dialogue that leads nowhere. In terms of the embodiment or figuration of speech, some of the voices are dissociated from the characters whose "speech" is outside of the diegesis. Images, in turn, are liberated from their representative role and given a semantic function, producing a kind of pictography by way of images reflexive on their own relationship to language.[94] In other words, speech and image are disjointed along with what is "sayable" and "visible". I further offer three kinds of speech: "lying speech," "stammering speech" and a third voice, a female voice that embodies "militant cinematic speech," which becomes the regime of enunciation of the collective that got together to make the film—the incipient DVG. The role of this voice is to make sense of what the two other voices are saying and to elaborate, self-critically, a program for the militant filmmakers.

[92] James Roy MacBean, *Film and Revolution* (Bloomington and London: Indiana University Press, 1975), p. 118.

[93] According to David Faroult, Godard and Henri Roger (with whom he had been working in previous DVG films) were approached by a rich Italian patron who wanted to bring together fashionable names to make a politico-collective film with figures such as Daniel Cohn-Bendit and Gian Maria Volonté. After a few days of shooting, most of the members of the group fled to Italian bistros and beaches with the money from the film. Godard asked Gorin to come and help him. They took over the "production team," and the result was *Le Vent d'Est*, their first film together. David Faroult in an interview with Jean-Pierre Gorin, cited in "Never More Godard: Le Groupe Dziga Vertov, l'auteur et la signature," *Jean-Luc Godard: Documents*, p. 123.

[94] Peter Wollen, "Godard and Counter-Cinema: *Vent d'Est*," in *Readings and Writings*, p. 80.

The first scene opposes *stammering*, depicted by students and workers who are the "acting minorities," to *lying*, depicted by revisionist or bourgeois discourse, embodied by the boss, his daughter, and the delegate. The worker's voice is dictated by another voice (presumably Godard's). The voices are superimposed on the images of Anne Wiazemsky and a young man, who are the Maoist activists. In a scene in which they are lying on the grass, the female "cinematic voice" states twice: "Il y a deux voix qui ont continué à mentir, deux voix qui ont continué à bégayer. Quelle est la nôtre? Comment le savoir? Que faire?"[95] This was the question asked by Maoist militants in September 1968, at the moment when they gathered to discuss what to do in the aftermath of the events of May, when they founded La Gauche Prolétarienne. The following sequence illustrates didactically the negotiation between workers and the factory owner through the mediation of the delegate. The background is a beautiful landscape populated by characters dressed up in nineteenth-century attire, depicting "the bourgeois," "the boss," (Gian Maria Volonté), "the delegate" and the "worker"; the latter is wearing "Red Indian" attire. The film stages the failure of the delegate to speak truthfully on behalf of the workers. For them, the delegate represents by translating: "Le délégué traduit dans la langue du patron la lutte ouvrière,"[96] and he fails because as the Renaissance exclamation attests, the translator is a deceiver (*traduttore, traditore*), "Quand le délégué traduit, il trahit."[97] In this scene, the delegate's efforts of translation and failure to rightfully articulate the workers' concerns are put forth didactically. The delegate speaks in Italian and the worker in English; we see that the former fails to convey adequately the workers' demands to the boss.[98] This delegate represents the CGT delegate, the target of the critique of the DVG and the Maoists. We know that he belongs to the

---

[95] "Two voices have continued to lie and two to stammer. Which one is ours? How to know it? What is to be done?"

[96] "The delegate translates workers' struggle into the language of the factory owner."

[97] "When the delegate translates, he betrays."

[98] Godard and Gorin bestow on the worker the "imperialist" language, English. The dialogue goes:
The delegate to the striker: "Che cosa vuoi? Che cosa vuoi?" [What do you want? What do you want?]
Striker: "Down with the moving lines! Power to the working class!"
The owner to the delegate: "Che cosa vuole?" [What does he want?]

PCF because, in the scene that follows, the delegate reads out passages from a book about May 1968 by one of the predominant militants of the PCF: Waldeck Rochet's *L'Avenir du Parti Communiste Français*. In an off-screen voice, we hear the voice of Anne Wiazemsky—the Maoist militant—shouting: "C'est faux!" and "il parle, il parle, il parle!"[99] Godard and Gorin sketch out didactically their position regarding militant practice, parallel at this point to the Maoists' position. The speeches of the workers, delegates and Maoists are laid out in this sequence, not as representing various diverging political positions but as *different languages*, and thus the problem of representation is presented as a process of mistranslation.

The following sequence is a staging of a General Assembly (*Assemblée générale*).[100] Following Michel de Certeau, during a General Assembly everyone has the right to speak *only* in his/her own name because the Assembly refuses to hear anyone identified with a function or speaking in the name of a group. In a General Assembly, "to speak is not to be the 'speaker' in the name of a lobby, of a 'neutral' and objective truth, or for convictions held elsewhere."[101] In this sequence, as in the previous one, we are given very little visually and we only know what is happening through the voice-over.

The delegate:	"Vuole migliori condizioni del lavoro ed essere pagato meglio; lo vede c'è un poveraccio d'indiano; lui a la moglie malata, gli figli malati. Secondo me, possiamo anche metterci d'accordo. Io non me ne posso occupare... lei è responsabile di portarli al campo di concentramento..." [He wants better working conditions and to be paid better. You can see that he is a pitifully poor Indian; his wife is ill, his children are ill. I think that we can reach an agreement. But I'm unable to take care of this, you are responsible for bringing him to the concentration camp...]

[99] "He is lying! He talks, talks and talks"

[100] On May 17th, 1968 the Parisian film community held their own General Assembly, the États Généraux du Cinéma (EGC). It was agreed that the filmmakers would interrupt the Cannes Festival in order to show solidarity with the striking workers and students, to protest against police repression and to contest Gaullist power along with the actual structures of the French cinematographic industry. The EGC published three bulletins and a dossier in *Cahiers du Cinéma*. At the end of May, it prescribed the total or partial nationalization of the cinematographic industry, administered through a self-managing scheme. Many collectives would be spawned by the EGC's efforts, such as SLON, ISKRA, the Groupes Medvedkine and Cinélutte. See the editorial of *Cahiers de Cinéma* no. 202 (June–July 1968), and the editorial and the dossier of the EGC published in the following issue of *Cahiers du Cinéma*, no. 203 (August 1968).

[101] Michel de Certeau, *The Capture of Speech and Other Political Writings*, trans. Tom Conley (Minneapolis and London: The University of Minnesota Press, 1997), p. 11.

We see everyone who is involved in the film production sitting or lying down, including Daniel Cohn-Bendit who is wearing a cowboy hat.[102] The purpose of this General Assembly is to find the "correct line" (*ligne juste*) of the film's political tendency. Specifically, the debate centers on whether the image of a Leftist tract, whose front page has the phrase "Wanted for murder" scribbled over an image of Stalin and Mao, could successfully signify repression, and whether the inclusion of Stalin's image in the film would compromise their pro-Sino-Soviet split position and rather indicate a pro-Soviet alliance, along the lines of the PCF (which, evidently, as Maoists, they were against).

During the sequence, we hear the members of the assembly talking but we cannot follow what they are saying. What we hear is an agitated cacophony of utterances, allegedly speaking out opposing views on whether to show the image in the film or not. When everyone speaks, Godard and Gorin tell us didactically, debate is hindered because no one listens to each other, and no one can agree on anything. The impossibility of making sense is one of the consequences of the capture/liberation of speech—a moment of loghorrea, in which the contradictions of democracy and the dangers of the relationship between logos, freedom and truth become evident.[103] In the General Assembly, soliloquy takes over productive debate; *doxa* (opinion) over *aletheia* (truth); and common interest is barred by the Assembly's format (because everyone must speak in his/her own name), resulting in a logorrheic state of confusion and disorder. This sequence allegorizes the crisis of Maoist politics while pointing at its dialogic condition. In *Le Vent d'Est*, all four modes of speech—lying, stammering, mistranslating speech and logorrhea—are taken to their limit, evidencing that none of them is an effective solution to the problems of representation and mediation. By portraying speech in crisis, Godard and Gorin explore how speech "normally" works. One of the conclusions of *Le Vent d'Est* is the articulation of the tasks of "progressive cinema," which are: first, to address the problem of filmic distribution as a question of commodity production; second, to "liberate" images

[102] Cohn-Bendit was the leader of the group of students from Nanterre, *Le mouvement du 22 mars*; he became one of the main figures of May 1968, known as "Dany Le Rouge" and famously stated: "Nous sommes tous des juifs allemands."

[103] See the section on "Parrhesia and the Crisis of Democratic Institutions" from Foucault's lectures at Berkeley in November 1983, *Truth and Discourse* available online at: http://foucault.info/documents/parrhesia/foucault.DT3.democracy.en.html

from sounds; and third, a call for the democratization of the instruments of production of images and sounds. The DVG critiqued Maoism again through self-critique by pointing out the limits of speech in *Ici et ailleurs*. When Godard states in the voice-over, "On a mis le son trop fort,"[104] the realm of enunciation of the "we" is Maoist. When we hear this in the voice-over, a hand is seen turning the volume up and down on a stereo playing *L'Internationale*, thus extending their critique to ideological French communism as well. Consistent with the theory that sound is more powerful than image, Godard and Miéville point here at the passage from the (Maoist) capture of *speech* to passion-action, and then to despotic sound or noise (ideology) as Leftist *voice*.

GUERNICA AND ICI ET AILLEURS, 1974

As we have seen, Godard's films of the DVG period show the political *actuality*, the now of political struggle, opposing in this way the logic of the avant-garde that envisions an emancipatory future world-image. In these films, Godard adopts a position as a "militant filmmaker" taking a different position from engaged, self-reflexive, materialist filmmaking (i.e., Agnès Varda, Carole Roussopoulos, Chris Marker, PLON, Marin Karmitz…). Creating *materialist fictions*, the DVG makes *real reflections* of political action resembling a political function, but that have a different origin than politics. Using Marxism-Leninism as the code and as the method, transforming the discourse of politics into a political enterprise, it seeks not to make political films but to make films politically. If for Breton and Debord the aesthetic is inextricable from representational politics aiming at emancipation, in Godard the aesthetic and the political coexist, insofar as one does not imply the other. The DVG's films seek to construct a mode of address in film that veers toward the political by means of pedagogy.[105] For the DVG, image and sound-making imply analyzing situations and exposing and sustaining their contradictions, as opposed to transitively letting images speak or stand for a given objective reality and denouncing it. Arguably, Godard's discursive reclamation of historical avant-garde positions was a strategic war of positions that allowed him to explore the transitive relationship between aesthetics and politics at a stage

---

[104] "We turned up the volume too loud."
[105] After Charlotte Nordmann in: *Bourdieu/ Rancière: La politique entre sociologie et philosophie* (Paris: Amsterdam Poches, 2006), p. 117.

in which avant-garde critique had become desirable only via self-critique. His war of positions led to a shift toward an analogical and reflexive relationship between the two. An example of this is his citation of Picasso's *Guernica* in *Ici et ailleurs*. As we have seen, the painting appears reproduced mechanically, much smaller than its actual size, and hanging on a wall in a "working class" home interior. The painting appears in an earlier DVG film, *British Sounds* (1969), in a sequence for which Godard and Jean-Henri Roger filmed a reunion of Trotskyite workers in London.[106] *Guernica* both punctuates the middle and stands at the other end of the bracketing of Godard's Leftist trip years.

Godard and Miéville's *Ici et ailleurs* is usually interpreted as putting forth a revisionist discourse that attempts to flush out or "correct" the DVG's "militant excesses": it has also been read as a repentant discourse sketching out an erroneous engagement in the "wrong" direction. These readings of the film entail that the disaster of the Black September massacres and wave of terrorism that ensued in Jordan made Godard realize the limitations of his previous engagement and compelled him to change the direction of his thought: a "turn" in his work. However, *Ici et ailleurs* does not differ drastically from other DVG films: it articulates an avant-garde attitude (here, the militant abroad), points at the contradictions inherent in the situation it analyzes, and proceeds to self-critique. Yet, instead of being a reflection of the political actuality, it is temporally and spatially larger in scope than other DVG films, encompassing the *transitional* and *transitory* moment opened up by the acknowledgment of the practical and theoretical consequences of May 1968.

Ici et ailleurs, and Godard and Gorin's collective project at the DVG, coincide with the moment between the capture/liberation and the recuperation of speech described above (1968–74). At this juncture, as we have seen, the Maoists sought to construct a revolutionary organization without becoming a dry, senile, despotic power-machine (like the CGT and the PCF, whom they critiqued), asking, as we have seen, two questions: *D'où tu parles?* which meant contesting the position of power from which the speakers spoke, and *D'où je parle?*, putting forth a self-reflexive, non-despotic and anti-hierarchical site for enunciation. This was also the moment of capitalism's transition from the production system of Fordism,

---

[106] According to Faroult, Godard and Roger wanted to hook up with Maoists in London but because they did not find any, they filmed the Trotskyite workers instead. David Faroult, "Never More Godard," p. 123.

characterized by mass assembly lines (as shown in *British Sounds* and *Ici et ailleurs*), mass political organization and welfare-state interventions, to a mode of production characterized by flexible accumulation or the pursuit of niche markets, decentralization and spatial dispersal of production and the withdrawal of the nation-state from interventionist policies coupled with deregulation and privatization. This moment of transition saw, as well, the emergence of the self-management model epitomized by the short experiment (1973–77) at the LIP factory in Besançon, France, which has a relevant role in *Ici et ailleurs*, where we see an image of a newspaper bearing the headline: "LIP: Failure Yesterday in Dijon." The headline has been encircled in red. Further, we see more images of newspapers, giving us news from LIP. LIP was (and is) a watch and clock manufacturing company, owned until 1971 by the Lipmann family, who had founded it in 1867. The administrators of the company that had acquired the factory wanted to close it and, in an effort to resist unemployment, the workers occupied it on June 12, 1973. The workers were able to organize themselves without the intervention of Maoist activists or union representatives,[107] and the occupation of the LIP factory became the paradigm for the struggle against unemployment as well as one of the most famous factory occupations in France, because the workers kept it functioning under the principle: "We work, we sell and we pay ourselves." On August 14 the factory was occupied by the police, people were arrested, but the workers continued to run the factory by themselves until 1977. If the Maoist enterprise was founded on symbolic action in order to accomplish material action, the LIP workers achieved both at the same time. Not seeking the power to take over the factory, they sought their own freedom of organization *without mediation*, rendering Maoist practice obsolete and becoming an icon of resistance against cumulative capital.[108]

[107] See *LIP 73*, edited by Edmond Maire and Charles Piaget, with texts and interventions by André Acquier, Raymond Burgy, Jacques Chérèque, Fredo Moutet, J.Paul Murcier and Claude Perrignon (Paris: Seuil, 1973) and *LIP 20 ans après (propos sur le chômage)* by Claude Neuschwander and Gaston Bordet (Paris: Syros, 1993). For a recent English source, see: Michael Scott Christofferson, *French Intellectuals Against the Left: The Antitotalitarian Moment of the 1970s* (London: Berghahn Books, 2004), 63. In the film, the reference to LIP signifies the struggles *here* in addition to the struggles *elsewhere*. LIP was also one of the most mediatized strikes in France, as even Henri Cartier-Bresson documented it. The collective Groupes Medvedkine from Besançon, France, made a movie about LIP in 1968 called *Classe de Lutte*.

[108] An account of the LIP strike from a Maoist point of view is articulated in the series of interviews between two Maoists, Philippe Gavi and Pierre Victor, and Jean-Paul Sartre in: *On a raison de se révolter* (Paris: Gallimard, 1974).

Ici et ailleurs builds up precisely during this transition, transubstantiating to the domain of film the liberation of speech, the emergence and the demise of Maoist activism,[109] and the shift from Fordism to the flexible accumulation of capital. Other recent historical events that appear in the film, pointing to the waning of Leftism around 1974, are Pinochet's anti-communist *coup d'état* in Chile and the dissolution of La Gauche Prolétarienne marked by its members' metamorphosis from activists to parachutists, appearing elsewhere as Médecins Sans Frontières (Doctors Without Borders) or as journalists, crystalizing their practice around the foundation of the newspaper *Libération* in 1973.[110] *Ici et ailleurs* differs from other DVG films in its spatio-temporality, partly due to the problems posed by the Palestinian footage I discuss in the next chapter, expanding *Pravda*'s self-critique against "political tourism" and Third Worldism. Editing the material three to four years after having shot it, Godard and Miéville articulate a position from which they analyze the immediate Parisian and Palestinian aftermath of May 1968, six and four years back, respectively, from Grenoble. In the voice-over, Godard declares:

> On a fait comme pas mal de gens. On a pris des images et on a mis le son trop fort. Avec n'importe quelle image: Vietnam. Toujours le même son, toujours trop fort, Prague, Montevideo, mai soixante-huit en France, Italie, révolution culturelle chinoise, grèves en Pologne, torture en Espagne, Irlande, Portugal, Chili, Palestine, le son tellement fort qu'il a fini par noyer la voix qu'il a voulu faire sortir de l'image.[111]

Here Godard and Miéville are addressing the predicament of May 1968: the putative speaker's position was problematized because the intellectuals had spoken out too loudly, drowning the voice inside images. According to Le Goff, the logic animating Maoists' denunciation of power was not theoretical but practical, a kind of "settling of accounts," denouncing oppression, exploitation and racism. Exploiting the potential of dissent,

---

[109] See Kristin Ross, *May '68 and its Afterlives* and Jean-Pierre Le Goff, *Mai 68, l'héritage impossible*.

[110] The La Gauche Prolétarienne dissolved on November 1, 1973 in what is known as "La Réunion des Chrysanthèmes."

[111] "We did what many others were doing. We made images and we turned the volume up too high. With any image: Vietnam. Always the same sound, always too loud, Prague, Montevideo, May '68 in France, Italy, the Chinese Cultural Revolution, strikes in Poland, torture in Spain, Ireland, Portugal, Chile, Palestine, the sound so loud that it ended up drowning out the voice that we wanted to emerge from the image."

Maoists created considerable mediatic events, putting forth the State as fascist. By many accounts (including those of Godard and Miéville) their goal of people's exercise of power without delegation or mediation led to their project's failure in an excess of dissent.[112]

The impending breakdown of activist practice at home was analogous to intellectuals' failure to engage with revolutionaries abroad. In the General Assembly sequence, sound is to image as militant ideology is to art. The image had been drowned out by political ideology. When Godard and Miéville say, "People always speak about the image and forget about the sound," it means that the ideology that informs the discourse of political art-making takes precedence over the image. We thus *enunciate* the image (see p. 130) as opposed to *seeing* it, forgetting the sound that has taken power over it. The citation of *Guernica* summons silence; with it, Godard and Miéville call for silencing Leftist ideology because in the face of the failure of the Palestinian Revolution, which embodies the failure of all revolutions, they are speechless.

Now their gesture of summoning silence is more allegorical than self-critical. In *Ici et ailleurs*, Godard and Miéville amalgamate the crisis of patriarchy with the revolutionary's responsibility to take part in revolutionary action *at home* (as opposed to going abroad), thus critiquing the intellectuals who had gone abroad and brought back materials to speak about others' struggles without looking at what was happening at home. Moreover, in the scene with *Guernica*, a call to action (or to help) gets postponed indefinitely. When Godard declares: "On a mis le son trop fort," he is making a further positioning move, this time with regards to Sartre. As we saw above, Godard took up Sartre's position of the separateness between art production and engaged activism working on bridging the gap between the two in his practice of "militant filmmaking," after first having contested him for being unable to bridge his double position as writer and intellectual. Citing *Guernica* enables Godard and Miéville to contest Sartre, this time regarding his skepticism about the power of visual images as a medium with which to effectively convey indignation and to denounce injustice, embodied by his dismissal of *Guernica*.[113] For

---

[112] See *Mai 68, l'héritage impossible* (Paris: La Découverte, 1998), p. 201.

[113] *Guernica* is the symbol *par excellence* of intellectual militant struggle. It was deprecated by Sartre in *Qu'est-ce que la littérature? [What is Literature?]* (1948) and championed by Adorno in his article "Commitment", *New Left Review*, I/87–88, 1974. In 1968 protests in America against the war in Vietnam used *Guernica* as a peace symbol; in 1967,

Sartre, insofar as images are mute, they are open receptacles of meaning and therefore invoke ambiguous readings, as opposed to conveying a clear, unified message, like writing. That is why for Sartre only literature can be successful as committed art, because the writer guides the readers through a description, making his audience see the symbols of social injustice and thereby provoking their indignation.[114] Godard and Miéville's view of *Guernica* is that it takes the form of a quiet, visual scream. At the same time, as we have seen, Godard and Miéville make a statement in favor of a flight from the prison of language, from *logocracy*, which, as we have seen, is the becoming noise of revolutionary speech. As they state in the voice-over in *Ici et ailleurs*:[115]

> Il y a un moment // un point dans le temps où un son prend pouvoir sur les autres // un point dans le temps où le son cherche// quasi désespérément à conserver ce pouvoir // Comment ce son a pris le pouvoir? Il a pris le pouvoir parce que à un moment donné il s'est fait représenter par une image // Celle-là par exemple...[116]

This fragment from the voice-over recalls scenes from *One A.M.*, the film that Godard filmed in 1968 in New York in collaboration with the documentary filmmakers Richard Leacock and D.A. Pennebaker, produced and edited in 1972 by the latter, who titled it *One P.M.* (or *One Parallel Movie* or *One Pennebaker Movie*). In one scene, a nervous and hesitant Godard interviews Eldridge Cleaver, who is both aloof and annoyed by the film-

---

some 400 artists and writers petitioned Picasso: "Please let the spirit of your painting be reasserted and its message once again felt, by withdrawing your painting from the United States for the duration of the war." In 1974, a young Iranian artist, Tony Shafrazi, sprayed *Guernica* with the words "Kill Lies All." See *Picasso's Guernica*, ed. Ellen C. Oppler, Norton Critical Studies in Art History (New York, London: Syracuse University, 1988).

[114] Jean-Paul Sartre, "What is writing?" in *What is literature?*

[115] Walter Benjamin calls the power of intellect "logocracy," an already established activist position in which the intellectual does not acknowledge his/her own role in the process of production. This position implies a system in which words are the ruling power. In "The Author as Producer," written in 1934 and published in *New Left Review* I/62, (July–August 1970).

[116] "There is a moment // A point in time when one sound assumes power over the others // A point in time where the sound seeks almost desperately to conserve its power. // How did the sound take power? It took power because at a given moment it made itself to be represented by an image // this one, for example..." While we hear this part of the voice-over, during which Hitler can be heard giving a speech, we are looking at the amplifier that is measuring the given sound's intensity (a fragment of the *Internationale*).

maker's questions. Throughout the film, a white actor dressed up at various times as an Indian, cowboy or policeman walks around the streets of New York with a tape-recorder, playing over fragments of Cleaver's speech and repeating after them. Through echolalia, revolutionary discourse is decomposed, disqualifying the syntagmatic quality of speech in favor of its phonetic quality. *Passing through* the (white) actor, (black) revolutionary speech (syntagm) becomes noise (phoneme).

Guernica is not a speech-act, and that is perhaps the reason why it became the epitome of an autonomous yet committed work of art, because while it remains separate from the social sphere (the domain of opinion, speech), it lets the German guilt/culpability surface, and at the same time, it does not have as an end Picasso's declaration of indignation.[117] While we can doubt with Sartre whether *Guernica* converted anyone to the Spanish Republican cause, this painting, like much of Godard's work posits a reflexive and analogical relationship between aesthetics and politics, as opposed to a transitive link. Transitivity is the effect of an action on an object: here, the effect is of politics on art or vice versa. Differently, an analogical relationship between art and politics implies a linking via aesthetics and ethics: if aesthetics is to ethics what art is to politics, each term necessarily acts individually. Arguably, Godard replaces an ideological and transitive relationship between art and politics with an analogical and reflexive link between the two. A reflexive or analogical link between aesthetics and politics implies a relationship that acknowledges the presence of the other: they are separate, but aware of each other. Such a link presupposes art's autonomy as relying on its having an end, as different from being an end, or being instrumental to a cause: art appeals to viewers calling for judgment or consideration like appearing in a court and interpellating the viewer.

This is Theodor Adorno and Pierre Macherey's position regarding the relationship between aesthetics and politics. For Macherey, art has an end insofar as it presupposes a subjective pact between viewer and author based on general trust: the author's word is to be believed because the receiver's is an act of faith. This implies that before the work appears, there is an abstract space presupposing the possibility of the reception of the author's word.[118] Godard echoes the conception of the artwork as based on trust

---

[117] According to Theodor Adorno in "Commitment." He further quotes an apocryphal anecdote about a Nazi officer coming into Picasso's studio and, pointing to a photograph of the painting, asking him: "Did you do that?" Picasso's answer being: "No, you did!"

[118] Pierre Macherey, *Pour une théorie de la production littéraire,* Collection "Théorie" par Louis Althusser (Paris: François Maspero, 1966), pp. 89–91.

when he states that for him, an image is like a proof in a process, and he compares filmmaking to "building a new proof."[119] Issues of trust and faith in the image will become recurrent themes in Godard's work. As he wrote in a collage he made for *Cahiers du Cinéma* in 1979: "L'image comme preuve. L'image comme justice, comme résultat d'un accord."[120]

The succession of combative positions assumed by Godard between 1967 and 1974 can be summarized as the production of contradictory images and sounds that appeal to viewers calling them to produce meaning *with* the film as readers/viewers, as opposed to consuming meaning. Name it a politics of address, a "the(rr)orising" pedagogy (Serge Daney) or Brechtian didacticism. Godard's collaborations with Gorin and Miéville call for a radical way of hearing and seeing. In their work the task of art is to separate and transform the continuum of image and sound meaning into a series of fragments, postcards and lessons, outlining a tension between visuality and discourse. Godard reconfigures Sartre's split between writing and commitment once more: if for Sartre the subjectivity of the *committed artist* is *universal*, as opposed to the tradition of speaking in the first person in the name of universal values, Godard articulates in his video-essays of the mid-1970s a depersonalized discourse, not as an intentional process but using the camera as a tool for encountering reality, thinking out loud while editing in video, positioning himself seeing = re-see-(v)ing-re-sending, formulating a site for enunciation in between the sites articulated by the double pragmatic expression: "Moi je suis un animal politique // Moi je suis une machine."[121]

Bibliography

Adorno, Theodor W. "On Commitment," in *Aesthetics and Politics* (London: Verso, 2006)

Aragon, Louis. "Qu-est ce que l'art, Jean-Luc Godard?" *Les Lettres Françaises* no. 1096 (September 9–15, 1965). Available at: http://tapin.free.fr/godard/aragon.html

---

[119] See "Économie politique de la critique de film: Débat entre Jean-Luc Godard et Pauline Kael," published originally in *Camera Obscura* nos. 8-9-10 reprinted in *Jean-Luc Godard par Jean-Luc Godard*, p. 481.

[120] "The image as a proof. The image as justice, as the result of an agreement." Jean-Luc Godard, *Cahiers du Cinéma* no. 300 (1979), p. 125.

[121] "Me, I am a political animal // Me, I am a machine." From the 1973 script of an unrealized film, *Moi, je*.

Aumont, Jacques. "The Medium," in *Jean-Luc Godard: Son + Image 1974–1991* (New York: MoMA, 1992)
Barthes, Roland. "From Work to Text" (1971) in *Textual Strategies: Perspectives in Poststructuralist Criticism*, ed. Josue V. Harari (Ithaca, New York: Cornell University Press, 1979)
Bellour, Raymond. *L'entre-images: photo, cinéma, vidéo* (Paris: La Différence, 2002)
Benjamin, Walter. "The Author as Producer," *New Left Review* I/62, (July–August, 1970)
Besançon, Julien. *Les murs ont la parole: Journal mural Mai 68 Sorbonne Odéon Nanterre etc....*, (Paris: Tchou, 2007)
Bordet, Gaston and Neuschwander, Claude. *LIP 20 ans après (propos sur le chômage)* (Paris: Syros, 1993)
Bourdieu, Pierre. "Sartre, l'invention de l'intellectuel total," *Libération*, 31 March 1983, pp. 20–21
Bourseiller, Christophe. *Les Maoïstes: La Folle histoire des Gardes-Rouges français* (Paris: Points, 2008)
Brenez, Nicole and Witt, Michael, eds. *Jean-Luc Godard: Documents* (Paris: Centre Georges Pompidou, 2006)
Breton, André. "Towards a Free Revolutionary Art," trans. Dwight MacDonald, in Charles Harrison and Paul Wood, eds. *Art in Theory, 1900–2000: An Anthology of Changing Ideas*, 2nd edition (Malden, MA: Blackwell Publishers, 2003), 533. Originally published in *Partisan Review* IV, no. 1 (Fall 1938), pp. 49–53
Breton, André. *Manifestes du Surréalisme*, édition complète (Paris: France Loisirs, 1962)
Cahiers du Cinéma, nos. 216–17 (October–November 1969)
Carroll, Kent E. "Film and Revolution: Interview with the Dziga Vertov Group," *Evergreen Review* 14, no. 83 (October 1970)
Christofferson, Michael Scott. *French Intellectuals Against the Left: The Antitotalitarian Moment of the 1970s* (London: Berghahn Books, 2004)
Cinéthique no. 5 (September–October 1969)
Comolli, Jean-Louis and Narboni, Jean. "Cinéma/idéologie/critique," *Cahiers du Cinéma* no. 216 (October 1969)
Daney, Serge. "Le thérrorisé (Pédagogie godardienne)," *Cahiers du Cinéma*, nos. 262–263 (January 1976), 32–39
De Baecque, Antoine. *Godard Biographie* (Paris: Grasset & Fasquelle, 2010)
De Certeau, Michel. *The Capture of Speech and Other Political Writings*. (Minneapolis and London: The University of Minnesota Press, 1997)
Debord, Guy. "The Role of Godard" (1966) *Situationist International Anthology* ed. Ken Knabb, (Berkeley: The Bureau of Public Secrets, 1989)
Debord, Guy. *La Société du Spectacle* (1967) (Paris: Gallimard, 1996)

Didi-Huberman, Georges. *Passées cités par JLG: L'Oeil de l'histoire*, 5 (Paris: Éditions de Minuit, 2015)
Fargier, Jean-Paul. "La parenthèse et le détour," *Cinéthique* no. 5 (September–October 1969)
Farocki, Harun and Silverman, Kaja. *Speaking About Godard* (New York: The University Press, 1998).
Faroult, David and Leblanc, Gérard. *Mai 68 ou le cinéma en suspense* (Paris: Syllepse, 1998).
Faroult, David. "Du Vertovisme du Groupe Dziga Vertov," in Brenez, Nicole and Witt, Michael eds. *Jean-Luc Godard: Documents* (Paris: Centre Georges Pompidou, 2006a)
Faroult, David. "Never More Godard," in Brenez, Nicole and Witt, Michael eds. *Jean-Luc Godard Documents* (Paris: Centre Georges Pompidou, 2006b)
Fields, Belden. *Trotskyism and Maoism: Theory and Practice in France and in the United States* (Brooklyn: Autonomedia, 1988).
Foucault, Michel. "La fonction politique de l'intellectuel," *Politique Hebdo*, 29 (November–December 1976) reprinted in *Dits et écrits*, volume III (1976–1979) (Paris: Gallimard, 1994)
Foucault, Michel. "Parrhesia and the Crisis of Democratic Institutions," lectures at Berkeley, November 1983a, *Truth and Discourse*. Available at: http://foucault.info/documents/parrhesia/foucault.DT3.democracy.en.html
Foucault, Michel. Preface to Deleuze and Guattari's *Anti-Oedipus*, trans. Brian Massumi (Minneapolis: University of Minnesota Press, 1983b)
Godard, Jean-Luc. "Pratique révolutionnaire," *Cinéthique* nos. 9–10 (Fall 1971)
Godard, Jean-Luc. "Manifeste," in Brenez, Nicole and Witt, Michael eds. *Jean-Luc Godard: Documents*, (Paris: Centre Georges Pompidou, 2006)
Godard, Jean-Luc. Interview with Marlène Belilos, Michel Boujut, Jean-Claude Deschamps and Pierre-Henri Zoller, first published in *Politique Hebdo*, no. 26–27 (April 1972)
Godard, Jean-Luc. *Jean-Luc Godard par Jean-Luc Godard* (Paris: Cahiers du Cinéma, 1998)
Godard, Jean-Luc. *Le Gai savoir: Mot-à-mot d'un film encore trop réviso* (Paris: Union Ecrivains, 1969)
Gramsci, Antonio. "State and Civil Society," in *Selections from the Prison Notebooks* edited and trans. Quentin Hoare and Geoffrey Nowell Smith (New York: International Publishers, 1971)
Grant, Paul Douglas. *Cinéma militant: Political Filmmaking & May 1968* (New York: Columbia University Press, 2016)
Hennebelle, Guy and Serceau, Daniel. *Écran* (Décembre 1975)
Jameson, Fredric. "Reflections in Conclusion," *Aesthetics and Politics* (New York: NLB, 1979)
Jameson, Fredric, "Periodizing the Sixties" *Social Text* no. 9/10 (spring-summer 1984)

Karmitz, Marin. "Towards a Proletarian Cinema: An Interview with Marin Karmitz," *Cinéaste* Vol. IV, no. 2 (Fall 1970), pp. 20–25

Kristensen, Stefan. *Jean-Luc Godard Philosophe* (Lausanne: L'Âge d'Homme, 2014)

Leblanc, Gérard. "Sur trois films du groupe Dziga Vertov," *VH 101*, no. 6 (September 1972)

Le Goff, Jean-Pierre. *Mai 68, l'héritage impossible* (Paris: La Découverte, 1998)

Lenin, Vladimir. *What Is To Be Done?*, printable edition produced by Chris Russell for the Marxist Internet Archive. Available at: www.marxists.org

Lesage, Julia. "Godard and Gorin's *Le Vent d'est*: Looking at a Film Politically," *Jump Cut*, no. 4 (November–December 1974)

Lesage, Julia. "Godard and Gorin's Left Politics," *Jump Cut*, no. 23 (April 1983)

Lesage, Julia. "*Tout va bien* and *Coup pour coup*: Radical French Cinema in Context," *Cineaste* 5, no. 3 (Summer 1972)

Linhart, Robert. *L'Établi* (Paris: Éditions de Minuit, 1978)

Lukács, Georg. "Realism in the Balance" (1938) trans. Rodney Livingstone, *Aesthetics and Politics*, ed. Ernst Bloch (London and New York: Verso, 1987), p. 33

MacBean, James Roy. *Film and Revolution* (Bloomington and London: Indiana University Press, 1975)

MacCabe, Colin. *Godard: Images, Sounds, Politics*, with Mick Eaton and Laura Mulvey (London: British Film Institute, 1980)

Macherey, Pierre. *Pour une théorie de la production littéraire*, Collection "Théorie" par Louis Althusser (Paris: François Maspero, 1966)

Maire, Edmond and Piaget, Charles. *LIP 73* (Paris: Seuil, 1973)

Manceaux, Michèle. *Les Maos en France* (Paris: Gallimard, 1972)

McDonough, Tom. *"The Beautiful Language of My Century": Reinventing the Language of Contestation in Postwar France, 1945–1968* (Cambridge, MA: MIT Press, 2007)

Mouffe, Chantal. "Hegemony and Ideology in Gramsci," in Chantal Mouffe, ed. *Gramsci and Marxist Theory* (London: Routledge & Kegan Paul, 1979)

Nordmann, Charlotte. *Bourdieu/Rancière: La Politique entre sociologie et philosophie* (Paris: Amsterdam Poches, 2006)

Oppler, Ellen C, ed. *Picasso's Guernica*, Norton Critical Studies in Art History (New York, London: Syracuse University, 1988)

Retort, *Afflicted Powers: Capital and Spectacle in a New Age of War* (London and New York: Verso, 2005)

Ross, Kristin. *May '68 and its Afterlives* (Chicago: The University Press, 2002)

Sartre, Jean-Paul, Pignaud, Bernard and Mascolo, Dionys. *Du rôle de l'intellectuel dans le mouvement révolutionnaire* (Paris: Le terrain vague, 1971)

Sartre, Jean-Paul. *Situations, VIII: Autour de 68* (Paris: Gallimard, 1972)

Sartre, Jean-Paul. *What is Literature?* trans. Bernard Frechtman (New York: Harper Colophon Books, 1965)
Silverman, Kaja. *Acoustic Mirror: The Female Voice in Psychoanalysis and Cinema*, (Bloomington: Indiana University Press, 1988)
Tse-Tung, Mao. "Where do Correct Ideas Come From?" (1957), *On Practice and Contradiction. Slavoj Zizek presents Mao* (London: Verso, 2017)
Tse-Tung, Mao. *On Practice and Contradiction* (London: Verso, 2007)
Vertov, Dziga. *Kino-Eye: The Writings of Dziga Vertov* (Berkeley: University of California Press, 1984)
Victor, Pierre. *On a raison de se révolter* (Paris: Gallimard, 1974)
Weil, Simone. *La Condition ouvrière* (Paris: Gallimard, 1951)
Weil, Simone. *Oppression and Liberty* (1955), (London: Routledge, 2001)
Witt, Michael. "Godard dans la presse d'extrême gauche," in Brenez, Nicole and Witt, Michael eds. *Jean-Luc Godard: Documents* (Paris: Centre Georges Pompidou, 2006)
Wollen, Peter. "Godard and Counter Cinema: *Le Vent d'est*," in *Readings and Writings: Semiotic Counter-Strategies* (London: Verso, 1982)
Wollen, Peter. *Signs and Meaning in the Cinema* (expanded edition), (London: BFI, 1998)

CHAPTER 3

Elsewhere: Dialogue of Points of View: Jean-Luc Godard and *Tiersmondisme*

The Third World in European Eyes

The relationship to revolutions elsewhere has been part of the history of the European Left since 1917. In the twentieth century, enthusiastic utopias and depressing realities became the core of the relationships between countries of developed capitalism and those of the Second and Third Worlds.[1] As early as Eisenstein's *Battleship Potemkin* (1925) and *¡Qué viva México!* (shot in 1931), filmmakers pondered their role in relationship to the revolution here and elsewhere, asking what political cinema is, what the most suitable genre (documentary, *vérité* or fiction) is and how an image producer and images play a role in revolutionary processes. In that regard, political cinema has its roots in the tradition of recording actuality, like the films of the Dutch documentary filmmaker Joris Ivens, especially *The Spanish Earth* (1937), *The 400 Million* (1939) filmed with Robert Capa in China or *How Yukong Moved the Mountains* (1976). As a socialist filmmaker, Ivens was a pioneering legend: between 1911 and 1988 he made about 50 documentaries, traveling from the Soviet Union (which he visited in 1930, invited by Pudovkin) to Spain (during the Spanish Civil War), Indonesia, Cuba, Chile, Vietnam, Laos and so on. Ivens is thus a forerunner in the twentieth century tradition of state-sponsored visits of Western sympathizers to socialist countries known as the *delegacija* or delegate system and who produced accounts about them for a Western public.

[1] Rossana Rossanda, "Les Intellectuels Révolutionnaires et l'Union Soviétique," *Les Temps Modernes* no. 332 (March 1974), p. 1523.

Famous accounts of visits to the Soviet Union include André Gide's *Retour de l'URSS* (1936) and *Retouches à mon retour de l'URSS* (1937), and Brecht's critique of Gide,[2] while those to China include *D'une Chine à l'autre* (1954), with photographs by Henri Cartier-Bresson and text by Jean-Paul Sartre.[3] Simone Weil contributed with poetry and documentation about the Spanish Civil War (as well as by fighting for two weeks as a volunteer for the Republicans).[4] Later on, revolutionary sympathy was channeled in the French Leftist political imaginary toward decolonization movements, side by side with a critique of imperialism. This was brought together under the umbrella of "Third World" struggles. In the 1960s, the term "Third World" designated a group of countries other than the capitalist and socialist industrialized, some of which were fighting revolutions characterized by armed struggle and a national (decolonizing) socialist or communist project. *Tiersmondisme* was a movement, a project, an ideology that was essential to the Western Left's imaginary: it was the means to catalyze issues of slavery, past and present colonialism, socialism and revolution. *Tiersmondisme* was furthermore inspired by Mao Tse-tung's revolutionary call to unite with the Third World against the "Paper Tiger" of imperialism, his emphasis on the revolutionary potential of the Third World's proletariat and lumpenproletariat, and by Che Guevara's call: "Hasta la victoria! Crear dos, tres, muchos Vietnam!" Frantz Fanon's *The Wretched of the Earth* (1961), Paul Nizan's *Aden Arabie* (1960), Leopold Sedar Senghor's *Anthology of New Negro and Malagasy Poetry* (1949) and Sartre's prefaces to these books are considered manifestos of *Tiersmondisme*.

Like the Soviet Union's delegate system, Third World struggles sponsored Western intellectuals' official visits, for example, to Cuba, Vietnam or Palestine, after which artists, writers, journalists and filmmakers produced accounts speaking for and about them. *Tiersmondiste* interventions mixed the genres of documentary, travel diary, photojournalism and reportage. Cinematic instances of accounts from trips engaging with struggles elsewhere include Agnès Varda's *Black Panthers – Huey!* (1968) and *Loin du Vietnam* (1967), made collectively by Varda, Jean-Luc Godard, Joris Ivens, William Klein, Claude Lelouch, Chris Marker and Alain Resnais. Dealing with the

---

[2] Bertolt Brecht, *Kraft und Schwäche der Utopie, Gesammelte Werke* vol. VIII (Frankfurt am Main: 1967), pp. 434–437.

[3] Jean-Paul Sartre and Henri Cartier-Bresson, *D'une Chine à l'autre* (Paris: Éditions Delpire, 1954).

[4] See Weil's "Lettre à Bernanos," "Journal d'Espagne," and "Non-intervention generalisée," in *Écrits historiques et politiques* (Paris: Gallimard, 1960).

post-colonial there are Gillo Pontecorvo's *La Bataille d'Alger* (1965)[5] and René Vautier's *Algérie en flammes* (1958). India could be another sub-genre, as there is Pasolini's travel *récit*, *L'odore dell'India* (1960), Roberto Rossellini's *India, Matri Bhumi* (1959), Louis Malle's *L'Inde Fantôme* (1969) and Marguerite Duras' *India Song* (1975). André Gide's and Marc Allégret's trip to the Congo in 1925–26 was an early intervention denouncing French colonization, after which they produced an anti-colonialist *récit* and documentary, respectively, both titled *Voyage au Congo*. A distinctive case that is at the crossroads of *cinéma vérité* and ethnography is Jean Rouch's work in Africa between 1958 and 1971, which includes *Moi, Un Noir, Jaguar, La Pyramide humaine* and *Les Maîtres fous*. Another case is Chris Marker, who visited and made films about countries that experienced socialist revolutions: *Sunday in Peking* (1956), *Lettre de Sibérie* (1957), *¡Cuba Sí!* (1961) and so on. *A Grin Without a Cat/Le Fond de l'air est rouge* (1977) is a summation of this era and the memory-images it left behind.

Contrary to Sylvain Dreyer's assertion that *Tiersmondiste* works were either a pretext to identify with exotic revolutionary causes while hiding the impasses of the French political movement, or empty slogans and a superficial fascination and mystification of the elsewhere,[6] we could make a parallel between Europeans sympathizing with the movement of Third Worldism and the enthusiasm experienced by the German spectators of the French Revolution: According to Immanuel Kant, their enthusiasm constituted evidence of the fundamental moral disposition in human nature to express solidarity with the ordeals of others. Thus, *Tiersmondisme* could be considered as a reassessment of how the West interpreted and produced new discourses about the "Other" beyond racism and in the light of Europe's post-colonial identity crisis and the ideological scission of the world during the Cold War. Third Worldism is thus a proto-global cartography characterized by a division of the world into First and Third and by ideological alliances with Marxism as the common code. These interventions were inspired by ideological kinship, which is the Marxist-Leninist belief in the revolutionary potential of Third World peasantry, coded through a global Western Marxism translated to local specificities. Most of these works are self-reflexive and thus inquiries about how to account for foreign struggles within the framework of state- or militia-sponsored visits.

[5] Which is not a documentary, but a reconstruction.
[6] Sylvain Dreyer, *Image & Narrative*, Vol. 11, No. 1 (2010).

The question of the politics of representation is evidently at the core of this body of work, and most authors (although not all of them) saw a double problem in the task of giving voice to struggles elsewhere: first, that of blind ideological identification, which endangers the viewer in not being able to see the contradictions or his/her position as outsider with regard to the struggle in question. As Hans Magnus Enzensberger wrote:

> No matter what attitude or position one takes toward these countries – and they run the gamut from blind identification to vitriolic dislike – the verdicts are invariably reached *from the outside. No one who returns from a sojourn in socialism is a genuine part of the process he tries to describe.* Neither voluntary commitment, nor the degree of solidarity with which one behaves, no propaganda action, no walk through the cane fields and schools, factories and mines, not to mention a few moments at the lectern or a quick handshake with the leader of the revolution, can deceive about the fact. *The less the traveller understands this and the less he questions his own position, the greater and more justified will be the animosity that the voyager into socialism encounters from the very onset – from both sides.*[7]

Therefore, for Enzensberger, the political task of the voyager is to question his/her own position in the encounter and to be aware that he/she is not part of the process being observed. The second problem arising from these kinds of interventions is the danger of reading the world from a unique point of view tinted by the interests and desires of the Occidental observer. This is what Gilles Deleuze termed the "Oedipus-in-the-Colonies" phenomenon, which he described as the "I came and I saw this" genre, which is recorded and filtered through the traveler's personal drama.[8] This implies that the specific geopolitical location of the observer assumes universal relevance, transforming Western subjectivity (or expertise—valuing insight over cognition) and objectivity into the same thing.[9] From the point of view of *Tiersmondiste* filmmaker Glauber Rocha, exchanges of gazes between the First and Third Worlds are grounded in a clash of realities characterized by an irreconcilable misunderstanding: while Latin Americans bemoan their own wretchedness, foreigners cultivate a taste for it and come to consider it a proper field of knowledge or information. That is the reason why these kinds of exchanges were dismissed in Latin America as *porno-*

---

[7] Hans-Magnus Enzensberger, "Tourists of the Revolution," p. 130. My italics.

[8] Deleuze, "Les Intercesseurs," reprinted in *Pourparlers* (Paris: Éditions de Minuit, 1990), p. 130.

[9] Martin Heidegger, "The World Picture," in *The Question Concerning Technology and Other Essays* (New York: Harper and Row, 1977), pp. 115–136.

miseria; therefore, filmmakers gave themselves the task of self-reflexively presenting the modern version of colonialism in the Third World, while problematizing this kind of cinema formally and politically. For example, in their 1978 film, *Agarrando Pueblo*, Luis Ospina and Carlos Mayolo highlight the viciousness behind the relationships established in these forms of exchange of gazes by filming the staging of a *pornomiseria* film geared at constructing a specific reality for a European concerned public in astute complicity with the wretched. Another problem that arises is that the filmmaker's position of privilege before the wretched is camouflaged as "objectivity." Thus, a third issue arises: the fact that the discourse of objectivity, which, as it is part of the information and mass communication industry, hides the fact that it produces surplus value. At the same time, objectivity is a regime of enunciation unable to denounce the links between power and knowledge, thereby ensuring a system of given interests. Therefore, and taking into account the dangers of blind naïve identification, objectivity becomes even more problematic: is it possible to go beyond the ideological veil imposed by the framework of the official visit? How is it possible to account for one's position as an external observer? Can the political emotions of sympathy and enthusiasm suspend the subject from the conditions of viewing and open up complex, interrelational points of view?

The risk that *Tiersmondiste* films run is that Third World wretchedness or idealized revolutions tend to become curiosities for a naïve European observer and viewer who is placed before "objective truths." For Godard, the problem with objectivity is the fact that the journalist or the filmmaker never speaks as "I," and this "I" carries the authority of testimony, of the "having been there," and thus an "it speaks" covers the relationships between appearances, discourse, power and the form of inscription of information.[10] As we will see, Godard's *Tiersmondiste* work is permeated by an anxiety about blindness and characterized by deconstructing objectivity and representation; moreover, his battle in solidarity with *Tiersmondisme* is aligned with anti-imperialism which is translated into a

[10] Unpublished material from an interview with Godard by Paula Jacques. The conference-interview was aired on June 22, 1976. Source: The archives at the Phonothèque at the Institut National de l'Audiovisuel, Paris. Date consulted: April 14, 2006. I would like to thank Mme. Amélie Briand-Le Jeune from the Phonothèque and Mme. Sylvie Fegar from the INA for granting me access to this material. For critical accounts of what I call the "mediatization of mediation" or the translation of the intellectual function to the mass media see: Régis Debray, *Le pouvoir intellectuel en France* (Paris: Ramsay, 1979) and Gilles Deleuze, "A propos des nouveaux philosophes et d'un problème plus général," *Deux Régimes de Fous* (Paris: Éditions de Minuit, 2003).

war against Hollywood films, a struggle that is ongoing in Godard's films as became evident with *Histoire(s) du cinéma*, *Éloge de l'amour* and *Film Socialisme*, *Les Trois désastres*, *Le Pont des soupirs*, *Lettre filmée de Jean-Luc Godard à Gilles Jacob et Thierry Frémaux* and so on.

Godard's *Tiersmondisme*

In his Dziga Vertov Group (DVG) films as well as in the Sonimage works, Godard sought to self-reflexively highlight his own point of view as European filmmaker in relationship to the struggles he engaged in (as in *Camera Eye*, discussed in the previous chapter). As a strategy to avoid blind identification with the struggle they sought to represent, Godard and Gorin insisted on aligning themselves with people with whom they disagreed, or whom they fought against ideologically. That is the reason why the DVG was associated with Fatah's Information Services Bureau as opposed to having aligned itself with the Popular Front for the Liberation of Palestine (PFLP), because as Godard stated in "Manifeste," they disagreed with the Fatah people most of the time; for him, Armand Marco and Gorin, the disagreement was positive, because it enabled them to learn more about the Palestinian Revolution.[11] Another example is Godard and Gorin's disagreement with Jane Fonda's brand of star activism and the tension and friction between them and Fonda came out in *Tout va bien* and *Letter to Jane*. Godard and Gorin were interested in conveying the tension of the disagreements through the images. Another aspect of the DVG's politicized filmmaking is that it posited filmic space as a political space, seeking to enable sharing and spreading of strategies and tools for political struggle. As Godard put it: "A [militant] film is a flying carpet that can travel anywhere. There is no magic. It is a political work."[12] Thus, the DVG insisted not on documenting the *reality* of struggles *elsewhere*, but on the revolutionary potential of making images transmigrate in the world to share political knowledge for emancipatory struggles across the globe.

In the Sonimage videos, Godard reconfigures political work as "journalism of the audiovisual" in accord with, but highly critical of, the French Left's shift to the mass media as a site for political action. This shift crystallized in the foundation of the newspaper *Libération* in 1973 and in former

---

[11] "Manifeste" (1970) reprinted in *Jean-Luc Godard: Documents*, edited by David Faroult (Paris: Centre Georges Pompidou, 2006) p. 138.
[12] Ibid., pp. 138–140.

Maoists becoming media figures, which for thinkers like Régis Debray and Gilles Deleuze was a clear symptom of the domestication of intellectuals post-May 1968. Therefore, the challenge for Godard became not how to represent struggles elsewhere, nor delve into what images represent, but to explore the *how* of images (*Comment ça va?*), in the sense of *how* they reach us, the networks in which images circulate, how they hide while showing states of affairs. With their project of "audiovisual journalism," it became necessary for Godard and Anne-Marie Miéville to observe the relationships between images and us, as two of their premises are: "On produit et on consomme notre image avec celle de l'autre" and "une image photographique est un regard, sur un autre regard présenté à un troisième regard, déjà représenté par l'appareil photographique."[13] Thus, they posit the issue of representation as a matter of exchanges of gazes, which for them are conditioned by the regime of visibility in which the image circulates. They further highlight the fact that there is always a difference between the photographer, the seen and the viewer, bearing in mind that this exchange of gazes is determined as well by the potential target market of the image. Moreover, in their view, to understand the relationship between two images is to see the *true* image of their relation, an image that emerges when we see the role we ourselves play in the "uninterrupted" chain of images circulating in the mass media. Thus, in the Sonimage films, Godard and Miéville gave themselves the task of deconstructing the discourse of objectivity in photojournalistic images and used the formula "2 to 1" (être deux pour regarder une image,[14] and 1 image + 1 image = a third image, as we will see in the next chapter). They also sought to explain pedagogically to their viewers the functioning of the economy of information and the circulation of images.

Godard had done a "Revolutionary Tour" between 1967 and 1970—(virtually) to Vietnam for *Camera Eye*, his contribution to the collective film in solidarity with the Vietnamese people, *Loin du Vietnam*, and actually to Cuba, Czechoslovakia, London, Italy, Québec, the United States and Palestine. In 1968 he visited Cuba and proposed a project which was turned down by the Cuban government.[15] He also met Cuban filmmaker

---

[13] "We produce and consume our images with those of others," and "A photographic image is a gaze upon another gaze that is presented to a third gaze, already represented by the camera's lens." Both are quotes from the voice-over of *Ici et ailleurs*.

[14] "To be two to see an image." From *Comment ça va?*

[15] Daniel Fairfax, "Birth (of the Image) of a Nation: Jean-Luc Godard in Mozambique" *Acta Univ. Sapientiae, Film and Media Studies* 3 (2010), p. 58.

Santiago Álvarez, whose work (especially his newsreels-assemblages-collages) arguably influenced his method of montage as much as Debord and Vertov did; especially his films such as *Now* (1965) and *Hasta la victoria siempre* (1967).

As we have seen, in the first official DVG film, *Le Vent d'Est* (1970), Godard and Gorin ask the question, "Quoi faire?" in regards to anti-imperialism and the Third World. In a scene in which a white cowboy shouts, "*Io sono il Generale Motors!*" while he tows an Indian tied to his horse, Godard and Gorin oppose Third World filmmaking to Hollywood film (whose archetypical genre is the Western). As the Indian declares: "I'm black! I'm Palestinian, I'm Vietnamese, I'm Indian, I'm Peruvian," we hear in the voice-over: "Quel film fait-on à Alger? Quel film fait-on à la Havane? On prétend qu'on lutte contre Nixon-Paramount; mais qu'en est-il en réalité?"[16] Evidently Godard was in dialogue with Third World filmmakers who were critical of *pornomiseria* filmmaking, and the scene asks the question of what kind of politics should militant cinema produced in the First and Third Worlds follow, and what would their relationship be. We see a subsequent scene in which Glauber Rocha, the Brazilian filmmaker who wrote what is considered to be the Third Cinema manifesto, "The Aesthetics of Hunger" (1965), plays himself. Rocha appears standing at a crossroads with extended arms in a crucifixion pose (chin down, making the peace/victory sign with both hands), chanting: "é preciso estar atento e forte // não temos tempo de temer a morte // é preciso estar atento e forte."[17] Coming from the horizon behind Rocha, we see the "militant filmmaker," a young pregnant woman played by Isabel Pons,[18] who approaches to ask him about his struggle, about the relation between film and politics. In the voice-over we hear: "Tu disais au début, une route que l'histoire des luttes révolutionnaires nous a apprise à connaître; mais où est-elle? Devant, derrière, à droit, à gauche et comment? Alors tu as demandé au cinéma du tiers-monde où était-elle?"[19] Then, Pons asks Rocha, "Excusez-moi camarade de vous

---

[16] "What kind of film do we make in Algeria? What kind of film do we make in Havana? We pretend to be struggling against Nixon-Paramount; but what's it all about, really?"

[17] "It is necessary to be attentive and strong; we have no time to fear death; it is necessary to be attentive and strong."

[18] Gorin's partner at the time, a member of the DGV, and assistant director on several of Godard's films prior to 1968.

[19] "You mentioned at the beginning the road that the history of revolutionary struggles has shown us; but where is it? In front of us, behind us, to the right, to the left, and how? So you have posed the question to Third World cinema, where is it?"

déranger...votre lutte, a-t-elle de l'importance dans la direction de la lutte de classes?"[20] Rocha points at two roads. The first one leads to a cinema aligned with power interests: "Para lá, é um cinema desconhecido ...um cinema d'aventura."[21] He points in the other direction and states: "para aqui é um cinema do terceiro mundo; é um cinema very good, um cine maravilhoso, é um cinema da opressão, da opressão fascista, do terrorismo é um cinema perigoso, divino e maravilhoso, é um cinema que vai construir tudo: a técnica e as casas de produção e de distribuição, os técnicos [...] é um cinema para todos [...] do terceiro mundo..."[22] In the voice-over we hear: "Et là, t'as senti la complexité de la lutte; t'as senti qu'il te manquaient les moyens de les analyser; t'es revenu a ta situation concrète: en Italie, en France, en Allemagne, à Varsovie, à Prague...t'as vu que le cinéma matérialiste n'aidera seulement au tiers monde à lutter contre le concept bourgeois de représentation."[23] Having realized that Third World struggles are too complicated for the European filmmaker because they are not concrete enough for her, as she lacks the means to analyze the foreign situation, the "militant filmmaker" decides to walk in a different direction than the ones pointed out by Rocha. After pondering the problems, the options and the history of revolutionary cinema, she realizes that her concrete struggle is against "the bourgeois notion of representation." The weapon, which is common to Third World filmmakers, is materialist cinema. Evidently the scene allegorizes the DVG's relationship to Third World cinema. Weary of idealizing struggles beyond its means to understand them (i.e., colonialism from the point of view of the colonized), it situates its struggle against Hollywood imperialism, side by side with Third World films and against representation. Godard and Gorin's position regarding cinema and Third World struggles could be described as self-critical

---

[20] "Sorry to bother you, comrade...your struggle—is it relevant to the class struggle?"

[21] "That way, there is an unknown cinema, a cinema of adventure."

[22] "This way is the road to a cinema of the Third World, it is a very good cinema, a marvelous cinema, it is a cinema of oppression of consumption and imperialism, it is a dangerous cinema, a cinema of fascist repression, of terrorism, a dangerous cinema; dangerous and divine and marvelous cinema, it is a cinema that will construct everything: technique and production and distribution houses, the technicians [...] it is a cinema for everyone [...] of the Third World..."

[23] "At that moment, you sensed the complexity of the struggle, you felt that you lacked the means to analyze it, you came back to your concrete situation in Italy, France, Germany, Warsaw, Prague...and you saw that materialist cinema is useful beyond the Third World, in the fight against the bourgeois concept of representation."

solidarity. In an interview from 1969 with Fernando Solanas, the Argentinian filmmaker and co-director, with Octavio Getino, of *La Hora de los Hornos* (1968),[24] both Godard and Solanas agree that the role of film is the liberation of man, to raise consciousness, to induce reflection and to clarify things,[25] and they discuss the potential unification of Third Worldists and Third World filmmakers in anti-imperialism: the position allegorized in Glauber Rocha's scene with Isabel Pons in *Le Vent d'Est*. We should bear in mind that Pons' encounter with Rocha is evidently imbued with anxiety of blindness—as will all of Godard's filmic encounters with Third World struggles, especially *Ici et ailleurs*, as we will see below.

For their part, *British Sounds* and *Lotte in Italia* (1969, 1970) are accounts of the struggles in London and Italy respectively, and *Pravda* (1969) is a film about the situation in Czechoslovakia that is highly critical of the Soviet occupation and of socialist capitalism and bureaucracy. These films were made self-critically, posing the question of political tourism. *One A.M.* (1968) was filmed in collaboration with the Newsreel collective from New York and, as we have seen, it included an interview with Black Panthers' leader Eldridge Cleaver.

Radical Tourism and the Palestinian Revolution: *Jusqu'à la Victoire*

In 1969, the DVG decided to make a film about the Palestinian Revolution, wanting to get to know its practice in order to derive "sensible knowledge" from it. It thought that the situation there was more complex and paradigmatic, less clear than elsewhere.[26] Back then, the Palestinian Revolution was perceived as new, insofar as it presented a perspective that was something other than the Orientalist image of the Arab world produced by colonial Europe. Differently from today, the fedayeen were seen from the inside barely as heroes, definitely not as martyrs, and from the outside, the Palestinian resistance was seen as "new" and "beautiful." In

---

[24] Solanas and Getino also wrote the manifesto "Towards a Third Cinema: Notes and Experiences for the Development of a Cinema of Liberation in the Third World" (1969).

[25] The interview is unpublished and it was recorded by the Third World Cinema Group in Paris (from Berkeley, it seems) in 1969. David Faroult kindly forwarded me a digital copy.

[26] As Godard wrote in "Manifeste," published in *El Fatah* (July 1970). Reprinted in *Jean-Luc Godard: Documents*, p. 138.

other words, Palestinians were perceived from the outside as the epitome of progressive artistic and political sophistication and were portrayed as "sexy" revolutionaries fighting for political self-determination. This was encouraged through the PLO's astute manipulation of the empathy of Third Worldists and European journalists, creating an exchange of gazes that posed the fedayeen for foreign cameras as patriotic heroes who were dedicated to recovering their stolen land.[27]

The DVG (Gorin, Armand Marco and Godard) filmed the refugee and training camps in Jordan, Syria and Lebanon between February and July 1970. Godard insisted in an interview that the "political" aspect of the film resided in the fact that it was aimed at being the result of political discussions and study of the thinking and working methods of the Palestinian Revolution. In other words, Godard held a theoretical-political position by arguing that he was not "putting himself at the service of the cause" based on political sympathy but insisted on dialogue and on political analysis *with* the Palestinians.[28] Under the banner of the Russian avant-garde, Godard posited himself neither as the bearer of an individual message nor as the spokesman of the fedayeen, but as a technician making use of a medium that he knows well in order to express the ideas of the Palestinian Revolution. From this interview, moreover, we can infer that in 1970, the film's explicit purpose was to show "just images and sounds" from the Palestinian camps, different from those that appeared in the Western press and television.[29] The original title of the DVG's film, *Jusqu'à la victoire* [*Until Victory: Working and Thinking Methods of the Palestinian Revolution*], underscores its effort to convey the logic of the Palestinian guerilla through revolutionary pedagogy. The film would conclude with lessons drawn from the Palestinian schema that could be useful to other revolutionary movements. In "Manifeste," a text published in July 1970 in *El Fatah* (a Palestinian journal published in France), Godard articulates the propagandistic aspect of the

---

[27] For instance, Armand Deriaz's book of photographs of refugees and fedayeen in relationship to the film *Biladi, une Révolution*, shot in Jordan in 1970, directed by Francis Reusser. The book, in which the photographs were accompanied by texts written by Palestinians, was published in Switzerland. There are also the photographs taken by Bruno Barbey for Magnum, one of them reprinted in a French journal analyzed by Godard and Miéville in *Comment ça va?* Barbey's images also illustrated a text by Jean Genet on the Palestinians in *Zoom* magazine in 1971.

[28] Interview with Michel Garin, "Godard chez les fedayeen," *L'Express*, July 27–August 2, 1970, 44–45, reprinted in *Jean-Luc Godard par Jean-Luc Godard*, p. 165.

[29] Ibid.

film as an educational enterprise, conveying to revolutionary movements elsewhere lessons from the Palestinian guerilla.[30] For Godard, furthermore, propaganda meant "political discussion and analysis" rather than reporting or documenting the revolution. He further emphasized his goal of showing relationships between images and sounds, as opposed to images of the struggle. In other words, Godard and Gorin were not interested in portraying the ideological propaganda of the Palestinian struggle in order to fit Fatah's agenda, as their image-making did not have as an *end* the image of the Palestinian Revolution; rather, they saw these images as *instruments*, in the sense of pedagogical tools for discussing revolutionary methods and their contradictions, that needed to be disseminated elsewhere.

The DVG filmed different aspects of Fatah's movement and, from the start, it claimed to seek to differentiate its images from those taken by journalists and reporters. This became supposedly the source of a political struggle with the Palestinians. According to Godard and Gorin, the Palestinians were used to receiving journalists and reporters who would come and create images of training camps or hospitals. For this reason, the Palestinians resisted the idea that for the DVG it was important to see these places only to be able to *build* pictures after, as opposed to *taking* pictures of these places: making the Palestinian images was, for the DVG, a political struggle in itself. Godard and Gorin's emphasis on the *construction* of images was based on Dziga Vertov's praxis of concrete analysis of a situation by the construction and analysis of images' signification.[31] Moreover, for the DVG it was pivotal that the images contain tension and that they resulted from contradiction, discussion and struggle.

Once the material for *Jusqu'à la victoire* had been filmed, Godard and Gorin intended to come back to Palestine in order to show the material to the fedayeen with the aim of concluding its political aspect in discussion with them and with Fatah militants in order to achieve the "definitive montage" of the material. This method follows Dziga Vertov's procedure of "editing before shooting, during shooting and after shooting" which consists of the following steps: the writing of the script, the orientation of the "disarmed" gaze (the eye without the aid of the camera), the organiza-

---

[30] David Faroult insists that we take into account that with this text Godard and Gorin were seeking to reassure the financial support of Fatah; and that is why they proved publicly their support to Fatah. See Faroult's "Du *Vertovisme* du Groupe Dziga Vertov," in *Jean-Luc Godard: Documents*, p. 134.

[31] Godard and Gorin, *Double Feature: Movies and Politics*, p. 45.

tion, within the director's mind, of what has been seen, montage during shooting, the orientation of the "armed" gaze, montage after shooting, definitive montage, and emphasizing the pivot [direction] of the film.[32] Vertov's method of "uninterrupted montage" was based on a notion of cinema as a "factory of facts," what we also know as the Soviet practice of *factography*. Factography aims at "integrating ideological systems by producing signification not as a mimetic reflection but as an act of productive labour."[33] In other words, factography implies a reduplication of reality as an act of signification, as a coding and production of reality drawn from the components of daily experience. Factography, moreover, is a model of production that seeks to reorganize the symbolic codes of language and art according to the new social configurations, ideological principles and forces of production that emerged in the post-revolutionary epoch in Soviet Russia. Factography as a genre is close to propaganda, insofar as it uses analogue images not as visual facts but as the *fixation* of visual facts, a kind of writing that is not only historically constituted from a subjective point of view.[34] We can infer from Godard's and Gorin's statements that they had Vertov's practice of factography in mind.

The DVG's images of Palestinians are framed in objective indirect or photojournalistic style (fixed-frames), a style characterized by a steady camera showing a point of view of someone who is external to the set.[35] Such a way of framing cuts out objects from "reality," determining artificially a closed system as slices of space and time. Fixed-frames predominate, except in a few instances in which the camera follows the action in long pans. This is where a critical distinction must be drawn between the genres of factography and documentary. The term "documentary" was coined in 1926 by the filmmaker John Grierson to designate the depiction of reality at its most objective, passive and impartial. Factography, in contrast, does not claim to reflect reality veridically, but to actively transform it. Factography is praxis, the outcome of a process of production. As a method,

---

[32] Dziga Vertov, *Articles, journaux, projets* (Paris: UGE '10/18', 1972), 102–103. Cited by Faroult in "Du *vertovisme* du Groupe Dziga Vertov," p. 135.
[33] Benjamin Buchloh, "From Faktura to Factography," *October* No. 30 (Fall 1984), p. 107.
[34] Ibid., p. 114.
[35] Deleuze gives a nominal definition of "objective" image, which is when a thing (or a set of things) is seen by someone external to the set. Deleuze, *Moving-Image Cinema 1*, translated by Hugh Tomlinson and Barbara Habberjam (Minneapolis: University of Minnesota Press, 2001), p. 71.

truth is an effort not to reflect human experience but to organize it.[36] Moreover, *signification* in factography is not a system of mimetic reflection but one of productive labor, an *inscription of facts*, a kind of writing (*écriture*), as opposed to a set of codes establishing a series of reality effects.[37] In sum, the difference between factography and documentary lies in recording facts as opposed to producing and inscribing facts.

The DVG had planned to bring the rushes back to the Middle East to discuss them with the fedayeen in order to organize the montage of the film. However, they were unable to return to the Middle East because of the Black September massacre of September 1970. Military action was taken by King Hussein of Jordan, with the support of Henry Kissinger; it led to the slaughter of a number of the fedayeen in the PLO's refugee and training camps in Jordan. The DVG had filmed extensively in these camps. Moreover, the massacres in Jordan and the Black September wave of terrorism that followed in 1970 were perceived as the failure of the Palestinian struggle for self-determination. In France, for example, the Palestinian impasse in 1972 was articulated as lacking a cohesive strategy to resist Israel, conflating the guerrillas' failure to defeat the enemy with a perceived incapacity to come up with a solution to the refugee problem.[38] After having been expelled from Jordan, the Palestinian resistance regrouped and concentrated in Beirut, initiating a new era in the history of the PLO.

From *Jusqu'à la Victoire* to *Ici et Ailleurs*

Two years after having shot the material for the film in the Middle East, Gorin declared that the material had become impossible to edit. In the DVG's view, the problem was that the footage had acquired historical status, and that the film could not become a "film-reportage" with a voice-over or a documentary with objective implications that would attempt to explain all the aspects and contradictions of the Palestinian struggle; rather, for Gorin, the material had the potential of becoming a "continuous addition" summing up all the aspects of the history of Palestine.[39] The DVG dissolved in 1972, and Godard edited the material in collaboration with Anne-Marie Miéville within the framework of their newly founded audiovisual workshop Sonimage.

---

[36] Devin Foe, "Introduction," *October* no. 118 (Fall 2006), pp. 3–5.
[37] Ibid., p. 8.
[38] See Gérard Chaliand, *Voyage dans vingt ans de guérillas* (Paris: L'Aube, 1988) pp. 110–115.
[39] Interview with Jean-Pierre Gorin by Christian Braad Thomsen, *Jump Cut* no. 3 (1974), pp. 17–19.

According to Miéville, they worked on editing the film every day for 18 months.[40] For many, this film is the intellectual peak of Godard and Miéville's collaboration. The question in *Ici et ailleurs* became, for both filmmakers, how to create a point of view to edit the Palestinian images, images in which the Palestinian people appear as a revolutionary movement now betrayed. According to film director Masao Adachi who, along with Koji Wakamatsu, also made a film about the Palestinian Revolution titled *Seikun-PFLP: Sekai Senso Sengen* (The Red Army/PFLP: Declaration of World War, 1971):

> *Ici et Ailleurs* manifests a spirit that we shared with comrades all over the world, mobilized as we were by the march towards the creation of a new world. The film recounts the shadows of the historical time and space as we lived it back then. It is an account that demonstrates the painful road travelled by those who marched without halt in the middle of those shadows, towards a confiscated goal.[41]

In this regard, the editing of *Ici et ailleurs* coincided with the end of the "French Cultural Revolution," with the failure of revolutions *elsewhere* and with the beginning of a new reactionary period in general, specifically in France.[42]

As we have seen, the years 1973 and 1974 mark in France the churning out of Marxist discourse and the demise of the revolutionary project and subject, provoked by a critique of Left-wing totalitarianism spawned by the publication in French of Solzhenitsyn's *The Gulag Archipelago* (in 1974).[43] The critique of totalitarianism also ensued from the collapse of Third World revolutions elsewhere and the disappointment at home, for instance, brought about by the fall of Salvador Allende's socialist regime in Chile in 1973. The discourses of Third Worldism and anti-imperialism drifted away, giving way to a new humanism. If Third Worldism had implied universalizing or giving a name to a political wrong that mobilized activists in the West, in spite of the fact that the relationships between the political problem of self-determination and military questions (the facts on

---

[40] In "Un entretien avec la réalisatrice: Il faut parler de ce que l'on connaît," interview with Miéville by Danièle Heyman, *Le Monde* 18, January 1989.

[41] Masao Adachi, "The Testament that Godard has never Written", in Nicole Brenez and Go Hirasawa (eds.) *Le bus de la révolution passera bientôt près de chez toi*, Editions Rouge Profond, Paris 2012, translated into English by Stoffel Debuysere, Mari Shields and available online: http://www.diagonalthoughts.com/?p=2067

[42] Deleuze, "Les Intercesseurs," *Pourparlers* (Paris: Les Éditions de Minuit, 1990), p. 165.

[43] See Jean Daniel and André Burguière, *Le Tiers monde et la gauche* (Paris: Éditions du Seuil, 1979).

the ground, i.e., war) were at times interchangeable or idealized, the relationship that this movement established with the Third World was *political*. The "wretched of the earth" emerged for a specifically historic period of time as a new figuration of "people" in the political sense: the Other became the immigrant worker, the Chinese barefoot doctor, the revolutionary from elsewhere.[44] Afterwards, the articulate Third World revolutionaries fighting for self-determination became victims unable to present solutions to their own political problems. A new Third World imaginary emerged with the collapse of the socialist ideal followed by a fear of radical politics and the death of the political as the grounds for relating to the elsewhere. The relationship to the Third World shifted from a political stance to an ethical one, under the discourse of human rights.[45]

Bearing in mind the historical impasse of the Palestinian Revolution in the early 1970s and the shifts in political engagement upon the demise of Third Worldism, commentators wanted to see in *Ici et ailleurs* a radical break in Godard's *oeuvre* at the level of his political commitment and aesthetic engagement, as they saw a qualitative and quantitative change in his engagement from the Marxist-Leninist period to the Sonimage years.[46] The changes in Godard's engagement were qualitative insofar as they responded to the actuality and to the shifting historical conditions prompted by the fall of *Tiersmondisme* and socialism as the containers for political change elsewhere. Therefore, *Ici et ailleurs* is not only an example of vanguardist political filmmaking, but a self-reflexive account of revolutions here and elsewhere and of militant cinema. Aside from positing film as a politicized space, it is an interrogation of the conditions of possibility of representation: the film ends revealing the limits of aesthetic practice grounded in the politics of the signifier and the signified. The politics of

---

[44] Kristin Ross, *May '68 and its Afterlives* (Chicago: University of Chicago Press, 2002), p. 11.

[45] Michael Scott Christofferson, *French Intellectuals against the Left*, p. 267.

[46] Christa Blümlinger called it "a radical farewell to militant filmmaking," in "Procession and Projection: Notes on a Figure in the Work of Jean-Luc Godard," *For Ever Godard*, edited by Michael Temple (London: Black Dog Publishing and Tate Modern, 2004), 182. For Raymond Bellour, it announces a radical break in Godard's work as "the end of militant politics, the exportation of concepts and the credo that images cannot embody words and that images bear upon them the task of expressing a political truth, that is, the political (*la politique*) like truth." Raymond Bellour, *L'entre-images: photo, cinéma, vidéo* (Paris: Éditions de la Différence, 1990), p. 117. For Serge Daney "nothing has protected him from the average illusions of his day (and when his films became more political, crafty though he was, he came up against the same naivety and dead-ends as any other 'Maoist' of the age)." Serge Daney, "The Godard Paradox," *For Ever Godard*, p. 70.

the signifier could be defined as formal Modernism, an ontological reflection of images tied to self-reflexivity of the cinematic apparatus. A politics of the signified implies a coding, decoding and recoding of images through ideological auto-critique. In the case of *Ici et ailleurs*, this translates to deconstructing the myth of objectivity, imbued with an anxiety of blindness. For this reason, in the new film Godard and Miéville created a multiplicity of points of view to look at the DVG's Palestinian footage guided by a main category: "Re-thinking about the *elsewhere* (Palestine), *then* (1970), from *here* (France), *now* (1973–74)," and assembled it in three main axioms: Palestine, France and the conjunction "AND." In creating this spatio-temporalizing, conjunctive and geopolitical axis, Godard and Miéville emphasized their French perspective (although they are both Swiss, they were residing in Grenoble and in dialogue with the Parisian intelligentsia), especially in relationship to the media, and began to explore the Palestinian material in relationship to the history of revolutions. The main category is further subsumed within a multiplicity of spatio-temporalities and points of view on the Palestinian Revolution including and problematizing the domains of journalism, documentary, Third Worldist intervention, history, cinema, Maoist discourse, materialist self-reflexivity, pedagogy, and (chastising) female and (repenting) masculine discursive voices. Not only different points of view co-exist through image/sound juxtapositions and voice-overs; also, different material forms of expression of the Palestinian conflict manifested *here* (France) appear in the film: newspapers, Gérard de Villiers' novels,[47] television, songs, cartoons and Palestinian revolutionary poetry ("I will resist" by Mahmoud Darwish (1968) and "Bisan and the Martyr" by Khaled Abu Khaled (1970)). Through montage, every point of view is defined in relationship to *series* of transformations, through which the images and sounds pass by means of repetition and juxtaposition. Working in series, Godard and Miéville make different versions of basic themes or categories, arranging the images and sounds accordingly. The Palestinian *visibilities* are thus included in the points of view, not as a window open into their struggle but as a *table of information*, which means that the images are opaque with layers of infor-

---

[47] In the film we see the character of a "French worker" flipping through Gérard de Villiers' books. De Villiers' books are sort of "proletarian pedagogical fictions" about conflicts in the Middle East and elsewhere, and they appear repeatedly in the film, as the fictive mode of the material existence of the Palestinian conflict in France.

mation.⁴⁸ The editors, then, make the table of information pass through a table of categories, using seriality as a method, peeling off and putting on layers of images within the images through fruitful juxtapositions to complicate their legibility and unearth what is hidden by the images themselves.

Exploring the exchanges of gazes inherent in the production of images in accord with Godard's politics of the image, as I mentioned, Sonimage starts from the premise that all images are always addressed to a third, and thus must be understood as immanent to an interlocutionary act, especially documentary and photojournalistic images, which conceal the mechanism of mediation through the myth of objectivity. Considering that the speaker belongs to a different discursive regime than the imaged, for Godard and Miéville, the speaker needs to displace him/herself spatio-temporally in order to be able to translate the codes. Vouching for a politics not of objectivity, but of "subjectivation,"⁴⁹ Godard and Miéville made it an imperative to acknowledge that the real does not speak in images in any instance.

Sonimage and Anxiety of Blindness

Michelangelo Antonioni addressed the relationship between engaged intervention *elsewhere*, reportage and objectivity after his 1972 visit to China, where he had been invited by the Maoist government to produce his documentary, *Chung Kuo - Cina*. In the introduction to the script, he poses the question guiding his film: "How to get to know the Chinese, how to deal with the 'idea' of China from books and images, is it possible to portray revolution and socialism, is documentary film possible?"⁵⁰ Three years after he filmed *Chung Kuo - Cina*, Antonioni made *The Passenger* or *Professione: reporter*, a fictional rendering of the contradictions inherent to intellectual engagement with Third World struggles in the 1970s. Asking similar questions to those raised by Godard, Gorin and Miéville, the script by Mark Peploe, Peter Wollen and Antonioni takes up

---

⁴⁸ The practice of stratigraphy implies the uncovering of strata, and Deleuze-Foucault defines strata "as historical formations, positivities or empiricities. As 'sedimentary beds' they are made from things and words, from seeing and speaking, from bands of visibility and fields of readability, from contents and expressions." Deleuze, *Foucault*, p. 47.

⁴⁹ In Deleuze's sense of *assujettissement*.

⁵⁰ Michelangelo Antonioni, "Est-il encore possible de tourner un documentaire? *Chung Kuo Cina, 1972*" (1974), *Écrits: Fare un film è per me vivere* (Paris: Éditions Images Modernes, 2003), pp. 272–273. See Susan Sontag's discussion of the film and its Chinese reception in *On Photography*. The film and her own experience in China became pivotal in her discussion on the difference between empirical knowledge and the knowledge offered by images.

the issue of political engagement within the context of the mediatization of the representation of revolutionary struggles elsewhere. Exploring the contradiction of militant engagement versus objective mediation, in *The Passenger* the figures of the journalist and the engaged *Tiermondiste* become folded into one another through the existentialist "passage" from journalist to arms dealer or, as some would put it, through an escape to a different order of experience. John Locke (Jack Nicholson) is a journalist working on a story about a guerrilla movement in Central Africa. His attempts to contact the rebels who want to overthrow the dictatorial government fail after his guide deserts him and his jeep gets stuck in the sand, causing him to shout: "I don't care!" Locke walks back to his hotel where he finds the corpse of Robertson, a fellow Englishman on a "business trip", who has died of a heart attack. Locke swaps identities with his compatriot and his life becomes determined by Robertson's appointment book and airplane tickets. After he meets with one of Robertson's contacts at the airport in Munich, he realizes that Robertson was an arms dealer helping the Chadian rebels. This turn of events recalls Arthur Rimbaud's activities selling weapons to a tribe in North Africa during the 1880s.[51] Poet and businessman, we can draw a parallel between the figures of Robertson and Rimbaud: while Locke is busy pasting his photograph into the dead man's passport in the process of becoming him, we see a flashback comprised of a shot of Robertson and Locke in a terrace facing the desert discussing the different ways in which they engage with the landscape. Locke asserts that Robertson does so in the manner of a poet.[52] The figure of Locke, the objective journalist, folds into Robertson-Rimbaud, the absolute sympathizer with the cause, poet and arms dealer. Locke continues Robertson's journey across Europe, now made out of

---

[51] See Rimbaud's letter of December 1887 to the Minister in which he demands permission to unload materials to fabricate rifles, cartridges and weapons of war in the Somali coast held by France, destined for King Ménélik of Choa. In *I Promise to be Good: The Letters of Arthur Rimbaud*, translated by Wyatt Mason (New York: The Modern Library, 2003), p. 292.

[52] Robertson: It's so beautiful here... It's the immobility – a kind of waiting, an eternal suspension.
    Locke: You seem unusually poetic – for a businessman.
    Robertson: Do I? Doesn't the desert have the same effect on you?
    Locke: I'm interested in men more than landscapes.
    Robertson: But there are men who live in the desert [...]
Mark Peploe, Peter Wollen and Michelangelo Antonioni, *Michelangelo Antonioni's "The Passenger": The Complete Script* (New York, Grove Press Inc., 1975), p. 27.

missed appointments, as no one shows up to the meetings marked in Robertson's agenda. Back in London, Locke's wife and his media agency colleague, Knight, discuss his African footage and his journalistic ethics, as they plan to edit this material into a posthumous homage to his journalistic career. Locke, we learn, in a self-reflexive vein, *always put himself in every shot* of his documentaries. Rachel and Knight show us three fragments from Locke's footage: an interview with Rama Fadeda (an outlaw from the Chadian United Liberation Front), Patrice Lumumba's execution, and an interview with the African president at a luxurious and kitsch hotel stating the official version regarding the repression of the rebels in the mountains. While we are shown this footage, Rachel points at the out of field (*l'hors champ*) images where the dilemmas of journalistic objectivity that her husband grappled with are located. "He accepted too much," she says, addressing the compromises that a reporter needs to make in order to get a scoop. Also, Rachel tells us, highlighting the dismissal of the aesthetic by the imperative *to inform*: "He thought all fiction was unnecessary, frivolous."[53] In a flashback to a previous meeting in Africa, she confronts Locke, directly accusing him of being only half-heartedly engaged with the struggles he spoke of the need to inform about: "You involve yourself in real situations but you have no real dialogue," and "Your neutrality becomes a form of acceptance."[54]

In *The Passenger*, engagement is figured by objective enunciation in the mode of journalism, as artistic enunciation is considered superfluous. Where do the ethics of political engagement remain as they are replaced by journalistic objectivity? Locke's outburst at the beginning of the film—"I don't care!"—is consciously symptomatic here. We can ask if detachment is the emotion that necessarily replaced enthusiasm and empathy after the generalized disappointment that followed the unmasking of totalitarianism and the betrayal of Third World struggles. Is detachment the emotion necessary to speak for a cause from a neutral point of view? Or is it the condition to overcome the contradictions of journalism? In the film, absolute sympathy is offered by the poet/arms dealer, but both men's pursuits become purposeless. Not only does the camera appear to wander aimlessly in the film's famous last sequence; so does this double character, a journalist who becomes a supporter for a rebel cause by proxy, in a pursuit that becomes senseless. Locke, now Robertson, fails to realize

---

[53] Ibid., p. 64.
[54] Ibid., p. 69.

that his adopted assignations to meet with the rebels across Europe have ceased to make sense, and he pays with his life. Facing the failure of Third World struggles and the waning of revolutionary ideology, in *The Passenger* the possibility of militant engagement abroad is figured in the aporia of a Westerner being either an impartial Rimbaudian *poète maudit* or an accepting journalist seeking to be neutral and objective. Further, the matter of the angle hiding a (Western) personal or ideological, non-reflexive intention—Deleuze's "Oedipus in the Colonies" phenomenon—is raised in *The Passenger* when Locke interviews Rama Fadeda, who responds to his questions with the following:

> Mr. Locke, there are perfectly satisfactory answers to all your questions … But I don't think you understand how little you would learn from them. Your questions are much more revealing about yourself than my answers would be about me… Mr. Locke, *we can have a conversation* but only if it is not just what you think is sincere, but also what I believe to be honest.[55]

One of the contradictions that Rama Fadeda addresses here is that the format of the interview is inevitably an effaced projection of the interviewer that inserts itself within the economy of information, expertise and opinion. Along similar lines, Godard and Miéville defined objective intervention as an instance of the author *hiding herself behind the image produced*, welding authorial disappearance with objectivity. In *Ici et ailleurs*, we hear: "On ne voit *jamais* l'image de celui qui *met en scène*,"[56] while we hear Godard's voice asking a young woman to tilt her head in the out of field. For Godard, documentary filmmakers and photojournalists seek to hide behind the images they film as a form of self-effacement; as the female voice-over states, it is the fascist form of representation.[57]

It is evident that Godard grappled with similar questions in *Ici et ailleurs* as did Antonioni in *The Passenger*, especially the "myth of objectivity." Having been hosted under the *delegate* system in Palestine, Godard and Miéville needed to account for the footage in relationship to the production of information about revolutionary struggles elsewhere in relation to journalistic objectivity, propaganda and ideology—most importantly,

---

[55] Ibid., p. 75. My italics.
[56] "We *never* see the image of she who realizes the *mise en scène*."
[57] Letter from April 12, 1979, first published in a special number in *Cahiers*, 1979, reprinted in *JLG Documents*, p. 289. Followed by Roussopoulos' answer in 2005.

because of the ethical and political problems raised by the Palestinian footage.

As I have mentioned, the myth of objectivity and the act of observation of political processes elsewhere raise the questions of blindness and seeing in Godard. According to Odile, one of the main characters in *Comment ça va?* (1978), objectivity is a crime since he/she speaking in the name of others does not use the other's voice. Speaking in the name of others implies occupying their place—Odile's is a critique of *vertreten* as a crime, as he/she who speaks in the name of others does not use the other's voice. Keeping his/her own place, the documentarist or reporter speaks in the name of others, which falsely implies occupying their place. For Odile, it is necessary to take responsibility in enunciation, by speaking in one's own name on behalf of others. But in order to speak in one's name *of others*, it is necessary to *see first*. Here Odile champions *darstellen*: a description of the other, speaking in one's proper name. In order to be able to *see*, a displacement (*translation* in French) must take place: one must lose one's place because to speak *of others* is an act of translation (*traduction* in French), considering that the speaker belongs to a different discursive regime than those being spoken of.[58] For Godard, the problem of objectivity is inextricable from the question of communication, which means to work *blindly*, unable to read or write.[59]

As I mentioned above, for Godard empathy and observation are inextricably related to the anxiety of blindness. Psychoanalysis grounds empathy in the possibility of sharing our experience with the object of desire by the way of an introjection—a projection inward—which prompts identification with what is seen, and which is the condition for empathy and the grounds for ethics. Along the lines of Vertov's *Kino-Glaz*, Godard privileges the camera as an epistemology of *seeing*, while designing his own discursive practice and a site of enunciation as reactive and pragmatic, starting with a *Je vois*.

---

[58] Sonimage's critique of photojournalism resonates with Susan Sontag's own critique, articulated in *On Photography* from 1977. She takes up the issue in *Regarding the Pain of Others* in 2003, where she provides a short history of war photojournalism on pages 36–39.

[59] Godard from an interview in *Le Monde*, September 25, 1975, cited in Philippe Dubois, "Video Thinks what Cinema Creates: Notes on Jean-Luc Godard's Work in Video and Television," *Jean-Luc Godard: Son + Image 1974–1991*, edited by Raymond Bellour and Mary Lea Bandy (New York: MoMA, 1992), p. 170.

Godard has stated that at the beginning of the "Sonimage period" he situated himself within the contradiction of cinema's resistance to the new and television's lack of originality. For him, to be within this contradiction is to be blind, unable to read or write as he seeks, stammering, to respond to the question of communication.[60] Insisting on expression, Godard and Miéville explored diverse tools and methods such as dialogue, pedagogy and emphasis on shifters—exploring designation and address as alternatives to the communication model. In their audiovisual/journalistic workshop they became self-managed producers working from a "library" of images and sounds and their studio became a factory for *seeing* and *thinking*. Sonimage's site of enunciation is situated within the "inter-media" realm of cinema, photography, television and the printed media, one that is made possible by video, which, because of its technical qualities, is able to integrate these media. Video is thus a virtual and operational site for moving back and forth between different media, a technical and mental place operating in between mobility, stillness and two monitors.[61]

What is crucial here is Godard's and Miéville's response to the intransitivity of the media (the absence of address) by creating their own mode of pragmatic enunciation activating a speaking subject in the act of seeing: *Moi, je vois*. Their starting point is blindness, and they privilege searching as an intensive way of seeing; they convey a subject that sees and speaks, a subject that gets sewn up in the utterance: "I try to see." Bearing in mind that *video* in Latin means "I see," an analogy can be drawn with the seer, Bernadette Soubirous, who appeared in Godard's *Passion* (1982). Like Soubirous, the seer confirms both the image's status as a sacred imprint and herself as a seer in an indicative speech act.

In *Ici et ailleurs*, Godard speaks in the first person and calls for an ethics of enunciation as a means of accounting for intransitivity as well as undermining the code of objectivity proper to the media.[62] Moreover, in Godard,

---

[60] Ibid.

[61] Raymond Bellour, *L'Entre-images*, p. 2.

[62] I am referencing here the linguist Oswald Ducrot, who argues that the *talking subject* introduces sentences (in enunciation) that necessarily contain the responsibility of the utterer; in other words, in enunciation the speaker is committed to the semantic content; that is why for Ducrot speech-acts constitute *expression*. Oswald Ducrot, *Logique, structure, énonciation: Lectures sur le langage* (Paris: Éditions de Minuit, 1989), and *Les Mots du discours* (Paris: Éditions de Minuit, 1980).

the condition of seeing is close to Rimbaud, for whom seeing implies a derangement of the senses, an "encrapulation" or intoxication of the self.[63] Rimbaud's violence to the senses (as a shock in thought, as Deleuze would put it, or as a shock as the beginning of thought, for Arendt echoing Aristotle) actualizes in Godard as an explosion of contradictions, as we hear in the voice-over/off in *Ici et ailleurs*: "Très vite, comme on dit, les contradictions éclatent et toi avec // et *je commence à voir* // et je commence à voir // et je commence à voir que moi avec."[64] Finally, Godard displaces the question of seeing and blindness to the mass media and spectacle. He formulates it as the uninterrupted "chains of images" in which we are all caught and from which we build our own images (Foucault's and Deleuze's subjectivation), and thus he and Miéville take up the task to slow down the chains of images and dissect them to enable themselves and viewers to find their own place within those chains.

In order to further problematize documentary and photojournalistic objectivity they insert in the film a multiplicity of points of view and a diversity of temporalities. For Godard and Miéville, as they put it in the voice-over in *Ici et ailleurs*, objectivity—along similar lines to the accusations Rachel puts to her journalist husband in Antonioni's film—is a doubling of silence, the hidden silencing of the already silent, and "un silence qui devient mortel parce qu'on l'empêche de s'en sortir vivant."[65] Thus, objectivity implies a situation that is "covered" in both senses: a journalist covers a story while simultaneously covering it up by making the story itself the event. Therefore, for them, objectivity is a form of silent complicity that in the case of the Palestinian resistance proved to be deadly. The ethical-political imperative became, first, to take enunciative responsibility: for them it implies *enunciating* images (see p. 130) by acknowledging authorship over them, accounting for the intentionality immanent within the act of speaking for and of others as an act of expression. Second, to make images speak and to open up a space in which the speech that had been taken away from the dead Palestinians could be restituted, as I will further explore in the

---

[63] Rimbaud, letter to Georges Izambard, *Letters of Arthur Rimbaud*, p. 28. The translator wrote "encrapulation" for *encrapuler* (similar to *débauchement, dérégler*) which in French means to intoxicate oneself, to become filthy, vulgar, dishonest, to live in the excess of carnal pleasures. Baudelaire put it as: *se délivrer à la crapule*.

[64] "Very quickly, as they say, the contradictions explode and you with them // and *I begin to see* // and I begin to see // and I begin to see that I explode with them."

[65] "A silence that is deadly because it is stifled."

following chapter. These forms of accounting for speech and image are absolutely different from confessional (*Ici et ailleurs* is sometimes dismissed as "highly confessional") or situated knowledges; in the manner of *écriture*, Miéville and Godard situate themselves in the film at the crossroads of the social techniques of television, the media, and cinema, sight, vision and speech.[66]

SONIMAGE, THE CARNATION REVOLUTION AND THE NEWLY INDEPENDENT MOZAMBIQUE

In *Comment ça va?* Godard and Miéville deconstruct a photo and a text by Serge July about the revolution in Portugal in April 1974 (also called the Carnation Revolution), published in the newspaper *Libération* on September 12, 1975. They juxtapose and superimpose the image with a similar one from May Events of 1968. In a letter to Palestinian historian Elias Sanbar, Godard wrote: "Une image ne sert à rien si elle n'est pas accompagnée par sa semblable dans une situation différente."[67] If in *Ici et ailleurs* they juxtapose two states of affairs (France and Palestine), *Comment ça va?* can be described as a reflexive *mise-en-scène* of Sonimage's efforts to examine the mechanisms proper to the transformation of knowledge and perception into information in the mass media, asking "Forme-in-formation: Comment ça va de l'entrée a la sortie?"[68] According to Nicole Brenez, to ask the question "Comment ça va?" is an act that persists throughout the work of Godard, parting from the *mise-en-scène* of the question in the film.[69] First, narratively or figuratively, "What is the form of information?" And second, to an ethical and formal order, "How should we look at that which concerns us?"

Journalistic practice as a mode of production of *visual* information is characterized by speed, velocity, immediacy and presence. In *Photo et*

---

[66] See Derrida's *Of Grammatology*, translated by G. Spivak (Baltimore and London: The Johns Hopkins University Press, 1997).

[67] "A single image is useless if it is not accompanied by a similar image in a different situation." The letter is dated July 19, 1977, and published in *Cahiers du Cinéma* no. 300 (special issue, 1979), pp. 16–19.

[68] "Form-in-formation, how does it work from the entrance to the exit?"

[69] Nicole Brenez, "The Forms of the Question," *For Ever Godard*, ed. Michael Temple, (London: Black Dog Publishing and Tate Modern, 2004), p. 165.

Cie, one of the chapters for their television series, *Six fois deux: Sur et sous la communication* (1976), Godard and Miéville deconstruct photojournalistic practice in an interview with the photojournalist Christian Simonpietri (from the Sygma Agency), whom they ask to describe the techniques of his profession. Simonpietri does so by telling the story behind a photograph he took in Dakar in December 1971, three days after the departure of the Indian troops at the end of the Indo-Pakistani war. To celebrate the independence of Bangladesh, a public meeting was held in Dakar. After the evening prayer, the prisoners that had been accused of collaboration with the Indian troops were beaten and then executed. Simonpietri took a photograph at the same time as did Michel Laurent, a journalist from Associated Press, whose very similar image won the Pulitzer Prize. Discussing the economy of information, Simonpietri and Godard address the qualities of photo-journalistic production. Simonpietri defines a good journalistic photograph as one that should be apprehended by the viewer instantaneously. Such an image has the power to "speak" right away, and presupposes a viewer who engages with it quickly, ready to receive information instantly, speedily, equating the image's "here and now" to the moment of viewing. Against the grain, Godard and Miéville in this context insist on the need to stop the circulation of images, by slowing down the viewing process: "On va plus lentement à décomposer en uniforme,"[70] says Odette (Miéville) in *Comment ça va?* in order to "Montrer des rapports, plutôt que des vérités."[71] Slowing down, decomposing and showing relationships are opposed to the usual immediacy of photojournalist images and are also actions that call for an active viewership. Evidently the mass media narrows if not hinders comprehension of the events presented by spatio-temporalizing empirical facts, turning them into events seen from a single point of view, coded by the information apparatus. This is why for Godard and Miéville, the image-event renders us powerless as viewers. As Godard wrote, it is about putting a stop to circulation of images in the mass media; working together with other people can remedy our impotent capability to make images.[72]

---

[70] "We break [the image] down more slowly, in order to provide a more consistent analysis [of what we are viewing]."

[71] "Show relationships, as opposed to truths."

[72] Godard in his letter to Elias Sanbar, *Cahiers du Cinéma* no. 300 (Special issue 1979), pp. 16–19.

After a few years of slow and detailed analysis of chains of images, how they circulate in the mass media and the exchanges of gazes embedded in them, Godard and Miéville were invited to Mozambique to conduct a project outlining the newly independent country's television industry. With the Carnation Revolution in 1975, Mozambique had been granted independence from Portugal and the Frelimo (Frente de Libertação de Moçambique) had established itself as a Marxist government under its leader Samora Machel. It is not difficult to understand why the invitation would be tempting for Sonimage: the country was absorbed in the process of building a socialist society. Godard and Miéville were invited to observe what was happening and to contribute to the cause by helping to build the newly independent country's national image. Sonimage went there, funded by a French producer, on a two-year contract with the goal of using its experience as raw material from which to produce a five-hour television series.[73] Godard and Miéville were hosted and also funded by the National Film Institute whose director was Cinema Novo filmmaker Ruy Guerra. Mozambique seemed to them to provide an ideal laboratory to explore with the Mozambicans the relationships between nation and image, propaganda and community, self and collective. After six months, however, the producer felt that Godard was spending too much money on theorizing as opposed to making films and cancelled his contract at the end of the year.[74] The project did not see the light of day and there is no filmic footage left. Traces of the project—an image-essay and diary entries from Sonimage's experience in Mozambique—were printed in a dossier in the 300th issue of *Cahiers de Cinéma* in 1979 titled *Le Dernier rêve d'un producteur: nord contre sud, ou naissance (de l'image) d'une nation*. In the dossier, Godard declared that Sonimage had wanted to take advantage of the audio-visual situation in Mozambique before it flooded the whole social and geographic corpus of the Mozambicans, and to study how the image and voice of a newly independent country gradually take shape.[75] As they put it:

---

[73] Daniel Fairfax, "Birth (of the Image) of a Nation: Jean-Luc Godard in Mozambique" *Acta Univ. Sapientiae, Film and Media Studies* 3 (2010) pp. 55–67.

[74] As stated by Manthia Diawara, "Sonimage in Mozambique" (1999), in *I Said I Love. That is the Promise: The TVideo Politics of Jean-Luc Godard*, Gareth James and Florian Zeyfang eds. (Berlin: oe + b Books, 2003), p. 105.

[75] *Cahiers du Cinéma* no. 300 (1979), p. 73.

> La voix du Mozambique.
> De quelle bouche sort cette voix?
> Quel est son visage?[76]

They further gave themselves the following tasks: "d'étudier l'image, le désir d'images (l'envie de se souvenir, l'envie de montrer ce souvenir, d'en faire une marque, de départ ou d'arrivée, une ligne de conduite, une guide moral/politique en vue d'une fin: l'indépendance)."[77] In a similar approach to the DVG's Palestinian images, Godard and Miéville insisted on the relational process of building images with the Mozambicans geared up at their emancipation. Godard also placed the emphasis on the moment of production, technique and the participation of the spectators and their desires in the making of the images. At that stage, however, this was difficult to realize due to the embryonic character of the audience. For instance, they describe the problem posited by taking a photograph of a woman and then showing it to her: the first image she had ever seen. Moreover, the project gave them an opportunity to shift from a politics and ethics of imaging others, elsewhere, to construct their image with them, not for a foreign audience, but for themselves. As Godard summed it up, "Une image de moi pour les autres, ou une image des autres pour moi,"[78] underscored by photographs of Mozambican women and children behind the camera—reminiscent of a scene from *Ici et ailleurs* in which the working-class mother and daughter stand behind still and movie cameras as producers of images. In Mozambique, Godard and Miéville were especially interested in the moment of production before the needs of distribution would distort the image, and before the spectators would cease to recognize themselves in the images and instead would begin to "trail behind" them, as they put it. In other words, Sonimage's goal was not to try to show the Mozambicans how to produce an image, but rather to show them how they would promote their

---

[76] "The voice of Mozambique. From which mouth does it issue? What is its face?" Ibid., p. 93.

[77] "To study the image, the desire of images (the wish to remember, the wish to show this memory, to make a mark of departure or arrival, a line of behavior, a moral/political guide toward one goal: Independence)." Ibid., p. 73.

[78] "An image of myself for the others, or an image of others for myself." Ibid., p. 79.

country by making images together.⁷⁹ Godard also states as his goal a similar exercise he had done for *Jusqu'à la victoire* and *Ici et ailleurs*: "enregistrer ce qui va, et le comparer avec ce qui ne va pas."⁸⁰ The lessons that Sonimage drew from the Mozambique experience resonates with *Ici et ailleurs* as well:

> Pouvoir des images.
> Abus de pouvoir.
> Toujours être deux pour regarder une image, et faire la balance entre les deux.
> L'image comme preuve.
> L'image comme justice, comme résultat d'un accord.⁸¹

Images are powerful and this is why representation is colonizing; therefore, they posited representation as an *agreement* between two in order to reach a balance and to avoid colonization. They further posit images as a mark, visual record or proto-archive, a concern that they also explore in *Ici et ailleurs*, as we will see in the following chapter. They further insist on the "being two" of images—in *Notre musique* (2004), as we will see, this "being two" of images is translated to the shot/reverse-shot logic in montage. "To be two" means not only juxtaposing two images to deliver a third, but as we have seen, in the sense Godard and Miéville had been working in their Sonimage films: as being two to see, to discuss, to enunciate an image. An image as the result of an agreement. Finally, one of the problems they considered to be at the beginning of the establishment of an audio-visual culture in Mozambique, was that of the "colonization of the screen," as it had already been colonized in developing countries; for them, this colonization was already announcing itself in Mozambique by the imperialism of the format (Sony, Secam…). They thus concluded that it is impossible to create autonomous images.

---

[79] Richard Dienst, *Still Life in Real Time: Theory after Television* (Durham: Duke University Press, 1994), p. 34.
[80] "Take notice of what works, and compare it with what doesn't". *Cahiers du Cinéma* no. 300 (1979), p. 115.
[81] "Power of images. Abuse of power. Always to be two to look at an image, and to make a balance between the two. The image as proof. The image as justice, as the result of an agreement." *Cahiers du Cinéma* no. 300 (1979), p. 125.

Comment Changer d'Image/Montrer une Image du Changement?

Television is the everyday while cinema is not, and Godard and Miéville, in their Sonimage videos, sought to analyze ordinary, everyday images contained in and produced by television by means of exploring the *techniques* of film and video, introducing creativity and thinking into the medium. In 1976 and 1978 they made two television series, *Six fois deux: Sur et sous la communication* and *France/ tour/ détour/ deux/ enfants*. *Six fois deux* was commissioned by Manette Bertin from the INA. According to Michael Witt, both series, especially *Six fois deux*, "seek to construct a 'softer' decentralized televisual practice, and to actively resist the centralized universalizing homogenization of broadcast television." *Six fois deux* was filmed in Grenoble and *France tour détour* in Rolle and broadcast was delayed for almost two years by the network that commissioned them, Antenne 2 (now France 2). "*France tour*, as opposed to *Six fois deux*'s complication of television's flow through a process of 'amateurisation' and intertextual cross-referencing, uses as its principal tactic the exaggeration and *redoubling* of familiar televisual codes, and especially the magazine format of the *journal télévisé*."[82] While *Six fois deux* is concerned with experimental ways of giving voice to individuals working in an array of different things, in *France tour détour* they examine, among other things, forms of power embedded in the education of children. Both series are also concerned with communication and the mass media.

In this context and beyond the vanguardist model, Godard and Miéville constructed a discursive site for asking not "What is to be done?" but "How can one *see* and provide a *means of seeing*?". The domain of appearances—their version of "Spectacle"—is defined by Sonimage, as we have seen, as: "N'importe quelle image quotidienne fait partie d'un système vague et compliqué, où le monde entier entre et sort à chaque instant [a commonplace, contemporaneous image, part of a vague and complex system reflecting events from around the world fleetingly and momentarily]." The domain of spectacularized television, furthermore, operates for them in a relationship between technique and public space, delivering new modes

---

[82] For a brilliant and detailed analysis of the Sonimage project see Michael Witt's doctoral dissertation for Bath University (1998): "On Communication: The Work of Anne-Marie Miéville and Jean-Luc Godard as 'Sonimage' from 1973 to 1979."

of perception and the inscription of memory. In the mass media, journalism creates events, transforming them into information, substituting history as a means to account for states of affairs and to make them public.

A political preoccupation of Godard and Miéville at this time concerned the use of video, a technology developed for television. They "dressed up" videos as films, shooting and editing in video, and then printing and projecting them as films in the cinema. Moreover, they used the *technique* of video to analyze the *techniques* of television, understanding *technique* as the materialization of a code of certain desires of the society that created the machines in question, in this case, man's fundamental desire to possess his/her own image. In this manner, they argue, the success of still photography to preserve an instant responds to man's instinct of self-preservation. Such desire to preserve the immediacy of images led to the invention of Polaroid and the video-tape recorder,[83] and Godard and Miéville analyzed this drive to preserve the instant, dedicating many minutes of screen time to still images. Hence photography's essential role in the early Sonimage films as an arrested image, as the atom of cinema.[84] Following Deleuze, television is a social technique, it is consensus *par excellence* and its social function is that of power and control; its immediacy and directness (by being "live," doing "broadcasts," emphasizing "presentness") imply that there is no delay between television and the social, and that is what renders it a "pure" social technique. In contrast, cinema has for Deleuze an aesthetic function that enables critique because, differently from television's immediacy, there is delay between the viewer and cinema.[85] Video in its manifestation as commercial television is a "whole flow," an apparently endless visual stream. Its mode of spectatorship is a continuous presence, the contents of the screen streaming before us all day long without interruptions, disabling the possibility of critical distance.[86] Not only the aesthetic and the non-everyday aspect of cinema becomes relevant for Godard,

---

[83] Godard in "Jean-Luc Godard fait le point," interview with Philippe Durand published in *Cinéma Pratique*, 1973, p. 156.

[84] Philippe Dubois, "Video Thinks what Cinema Creates: Notes on Jean-Luc Godard's Work in Video and Television," *Jean Luc Godard: Son + Image, 1974–1991*, p. 173.

[85] Gilles Deleuze, "Lettre à Serge Daney: Optimisme, Pessimisme et Voyage," first published in Serge Daney, *Ciné-Journal*, preface, ed. *Cahiers du Cinéma*, reprinted in *Pourparlers*, p. 105.

[86] Fredric Jameson, "Video: Surrealism Without the Unconscious," *Postmodernism: Or, the Cultural Logic of Late Capitalism* (Durham, NC: Duke University Press, 1991), p. 70.

but also its ontology in the sense that it progresses intermittently, frame-by-frame.

By the late 1970s, the mediatic post-Maoist intellectual in France had taken his/her public role back as the "speaker of truths" with a vengeance, refusing to distinguish between voice and appearance while incarnating authority. In a television programme broadcast in 1978, Jean-François Lyotard was invited to discuss his role as an "intellectual". As he spoke, his voice and image were artfully desynchronized. This was designed to confound expectations about how an intellectual should address an audience on television.[87] Making a distinction between scientific expertise and philosophical "simple opinions," objectivity as empiricist omniscience (knowledge of all things, whether real or apparent knowledge), Lyotard defines expertise as both provided and portrayed by someone who believes and who is believed to know what he/she is talking about: thus, expertise on a subject is having authority over given matters and authority to speak freely about them. For Lyotard, the paradox of philosophical expertise lies in the fact that the philosopher precisely ponders on the matter of authority while drawing a distinction between philosophy and scientific knowledge, saying that philosophers and intellectuals' discourse does not purport objective knowledge but belongs to the domain of opinion. Lyotard is pointing out the paradox of the disappearance of the intellectual as a public figure, problematizing the authority bestowed on "opinion", given the public's need to believe in figures who display authority and knowledge.[88] A figure embodying the solution to satisfying this need (which is also the need to consume opinion), was provided by the ostensibly expert, objective journalist. Years later, on May 22, 1982 Godard intervened along the same lines as Lyotard in a news broadcast from Antenne 2 Midi.[89] Differently from Lyotard, who emphasized the distinction between knowledge, information, philosophy and opinion, Godard did so from the point of view of *image* and *sight*. Via live satellite transmission, he introduced his film *Passion* from Cannes in the programme; he then intervened to comment on the images shown, positing

---

[87] The programme was part of a series entitled "Tribune Libre" that appeared on the French network FR3 on March 27, 1978. See Lyotard, "A Podium without a Podium: Television According to J-F. Lyotard," in *Political Writings: Jean-François Lyotard*, translated by Bill Readings and Kevin Paul (Minneapolis: The University of Minnesota Press, 1993).

[88] Lyotard, "Podium Without a Podium," 1978, p. 25.

[89] Available for consultation in the archives at the Institut National de l'Audiovisuel, housed at the Bibliothèque Nationale in Paris.

his critique in terms of the inverse ratio between image and speech. For him, televisual speech is as profuse as the images portrayed are poor: "C'est difficile avec vous à la télé. *Vous parlez beaucoup*. Vous montrez quelques images pauvres qui ne *peuvent pas dire* grand-chose." He further articulates his relationship to television, raising the matter of *seeing*: "Si j'étais à la télévision je me servirais des images pour *voir* quelque chose." In the broadcast, Godard brings up the subject of images of the Malvinas (Falklands) war, lamenting the fact that war images shown on television are provided by the army. He further critiques the kind of viewership that television has created, comparing the future of images of war shown live on television to the circus: "Moi je pense que ça passionnerait les gens de voir la guerre en directe, on y viens voir les gens du cirque; moi je pense que la guerre est faite pour être montrée en télévision [...]." Godard's intuition and protest—there were drastic restrictions to media access, as Prime Minister Margaret Thatcher granted access to the campaign only to two photojournalists and no live television transmission was permitted[90]—became realized in 1989 when the Romanian "revolution" was televised and two years later with CNN's 24-hour live coverage of the Gulf War. Finally, Godard draws a distinction between *information* and *seeing*, pushing the anchor to admit "*Je n'ai pas vu* ce qui s'est passé aux Malouines."[91] In his Antenne 2 Midi intervention, Godard sums up his "journalism of the audiovisual" program: to privilege images over speech by *enunciating images*, to use images to *see* something, and highlights the issue of the difference between information, knowledge and seeing.

In a short video he made that same year, *Changer d'image* (1982), Godard recalls the Mozambique experience. The video begins with Godard seen from behind, sitting before a blank screen, when Miéville's voice asks him if it is possible to deliver an image of change, if it is possible for an image of change to exist and if an image can change things. Further on, a third voice describes Godard as the "imbécile" who needs to feel humiliated because he has failed in his project of delivering a film

---

[90] Susan Sontag, *Regarding the Pain of Others* (New York: Farrar, Straus and Girous, 2003), 65.

[91] "When on TV it's hard. One talks a great deal while showing rather poor images that don't say anything of importance." http://debordements.fr/Grandeur-et-decadence-d-un-petit-commerce-de-cinema-Jean-Luc-Godard; "If I was on television I would use images to *see* something"; "I think that people would be passionate about seeing war live [in much the same way} as we go to see performers at the circus; I think war is made to be shown on television"; "*I did not see* what happened at the Malvinas Islands." My italics.

of change: "il est vrai que la vie de cet imbécile va et viens entre la vie des images [...] il y avait montré qu'il n'y a d'images mais des chaînes d'images... une image de la façon que nous avions de nous inscrire ou de nous faire inscrire au centre ou à la périphérie de l'univers...."[92] Godard posits First and Third World relations as a *way of inscribing ourselves or being inscribed either at the center or the periphery*. We further hear that three or four years back, Godard had to come to a "Latin American or African country" as a sympathizer and as a specialist of images to inquire about how to build a television network that would serve the people without serving power. The film ends with the questions: "What is the formula of 'good' television?" and "What is the formula of the change of images and of images of change?" Godard's declaration, also toward the end of the film: "Moi je me sens en territoire occupé"[93] both crystalizes his Sonimage work and outlines his aesthetico-political project for years to come. While Godard would posit the periphery or those "out of the frame" as an aesthetico-political problem in later films, "occupation" as a form of oppression would become his model to understand aesthetico-political challenges toward the end of the twentieth century and the beginning of the twenty-first, and he thus gives himself the filmic task to "montrer la resistance d'une image du changement; *entre* les images on peut changer; ce qu'on peut montrer c'est l'entre, un intervalle."[94] Indeed, like the "pauvre con révolutionnaire, milliardaire en images d'ailleurs"[95] from *Ici et ailleurs*, the "imbécile" in *Changer d'image* failed in his quest to show images of change/change things with images, but what can be shown is the *in-between* or the interval, a concept derived from Dziga Vertov's theory and practice of montage that becomes pivotal in Godard's materialist filmmaking.

In retrospect, we could think of Third-Worldism as the last utopia in the sense that utopia (lit. "nowhere") can also be considered an imagined, potentially ideal, place. The ephemeral frame within which the term "Third

---

[92] "It is true that the life of this idiot is largely dedicated to images [...] having demonstrated that there are no images but sequences of images...an image of the way we have of inscribing ourselves or having ourselves inscribed at the center or the periphery of the universe."

[93] "I feel in occupied territory."

[94] "To show resistance in an image of change; we can change *in between* images; what we can show is the in-between, the interval."

[95] "The poor stupid revolutionary, millionaire in images of elsewhere."

World" was coined—the Cold War—has disappeared, and the new frame that came to substitute it (human rights, development and economic growth, cultural intervention, wars in the name of democracy, even social responsibility) has failed just as Third-Worldism did in highlighting the pressing issues that were (and are) at stake: the incredible polarization and massive dispossession and displacement brought about by the globalization of the free market economy, capitalism's financial structural crisis and the hegemony of ideological neoliberalism. Since then, states of affairs regarding the geopolitically sensible imaginary have been configured from the points of view of the European Third-Worldists as well as from Third World filmmakers. Third Cinema has been institutionalized as the genre of films "from elsewhere," characterized by hybridity and by having self-representation and counter-hegemonic narratives as mandates related to the issue of nationalism and to the rewriting of the narratives of formerly colonialized states.[96]

In the 1980s, the colonial distinction between center and periphery became irrelevant: cultural production and capital began to celebrate decentralization, rendering the distinction between First and Third Worlds

[96] The main theorists in the Anglophone world regarding "Third Cinema" are Ella Shohat and Robert Stam. The latter, in his article "Beyond Third Cinema: The Aesthetics of Hybridity," defines this kind of cinema as emerging in the late 1960s and 1970s as an alternative to Hollywood at a time when Third World intellectuals called for a tricontinental revolution (with Ho Chi Minh, Che Guevara and Frantz Fanon the main referential figures). The principles of Third Cinema were established in a series of manifestos: Glauber Rocha's "Aesthetics of Hunger" (1965), Fernando Solanas and Octavio Getino's "Towards a Third Cinema" (1969) and Julio García Espinosa's "For an Imperfect Cinema" (1969). Stam sums it up in this manner: "Rocha called for a 'hungry' cinema of 'sad, ugly films,' Solanas and Getino called for militant guerilla documentaries, and Espinosa called for an 'imperfect' cinema energized by the 'low' forms of popular culture, where the process of communication was more important than the product, where political values were more important than 'production values.'" The themes of Third Cinema were in general Fanonian: "the psychic stigmata of colonialism, the therapeutic value of anti-colonial violence, and the urgent necessity of a new culture and a new human being, stressing anti-colonial militancy and violence, literal/political in the case of Solanas-Getino, and metaphoric/aesthetic in the case of Rocha." Robert Stam, *Unthinking Eurocentrism* (London: Routledge, 1994), p. 248. See also *Rethinking Third Cinema*, edited by Anthony Guneratne and Wimal Dissanayake (London: Routledge, 2003), p. 31. Today Third Cinema is considered as consisting of a wide range of alternative cinematic practices, and the genre may include films that adopt the diasporic point of view. See also Ella Shohat's "Framing Post-Third-Worldist Culture: Gender and Nation in Middle Eastern/North African Film and Video," *Jouvert* 1, no. 1 (1997).

obsolete, at a moment in which the Other had been rendered transparent by ethnography and journalism. The globalized market, with its ability to go beyond national divisions, integrated First and Third Worlds, forcing certain areas of the Third World to "develop," creating pockets of the wretched of the earth, wealth and cultural sophistication within the Third World, and areas of destitution and misery within the First.

Facilitated by the democratization of tourism, culture and information, encounters with the Other have been substituted by encounters with *different forms of life* now mediated by the mass media, tourism, and interventions based on aesthetic or humanitarian considerations, often involving NGOs. At the beginning of the twenty-first century, while the Other has been made transparent due to a series of discursive mutations, global connectedness has rendered the "elsewhere" immediate. For example, Congo—and even an "ethical" relationship to Congo—may be in the "free trade" coffee you sip every morning, or Colombia is in the coke you snort at a *vernissage*. As a consequence, the *elsewhere* or the form of alterity inherent in the globalized world has mutated into *different forms of life* (which are different in the quantitative sense: they are more or less equal, more or less privileged, with more or less access to jobs and commodities). Some questions that arise under this New World Order are: How to *see* the differences between *different* life worlds coexisting side by side and how to account for their interaction? Is the *outside* of gated communities—now a cliché in Hollywood films such as *Upside Down, World War Z, The Hunger Games, Elysium* (all from 2013) and so on—the actual paradigm of aesthetico-political engagement? In *Adieu au langage* (2014), Godard would make a plea, yet again, for those who remain on the periphery, outside of the frame of the film.

Bibliography

Adachi, Masao. "The Testament that Godard has never Written" (2002). French translation in Nicole Brenez and Go Hirasawa (eds.), *Le bus de la revolution passera bientôt pres de chez toi* (Paris: Editions Rouge Profond, 2012)

Antonioni, Michelangelo. "Est-il encore possible de tourner un documentaire? *Chung Kuo Cina, 1972*" (1974), *Écrits de Michelangelo Antonioni: Fare un film è per me vivere* (Paris: Éditions Images Modernes, 2003)

Antonioni, Michelangelo, Peploe, Mark and Wollen, Peter. *Michelangelo Antonioni's The Passenger: the Complete Script* (New York: Grove Press Inc., 1975)

Bellour, Raymond. *L'entre-images, photo, cinéma, vidéo* (Paris: Éditions de la Différence, 1990)
Blümlinger, Christa. "Procession and Projection: Notes on a Figure in the Work of Jean Luc Godard," in *For Ever Godard*, ed. Michael Temple (London: Black Dog Publishing and Tate Modern, 2004)
Brecht, Bertolt. *Kraft und Schwäche der Utopie, Gesammelte Werke*, vol. VIII (Frankfurt am Main: 1967)
Brenez, Nicole. "The Forms of the Question," in *For Ever Godard*, ed. Michael Temple (London: Black Dog Publishing and Tate Modern, 2004)
Buchloh, Benjamin. "From Faktura to Factography," *October* No. 30 (Fall 1984)
Burguière, André and Daniel, Jean. *Le Tiers Monde et la Gauche* (Paris: Éditions du Seuil, 1979)
Cartier-Bresson, Henri and Sartre, Jean-Paul. *D'une Chine à l'autre* (Paris: Éditions Delpire, 1954)
Chaliand, Gérard. *Voyage dans vingt ans de guérillas* (Paris: L'Aube, 1988)
Christofferson, Michael S. *French Intellectuals Against the Left: The Antitotalitarian Moment of the 1970s* (London: Berghahn Books, 2004).
Debray, Régis. *Le pouvoir intellectuel en France* (Paris: Ramsay, 1979)
Deleuze, Gilles. "La Gauche a besoin d'intercesseurs," in *Pourparlers (1972–1990)* (Paris: Éditions de Minuit, 2003)
Deleuze, Gilles. "A propos des nouveaux philosophes et d'un problème plus général," in *Deux Régimes de Fous* (Paris: Éditions de Minuit, 2003)
Deleuze, Gilles. "Lettre à Serge Daney: Optimisme, Pessimisme et Voyage," in *Pourparlers* (Paris: Éditions de Minuit, 1990)
Deleuze, Gilles. *Foucault* (Paris: Éditions de Minuit, 2004)
Deleuze, Gilles. *Moving-Image Cinema 1*, translated by Hugh Tomlinson and Barbara Habberjam (Minneapolis: University of Minnesota Press, 2001), p. 71.
Derrida, Jacques. *Of Grammatology*, translated by G. Spivak (Baltimore and London: The Johns Hopkins University Press, 1997)
Diawara, Manthia. "Sonimage in Mozambique" (1999), in *I Said I Love. That is the Promise: The TVideo Politics of Jean-Luc Godard*, Gareth James and Florian Zeyfang eds. (Berlin: oe + b Books, 2003)
Dienst, Richard. *Still Life in Real Time: Theory after Television* (Durham, NC: Duke University Press, 1994)
Dissanayake, Wimal and Guneratne, Anthony. *Rethinking Third Cinema* (London: Routledge, 2003)
Dreyer, Sylvain. "Autour de Mai '68 en France et ailleurs," *Image & Narrative*, Vol. 11, No. 1 (2010)
Dubois, Philippe. "Video Thinks what Cinema Creates: Notes on Jean-Luc Godard's Work in Video and Television," in *Jean-Luc Godard: Son + Image 1974–1991* (New York: MoMA, 1992)

Ducrot, Oswald. *Les mots du discours* (Paris: Éditions de Minuit, 1980)
Ducrot, Oswald. *Logique, structure, énonciation: Lectures sur le langage* (Paris: Éditions de Minuit, 1989)
Enzensberger, Hans-Magnus. "Tourists of the Revolution," in *Critical Essays* (London: Bloomsbury, 1997)
Fairfax, Daniel. "Birth (of the Image) of a Nation: Jean-Luc Godard in Mozambique" *Acta Univ. Sapientiae, Film and Media Studies* 3 (2010), p. 58
Foe, Devin. "Introduction," *October* no. 118 (Fall 2006)
García Espinosa, Julio. "For an Imperfect Cinema," trans. Julianne Burton, *Jumpcut* No. 20, 1979, pp. 24–26
Getino, Octavio and Solanas, Fernando. "Towards a Third Cinema," *Tricontinental* No. 14 (October 1969)
Godard, Jean-Luc. "Jean-Luc Godard fait le point," entretien avec Philippe Durand, *Cinéma Pratique*, 1973
Godard, Jean-Luc. "Lettre à Elias Sanbar," *Cahiers du Cinéma* no. 300 (Numéro spéciale 1979)
Gorin, Jean-Pierre. "Interview by Christian Braad Thomsen," *Jump Cut* no. 3 (1974)
Heidegger, Martin. "The World Picture," in *The Question Concerning Technology and Other Essays* (New York: Harper and Row, 1977)
Jameson, Fredric. "Video: Surrealism Without the Unconscious," in *Postmodernism: Or, the Cultural Logic of Late Capitalism* (Durham, NC: Duke University Press, 1991)
Lyotard, Jean-François. "A Podium without a Podium: Television According to J-F. Lyotard," in *Political Writings*, translated by Bill Readings and Kevin Paul, (Minneapolis: The University of Minnesota Press, 1993)
MacCabe, Colin. *A Portrait of the Artist at 70* (London: Bloomsbury, 2003)
Rimbaud, Arthur. *I Promise to be Good: The Letters of Arthur Rimbaud*, translated by Wyatt Mason (New York: The Modern Library, 2003)
Rocha, Glauber. "The Aesthetics of Hunger" (1965). Available at: http://www.tempoglauber.com.br/english/t_estetica.html
Ross, Kristin. *May '68 and its Afterlives* (Chicago: University of Chicago Press, 2002).
Rossanda, Rossana. "Les Intellectuels Révolutionnaires et l'Union Soviétique," *Les Temps Modernes* no. 332 (March 1974)
Shohat, Ella and Stam, Robert. *Unthinking Eurocentrism: Multiculturalism and the Media* (London: Routledge, 1994)
Shohat, Ella. "Framing Post-Third-Worldist Culture: Gender and Nation in Middle Eastern/North African Film and Video," *Jouvert* 1, no. 1 (1997)
Sontag, Susan. *On Photography* (New York: Picador, 2001)
Sontag, Susan. *Regarding the Pain of Others* (New York: Farrar, Straus and Giroux, 2003)
Vertov, Dziga. *Articles, journaux, projets* (Paris: UGE '10/18', 1972)

Weil, Simone. *Écrits historiques et politiques* (Paris: Gallimard, 1960).
Witt, Michael. "On Communication: The Work of Anne-Marie Miéville and Jean-Luc Godard as 'Sonimage' from 1973 to 1979," doctoral dissertation for Bath University (1998). Available at: http://www.mediafire.com/file/d4os8rc-qb01ubst/Michael+Witt%2C+ON+COMMUNICATION+-+THE+WORK+OF+ANNE-MARIE+MIEVILLE+AND+JEAN-LUC+GODARD+AS+%27SONIMAGE%27+FROM+1973+TO+1979.pdf

CHAPTER 4

Technique and Montage: Saying, Seeing and Showing the Invisible

Materialist Filmmaking and Spectacle

As we have seen, in the 1960s, artists and filmmakers shared the problem of the explosion of the mass media and information, and of addressing an audience from an educated middle class that emerged as consumers of cultural products. The transformations in perception and knowledge brought about by mechanical reproduction and its links to capitalism are inseparable from the emergence of new social identities and subjects of history brought about by Spectacle. Spectacle has been defined by Jean Baudrillard as a moment in history in which the regime of appearances becomes indistinguishable from the consumption and production of the signs of equality.[1] Guy Debord defined Spectacle as a stage of capitalism in which everything becomes its own simulacral inverted image (in the negative Platonic sense),[2] a regime in which a highly literate society produces and consumes its own desires as false images having fused memory, perception and appearance. Spectacle is further an economy that obliterates representation in favor of self-representation subjugating the masses

---

[1] Jean Baudrillard, *La Société de consommation: ses mythes, ses structures* (Paris: Gallimard, 1974), 60. Quoted by Jonathan Crary, "Spectacle, Attention, Counter-Memory," in *Guy Debord and the Situationist International: Texts and Documents*, edited by Tom McDonough, (Cambridge, MA: MIT Press, 2004), p. 256.
[2] Guy Debord, *La Société du Spectacle* (Paris: Gallimard, 1996), p. 9.

because the sign-making machinery is aligned with power interests.[3] Spectacle is also the emergence of "perceptual consumption," defined by Jonathan Crary as a shift in the relationships between memory, shock, attention and perception. For Crary, this shift is presupposed by the rift between memory and perception that occurred at the end of the nineteenth century, when memory acquired the capacity to rebuild the object of perception primarily as redundancy. This form of perception was offered by mechanical reproduction, which led, according to Crary, to the inhibition and impoverishment of memory and to a standardization of perception.[4]

Bearing this in mind, in their Sonimage work, Jean-Luc Godard and Anne-Marie Miéville reconfigured aesthetico-political representation not as the challenge of "speaking on behalf of others" but as showing and saying, as seeing and providing the means to see *(donner à voir)* the power interests behind the sign-making machinery materialized in television and information, masked by the myth of objectivity and by the image as merchandise. For them, a critique of spectacle following Debord's indictment of the "totalitarianism of the mass media" was not pertinent, primarily because such a critique burdens images with the weight of truth and is predicated upon the notion of the need for fixed forms of representation which appeal to the utopia of social authenticity. Godard and Miéville also reject this analysis because it is based on a totalizing conception of a world in which it is impossible to separate life, capital and appearance, imbued with the negativity of the false. Godard and Miéville would not disagree with the idea that perception has been rendered redundant by mechanical reproduction or that capitalism has reached the stage of the preponderance of sign-exchange value. However, for them, images are neither true nor false; rather, images are events that transmigrate autonomously in the media, constantly transforming each other: "N'importe quelle image quotidienne fait partie d'un système vague et compliquée où le monde entre et sort à chaque instant."[5] This definition coincides with the notion of the nomadic post-modern image circulating values and disseminating detached signifiers within which we happen. Godard and Miéville further state in the voice-over

---

[3] Len Bracken, *Guy Debord: Revolutionary, A Critical Biography* (Venice, CA: Feral House, 1997), p. 131.

[4] Jonathan Crary, "Spectacle, Attention, Countermemory," pp. 455–466.

[5] "Any everyday image is part of a vague and complicated system in which the world enters and leaves at every instant."

in *Ici et ailleurs* (1976): "Le monde c'est trop pour une image // Non, dit le capitalisme, le monde ce n'est pas trop pour une image."[6] Hinting at capitalism's collapse of world and image, they do seem to be in dialogue with Guy Debord. For Debord, Spectacle is not to be confused with media images, which are for him only a "glaring superficial manifestation of spectacle." Spectacle is not, echoing Marxist analysis, a collection of images but "a social relationship among people mediated by images."[7] Similarly, for Godard, images are social relationships insofar as images are *subjects* and create subjects: "On produit et on consomme son image avec celle de l'autre."[8] Unlike Debord, however, who in his film *La Société du Spectacle/ The Society of the Spectacle* (1973) confronts society with the images it uses to depict itself, providing a form of self-incrimination,[9] Godard and Miéville insist on an understanding of images relationally as acts of communication. For Sonimage, the act of vision must be considered as three-dimensional and *subjectifying*, based on an exchange of signs that is proper to consumption. In order to do so, for instance, they use a recurring image in the Sonimage films, that of a mother and her child; or they experiment with address and the technique of video, with a semiotic approach to images, focusing on the language-operation inherent in the act of *imaging* (*mise en image*). For them, the exchange of signs that underlies images presupposes a virtual viewer because images are always addressed to a third person (*objectif*), represented by the camera's lens. This leads to the inference that the first person is the photographer and the second is the subject/object of the photograph. The third is the viewer, to whom the first gaze is addressed. The problem that they highlight is that in the dynamic of the communication of information, there is no possibility for the exchange of signs, and the viewer is rendered powerless, confronted with the events he/she is shown on the screen. This is the ground for their experiments with direct address, with which they sought to challenge the intransitivity of the mass media, alongside first, designing a site of enunciation that I call "videographic machinic expression" and second, with cinematic montage, which is systematically opposed to the social technique of television, as we will see below.

[6] "The world is too much for one image // No, says capitalism, the world is not too much for one image."
[7] Guy Debord, Thesis No. 4 from *La Société du Spectacle*.
[8] "We create and consume our images using those of others."
[9] Len Bracken, *Guy Debord: Revolutionary, A Critical Biography*, p. 190.

For Godard and Miéville, montage begins with gleaning single images from the mass media with the purpose of stopping the flow of information; then they *enunciate* images, uncovering and examining the layers beneath them.[10] Like stratigraphers uncovering layers, the methods they employ do not pose questions such as, "What is there to see behind the image (the image as a door/window behind which...)?" and "How can we see the image in itself (the image as a frame-plane in which...)?"; rather, they interrogate how we as viewers insert ourselves as accomplices, victims or impotent witnesses inside the images and are placed either at the center or at the periphery, as we saw in the previous chapter.[11] In this sense, the Sonimage project is materialist at its core insofar as it posits images as subjects with the purpose of analyzing the relationships of production with regards to subjectivity, signification and surplus value. Therefore, Godard and Miéville point to a global system arranged around the control and flow of information and our position within, giving themselves the task to understand images that they call "brand images," which are images that have become emblems of historical events and have thus solidified power. Therefore, they seek *to enunciate images*, to give images back the voices that have been taken away from them, to speak on behalf of the part of the image that is *out of field*, that is concealed by the apparatus that transforms images into information or emblems of historical events. Godard and Miéville's aesthetico-political task becomes therefore to see and provide a means to see the power relations embedded in the circulation of images in accord with the new political challenges that arose in the 1970s.

Parallel to the demise of anti-imperialism and to the humanitarian turn in the 1970s as a frame to relate to formerly colonized countries and subjects, the working class began to slowly disappear from the political arena in Europe. The Marxist principles of the working class as the motor of history and the emancipatory spontaneity of the masses had been put out of work; dialectical exhaustion gave leeway to a new reactionary period characterized by a pervasive disenchantment with the social, a retrenchment on individualism and confrontation with the failure of the Left to substantially reform capitalist society. At the same time, an imbalance of power relationships between the exploiters and the exploited was deepened

---

[10] Similar to Serge Daney's notion of thick or thin images, which implies that "the bottom of an image is always already an image." See also Nelson Goodman's *Languages of Art: An Approach to a Theory of Symbols* (Indianapolis: Hackett, 1976), and Pascal Bonitzer, "La surimage," *Cahiers du Cinema* no. 270 (September–October), 1976.

[11] Gilles Deleuze, "Lettre à Serge Daney: Optimisme, Pessimisme et Voyage," first published in Serge Daney, *Ciné-Journal*, reprinted in *Pourparlers* (Paris: Éditions de Minuit, 1990), pp. 101–107.

by the incipient transnationalization of capitalism, the increase of power in private and public capitalist formations, and the colossal accumulation of capital that began to take place outside of political regulation.[12] According to Félix Guattari, at the beginning of the 1980s, world society had become flabby; it had lost its outline along with the capability of proposing solutions to the problems that confronted it, while misery fermented in the Third World like a biblical plague and unemployment exploded in the First. For Guattari it was clear that no common program and no political formation organized in the classical sense would be able to represent the incipient social formation, the new composite mass society where all classes, races, sexes and cultures had begun to overlap.[13] In this context, Godard and Miéville had given themselves the task of exploring the relationship between the image and the visible, to analyze the latter as it is specifically rendered visible by the screen and experimented with new forms of the political in relationship to the image. In *Ici et ailleurs*, Godard established his technique of montage and with Miéville, a theory of enunciation. Systematically they would ponder, "How to share a space in common in relationship to visibilities as they are given to us by the mass media?" "How to potentialize the ambivalence of the visible?" "What is the relationship between image, text, sound and discourse?"

Toward New Forms of the Political

As unemployment and misery began to spread in Europe, Godard in his Sonimage work began to outline the chains of *assujettissement* (subjection) and disciplining of capitalistic machinery. For him, the semiotic chains of production of subjectivity were something akin to DNA chains, hotel chains, factory production chains. In that sense, *Comment ça va?* (1975), *Numéro deux* (1976), *Six fois deux: Sur et sous la communication* (1976) and *France tour détour* (1978) inaugurate experimental forms of politics and of critical thinking. *Numéro deux* and *Six fois deux* are works in which Godard and Miéville let non-traditional political subjects speak from the domestic realm. In that regard, Godard states in his monologue at the beginning of *Numéro deux* that it is not a political film but *un film du cul*;[14]

---

[12] Félix Guattari, *Les années d'hiver (1980–1985)* (Paris: Barrault, 1986), p. 10.
[13] Ibid., pp. 27–33.
[14] Literally, "a film about ass." *Une histoire du cul* is a story about sex which is shared privately among women. Such storytelling has, in consequence, become gendered as an activity.

aligned with second wave feminism, the domestic sphere, the private posited as the political. All the characters in *Numéro deux* are shown working at home: the young mother peels carrots, looks after her children, does the laundry; the father paints the staircase, the grandmother washes the bathroom, the children help around the house. Sandrine (the mother) declares that the washing machine, the home, is the factory. Godard and Miéville thus depict the form of labor that has largely remained invisible from political struggles throughout history: reproductive or care labor, the form of labor that is necessary to sustain workers, which is unpaid work by women. Not by chance, Sandrine is unable to enjoy sex and is constipated, as we see her solitude and a potential social metamorphosis grounded in women's revolt. Furthermore, in *Numéro deux* we hear a worker speak: the grandfather tells his story not from his position as a proletarian, but his own *histoire du cul*. Now retired, he recounts how he was a delegate for the CGT (General Confederation of Labour) for 30 years and a worker at a Swiss factory in Zurich; after that, he worked on the confectionary counter at a Gaumont cinema. He also tells a story about a trip to Singapore and Argentina in his capacity as a delegate; during the former, police approached them and they had to give away to Singaporean peasants political tracts they were carrying in Spanish for the Argentinian workers. It is interesting how in the anecdote, the message the delegates were carrying was delivered to the wrong addressee, in the wrong language, and yet the message concerned the peasants. This reflects another aspect of the crisis of May 1968 that I discussed in Chapter 2: the misaddress and mistranslation inherent in the relationship between union delegates and workers.

In *Six fois deux*, Godard and Miéville "donnent la parole"[15] to, among others, a worker, a cleaning lady, a prostitute, a painter, a photo-journalist. These *enquêtes* were meant to give visibility and voice to those who did not usually have the chance on television. We are made aware that Godard and Miéville paid them for the interviews, the equivalent of an hour's wage, calling attention to the relationship between work and the act of taking over speech as labor. *Comment ça va?* (1975) features a specialist in computer science and veteran delegate from the CFDT (French Democratic Confederation of Labour), and a journalist who works for a Leftist newspaper, *Le Parisien libéré*. Odette (Miéville) wants to make a political film about current events in Portugal in the context of the communist party. In her view, to discuss Portugal it is necessary to talk about events in contemporary France.

---

[15] "Pass the mic."

Joining forces, they go through the process of making an "engaged" video to show to their comrades in the Parisian *banlieue* that will explain how information is selected, written, and communicated in their newspaper. The video has as its objective to shed light onto how information works and has as its target the newspaper *Libération*, recently co-founded by Sartre and the former Maoist, Serge July. *Comment ça va?* is a critical exploration of the politics of counter-information questioning the Leftist belief of the emancipatory potential of activism in mass media, calling for new forms of politicization.

The Sonimage videos underscore Godard and Miéville's exploration of new forms of politics to counteract incipient capitalist formations translated into the acceleration of social relationships and the diversification of the means of production as well as the industrial and individual production of collective and individual subjectivity embedded in the new power imaginaries grounded in semiotic production. In this new socio-political context, the state was no longer a monster to be feared or tamed, but rather, it began to materialize everywhere, starting with the self, at the root of the unconscious.[16] Godard hints at this in his monologue at the beginning of *Numéro deux*, when he describes the film in the following manner: "*Numéro deux* n'est pas un film ni à gauche ni à droite mais devant et derrière: devant, il y a les enfants (de la patrie) et derrière il y a le gouvernement."[17]

As we saw in the previous chapter, in *Changer d'image* (1982) Godard revisits his failed Mozambique experience and designates himself (in the third person) as "cet imbécile," stating in front of a blank screen that he is trying to find, not an image that would change things, but that could *give an image of change*. In that regard, we could describe Godard's work in the late 1970s and early 1980s as an ongoing search for "an image" grounded in the study, creation and juxtaposition of images. Positing himself as a seer, he gives himself the task of showing things, relationships amongst things, that are invisible (as in *Je vous salue, Marie*; *Passion*; and *Soft and Hard*). For his part, Godard would convey the ongoing crisis in aesthetico-political representation of *les années d'hiver* as difficulty in speaking, as the worker's lack of speech. This is why in *Passion*, Isabelle, the

---

[16] Félix Guattari, *Les années d'hiver, 1980–1985*, p. 69.

[17] "*Numéro deux* is neither on the left nor on the right but in front and behind; the children (of the fatherland) are in front and the government is behind."

worker, stammers, reflecting the lack of discourse and thus of direction of the working class. As Godard stated in his Antenne 2 intervention on May 22, 1982 when he introduced via satellite from Cannes his film *Passion*:

> [...] si le patron a du mal à parler et que le travailleur bégaie c'est que la parole ouvrière bégaie et qu'il y a du mal dans la parole [...] le syndicat ne peut pas parler pour les autres comme papa et maman il faut aller voir sur place; il faut prendre du temps pour voir il faut aller voir sur place ça prends du temps; un jardinier prends le temps de voir la fleur qui pousse. *Ça prends* du temps *on ne peut pas tout toujours dire*.[18]

The general lack of political direction during *les années d'hiver* characterized by Leftist defeat and of the falling short of traditional forms of political organization to deal with the incipient subjection of the social to economic imperatives in the late 1970s and early 1980s, translates in Godard's work to the aesthetico-political necessity to "go there to see," although "we cannot always say" (or we say stammering), to a search for light, for beauty, for radically different forms of inhabiting the world (i.e., from the countryside), for light (*Passion*).[19] The subjection of the social to the economic caused worldwide unemployment and the marginalization of young people, the reinforcement of existing hierarchies and forms of segregation. The clear inability to propose strategies of emancipation and conquering spaces of freedom, or inability to create significant struggles, was translated in Godard's work to a search for images to provide a means to see, in a quest to resacralize the image.

---

[18] "If the boss has problems speaking and the worker stammers it is because working class speech stammers and because there is a malady with speech itself; the union is unable to speak on behalf of others like mom and dad, one has to go *see*; one has to take the time to go (there to) see, and that takes time; a gardener takes the time to see a flower that grows. It takes time, and we cannot always speak/say."

[19] In that regard, Daniel Morgan argues that Godard's late work, starting in the 1980s, begins to draw on the tradition of German Romanticism and Idealism, to rethink basic aspects of cinematic practice, intellectual interests and political concerns. Morgan further observes that at this moment Godard takes an interest in using images of nature to evoke the category of the sublime, to move it into the realm of the divine (or the unrepresentable), transposing familiar stories and iconographies onto one of the foundational narratives of Western culture (specifically, in *Passion* and *Prénom Carmen*). See Daniel Morgan, *Late Godard and the Possibilities of Cinema* (Los Angeles: University of California Press, 2013), pp. 13, 22.

How to See and to Provide A Means to See? Cinematic Voice and the Regime of Enunciation

As aesthetico-political representation was brought into a crisis by asking "Who speaks and acts, from where, for whom and how?". In May 1968, Godard designed in each of his films a complex site from which to speak. As I mentioned, in the Dziga Vertov Group (DVG) films, Godard and Gorin took the position of militant filmmakers, a regime of enunciation carved out from a historical and contemporary revolutionary constellation. As opposed to speaking in the name of a cause, and for the purpose of self-reflexivity and experimentation, they adopted the master discourse of Marxism and branched out in an array of diverging positions. Following Serge Daney, self-critically and pedagogically, Godard and Gorin adhered to a Marxist-Leninist position in *Pravda* and *Le Vent d'Est*; Althusser's lesson on ideology in *Lotte in Italia/Struggles in Italy*; Brecht's comments on the "role of intellectuals in the revolution" in *Tout va bien*, feminist discourse in *Numéro deux*,[20] counter-information in *Comment ça va?* The aesthetico-political task to design a complex site from which to speak is furthered in the Sonimage project as *enunciating images* and *providing the means to see*, resulting in omniscient voice-overs. Godard and Miéville, however, were challenged by critics and colleagues for their immanent presence in the diegesis or filmic space, mastering their images, articulating a discourse from a subjectivizing point of view while asserting their authorial presence as "voices coming from above."[21] But in order to begin to explain how voice-overs work for Godard and Miéville (as inextricable from montage), we must first note that in their films a female voice inverts the relationships between discourse, traditionally gendered by modernism as male, and speech, traditionally gendered as female. As we saw above, in *Numéro deux* the grandfather, instead of voicing political discourse, delivers his life story, his *histoire du cul*. Moreover, in Godard's films a female voice always lays out problems, plays devil's advocate, figures out a program for

---

[20] Following Serge Daney in "Le thérrorisé (pédagogie godardienne)," p. 36. Below I problematize Daney's insistence on Godard's repetitious gesture as a means to avoid his own discourse, as Daney highlights the differential potential of repetition in Godard's method of "correct appropriation".

[21] See Pascal Bonitzer, "J.-L. G. et J.-M. S.," in *Le regard et la voix* (Paris: Union Générale d'Éditions, 1976), 68, and "The Silences of the Voice" (1975), in *Narrative, Apparatus, Ideology: A Film Theory Reader*, edited by Philip Rosen (Columbia: The University Press, 1986), p. 324.

action and is critical of the male filmmaker. For instance, in *Ici et ailleurs*, Miéville's voice chastises, advises, teaches, and contests the militant filmmaker's speech.

The inversion of the traditional gendering of speech and discourse is related to Sonimage's experiments with enunciation, which include a concern with direct address that stems from their critique of the false "objectivity" of documentary voice-overs and journalism, discussed in the previous chapter. To account for the severance of the viewer in the communication process, they sought to undermine the traditional communications model of the media, which implies a source, a message, a transmitter and a receiver, and which produces unilateral speech acts, blocking feedback. Godard and Miéville took into consideration the absence of any possibility of feedback in three ways. First, by way of pedagogy, deconstructing the many components of the mass media and analyzing them one by one, as we have seen. Second, they use montage as a way of countering the media's reduction of information to an objective and scientific structure—to a series of given codes. Their third strategy is to stage direct address, in order to emphasize not the communicative potential of language but its role as the basis for intrasubjective relationships.[22] In *Soft and Hard* (1985), Godard explicates the intransitivity of television that subjectifies (*assujettisation*, in Foucault's sense) the viewer:

> Le sujet c'est le 'je' qui se projette dans le monde ou dans l'autre // celui qui dit 'je' ouvre la bouche et fait un angle // le 'je' se projette dans la télévision // on la reçoit et on est assujetti.[23]

When we, as televisual spectators, receive the "I" that has been projected from the televisual screen toward us, we are subjected in Foucault's sense, meaning that television is a form of asserting power by imposing certain modes of subjectivity on the viewer. Here Godard is posing the problem of subjectivation as the intransitivity of the media, that is, the absence of address. Godard and Miéville tackle this problem by staging direct address in *Ici et ailleurs* and by locating the speaking subject at the juncture of the broadcaster/interface, diffusing information, receiving/

---

[22] For a description of the staging of direct address in other Sonimage films see Dubois, "Video Thinks what Cinema Creates," p. 170.

[23] "The subject is the 'I' projecting herself into this world or an alternate one // he/she who says 'I' opens his/her mouth and takes a position // the 'I' is projected in television // we receive it and we are subjected."

broadcasting/resending images, and decoding and recoding them by means of direct address. This means that when Godard states—we filmed *this*, we saw *that*, they showed us *that*—he is performing indexing, pointing at things and places, making his "I" inextricable from what he shows. With this gesture, an opening is created in which the sensible happens. Following Jean-François Lyotard, pointing at something (indicating, indexing) is not a simple reference through which the thing shows itself unequivocally; rather, it is a movement that engenders a *here*. That is why Godard's speech cannot have meaning if it is not placed in a spatio-temporal situation (now, France). To indicate is a way of escaping *saying* (for Lyotard, *dia-deictics*, the dialectic of space and time), of putting forth *Dasein* (being-there) and different from *Sinn* (or meaning).[24] A "here" is thus grounded in the body, and indicates a correlative function between body and space, incommensurable with the experience of language and of a specific enunciating subject, drawing on shifters to indicate spatial and temporal location.[25] In other words, the referent is dissolved in its spatio-temporalization. "Godard" becomes part of the diegesis as a broadcaster, uttering his own actions of seeing and filming. In this manner, the act of communication is accounted for as an act of expression that implies taking responsibility not only for the speech-act but also for the images filmed, edited and seen. Instead of reporting on what the DVG filmed in Palestine in the journalistic form of "it speaks" or "someone said," Godard in *Ici et ailleurs* speaks *and shows* in his (proper) name, reflecting upon the ways in which his own discourse (or angle) affects the bodies and the actions (in the images) he is designating. In other words, that which is *expressed in the speech act* contains the actions and the multiple temporal displacement of the point of view of the subject of speech, affecting the bodies, constituting the expression.[26]

Godard's speech in the first person, calling for an ethics of enunciation accounting for the intransitivity of the media as well as undermining its code of objectivity in *Ici et ailleurs*, was foregrounded in the script for *Moi, je*. In this unrealized film from 1973, Godard articulates a regime of enunciation through a double statement: *Moi, je suis un animal politique // Moi,*

---

[24] Jean-François Lyotard, *Discours, Figure* (Paris: Klincksieck, 1971), pp. 39–41.

[25] D.N. Rodowick, *Reading the Figural, or, Philosophy After the New Media* (Durham, NC: Duke University Press, 2001), p. 6.

[26] Oswald Ducrot, *Logique, structure, énonciation: lectures sur le langage* (Paris: Éditions de Minuit, 1989), p. 44.

je suis une machine.[27] This is related to Godard and Miéville's concern with experimenting with new communication technologies to enlarge and enliven human exchanges. The first *je suis* is a reference to Aristotle, for whom man is a "political animal" living in the *polis*. The *polis* is the "natural" state of the human animal, as opposed to the idea that civilization is artificial. What differentiates humanity from the animals is the faculty of speech, which enables humans to pronounce ethical and moral judgments about the society in which they live. Using reason and speech, humankind must figure out how to live together, by creating laws that make it possible for a human community to survive. For Aristotle, the political man says "I" as an individual in the domain of the *polis*. The domain of action, for Godard in the Sonimage films, is a kind of *shared* space composed of discursive practices in which the Aristotelian *polis* is transformed into a subjectifying realm for speech, a space that contains a systematized field of objects: the phantasm, the group, the production, desire, the social, and capital. As a way to explain how he is tackling the problem raised by the systematized field of objects—which is the question of communication and the mass media—Godard tells us that his method is to bring these objects together, making them interact through the perspective that is facilitated by the work and methods of Eisenstein and Vertov, and through the activities of seeing and listening (which are the videographic apparatus). The systematized field of objects I listed above appears in a drawing/diagram in the upper-left corner of page 9 of the script, where the field of objects appears "outside,"[28] and "Jean-Luc Godard" "inside." This can be interpreted as Godard's rendering of himself as immanent within the videographic apparatus—illustrating the second statement: *Moi, je suis une machine*.

Moreover, in a rather dense yet poetic passage from the same script, he situates "his" realm of enunciation—which is the matrix of enunciation for the Sonimage films—within "the social," so that the "I" is part of what he calls "shared phantasms." The acknowledgement of shared phantasms makes "him" hope that they will open up "his right" to criticize the social regime to which "he" belongs and where "his motor" (or drive) is "pack-

---

[27] From David Faroult, "The Dziga Vertov Group filmography," *Jean-Luc Godard: Documents* (2006).

[28] It must be noted that, in the conversation between Sartre, Gavi and Victor, discussed earlier (see p. 76), their theorization of the New Political Man was also based on Aristotle's "Political Animal."

aged." Moreover, Godard uses direct address and speaks in his name in the first person, thus emphasizing the objective activation of an addressee inherent to the speech act:[29]

> C'est parce que je suis groupé avec la représentation de ces fantasmes, parce qu'il y a une *filiation* directe entre le "je" et le "il" qui l'objective, parce que "je" est un autre (un autre je comme un autre il ou elle et il et elle comme un autre nous comme des autres ils comme des autres elles) que je puis enfin critiquer réellement cet "il" dont "je" fais partie, et que c'est parce que j'en fais partie et que je ne le cache plus que j'ai maintenant réellement le droit de critiquer ce régime (social) ou "il" fait s'emballer "mon" moteur (désir).[30]

In this passage, Godard invokes Rimbaud's site for objective poetry: "I is someone else,"[31] an aphorism that would appear repeatedly in Godard's films from then on and would take different significations. In this particular case, "I" is posited inextricably from "he" because, when uttered, it activates the position of another, highlighting the interrelationality inherent in the act of communication and making subject and object coincide in the speech-act, highlighting the place from which the characters speak in a particular instance of communication, effectuated with the use of shifters. In that manner, Godard draws a distinction between language as a form of communication, which implies an emitter/message/receiver, from understanding language as the basis for dialogue, as an illocutionary act that implies a relationship between the addressee/locutor. In that regard, Godard and Miéville emphasize a use of language not as a code for communication but a pragmatic relational act, presupposing an addressee.[32]

---

[29] Émile Benveniste, *Problèmes de linguistique générale* 1 (Paris: Gallimard, 1966).

[30] "It is because I am part of the group of the representation of these phantasms, because there is a direct *relationship* between the 'I' and the 'he' that it objectivates, because the 'I' is an other (another 'I' like another he or she, and he and she like another we, like another they) that I can finally really critique this 'he' of which 'I' am a part, and it is because I am part of this that I do not hide it anymore and that now I really have the right to critique this regime (social) where 'he' gets carried away with 'my' motor (desire)." From the script of *Moi, Je*, p. 6.

[31] Rimbaud's famous phrase *Je est un autre* comes from his letter to Georges Izambard, in *The Letters of Arthur Rimbaud* (New York: The Modern Library, 2003), p. 28.

[32] Oswald Ducrot, *Logique, structure, énonciation: Lectures sur le langage* (Paris: Éditions de Minuit, 1989), p. 162. See also his *Les mots du discours* (Paris: Éditions de Minuit, 1980).

Technique and Video: An Epistemology of Seeing

Godard's experiments with delineating regimes of enunciation from which to speak in order to challenge the "crime of information" are inextricable from an epistemology of seeing grounded in the technique of video and montage as an antidote to the "anxiety of blindness." *Ici et ailleurs*, *Comment ça va?* and *Letter to Jane: An Investigation About a Still* were described by Godard as *vidéo-essais*: literally, "attempts to see." *Video* is Latin for *I see*, and *essayer* means to try. In the Sonimage videos, Godard and Miéville's "videographic machinic expression" gives primacy to the act of seeing and listening; it could also be understood as a means of providing audible commentary while they look at images together. We must consider that video lends itself to a particular form of editing different from that of cinema because it is done in front of two monitors: while one monitor shows the already edited material, the other shows the raw material *live*.[33] This particularity of video editing enables the editor to look at images side by side, a particularity that is materialized not only in the matrix of *Ici et ailleurs*, but also on the screen: Godard and Miéville film screens and other supports containing an array of images they seek to juxtapose. Moreover, by privileging video as a medium because it allows images to be juxtaposed before they are edited on a single screen, Godard highlights limitations in the *medium* of cinema. As they show pedagogically and self-reflexively in *Ici et ailleurs*, in any analogue filmic projection it is technically impossible to show images side by side, as cinema is made up of a procession of images that follow one after the other. Godard's use of the video-machine could be understood in a similar manner to the way in which Diderot's blind man describes the looking glass, a reflective/reflexive machine "that places things in relief from out of ourselves if properly placed: it is like my hand, which I must place properly to see an

---

[33] One must bear in mind that this is the apparatus of video in the 1970s. For an interview with Godard in which he talks about the technical aspects of video and Sonimage's video studio in Grenoble, see Wilfried Reichart, "Interview mit Jean-Luc Godard", *Filmkritik* no. 242, February 1977, reprinted in *Video Apparat/Medium, Kunst, Kultur, ein internationaler Reader*, edited by Siegfried Zielinski (Frankfurt: Peter Lang, 1992), pp. 198–208. For an account of Godard's first experiments with video in the Parisian context, see Jean Paul Fargier, "Histoire de la vidéo française: Structures et forces vives" (1992) in *La vidéo: entre art et communication*, edited by Nathalie Magnan (Paris: École Nationale Supérieure des Beaux-Arts, 1997), pp. 50–51.

object."[34] The looking glass is thus a machine that enables us to examine things closely, but only insofar as the latter are placed properly in front of the machine in the same way that things are distanced from us by the looking glass. Here the hand becomes a tool for seeing because while it designates the seen, it links images together. This translates to an aphorism that appears often in Godard's films: "Voir avec les mains,"[35] and to a gesture he repeats in his films of the early 1980s, that of waving his hands before a blank screen, "trying to see." In the script for *Moi, je*, Godard portrays diagrammatically his relationship to the visual and the aural in filming and editing in much the same way as the blind man describes the looking machine[36]:

$$(\text{re})\text{voir } (\text{re})\text{entendre} \leftarrow\rightarrow\rightarrow (\text{re})\text{lire}$$
or
$$\text{image(s) son(s)} \leftarrow\rightarrow \text{lecture.}[37]$$

As we can see/read, for Godard, "reading" images and sounds consists of an epistemological inquiry that implies the repetition of the activities of seeing and listening that occur in the first instance as *filming*; then the actions are reiterated in the process of montage. This mode of seeing, reading and listening to images and sounds is inextricably related to Godard's camera-eye, influenced by Dziga Vertov. As we have seen, the Kino-Eye implies that the camera has a consciousness of its own that *sees* reality and shows it to us. The Kino-Eye is for Vertov an x-ray of reality, an "assault" on the visible. The camera-eye operates by transmitting visual phenomena and as a factory of facts producing visual thinking. In Vertov, epistemological inquiry and cinematic consciousness converge in a dialectical image, seeking something from

---

[34] Denis Diderot, *Diderot's Early Philosophical Works*, trans. Margaret Jourdain (New York: Burt Franklin, 1972), p. 144.
[35] "To see with hands."
[36] While Godard is concerned with aspects of production and distribution relating to video and exploring its potential, I do not think that he is interested in the ontology of video. Video functions for Godard as the "other" of film as a way to explore an ontology of *translation* from cinema to video, from an analogical process to its transformation into data. For Godard it is also obviously a tool and a technique for seeing and thinking with which, over the years, he experimented repeatedly.
[37] (re)see (re)hear $\leftarrow\rightarrow\rightarrow$ (re)read
or
image(s) sound(s) $\leftarrow\rightarrow$ reading

which things and processes derive rather than what is revealed through its appearance.[38] With montage, as I will discuss below, Godard seeks to transform the invisible into an image of thought, by imposing an angle of vision through the passage from shot or frame to fragment. The image of thought is then delivered in the sense of Walter Benjamin's dialectical montage. In this regard, it could be said that Godard adds one extra step to Vertov's dialectical formula of the Kino-Eye that consists of seeing/re-*see*-ving/re-sending the visual through fruitful juxtapositions in the form of a potential Image of the *unthought*. In sum, Godard seeks, with the technique of video, a machinic vision that acknowledges the philosophical phantasm of the reflexive consciousness of the eye that sees, an eye that apprehends itself through its own constitution of the world's visibility. Godard's *seeing eye* is, furthermore, the expression, the utterance, it is the speech act: *Je vois*. The speech act is effectuated not in the recognition of the Self in the constitution of the world's visibility, but in montage, in a spatio-temporal passage between the two monitors, here and elsewhere, now and then. Godard's eye is not a reflexive consciousness but an eye that jumps, decoding and recoding reality, opening up the potential for the actualization of the image of the unthought.

Brand Images

In the 1970s, Godard used the term *image de marque* (brand image) to designate emblematic images that acquire power by means of circulation in the regime of visibilities; this circulation makes them part of history, contributing to collective historical consciousness composed of mechanically reproduced images. The problem is that brand images simplify the facts; they are images made out of events conceived to circulate in the first place in the mass media. These images are incomplete, carry solidified meaning and embody fixed signifiers. In 1976, a special issue of *Cahiers de Cinéma* was published, inspired by *Ici et ailleurs* and devoted to brand images.[39] According to the editors, Serge Toubiana and Serge Daney, the brand image has a power of its own and is marked by power relationships, thereby becoming an emblem; as an emblem, a

---

[38] Annette Michelson, "From Magician to Epistemologist: Vertov's *The Man with a Movie Camera*," *Artforum* (March 1972), 63. See also Dziga Vertov's "The Birth of Kino-Eye" (1924), "Factory of Facts" (1926), and "On *The Eleventh Year*" (1928), in *Kino-Eye: The Writings of Dziga Vertov* (Berkeley: University of California Press, 1984).

[39] Serge Daney and Serge Toubiana, "Présentation," *Cahiers du Cinéma*, nos. 268–269, special issue "Images de Marque" (July–August 1976), p. 4.

brand image is an instrument not of domination but solidified power. In the same issue of *Cahiers*, Alain Bergala defines brand images as stereotypical historical photographs, images that come back in the information apparatuses. For Bergala, the existence of these images is inseparable from the apparition of photographic reportage, which has been used to construct a historical imaginary of official history.[40] These images are dominated by written discourse, thus making the photographer into a secondary, imaginary figure, while forming a consensus created by their continual appearance as simulacra within collective memory.[41] In this sense, brand images may come from the mass media and share with them the trait of being *figural* (in Rodowick's sense of the mass image that is addressed to the atomized collective) or *textualized*: the semiotic regime of electronic and digital communication where the world of things is penetrated by discourse.[42] Brand images in Godard imply power, repetition, circulation and the stereotypical vision of events that conceal other aspects of history while constructing a collective visual historical consciousness. The concept of brand images, furthermore, points to the fact that the distinction between publicity and information is no longer relevant because the image has entirely swung to the side of power. What concerns Godard, moreover, is the potential of cinema and video to function as the other of the mass media that could bring into question how the *actualities* are delivered to us, as ready-made facts in the form of the traffic of grammatical propositions that affirm events—and that potentially write history. Following Michael Witt, Godard's work is a theory and practice of audiovisual history that simultaneously encompasses the history of cinema, the history of thinking about film, the history of the twentieth century, the interpenetration of cinema and that century, Godard's life and that place within these histories. For Witt, as for Godard, cinema assumed, on the one hand, the role of historian of the twentieth century as it documented it from beginning to end; on the other, every moment of the past remains potentially available to history. In his *Histoire(s) du cinéma*, Godard thus takes up the task of writing a polysemic history based on the principle of montage, of which

---

[40] Which Godard problematizes through his parades of cut-out images from journals such as *L'Express* and *Le Nouvel Observateur*.

[41] Alain Bergala, "Le pendule (La photo historique stéréotypée)," *Cahiers du Cinéma*, nos. 268–269, "Images de Marque" special issue (July–August 1976), pp. 40–46.

[42] David Rodowick, *Reading the Figural, Or, Philosophy After the New Media* (Durham, NC: Duke University Press, 2000), p. 8.

Ici et ailleurs is arguably the genesis.[43] For Godard, cinema is capable of "touching" and relating to the events themselves.[44] This is possible through montage, which has the potential not only of remembering, but of reviving the obliterated portrayals of states of affairs by delivering forgotten virtualities.[45] For Godard, montage is the site for a redemptive virtuality which, when it is actualized, creates the "real" or truth in the present (an Image). In *Ici et ailleurs,* which is different from *Histoire(s)* in that it excludes the history of cinema, Godard's own version of history operates within the relationships between historical (brand) mechanical images and reproducible sounds, the actuality of the mass media and the present.

For both Gilles Deleuze and Jean-Luc Godard, an image, including a film image (and especially a brand image), is always incomplete because when perceived, only one of an image's faces is actualized (or made accessible to consciousness). Following Deleuze, with his montage method of the "in-between," Godard proposes that prehension equals images and the whole that is stored in them. Having been influenced by Benjamin and Breton, for Godard the potential actualization of an image is only possible at the juncture of two others: "Film is not one image after another, it is an image plus another image forming a third—the third being formed by the viewer at the moment of viewing the film."[46] Godard's films are not articulated through images carrying a given code, rather, they are a *mélange* (mixture) of materials of expression (i.e., diegetic, didactic, documentary) and forms of content (i.e., series, categories, genres). It is this form of assemblage and his montage method of the "in-between" that renders Godard's films reflexive and at the same time generative of subjects. Godard's method of the "in-between" is operative and exposed pedagogically as the matrix of *Ici et ailleurs*. In this film, Godard exposes his

---

[43] See: Michael Witt, *Jean-Luc Godard, Cinema Historian* (Bloomington, IN: Indiana University Press, 2013).

[44] Youssef Ishaghpour, *Archéologie du cinéma et mémoire du siècle* (Tours: Farrago 2000), p. 19.

[45] Evidently this means forgetting other virtualities, which is Péguy's paradox. In Godard, montage is a means of bringing together and connecting virtualities by means of citation and juxtaposition, methods which Godard has mastered by being able to evoke an entire work or historical event by portraying only a small part of it. See Aumont, Jacques, *Amnésies, Fictions du cinéma d'apres Jean-Luc Godard* (Paris: POL, 2012), p. 155.

[46] "Le cinéma n'est pas une image après l'autre, c'est une image plus une autre qui en forment une troisième, la troisième étant du reste formée par le spectateur au moment où il voit le film." Godard, Jean-Luc, "Propos Rompus," in *Jean-Luc Godard par Jean-Luc Godard* (Paris: L'Étoile et Cahiers du Cinéma, 1985), p. 460.

non-dialectic method of montage pedagogically, through which the concept "brand image" emerges.

Ici et ailleurs is a film about utterances and figures eliding into one another in relation to cinematic voice, speech, discourse and expression as they become information. In the film we see a panoply of open mouths of politicians, militants and people speaking out: Henry Kissinger, Nixon, Golda Meir, Léon Blum, Hitler, students, Palestinians.[47] We hear an array of sounds, speeches and discourses proper to revolutionary songs, sounds, revolution, nations and history. As we have seen, the film registers major epistemological changes that took place in the 1970s prompted by the reconfiguration of representation, nationalism, Third Worldism, socialism and communism as ideological vehicles for revolutionary politics. In *Ici et ailleurs*, the act of mourning the failure of the Palestinian Revolution—in the face of the Black September massacres in the refugee camps in Jordan, and the wave of terrorism that followed—becomes the allegory of failure of all revolutions, from which a lesson is drawn. Further, working through the collapse of the revolutionary project and *imaging* of Palestinian resistance became for Godard a matter of the restitution of speech to the absent and to the dead Palestinians—to whom, as Godard laments in the film, their comrades had not listened.

One of Godard's concerns is to posit reproducible images and sounds as a form of historical memory; such a concern is clearly in dialogue with Guy Debord's articulation of Spectacle as the annihilation of historical knowledge, in particular, the destruction of the recent past.[48] For Debord, "Spectacle has irradiated into everything and has absolute control over production and perception, and especially over the shape of the future and the past."[49] In the age of Spectacle or of hyper-reality, "remembering" is not to recall a story, but to be able to invoke an image.[50] Spectacle is thus the reign of a perpetual present dominated by the economy of information, which, by selling the "here and now" as novelty, annihilates and

---

[47] I will address the controversy that arose from Godard's juxtaposition of Golda Meir and Adolf Hitler in the following chapter.

[48] According to Agamben, Godard and Debord share this paradigmatic messianic attitude toward cinema, and they both use repetition and montage in order to construct a restitutive memory. See Giorgio Agamben, "Le cinéma de Guy Debord," *Image et mémoire: Écrits sur l'image, la danse et le cinéma* (Paris: Desclé de Brower, 2004), p. 89.

[49] Jonathan Crary, "Spectacle, Attention, Countermemory," *October* 50 (Autumn 1989), p. 462.

[50] Susan Sontag, *Regarding the Pain of Others* (New York: Farrar, Straus and Giroux, 2003), p. 89.

replaces history.[51] An interesting link could be drawn here to Alfonso Cuarón's film *Children of Men* (2006). The narrative of the film takes place in 20 years' time in an apocalyptic future, which is rendered visible by mixing signs of the recent past of war, oppression and disaster *elsewhere* that have circulated in the Western media—Gaza, Abu Ghraib, Guantánamo, Baghdad, polluted landscapes—all of them extricated from their geographical and historical context, thus rendering the "actuality" elsewhere, as Britain's doomsday. The fusion of these images implies a further stage of Debord's Spectacle in which "false appearances" and their indistinguishability from life have proliferated into signs of oppression purporting a false, terrifying, "real" present in the privileged zones of the First World.

This should be understood in terms of how mechanized memory has changed the way in which we remember, hindering our capacity to imagine the future. Borges's short story "Funes el memorioso"[52] lays out the obliteration of the present and of analytic thinking by the impossibility of forgetting prompted by mechanical reproduction. In the story, Ireneo Funes is a boy of humble origins with a prodigious memory enabled by a fall that has given him clarity of vision of the present and of the past. He is not only able to memorize everything in complete detail, but he can also recall sounds and visual memories in real time. His powerful memory, however, prevents him from being able to analyze, think abstractly, or truly be in the present. He recites sections of Pliny's *Natural History* in Latin and can be seen as embodying the encyclopedic nature of this work.[53] Like Funes, this compendium does not claim to analyze or to give an opinion on the facts that have been recorded, and they are conveyed as information with a pedagogical voice. In Funes' case, the possibility of fully documenting the world through visual and aural memory is realized, similar to today's analogue (and digital) inscriptions and projections. When Funes remembers in real time, he is subtracted from the present because his ability to remember the *core of events* is accomplished by registering and reproducing duration. This recording is previous to history, as Funes' memory is an unmediated witness of events capturing not

---

[51] Guy Debord, *Commentaires* (1988), pp. 17–19, cited in Jonathan Crary, "Spectacle, Attention, Countermemory," p. 463.

[52] Jorge Luis Borges, *Ficciones* (Buenos Aires: Emecé, 1958).

[53] Pliny the Elder, *Natural History*, available at http://www.perseus.tufts.edu/cgi-bin/ptext?lookup=Plin.+Nat.+toc

only their immediate traces but duration itself, transcending subjectivity and testimony, a document, a kind of public (objective) duration. Funes' memory is not unlike a movie camera registering events that have the potential to become history. Following Péguy (who influenced Godard's notion of history), history, event and memory must not be confused, rather: "History and memory make a right angle. History is parallel to the event, and memory is central and transversal to it."[54] Therefore, Péguy considers writing history in two manners: one, as a parallel to the course of the event and its unfolding; two, to go back to the event, taking one's place within it stretching in two directions—one into the past and another into the future—this axis is memory. Memory is capable of traversing the event, like geological aging. For Péguy, however, the remembrance of the survivor is a narration (*un récit*), not a testimony, but fiction.[55] With Funes, we see the symbiosis of memory, event and testimony of mechanical reproduction. Evidently, the ability to register real duration through mechanical memory (a recording) has changed the way in which we perceive, remember and write history, although mechanical memory itself cannot remember. We could understand Funes' non-differential remembrance in real time as the hypostatization of Fredric Jameson's televisual "total flow" because "nothing haunts the mind or leaves after images… structurally memory (remembering) is excluded and so is critical distance."[56]

Accounting for that shift in memory and perception and influenced by Bergson (who defined consciousness as a dark plate on which images develop) and Péguy, Deleuze defines memory in the age of mechanical reproduction not as a matter of remembering but of *actualizing* the hidden virtualities contained in an image. For Deleuze, an *image* is never in the present: what is in the present is whatever the "image" represents. Because the image is made of temporal relations, images contain the potentiality to render visible these relations that cannot be reduced to the present. In other words, a multiplicity of durations co-exists in an image and their common denominator is the present.[57] Deleuze does not draw a distinction between the images we perceive empirically and those

[54] Charles Péguy, *Clio: Dialogue de l'histoire et de l'âme païenne* (Paris: Gallimard, 1932), p. 231.
[55] Ibid., p. 242.
[56] Fredric Jameson, "Video: Surrealism without the Unconscious," *Postmodernism: Or, the Cultural Logic of Late Capitalism* (Durham, NC: Duke University Press, 1991), pp. 70–71.
[57] Gilles Deleuze, "The Brain is the Screen: An Interview with Gilles Deleuze on the Time Image," *Discourse* Vol. 20, No. 3 (Fall 1998), pp. 55–71.

we perceive in cinema, photographs or on television. In his account, perceptions and memories are made out of stored memories. In their actualization, mechanized streams of memories or chains of images can be invoked to account for events. Along similar lines, one of the problems Godard posits and explores in his films is not how to write history using mechanized memory, but how to account for mechanized memory as it is written with "brand images." While for Cuarón and Debord reality and media images have become inseparable, collapsing actuality, memory and reality having become a single register of visibility, Godard's montage activates the relationships between the three.

As he is a materialist filmmaker, Godard's perception of the world is shaped by his historical consciousness of it. Thus his film practice aims at exploring how the mechanical reproduction of the material world can affect consciousness and memory, and how images shape historical consciousness by becoming emblematic of historical events. These attitudes crystallize in his monumental film *Histoire(s) du cinéma* (1988–1998), in an exploration of the relationship between cinema and history throughout the twentieth century. Godard addresses embryonically the problem of "History" in *Ici et ailleurs*, by exploring the images (and sounds) that have shaped the historical consciousness of "Revolution(s)," conceptualizing them as brand images. Examples that appear in Godard's films include the photograph of Che Guevara on his deathbed, or the little girl burned by napalm at Trảng Bàng, Vietnam. For Godard, there are also brand sounds, such as "L'Internationale," Hitler's discourses, and "Patria o muerte, ¡Venceremos!," which we hear in the soundtrack of *Ici et ailleurs*. The concept of the brand image—or sound—has evident market connotations, as it denotes the recognizable logo or mark of a company in the public domain, that is, as images that carry and leave traces, and that go on to become part of history. These kinds of images, first of all, evidence the paradox of photography as John Berger put it, namely, that a photograph is an automatic record of a given event which uses the event to explain or to justify its recording, thereby rendering the process of observation self-conscious.[58] As we have seen, a photograph may also become emblematic by acquiring power through its circulation in the regime of visibilities. In other words, events make images and then their circulation makes them part of history, thus forming a collective historical consciousness composed of

---

[58] John Berger, "Understanding a Photograph" in Nikos Stangos (ed.) *The Look of Things* (New York: The Viking Press, 1972), p. 180.

mechanical reproductions. In this sense, brands are characterized by being easily recognizable because they have simplified the facts.[59]

In *Ici et ailleurs*, the "now" and "then" are the "here" and "elsewhere," in 1970 and 1974–75, in Grenoble and the Middle East, respectively. By putting forth these spatial and temporal relationships rather than by situating themselves *in* the present, Godard and Miéville counter the temporality of the mass media (which is that of actuality and urgency) and introduce the time of history while they draw a Revolutionary cartography. Godard and Miéville interweave in the film two kinds of history: "recent history" (the news on television) and "far away history" (the history of all revolutions from 1789 to 1973). As we have also seen, in 1972, Jean-Pierre Gorin described the then-unrealized montage of *Jusqu'à la victoire* as the "somme continue de tous les aspects de la Palestine."[60] Following this premise, the histor(y)ies of all revolutions are accounted for as an addition of images and sounds. In the movie, there is a scene showing a hand "adding up mistakes" in a "calculator." The operations performed with the calculator are:

$$1789 + \mathbf{1917} + 1936 = \text{May } 1968$$
$$1789 + \mathbf{1917} + 1968 = \text{September } 1970$$

By way of the two additions of dates, Godard renders two parallel histories, tracking what is common to the French, and to the Palestinian Revolution—specifically 1917, which is the year that arguably defined the twentieth century, the year of the Russian Revolution and of the Balfour Declaration. The Stalinization of the former and the triumph of the latter led to the outcome of the Palestinian Revolution in 1970. These dates lay out as well what Alain Badiou recently called the "two sequences of the Communist hypothesis."[61] The first sequence runs from 1792 to 1871,

---

[59] Remi-Pierre Heude, *L'Image-marque* (Paris: Eyrolles, 1989). An obvious reference regarding a more recent consideration of brands is Naomi Klein, *No Logo* (New York, HarperCollins, 2000), which explores "branding" as the creator of surplus value as opposed to commodities.

[60] "The continuous sum of all the aspects of Palestine." Jean-Pierre Gorin interviewed by Christian Braad Thomsen, *Jump Cut* no. 3 (1974), pp. 17–19.

[61] Alain Badiou, "The Communist Hypothesis," *New Left Review* 49 (January–February 2008), available online: http://newleftreview.org/II/49/alain-badiou-the-communist-hypothesis

bookended by the French Revolution and Paris Commune, popular mass movements in which the seizure of power is accomplished through the insurrectional overthrow of the existing order and by the abolition of the old forms of society, leading to the installation of a "community of equals." This sequence ends with the Paris Commune, because its failure demonstrated the limits of working-class leadership and armed insurrection. The second sequence runs from 1917 to 1976, from the Bolshevik Revolution to the end of the Chinese Cultural Revolution. The problems posed by the second sequence were: "How to hold out?" and "How to protect the new power against the onslaught of its enemies?" In other words, these questions sought to realize in the twentieth century what the nineteenth had dreamt of, making the revolution prevail either through insurrection or prolonged popular war (Russia, China, Czechoslovakia, Korea, Vietnam, Cuba), implying not only the establishment of a new order but its preservation by means of the party. After Badiou, this second sequence created a new problem that could not be solved using the methods developed in response to the problems of the first: the problem was that the party-state, which developed into a new form of authoritarianism (the police-state), was characterized by corruption and ineffectiveness. The end of the second hypothesis came with the Cultural Revolution and May 1968, which were both attempts to deal with the inadequacy of the party. Since the mid-1970s, the ideas of Marxism-Leninism, revolution, the workers' movement, mass democracy, the party of the proletariat, and the socialist state—all inventions of the nineteenth and twentieth centuries—have no longer been useful at the level of practical politics.

In *Ici et ailleurs*, Godard constructs the history of revolutions along similar lines as does Badiou, by evoking images such as that of Léon Blum when the Popular Front government took power during the Bastille Day celebration on July 14, 1936.[62] The image signifies the coalition of Socialists and Communists for the first time in France, which led to negotiations between factory owners and workers under the aegis of the French state, an image that points to a historical double victory for the Left.[63] Another image in Godard's history of revolutions is that of a young

[62] On July 14, 1936, Socialists and Communists celebrated the end of the strikes of May/June that reunited two million strikers in France, when they voted for the 40-hour week, paid vacation and a pro-union law.
[63] See Georgette Elgey's commentary on the images taken by Robert Capa, David Seymour and Henri-Cartier Bresson documenting these events, reprinted in Georgette Elgey, *Front Populaire* (Paris: Chêne/Magnum, 1976).

woman behind the gates at the Renault Factory in Flins in 1968, that appeared frequently in other Sonimage films, as well as being restaged in *Soigne ta droite* (1987) and in *Adieu au langage* (2017). The original image denotes June 7, when the striking Renault workers, with the help of students, prevented replacement workers from entering the factory. This image stands, therefore, for the mythical alliance between proletarians and students in 1968. In *Ici et ailleurs*, the addition of the historical dates, and of the images and sounds of betrayed or failed revolutions (or "mistakes," as Godard puts it), lays out the history of Palestine in relationship to European history and especially to the Shoah. In order to do this, Godard makes a controversial juxtaposition of Golda Meir and Hitler in a video-collage, as well as quotes from Alain Resnais' archival footage of the Nazi concentration camps from *Nuit et brouillard* (1955). Here, Godard's conception of history is close to Walter Benjamin's dialectical image.[64] For Benjamin, the historical mark that images carry (*der Historische Index der Bilder*) not only indicates that images belong to a given era but that they are only legible at that time.[65] For Godard, an image never exists by itself because the historical mark that images bear can only be read within an ensemble of images. For the filmmaker, it is not chronological history that needs to be activated, but a Benjaminian messianic history that implies that something needs to be saved, an eschatological history seeking to accomplish something in a different temporality.[66] Attributing to cinema the power to re-establish a redemptive past, a past that cinema itself failed to capture, Godard juxtaposes critical historical periods, transforming by way of montage both the subject and the object of history and actuality.[67] In this manner, cinema saves the real because *it makes the real*.[68] The messianic *jetzt* (now) of the recognition of the historical images takes place at the interstices between the addition of images and sounds by way of Godardian montage. These additions "un-mark" or decode brand images and sounds, inscribing them in a movement within a process of crystallizations and metamorphoses that recalls the origin of brand images themselves.

[64] As he discusses in the interview with Ishaghpour.
[65] Walter Benjamin, (N3, I) *Das Passagen-Werk* (Frankfurt: Suhrkamp, 1982), pp. 577–578.
[66] Giorgio Agamben, "Le cinéma de Guy Debord," in *Image et mémoire: Écrits sur l'image, la danse et le cinéma* (Paris: Desclée de Brouwer, 2004), p. 89.
[67] Junji Hori, "Godard's Two Historiographies," in *For Ever Godard,* ed. Michael Temple (London: Black Dog, 2004), p. 340.
[68] Aumont, *Amnésies*, p. 248.

Perception, History and Montage

Godard's montage method consists not only of linking and chaining but dechaining and rechaining images and sound-images. His method is comparable to photomontage, described by John Berger as "cutting out with scissors events and objects (drawings or verbal slogans) from the scenes to which they originally belonged, in order to arrange them in a new, discontinuous scene."[69] With photomontage, for Berger, we look at *things* and then at the symbols that are achieved through bringing them together. Dechaining (or cutting out with scissors) implies taking the image/sound out of its commonsensical chain of signification,[70] and rechaining it on the basis of a break with the former codes. Here we must bear in mind the paradox of photographic and filmic images: they have an indexical relationship to the objects they depict and yet they are messages without a code because they are coded in regards to the context in which they appear. When an image is dechained or displaced, the world to which the image belongs is destroyed and the out of field disappears or undergoes a transformation. We can also compare Godard's decoding/dechaining method with Guy Debord's *détournement* (rerouting), which is based on the appropriation of ads, news photographs, media clips, film footage, texts, and soundtracks, by which he seeks to expose the ideological nature of mass-cultural images by infusing them with critical negativity. Each *rerouted* element may lose its original meaning for the sake of becoming part of a new meaningful whole, as the Situationists liked to put it: the old elements are sublated into a higher ensemble through dialectical juxtaposition. Godard, however, is not a dialectician. He also differs from the notion that the relationship between the signifier and the signified is arbitrary; for Godard, like for Bazin, images *are imprints of the real*: cinema is "reality 24 times per second," is another of his well-known aphorisms. In Godard, dechaining an image implies removing it from its usual chain of signification, which is always either defective or superfluous.[71] Once two incommensurable images are rechained on Godard's editing table,[72] they

---

[69] John Berger, "Understanding a Photograph" in Nikos Stangos (ed) *The Look of Things* (New York: The Viking Press, 1972), p. 185.

[70] Godard does not make a distinction between the images he appropriates or those he films.

[71] Gilles Deleuze, *Time-Image Cinema 2*, trans. Hugh Tomlinson and Robert Galeta. (Minneapolis: The University of Minnesota Press, 2001), pp. 179–80.

[72] After Deleuze, Godard's *table de montage* is understood as the Kantian *Table of Categories*.

enter into disparity and a potential thirdness emerges.[73] In other words, an Image (the unthought) emerges at the interstices between images in a spacing out that can cause it to be extracted in a differential operation. For Godard, having been influenced by Benjamin and Breton, the potential actualization of an image is only possible at the junction of two others.

In *Ici et ailleurs*, Godard and Miéville expose this method of montage pedagogically. In one of the sections of *Ici et ailleurs*, they lay out a series of binary additions. We hear in the voice-over: "Révolution Française *et*, et révolution Arabe, ici *et* ailleurs, dedans *et* dehors, national *et* étranger, lente *et* vite."[74] This sequence is interspersed with images of newspaper headlines about terrorism in the Middle East and about the LIP factory strikes. "Parlant de riches *et* de pauvres,"[75] Godard says, while we see images of Nixon, Vietnam, an African woman, Prague 1968 and LIP. The soundtrack is composed of a Chinese hymn, the Shoah *lied* "Auschwitz, Madjanek, Treblinka," the Cuban revolutionary song "Déjame estrechar

---

[73] For Deleuze, thirdness is double-edged: it can evoke either a cliché (a dialectical image) or the unthought. Thirdness is where signs take part in mental operations that make general statements about qualities and events: it is the realm of interpretation and symbolization. Charles Sanders Peirce's semiotic terms associated with thirdness are first, the sign itself, namely, the *legisign*, an agreed-upon general type; second, the relation of the sign to its object, which is symbolic, that is, the sign denotes the object through its relation to an interpretant; and third, how the interpretant represents the sign, namely, as an *argument*—for Deleuze, a *mental image* or *relation image*. A mental image "takes as objects *of* thought objects which have their existence outside of thought, just as the objects of perception have their own existence outside perception." Gilles Deleuze, *Cinema 1: The Movement-Image* (Minneapolis: University of Minnesota Press, 1986), p. 189. The mental image intervenes in the clichés of the sensory-motor schema by making us aware of the subtractive nature of perception. The mental image either reinforces clichés, or opens the film to the whole, to the outside (toward the unthought). Thirdness tends to degree zero. See also Laura Marks, "Signs of Time" in Gregory Flaxman (ed.) *The Brain is the Screen* (Minneapolis: The University of Minnesota Press, 2000), p. 199. "Thirdness" here is not to be confused with Barthes' "third meaning," which is not far from Deleuze. For Barthes the "third meaning" is an obtuse meaning, a field of permanences and permutations, a trace which by difference compels a vertical reading, an aleatory combination, *a signifier prompted by chance*, something that seems to open the field of meaning totally, extending outside culture into the infinity of language. It is the supplement, the "too many" that one's intellect cannot succeed in absorbing. Barthes linked this concept to Kristeva's *signifiance*, which he calls "a word which has the advantage of referring to the field of the signifier (and not by signification)," a semiotics of the text. Roland Barthes, "The Third Meaning," in *Image, Music, Text* (New York: Hill and Wang, 1977), pp. 54–55.

[74] "French Revolution *and*, and Arab Revolution, here *and* elsewhere, inside *and* outside, national *and* foreign, slow *and* fast…"

[75] "Speaking of rich *and* poor."

tu mano" and the Nazi song "Adolf Hitler soll uns führen...." Lastly, Godard shows us images of contemporary revolutionary struggles here and elsewhere: LIP *and* Palestine. Differently than in the voice-over, these "binaries" are asymmetrical, as Godard anti-dialectically states that dividing the world in two: "c'est trop simple et trop facile."[76] The way in which the images and sounds are linked is through an additive logic of non-opposing binaries, the method of the *in-between*. This method is operative and could be understood as the matrix of *Ici et ailleurs*. As I have already mentioned (see p. 115), the film is composed of heterogeneous materials of expression; it includes didactic sequences, non-diegetic elements of different kinds, a narrative centered on a French working-class family and documentary images of the Palestinian struggle. We also saw that the word *ET* ("AND") appears as a sculpture on a pedestal throughout the film. The "AND" is literally placed in between images; it is the re-creation of the interstice, bringing together the socio-historical figures along with the diverse materials of expression in the film. Through montage, the syntax of the film, as expressed by the film's title, is rendered visible.[77] Therefore, the French family enters into a relation of disparity with the group of Palestinian fedayeen: as socio-historical figures, these two figures (French/fedayeen) are meant to be perceived as irreducible. The conjunction/disjunction of these figures creates a fissure in the film's signifying chain of association. The interstice between the states of affairs of the two figures allows resemblances to be ranked, and a difference of potential is established between the two.[78] The word "AND" is a syncategoreme, which means "a category-with."[79] In Borges's Chinese encyclopedia as evoked by Foucault in *The Order of Things* (1966), there is a division between *words* and *things*; the use of the word "AND" allows for a heterogeneous taxonomy. It implies a juncture/disjuncture, announcing association/dissociation. "AND" has a linkage function that authorizes

---

[76] "It's too simple and too easy."

[77] Another instance in which Godard juxtaposes two socio-historical figures is in *One Plus One: Sympathy for the Devil* (1968), where he brings together staged, diegetic images of the Black Panthers with documentary images of the Rolling Stones in the studio recording their famous song.

[78] Gilles Deleuze, *Time-Image*, p. 198.

[79] See Jacques Derrida, *Et cetera (and so on, und so weiter, and so forth, et ainsi de suite, und so überall, etc.)* (Paris, L'Herne, 2005).

heterogeneous enumerations, allowing for divisions, for chaining unities together or to postulate relationships without relationships.[80]

The mixture of images, texts and sounds joined with "AND" allows Godard to bring together sounds and images in relationships that are far more complex than identity or contradiction. "AND" is the glue of the film, but it also means consequence, consecution, conjunction, disjunction, connection, opposition, strategic alliance or juxtaposition.[81] The manner in which Godard assembles images in *Ici et ailleurs* recalls the manner in which Vertov, in *Three Songs about Lenin* (1933), structures a combination of documentary images and staged images based on a systematic play of binary alternation by progressive substitution of one visible series for the other.[82] *Three Songs* is a homage to Lenin expressing the fact that the Soviet people live and work for their leader and for the Soviet future. The logic inherent in the film is that of the passage from the "masses" to the "people," resulting directly from the new relationship established between the people and power after the Revolution. The assemblage of images is realized according to a visual formula describing the logic of a totality. This formula is composed of logical relationships established between the signifying regimes: "Masses," "Lenin," "USSR," "Work" and "People." Through the juxtaposition of images of the leader, the people, agricultural technology, women, workers and so on, what becomes intelligible is a propagandistic effort in favor of communism. Unlike Vertov (and Debord), as we have seen, Godard is not a dialectician, and in the filmic syntax of *Ici et ailleurs* Godard does not associate images in a chain of signification, but *differentiates* them so that their signifiers enter into disparity. Following Deleuze, the juncture of two images with the syncategoreme "AND" allows signification to emerge at the interstices between the images. Unlike the (Vertovian) interval, which is a dissociative force, the interstice creates an accumulation of images, resulting in a series of heterogeneous spaces that are incommensurable with each other and which establish incomparable, open relationships.[83] The distinction between the Godardian interstice and the Vertovian interval as principles of montage lies in the fact that, in Vertov, the construction of the object-

---

[80] Ibid., p. 42.
[81] Derrida, p. 55.
[82] Gilles Delavaud, "Composer (avec) le réel: *Trois Chants sur Lénine*," in Jean-Pierre Esquenazi (ed.) *Vertov, L'invention du reel!* (Paris: L'Harmattan, 1997), p. 245.
[83] See David Rodowick's discussion of *Ici et ailleurs* in *Reading the Figural*, pp. 195–197.

film is done by intervals, a visual and auditory gap opened up between two actions that becomes a signifying space. In order to make the film visible to the viewer, Vertov sublates the multiplicity of intervals to a single equation or global visual formula that expresses the film-object in those signifying spaces. For example, *Man with a Movie Camera* (1929) is based on the relations between planes, foreshortenings, movement, light and shade and speed. The composition of the relations points to Vertov's dialectic of the Kino-Eye, which oscillates between cinematic consciousness and epistemological research: the dialectic of the filmmaker is between magician and epistemologist.[84] Differently, the Godardian interstice is a crevice opened up in between two states of affairs, images and sound-images, destabilizing their signifiers, opening them up to *signifiance* (significance). *Signifiance* is a model of meaning that fluctuates between the expulsion and the mastery of signifiers, implying a passage and a fluidity of meanings. Through the conjunction of images, the expulsion dislocates the sign without annulling the markings or its indexicality, differentiating rather than mastering meaning.[85] That is why the images and sounds in *Ici et ailleurs* function as more or less autonomous units, because in this case an image's meaning does not depend on the image following or previous to it, nor on the sound put "on top" of it. The interstice "AND" is thus a provisory zone of indiscernibility in which the fluxes of meaning are exchanged, allowing simultaneous readings of the images in which past and present co-exist: actualization does not stop. This is because the assemblage destroys the images' identities, insofar as "AND" substitutes

[84] Annette Michelson, "From Magician to Epistemologist: Vertov's *The Man with a Movie Camera*," *Artforum* (March 1972), pp. 62–72.

[85] Julia Kristeva's use of Plato's concept of the *chora* (as matrix, mobile, merging, contradiction) functions similarly to the way in which Deleuze conceptualizes Godard's "ET" as the matrix; as in the *chora*, the elements are without identity or reason and the idea of *chora* is the site of a chaos: "The contradiction between expulsion and mastery engenders precisely the process of *signifiance* which traverses any finite formation and presents itself as passage, fluidity, effacement of the limits between inside and outside, assimilation of an 'object' in a 'self without contours.' The process of *signifiance* is precisely that *Va-et-vient* between mobility and resistance: expulsion itself pushing on and away its semiotic moments of stasis. It is their struggle which assures *life* and *text*. Expulsion works precisely on those elements of the natural and social environment with which the individual tends to identify under biological and social constraints. In the family structure, it is the parent of the same sex who is subject to expulsion." See Julia Kristeva, "The Subject in Process" in Patrick Ffrench and Roland-François Lack, *The Tel Quel Reader* (London and New York: Routledge, 1998), pp. 156–160.

the ontological attribution of those images: their *this is*, the *eidos* of images: their Être = ET (being = and) is taken over by "signified AND signified AND...."

Sometimes resorting to repetition, Godard produces a sort of mnemotechnics that enables us to recognize images and sound-images and to link their signifiers in diverse contexts. Repetition and juxtaposition become tools to pull out what the signifiers lack or to push out any excess of meaning, allowing us to see the images as multiplicities, instead of showing us a single face of the thing, as in ordinary representation or description.

Godard and Gorin present pedagogically in *Tout va bien* their conception of images as a multiplicity or as a collection, in a scene where the characters Suzanne (Jane Fonda) and Jacques (Yves Montand) have an argument about their crisis as a couple. When they talk about how they "see" their relationship, Montand describes it as: "On va au boulot, on mange, on va au cinéma ou pas, on couche ou pas."[86] Fonda's taxonomy of the relationship includes more images: "On se réveille, on va au boulot, on bouffe, on se dispute ou pas, on va au cinéma ou pas, on couche ou pas."[87] She then states that in order to be able to think about and understand their crisis, she needs to add an image of Yves at work, and an image of herself at work. The "unthought" image in this particular scene is crystallized in a photograph of a woman's hand holding a penis, which Fonda asks Montand to hold on his forehead while she tells him: "Ça te satisfait moins maintenant qu'il y a trois ans."[88] While the referent remains, an ambiguity is instituted: what is it that satisfies him less? Their sex life or his job?

As we have seen, for both Deleuze and Godard, an image is always incomplete because, when it is perceived, only one of its faces is accessible to consciousness. Here I would like to draw on Deleuze's model of *prehension*, which is the data of perceptions, defined in *The Fold* (1988) as a concretion of elements and as the function of the point of view. The movement from the prehending datum to the prehending subject is a subtractive operation insofar as prehension is a movement of framing in itself. The prehending subject selects what she can *manage*: the subject perceives an

---

[86] "We go to work, we eat, we go to the cinema or not, we have sex or not."

[87] "We get up, we go to work, we eat, we fight or not, we go to the cinema or not, we have sex or not."

[88] "This satisfies you less now than three years ago."

image minus what does not interest her, minus what she does not know, minus what she does not need to perceive. Following Deleuze, with his method of the "in-between," Godard means that prehension equals images and the whole that is stored in them. According to Deleuze, in Godard "[The] whole is the outside."[89] Godard's films, as I discussed, are not articulated through images carrying a given code, but are rather a mixing of the materials of expression (i.e., diegetic, didactic and documentary) and of the forms of content (i.e., series, categories and genres). For Deleuze "readable" images are "pure images"; they are a form of visual communication that demands a specific use of eyes and ears. In the case of *Ici et ailleurs*, the spectator is obliged to appreciate the series through pedagogy,[90] which is based first on the appropriation and repetition of "that which others have said," as we have seen: citations, slogans, images, cartoons, jokes, and so on, and second, in seeking another enunciation, sound, image, or text that could induce a certain effect (distantiation, the unthought) in the first appropriated element. As I mentioned, for Godard-Deleuze an image is only one face of the thing, if we understand an image as a picture, as depicting something it carries with it as a discourse, a verbal code. For Godard, what is denoted in the pictures (the signified, the verbal code) are categories that constitute genres. The categories and genres introduce a reflection upon the image itself, expelling the signifier. If we understand figuration as a form of *signifiance* as opposed to the *figural*, the image becomes a movement of figuration, because through montage, images are both inside and outside discourse. At his editing table Godard works through categories and establishes genres and discourses, reshuffling, separating and defamiliarizing images. Categorization, unlike a simple listing of items or a collage procedure, is a method for the constitution of series, each one in turn marked by a genre. Godardian categories are words, things, people and actions. These categories are redistributed, remanaged, and reinvented in every one of his films.[91] In *Ici et ailleurs*, the categories are "Palestine," "France," "Revolution," organized deictically,

---

[89] Gilles Deleuze, *The Time-Image*, p. 179. The whole implies not petrified meaning but ever-changing matter, animated by peristaltic movements, folds, and foldings that constitute the inside and the inside of the outside. The outside is a redoubling of the Other, a differential repetition.

[90] Gilles Deleuze, "Portrait of the Philosopher as a Moviegoer," in *Two Regimes of Madness*, p. 217.

[91] "In *Les Carabiniers* (1963), Godard films the categories of the war film genre: 'occupation, countryside, resistance.' In *Sauve qui peut (La vie)* (1980) the categories are: 'the

creating a cognitive map of Palestine as *seen from* the point of view of "France," necessarily and inevitably through the mass media. Palestine is divided into "then" and "now" for the purpose of presenting the differences between the Palestinian revolutionaries *then*, before the Black September massacres in Jordan (1970), and *now* (1974). The "here" is visually presented through the television monitors, which show images of the casualties of the massacres. "France" is further divided into the categories of "labor," "family," "leisure," and "media." The genres in the film are photojournalism, documentary, Brechtian epic, and "blackboard didactic" film. As we have seen, the Palestinian images resemble mass media images of the Palestinian conflict insofar as they have been filmed in an "objective" style; they are fixed frames that stylistically attest to their own indexicality, and that signify mutely the authenticity and immediacy of the "Palestinian Revolutionaries in action." Arguably, mass media and documentary images are "image-acts," analogous to "speech-acts," because they carry a judgment within them, and such judgments centralize the image by rendering it commonsensical.

Such "centralization" is the signifier as such, centralized in the face. For Deleuze, an image is pre-linguistic, however, insofar as it corresponds to signs and utterances; and language (signs and utterances carrying *information*) always centralizes images. Deleuze compares language to *un coup de tampon* (stamping): language authorizes and certifies images, normalizing them, subtracting that which we "should not" perceive in them.[92] For Deleuze language is neither communicational nor informative, but the transmission of order-words (Brian Massumi's translation of *mot d'ordre* from the French, literally *slogan* or *command* in English); language is pragmatic, and every statement accomplishes an act—that is why language authorizes or approves a state of affairs.[93] If language is the vari-

imaginary,' 'fear,' 'commerce,' and 'music,' which constitute the big problem of 'What is Passion?'—the next film moves on to explore that." Gilles Deleuze, *The Time-Image*, p. 185.

[92] Gilles Deleuze, "Trois questions sur *Six fois deux: A propos de sur et sous la communication*," *Cahiers du Cinéma* No. 271 (Novembre 1976), p. 10.

[93] "A distinction is sometimes made between information and communication; some authors envision an abstract *signifiance* of information and an abstract subjectification of communication. None of this, however, yields an implicit or primary form of language. There is no *signifiance* independent of dominant significations, nor is there subjectification independent of an established order of subjection. Both depend on the nature and transmission of order-words in a given social field. There is no individual enunciation. There is not even a subject of enunciation." Gilles Deleuze, *A Thousand Plateaux* (Minneapolis: The University of Minnesota Press, 2003), p. 79.

able and pragmatic application of a *pre-existing syntax*,[94] images can be said to behave in the same way—particularly mass-media and documentary images—by accomplishing certain actions. In *Ici et ailleurs*, an example of the pragmatics of the image is "The Palestinian Revolution." According to Deleuze-Godard, each subject has its own place in a chain of images and is trapped in it; this chain is a network of ideas that behave like order-words (or slogans/commands). Ideas function like order-words by being incarnated in images and sound-images, thus dictating what should interest us through images that direct our perception, in-*forming* us (subjectification, in Foucault).

When we look at an image in a film, it becomes a *crible* or "filter,"[95] mapping out "prehensions of prehensions" that refuse to distinguish affective forces from visible lexical forms.[96] On the one hand, Godard in *Ici et ailleurs* reflects upon the forces that constitute images (through categories and genres) and on the other, through Godard's additive-yet-dissociative montage. Predicated upon the logic of the "in-between," the film's montage aims at reaching a high degree of concretion by means of the prehension of a state of affairs, by way of accretion of data. In a way, Godard's method attempts to restore the exterior of images to the whole, making our perception equal to the image and all that is stored in it, thereby providing a way to fight against the authorization of order-words of the mass media's image-acts.

---

[94] Ibid., 78–79.

[95] Crary has brought up the genealogy of the notion of concretion: "The physicist André-Marie Ampère in his epistemological writings used the term *concretion* to describe how any perception always blends with a preceding or remembered perception. The words *mélange* and *fusion* occur frequently in his attack on classical notions of 'pure' isolated sensations. Perception, as he wrote to his friend Maine de Biran, was fundamentally 'une suite de différences successives.'" Ampère quoted by Jonathan Crary, "Techniques of the Observer," *October* 45 (Summer 1988), p. 11.

[96] See Tom Conley's introduction to his translation of Gilles Deleuze's *The Fold: Leibniz and the Baroque* (Minneapolis: The University of Minnesota Press, 1992). Furthermore, "The image is not in the present. What is in the present is whatever the image 'represents,' but not the image itself. The image itself is a bunch of temporal relations from which the present unfolds, either as a common multiplier, or a common denominator. Temporal relations are never seen in ordinary perception, but they can be seen in the image, provided the image is creative. The image renders visible, and creative, the relations which cannot be reduced to the present." Gilles Deleuze, "The Philosopher as a Moviegoer," in *Two Regimes of Madness: Texts and Interviews 1975–1995*, translated by Ames Hodges and Mike Taormina (New York: Semiotext(e), 2006), p. 290.

Bearing the historical traces of the failure of all revolutions, the expressions are molded from objective document into allegory, from slogans, or brand images, to figures of the failure of all revolutions. As allegories (*theorems*, in Deleuzean), the images are opened up to the outside: they have different layers of meaning, and different kinds of signs collide in and across them. Images then can be said to function like signals, but differently than signs, insofar as a signal is a structure by which differentials of potential are distributed, a switching mechanism that assures the communication by way of *rapprochement* of distant, uneven images enabled here by Godard's method of the *in-between*.

Appropriation, Stoppage, Défilé

As we have seen, in the late 1960s and 1970s Godard began to appropriate images seeking to counter the speed of the transmission of information and visualities in the mass media, sometimes devoting considerable screen time to discussing and analyzing still and halted images. Notably for 52 minutes, in the controversial *Letter to Jane: An Investigation About a Still*, Godard and Gorin discuss an image that appeared in the French journal *L'Express* of Jane Fonda's (1972) visit to Hanoi to support the communist struggle. For some, the film is a misogynous lynching of the actress' political efforts; the film can also be read as an analysis of the contradictions of activism unaware of the power relations at stake, which the filmmakers make it their task to render legible. Another device Godard has used is the staging of the autonomous transmigration of images, making processions of cut-out images from journals and magazines or with postcards that he passes under the camera's lens. The early versions of the procession for example, in *Les Carabiniers* (1963) were a reference to André Malraux's *musée imaginaire* (which he first conceived in 1947) for which he would assemble, disassemble and reassemble montages of photographic images. Malraux's "museum without walls" accounts for the new status of art on the eve of mechanical reproduction and so does Godard with these early processions. Arguably, Godard's processions from the 1970s, which also implied slowing down images, for instance, in *Ici et ailleurs, Comment ça va?, Six fois deux*, and *France tour détour* seek to account for images being seen as 'events' and 'information' as opposed to 'presences'. As we have also seen, Godard and Miéville posited the "chains of images" in the mass media as analogous to DNA chains, to hotel chains, to assembly chains and to chains of subjects. As the voice-over of *Ici et *ailleurs*, Godard asks, "Comment s'organise une chaîne?"[97] "How is a chain organized?" refers not only to the economy of images and to their transmigration in the media, but to montage and to the genetic element of cinema: the chains of still images or "photograms" in the filmstrip. In Vertov's *Man with a Movie Camera* (1929), there is a sequence in which we are shown a piece of filmstrip followed by a series of static images from other sequences from the film singled out and repeated. As the images begin to move, Vertov underscores the photogram as the genetic element in film. Here, the photogram is the source of movement in cinema insofar as it is "chained" to a mechanical procession of still images from the filmstrip. According to Thierry Kuntzel, the function of the parade of photograms is of the dialectical order of the presence/absence of the image, underscoring that what defines the filmic apparatus is neither movement nor stasis, but what is in between the film projecting and the photograms chained in the film strip: the parade of the virtual and mechanical passage of photograms that is being made visible in the projection.[98] Taking Kuntzel further, Serge Daney argues that the apparatus of the procession of photograms has a double sense, as in the double meaning of the word *défiler* in French: parade *and* procession.

Serge Daney theorized Godardian processions, which are not exclusively made of appropriated or stopped images, but also of people walking in front of the camera. The first such procession appears in *Tout va bien* during the demonstration accompanying the funeral of the Maoist activist Pierre Overney. One by one, the activists pass in front of the camera, hands up in the air.[99] In *Ici et ailleurs* we see procession staged in the studio: five actors line up to walk in front of the camera, holding enlarged stills of the Palestinian Revolution's images. The procession is repeated four times, enacting not only the succession of the cinematic frames in the filmstrip but the becoming image of bodies, figures and events in film: the transformation or *translation* of flesh and the space it occupies into time. The parade sequence of bodies and photograms from *Ici et ailleurs* has been extensively commented on, and it is not only a reference to Vertov's *Man with a Movie Camera* but to the first Lumière brothers film from

---

[97] "How is a chain organized?"
[98] See Thierry Kuntzel, "Le défilement," in *Cinéma: Théorie, Lectures*, edited by Dominique Noguez (Paris: Klincksieck, 1973).
[99] See Christa Blümlinger, "Procession and Projection: Notes on a Figure in the Work of Jean-Luc Godard," in *For Ever Godard* (London: Tate, 2004), p. 178.

1895, which depicts a parade of workers coming out from a factory. The Lumières made other "défilé" movies, filming parades of the army, cyclists, schoolchildren and so on.[100] In these procession-films, the camera is conventionally placed in such a way that the bodies come out from the vanishing point in the frame and move toward the viewer before passing the camera and going out of field.

In the processions in *Ici et ailleurs*, every image is represented by a body, and each image is accompanied by one of the five slogans that frame the Palestinian images (turning them into slogan-images): "The People's Will," "The Armed Struggle," "The Political Work," "The Long War" and "Until Victory." After Godard asks in the voice-over: "Comment s'organise une chaîne?" he asks, "Comment construire sa propre image?"[101] to draw a link between the procession of bodies before the camera and the projection of photograms; as Christa Blümlinger noted, Godard is highlighting here the becoming visible and utterable of the visible and the sayable.[102] In the meta-cinematographic episode of *Ici et ailleurs*, the procession may be further read as a sequence of immobile images that, as coded in film, cannot be placed next to each other or halted during the projection. Thus in *Ici et ailleurs*, Godard privileges video over cinema because, as we have seen, the video editing suite enables not only seeing two images simultaneously, but also to halt, rewind, fast-forward, juxtapose, superimpose and intervene in them. With the parade of bodies in front of the camera, moreover, Godard highlights the fact that film converts spatio-temporal "reality" into linear time in cinema, becoming a sum of temporal translations, transformations and displacements: "Cet espace n'est plus un tout, mais une somme de translations, une sorte de somme de traductions, une sorte de sentiments qui sont dans l'espace, c'est-à-dire, du temps // Et le film, c'est-à-dire, une somme des images à la chaîne // rend bien compte, au travers de cette série // d'images de ma double identité // espace et temps, enchaînés l'un à l'autre, comme deux travail-

---

[100] The workers' procession in the Lumière brothers' film is included in Harun Farocki's *Arbeiter verlassen die Fabrik* (1995), a film that cites instances of workers leaving the factory in the history of cinema, from *Metropolis* (1927), *Modern Times* (1936) and *Il deserto rosso* (1964). In Allan Sekula's *Untitled Slide Show* (1972) workers are shown coming out from a factory as well; some of them look directly into the camera lens as a way to acknowledge the engaged artist making their image.

[101] "How is a chain organized?" and "How does one construct one's own image?"

[102] Christa Blümlinger, "Procession and Projection," p. 178.

leurs sur la chaîne où chacun est à la fois la copie et l'original de l'autre."[103] Or, as Gilles Deleuze would put it: "Cinema does not reproduce bodies, it produces them with particles, and these are particles of time."[104]

The double movement of human forms and projected images that results from the *mise en scène* of images crossing the visible field shows the passage of the living to the moving image, or the "becoming image" of bodies. Another means by which Godard depicts this is by positing his characters as studies of the faces of the actors as they portray their role, for instance, Hanna Schygulla in *Passion* (1982). Godard's underlining of the process of the becoming images of bodies and faces is directly tied to his subscription to the paradigm of the iconic image. In *Passion* he tells for the first time the story of Bernadette "the seer." Shown going through a book of art history images of the Virgin Mary, Bernadette is the little shepherd girl who sighted the Virgin of Fatima. As the story goes, the nuns at a nearby convent asked Bernadette what the Virgin looked like. The girl was unable to describe her so they gave her a book of plates with reproductions of religious paintings. Bernadette recognized the lady she had seen in the grotto, pointing at the Cambrai Madonna, a Byzantine icon. Icon-sighting presupposes faith and it implies a becoming, not only as the image's status gets confirmed as a sacred imprint, but when the subject recognizes herself as a seer. With his experiments with the becoming bodies of images, Godard asks: what does it mean to make a person visible? Is it to incarnate an essence or to personify? Is it to make her voice audible? As we will see in the next chapter, one of Godard's concerns is that mass media and objectivity steal away voices from the bodies that utter them, thus he would make it his task to restitute the verb to the flesh, experimenting with bodies and discourses.

There are other processions in Godard's films: in *Grandeur et décadence d'un petit commerce de cinéma* (1986) we see a procession of unemployed extras, a parade of bodybuilders in *Armide* (1987) and fashion parades in the films that were commissioned by the Swiss fashion designers Marithé et François Girbaud (*On s'est tous défilé* and *Closed Jeans* series 1

---

[103] "This space is not a whole anymore, but a sum of translations, a kind of sum of translations, a kind of feeling in space, that is to say, in time. And the film which is, one might say, a sum of chained images, provides a good account throughout this series of images of my double identity, space and time, chained to each other like two workers on an assembly line where each is at the same time the copy and the original of the other."

[104] Pascal Bonitzer et al., "The Brain is the Screen: An Interview With Gilles Deleuze," in Gilles Deleuze, *Two Regimes of Madness*, p. 291.

and 2). In these parades, Godard posits the question of the becoming brands of images, their becoming information, their becoming commodities, which for him means their desacralization; or, the fact that images no longer render present bodies, but transform them into things to be consumed. This is why for Godard the "becoming image" of bodies becomes an obsession; how to transform bodies into presences-images? Beyond information, merchandise, events? This is why he ceaselessly films "parades" of bodies passing in front of the camera, so as to study "the becoming image of bodies". In other words, his exploration of "brand images" in relationship to history and the mass media in *Ici et ailleurs* is translated in these films into an inquiry about the relationship between commodification, image and subjectivity. *Grandeur et décadence d'un petit commerce de cinéma* (1986) is a feature-length film in which Godard explores relationships between voice, text and body and their becoming image. To create the *défilé*, Godard uses the format of the casting; the narrative revolves around a search for actors in a film for public television based on *The Soft Centre* (1964) by noir novelist James Hadley Chase. The extras of the film are played by unemployed people from the ANPE (the French Unemployment Agency), and parallel to the search for actors is a search for a film and thus a search for the birth of images and narrative. Gaspard Bazin (Jean-Pierre Léaud) is a frustrated screenwriter, now devoted only to doing screen tests, who discusses with Jean Almereyda (Jean-Pierre Mocky), a producer, the meaning and purpose of the *petit commerce du cinéma* before the industry of television that is destroying it. The film begins with people lining up in the street outside a door; once a woman lets them in, they begin to pass in front of the secretary, facing the camera, to tell her their age and phone number. As in *Ici et ailleurs*, we see different regimes of images co-existing in the film: the actors' portraits in black and white pass through the screen, and then their images in the video camera's small screen as they walk in front of it. We also see Léaud flipping through an art history book where he points at Tintoretto's *The Origin of the Milky Way* (1575) (which, as we learn from *Scénario du film Passion*, is the analogical origin of *Passion* as it is of the fragmented sub-narrative in *Grandeur et décadence*). Two characters (whom we learn later are unemployed actors, *chômeurs*) watch Dita Parlo in Jean Renoir's *La Grande illusion* (1937) which we know will take a predominant role in *Histoire(s) du cinéma*, and review a poster of Antonioni's *L'Avventura*, as well as a self-portrait by Rembrandt (in which, we hear, he "resembles Molière"). The *chômeurs* pass by the camera a second time shot from the side and each utters a sentence from a passage from Faulkner's "Sepulture South: Gaslight" (1940). In the short story, a four-year-old boy contemplates a state funeral procession foregrounded by the passage of the Stations succeeding one another. The child describes their empty looks as if they were defending their own weight against the dead, defenseless against the anguish and pain of inhumanity. Godard here juxtaposes life and death as well as "true" and "untrue," "original" and "facsimile" actors and images. The representativity of those "on the periphery"—the *chômeurs* who appear in the film—is fragmented in *Grandeur et décadence*: we only learn that the actors are unemployed from the credits at the end, so they appear as images of themselves but stripped of working-class discourse. Rather, they embody Faulkner's words: the literal passage of the anguish and the pain of humanity before the camera. We get a hint of where the working class is at when we hear in the soundtrack a fragment of Janis Joplin's song "Mercedes Benz." The consumerist society is the background of the film and is not only the cause of the *décadence* of independent cinema, but where the dreams and desires of the working class are now deposited.

The becoming merchandise of images, bodies and subjectivity—and the investment of images in the libidinal economy—is a sign of the capitalist integration of an array of mechanisms that have melded together the economic and the social. In *Schick Aftershave* (1971), a commissioned commercial, Godard and Gorin show a couple beginning their morning routine that ends in him shaving using "Schick"; the actors react comically and in wonder to the aftershave, while their routine is intermittently interrupted by a radio transmission informing them about a raid, presumably in the Palestinian Territories. Godard and Gorin parody the commodity's status as fetish, while they divert the viewer's attention *outside* of the advertisement space and toward the space of transnational politics. But as the economy and the social became indissociable by the 1980s, the ads designed by Godard and Miéville for the Swiss fashion designers Marithé et François Girbaud would reflect the incipient semiotization of production, a specific procedure of valorization of merchandise, activities and services based on systems of symbolization and particular syntax.[105] In these ads, Godard explores the links between merchandise and the becoming images of bodies, which also feature *défilés*. *On s'est tous défilé* (1988) is composed of heterogeneous elements that deliver complex associations; it shows a fashion parade by the Girbauds juxtaposed with Mallarmé's texts from *Divagations* (Mallarmé wrote fashion articles, it seems). Godard

---

[105] Félix Guattari, *Les années d'hiver*, pp. 167, 168.

further juxtaposes an ad for Charles Jourdan shoes with the nude figure painted by Michelangelo above the Persian Sybil in the Sistine Chapel, and images of people walking on the streets of Paris juxtaposed with Rococo portraits by Pietro Longhi depicting the banalities of the daily lives of eighteenth-century Venetians (including scenes of hairdressing, dressmaking, dancing, bowing when greeting, drinking coffee, gambling and flirting) as well as paintings by Cranach, Velázquez, Goya and so on. The shots of the Parisians on the street are the images of the atomized French consumerist society of the 1980s, which the voice-over compares or designates as "specters," highlighted by the film's communication of anxiety and the impending need to escape (*se défiler* means to slip away in French). We also see close-ups of the face of François Girbaud juxtaposed with the image of one of the models undoing her sandal. In the film, Godard uses extreme slow motion and reverse motion to distend the sequences, conveying a sensation of rawness; in between movement and stasis, the images oscillate between pre-fabricated images (or clichés, the essence of advertising, a brand image) and the becoming image of bodies passing in front of the camera. The slowing down of the images can be understood as a visual attack on the televisual flow of images, and Godard's experiments with decompositions into broken movements as an actual, self-reflexive destruction of the defilement as the televisual flow of images. The parade is further decomposed when the succession of images/bodies is alternated with shots of different elements. The formal strategies Godard deploys here make visible to the viewer the practice of gazing, of contemplating, as opposed to consuming images.[106] Finally, in *On s'est tous défilé*, Godard experiments with the reduction of figures to single semiotic matter and their disjunction from the background; the image of the figure of history to come is in the gap between stasis and movement, slowing down and *vidéo-mélange*. What comes across with the slowed-down figures are the pre-fabricated capitalist identities inextricable from production relations and welded with state and commercial infrastructure. The first series of *Closed Jeans* (1988) also shows a parade of images: a model and stand-in for Bernadette de Soubirous flips through an art history book saying "no" to paintings by Velázquez, Manet, Renoir, El Greco and finally "yes" to an ad of Girbaud "Closed Jeans." This sequence is repeated a few times and, in between them, we see photographic sessions with the models. Here Godard emphasizes the becoming merchandise of bodies, subjectivities and images, the subjectivities pre-fabricated by the mass media contrasted

---

[106] Christa Blümlinger, "Procession and Projection," 178.

with the history of painting. The parades of art history images qualified by "yes" or "no" pre-figure Godard and Miéville's *Vrai faux passeport* (2006), in which they juxtapose an array of images to be qualified as "good" or "bad," "true" or "false."

Passion and *Le Rapport Darty*: Materialist Filmmaking, *Encore*

On May 22, 1982 Godard was invited to present his film *Passion* via satellite from Cannes in the Antenne 2 Midi program, interviewed by the anchor Philippe Labro (see page 119). Live on air, Godard was asked to comment on the news given about the Falkland wars, about which the French broadcaster had received contradictory information from both sides. Godard stated that the images they had shown in the broadcast were poor and could not say a lot. He also established two things that are relevant to understand his filmic practice of the 1980s: first, that he *works with images* and that he uses images to *see things*. Second, that in cinema he seeks to show the invisible: moments like passion between two workers at Citroën, which he makes analogous to the Argentinians and the British. He states: "my job is to see, I am a scientist, poets are *voyants* (seers)." In *Scénario du film Passion*,[107] we see him filmed from behind sitting in front of a blank screen as he declares: "Avant de parler, je veux voir. J'ai cherché à voir."[108] In more ways than one, *Passion* marks a shift in Godard's work: the blank screen or blank canvas would begin to appear regularly in his films from then on. For Serge Daney, the blank screen is an analogy for the director: as a result of his own method of appropriating images, texts, sounds and quotes, Godard is himself the medium, the blank screen on which images and sounds co-exist, neutralize, recognize, designate and struggle with each other.[109] Taking this further, as we have seen, Kaja Silverman posits Godard as the embodiment of a blank screen, a "pure receiver." Similar to

---

[107] The "*scénario*" is a genre invented by Godard, generally videos; in them Godard annotates, explores, explicates and reflects upon his films, technique, sources. His first *scénario* could be said to be his seven minute monologue at the beginning of *Numéro deux*. Later ones are: *Passion, le travail et l'amour: introduction à un scenario,ou Troisième état du scénario du film Passion, Quelques remarques sur la réalisation et la production du film 'Sauve qui peut (la vie),' Petites notes à propos du film Je vous salue, Marie.*

[108] "Before speaking, I want to see. I have sought to see."

[109] Serge Daney, "Le thérrorisé (pédagogie godardienne)," p. 33.

Veronica's veil, the director becomes the embodiment of surface onto which perceptual phenomena project themselves and at the same time, the wall from which such phenomena bounce back toward the spectators. Here *techne* "brings into being" and *poiesis* "brings into presence" and "unveils." In Silverman's Heideggerian reading of Godard, his double function as receptacle and reflector *offers* his own authorial death so that the world can appear.[110]

Godard's recourse to the blank screen as an analogy for authorship and as the origin of his search for "an image" is without a doubt linked to his turn to painting as providing the genealogy and acting as interlocutor (in the sense that mass media images were his and Miéville's interlocutors in the Sonimage films) of his work. Following Daniel Morgan, in the 1980s Godard turned to painting as a strategy to displace assumptions about the ontology of cinema (André Bazin's theory of the filmic image as the imprint, as a trace of the real) onto a more complicated relationship between the image and the historical world, based on classical representation and narrative strategies. That is to say, Godard's shift to painting, which is linked to the appearance of the blank canvas in his films, shows a concern with the appearances of images and our experience of them beyond a referential relation to the world,[111] and beyond the regime of the mass media. In *Passion*, Godard uses the history of painting and restaging paintings as a tool, on the one hand *to see*, and on the other, to *recount* the great moments of humanity registered in the history of painting, as we learn from *Scénario du film Passion*. *Passion* is composed in part of a collage of *tableaux vivants* of great paintings of European art history, for instance, Rembrandt's *Night Watch* (1642), Goya's *Execution of the Defenders of Madrid, 3rd May, 1808* (1814), Delacroix's *Entry of the Crusaders into Constantinople* (1840) and paintings by El Greco, Ingres, and others. In *Scénario* Godard states that the origin of the film is the love scene between a man and two women depicted by Tintoretto in *The Origin of the Milky Way* (1575). The man is Jerzy (Jerzy Radziwiłowicz), a filmmaker and the women are Isabelle (Isabelle Huppert), a rebellious factory worker, and Hanna (Hanna Schygulla), the wife of the factory owner. The world of staged paintings unfolds in a film studio

---

[110] Kaja Silverman, "The Author as Receiver," *October* no. 96 (Spring 2001), pp. 17–34, and Silverman's interview with Gareth James, in *I Said I Love. That is the Promise: The TVideo Politics of Jean-Luc Godard* (Berlin: oe + b Books, 2003).

[111] Daniel Morgan, *Late Godard and the Possibilities of Cinema* (Los Angeles; University of California Press, 2013), p. 26.

under the direction of Jerzy who is looking for a script or a story, and is juxtaposed with the world of a factory. Both worlds come together as the workers move in between the factory and the film studio: Jerzy hires some of the factory's workers as actors to appear in his staged paintings and falls in love with Isabelle. *Passion*, like *Ici et ailleurs*, is avowedly about the "in-between," borne out of the juxtaposition of heterogeneous elements. For instance, the spaces "in between" the factory and the world of cinema are a gas station, a hotel, Jerzy's hotel room, a restaurant, a highway, which are all places where the film's narrative develops. "Passion" itself is situated by Godard at the crossing of work and love. Furthermore, for Godard, between film work and factory work there is "artifice." Aside from juxtapositions, there are other tropes such as analogy: the factory is analogous to cinema; the film's narrative is analogous to Tintoretto's painting; Jerzy is a stand-in for Godard; Hanna Schygulla's is analogous to the screenshots Jerzy makes of her; and service is analogous to entertainment when a young waitress brings food to Jerzy's room and then performs a gymnastics act. There are also hypostatizations: power relations hypostatize into physical struggles and tensions into violence; and money into the image, and to the image of film equipment. Godard also juxtaposes a metaphor, or illusion with reality, when we see a scene toward the end in which a boat that is used as a prop in the *mises en scène* of paintings crosses an outdoor field populated by characters, ready to pose for the paintings.

The world described by *Passion* is gradually brought into existence on a blank screen: a form of work, the work of seeing the passage from the invisible to the visible. Because of the fact that the film is not based on a script—as are some of his other films from that period—Godard privileges the primacy of the act of *trying to see* facing the blank screen and before speech (the narrative of many of Godard's films from the 1980s is the search for the narrative, for a story, for a script). The search for speech, for text, reflects the crisis of the workers' representativity hypostatized in Isabelle's stammering speech and in the failed strike that unfolds in the film when a group of female workers attempts to impede the entrance of a car driven by the owners into the factory.

By 1982 the Marxist narrative of the proletariat leading to emancipation and change, together with its role as the key historical and political figure, had waned. As Félix Guattari put it, militantism came to be impregnated by a rancid church smell that elicited a legitimate gesture of rejection.[112] And yet Godard would invoke Marx by superimposing his engraved portrait over a factory machine, over employees from a retail shop, over children in toy cars in his and Miéville's 40-minute video-essay *Le Rapport Darty* (1989).

As we hear in the voice-over, the film was commissioned by "Nathanael and Mme. Clio," the stand-ins of Godard and Miéville, by the CEOs at Darty—a multinational electrical retail company that by 1988 had opened its one hundredth store in Europe—to do an *enquête* or investigation into the identity and history of their stores. The film begins with an image of a Darty store while we hear a group of employees discussing their time of leaving the store with their manager: the store closes at 19.30, but they can never leave on time. In that regard, *Le Rapport Darty* is a portrait of an incipient new class of workers and forms of capitalist relationships. The film shows how economic relations are linked to material forces and to human labor, and how social relations and the investment of desire are the raw matter of capitalism. By 1989, capitalism was *everywhere* and had integrated all kinds of technical, economic, conceptual, religious and aesthetic mechanisms. In Guattari's words, capitalism had become a mode of semiotization, incorporating language, syntax, desire and subjectivity into the production processes.[113]

In their *enquête*, Mme. Clio and Nathanael give themselves the task of delving into the identity of the store, parting from Paul Gaugin's existential questions which serve as the title of his 1897 post-impressionist painting that depicts the life of Tahitian aboriginals: "D'où venons-nous? Que sommes-nous? Où allons-nous?"[114] As in *Passion* and other films from the 1980s, the source of the film is an image from the history of painting; here, the Darty corporation and Tahitian aboriginals are rendered analogous as neither has a history of their own, in the Western sense of the word. Reminiscent of Godard's working method since *Le Gai savoir*, the couple states that they have taken up the task to see images, to listen to sounds, to see sounds and to listen to images. In this video-essay, while Mme. Clio's voice is unfaltering and clear in her declarations, statements

---

[112] Félix Guattari, *Les années d'hiver*, p. 67.
[113] Ibid. p. 169.
[114] "Where Do We Come From? What Are We? Where Are We?"

and analyses about consumerism and capitalism, the male voice lacks a text, a speech. Nathanael, the first disciple to express belief in Jesus Christ as the Son of God, *a seer,* stammers or repeats in slow motion whatever Mme. Clio has said. They further declare as their mission: "To listen to (capitalist) speech that is said as an order" and to "seek for a prophetic speech to see beyond this (capitalist) speech." Here, Godard's effort to create chains of relationships between images and sounds, texts and speech seems to be non-existent. Images can only be superimposed, one on top of the other, in a metaphor of capitalist power relations and the specter of class struggle. We see *superimpositions* of Darty shops and workers inside dealing with clients or in meetings with their bosses. Like scientists or researchers, Godard and Miéville seek to observe in the footage they took of the Darty shops and employees the new social relationships. The film is a *rapport* in the double sense of the word: a report of the state of affairs and a relationship (new social and production relations). When we see footage of workers interacting with customers, they state: "C'est de la mise en charme",[115] pinpointing the new forms of labor—affective, cognitive, based on communication skills and relationships—brought by capitalist semiotization, what Franco (Bifo) Berardi would theorize two decades later from a post-workerist standpoint as "Semiocapitalism." What is now incorporated into the capitalist process are relationships of credit, trust, hope, and what is exchanged, according to them, are "civilities" (affective labor), not merchandise. Another superimposition that reflects the new relationships is footage of a Hollywood film showing a medieval knight on his horse superimposed on a Darty salesman: the new consumerism is a "chevalier" attack on the social, as inequality deepens, misery grows and raw desire is materialized in commodities. As they write "Capitalism as Public Happiness" on the screen, they highlight the incipient displacement of the state by the corporation, and the fact that the present forms of riches are decomposing and mocking humanity, leading to misery. As might be expected, the film's commissioners are not pleased with the "mirror" of Darty that Godard and Miéville have presented to them. The film ends with Godard declaring his ongoing search for images in the context of a consumerist society posited as a loss of direction, analogous to Gaugin's interrogation: "D'où venons-nous? Que sommes-nous? Où allons-nous?"

---

[115] "It is about being charming."

Bibliography

Agamben, Giorgio. "Le cinéma de Guy Debord," in *Image et mémoire: Écrits sur l'image, la danse et le cinéma* (Paris: Desclée de Brouwer, 2004)
Aumont, Jacques. *Amnésies: Fictions du cinema d'après Jean-Luc Godard* (Paris: POL, 1999).
Badiou, Alain. "The Communist Hypothesis," *New Left Review* 49 (January–February 2008). Available at: http://newleftreview.org/II/49/alain-badiou-the-communist-hypothesis
Barthes, Roland. "The Third Meaning," in *Image, Music, Text* (New York: Hill and Wang, 1977)
Baudrillard, Jean. *La societé de consommation: ses mythes, ses structures* (Paris: Gallimard, 1974)
Benjamin, Walter. (N3, I) *Das Passagen-Werk* (Frankfurt: Suhrkamp, 1982)
Benveniste, Émile. *Problèmes de linguistique générale* 1 (Paris: Gallimard, 1966)
Bergala, Alain. "Images de Marque," *Cahiers du cinéma* special issue (July–August 1976)
Bergala, Alain. "Le pendule (La photo historique stéréotypée)." *Cahiers du Cinéma*, nos. 268–269
Berger, John. "Understanding a Photograph" in Nikos Stangos (ed.) *The Look of Things* (New York: The Viking Press, 1972)
Blümlinger, Christa. "Procession and Projection: Notes on a Figure in the Work of Jean-Luc Godard," in *For Ever Godard* (London: Tate, 2004)
Bonitzer, Pascal. "The Silences of the Voice" (1975), in *Narrative, Apparatus, Ideology: A Film Theory Reader*, edited by Philip Rosen (Columbia: The University Press, 1986)
Bonitzer, Pascal. "La surimage," *Cahiers du Cinema* no. 270 (September–October), 1976
Bonitzer, Pascal. *Le regard et la voix* (Paris: Union Générale d'Éditions, 1976)
Borges, Jorge-Luis. *Ficciones* (Buenos Aires: Emecé, 1958)
Bracken, Len. *Guy Debord: Revolutionary, A Critical Biography* (Venice, CA: Feral House, 1997)
Crary, Jonathan. "Spectacle, Attention, Counter-Memory," in *Guy Debord and the Situationist International: Texts and Documents*, edited by Tom McDonough, (Cambridge, MA: MIT Press, 2004)
Crary, Jonathan. "Techniques of the Observer," *October* 45 (Summer 1988)
Daney, Serge and Toubiana, Serge. "Présentation," *Cahiers du Cinéma*, nos. 268–269, special issue "Images de Marque" (July–August 1976)
Daney, Serge. "Le thérrorisé (pédagogie godardienne)," *Cahiers du Cinéma*, nos. 262–263 (January 1976), 32–39
Delavaud, Gilles. "Composer (avec) le réel: *Trois Chants sur Lénine*," in Jean-Pierre Esquenazi (ed.) *Vertov, L'invention du réel!* (Paris: L'Harmattan, 1997)

Deleuze, Gilles. *Cinema 1: The Movement Image* (Minneapolis: The University of Minnesota Press, 1986)

Deleuze, Gilles. "Portrait of the Philosopher as a Moviegoer," *Two Regimes of Madness: Texts and Interviews 1975–1995*, translated by Ames Hodges and Mike Taormina (New York: Semiotext(e), 2006)

Deleuze, Gilles. "The Brain is the Screen: An Interview with Gilles Deleuze on the Time Image," *Discourse* Vol. 20, No. 3 (Fall 1998), pp. 55–71

Deleuze, Gilles. "Trois questions sur *Six fois deux: A propos de sur et sous la communication*," *Cahiers du Cinéma* No. 271 (Novembre 1976)

Deleuze, Gilles. *A Thousand Plateaux* (Minneapolis: The University of Minnesota Press, 2003)

Deleuze, Gilles. *The Fold: Leibniz and the Baroque* (Minneapolis: The University of Minnesota Press, 1992)

Deleuze, Gilles. *Time-Image Cinema 2*, trans. Hugh Tomlinson and Robert Galeta (Minneapolis: The University of Minnesota Press, 2001)

Derrida, Jacques. *Et cetera (and so on, und so weiter, and so forth, et ainsi de suite, und so überall, etc.)* (Paris, L'Herne, 2005)

Diderot, Denis. *Diderot's Early Philosophical Works*, trans. Margaret Jourdain, (New York: Burt Franklin, 1972)

Ducrot, Oswald. *Logique, structure, énonciation: Lectures sur le langage* (Paris: Éditions de Minuit, 1989)

Elgey, Georgette. *Front Populaire* (Paris: Chêne/Magnum, 1976)

Fargier, Jean-Paul. "Histoire de la vidéo française: Structures et forces vives" (1992), in *La vidéo, entre art et communication*, ed. Nathalie Magnan (Paris: École Nationale Supérieure des Beaux-Arts, 1997)

Godard, Jean-Luc. "Propos Rompus," in *Jean-Luc Godard par Jean-Luc Godard*, (Paris: L'Étoile et Cahiers du Cinéma, 1985)

Goodman, Nelson. *Languages of Art: An Approach to a Theory of Symbols* (Indianapolis: Hackett, 1976)

Gorin, Jean-Pierre. "Interview by Christian Braad Thomsen, *Jump Cut* no. 3 (1974), pp. 17–19

Guattari, Félix. *Les années d'hiver 1980–1985* (Paris: Barrault, 1986)

Heude, Remi-Pierre. *L'image-marque* (Paris: Eyrolles, 1989)

Ishaghpour, Youssef. *Archéologie du cinéma et mémoire du siècle* (Tours: Farrago, 2004)

Klein, Naomi. *No Logo* (New York: HarperCollins, 2000)

Kristeva, Julia. "The Subject in Process" in Patrick Ffrench and Roland-François Lack, *The Tel Quel Reader* (London and New York: Routledge, 1998)

Kuntzel, Thierry. "Le défilement," in *Cinéma: Théorie, Lectures*, edited by Dominique Noguez (Paris: Klincksieck, 1973)

Lyotard, Jean-François. *Discours, Figure* (Paris: Klincksieck, 1971)

Marks, Laura U. "Signs of Time" in Gregory Flaxman (ed.) *The Brain is the Screen* (Minneapolis: The University of Minnesota Press, 2000)

Michelson, Annette. "From Magician to Epistemologist: Vertov's *The Man with a Movie Camera*," *Artforum* (March 1972)

Morgan, Daniel. *Late Godard and the Possibilities of Cinema* (Los Angeles; University of California Press, 2013)

Péguy, Charles. *Clio: Dialogue de l'histoire et de l'âme païenne* (Paris: Gallimard, 1932)

Pliny the Elder, *Natural History*. Available at http://www.perseus.tufts.edu/cgi-bin/ptext?lookup=Plin.+Nat.+toc

Reichart, Wilfried. "Interview mit Jean-Luc Godard," *Filmkritik* no. 242, Februar 1977) reprinted in *Video Apparat/Medium, Kunst, Kultur, ein internationaler Reader*, edited by Siegfried Zielinski (Frankfurt: Peter Lang, 1992)

Rodowick, David. *Reading the Figural, or, Philosophy After the New Media* (Durham, NC: Duke University Press, 2001)

Silverman, Kaja. "The Author as Receiver," *October* no. 96 (Spring 2001)

Silverman, Kaja. Interview with Gareth James, in *I Said I Love. That is the Promise: The TVideo Politics of Jean-Luc Godard* (Berlin: oe + b Books, 2003)

Sontag, Susan. *Regarding the Pain of Others* (New York: Farrar, Straus and Giroux, 2003)

Vertov, Dziga. *Kino-Eye: The Writings of Dziga Vertov* (Berkeley: University of California Press, 1984)

Witt, Michael. *Jean-Luc Godard, Cinema Historian* (Bloomington and Indianapolis: Indiana University Press, 2013)

CHAPTER 5

Representing the Unrepresentable: Restitution, Archive, Memory

Witness-Images, Alienated Subjectivities and Restitution

In an article written in 1991, Elias Sanbar, the Palestinian intellectual, translator and Middle East liaison for the Dziga Vertov Group, recalls being present during the filming in Jordan of four fedayeen discussing a failed operation in the Occupied Territories.[1] This shot became the last 10 minutes of *Ici et ailleurs*. As Sanbar recalls, Jean-Luc Godard had wanted to film "live" the statement of account of a commando unit that had just returned from an operation in the Territories. Sanbar describes the four men covered in sweat, displaying bodily tension, on the verge of a breakdown. Two members of the commando unit were lying prostrate with exhaustion and the rest were directing their anger toward the commander. After that, Sanbar tells us, Godard asked them to sit down in front of the camera to discuss their operation in terms of self-critique. Sanbar further recalls sitting beside Godard at his editing table two years after filming, translating the conversation amongst the fedayeen: "Vous êtes des inconscients, notre ennemi est féroce et ne prend pas les choses à la légère (comme vous). Cela fait trois fois que les unités de reconnaissance nous font traverser le Jourdain au même endroit et cela fait trois fois que

---

[1] Elias Sanbar, "Vingt et un ans après," *Traffic* no. 1 (1991), pp. 115–122.

l'ennemi nous y attend et que nous perdons des frères...."[2] Then, they insulted each other, an action rather removed from the Marxist-Leninist self-critique the DVG wanted to film. Looking at this material in 1972 was shocking for both Godard and Sanbar; for the former, because he realized that he had not "listened" to the revolutionaries. For the latter, he says, because he had been deafened by theories and unfaltering convictions that had caused him to idealize the struggle in spite of the fedayeen's discussion being in his own language. In other words, theories and convictions had "covered" up what the fedayeen were saying along with the fact that their dialogue was not self-critique, but a matter of survival. It is true that in the euphoric eruption of revolutions and enthusiasm that fuel them, the necessary risks and sacrifices are forgotten as well as the fact that political struggles are, in truth, a matter of life and death.

In the voice-over that accompanies this scene, Godard reiterates that "his" voice as a Maoist had covered up the voices of the men and women they had filmed, denying and reducing them to nothing. While they highlight the need to show and listen to images of Palestinians, Godard and Anne-Marie Miéville draw a line in the film in their engagement with their cause. Like other Western sympathizers, they condemn and lament the wave of terrorism that followed the Black September massacres of the fedayeen and refugee bases in Jordan. At the end of *Ici et ailleurs* (referencing the terrorist operation in Munich in 1972), they state: "on est sûrs qu'il y avait autre chose à faire... on trouve con le fait de devoir mourir pour sa propre image... ça nous fait peur."[3] Along similar lines, Sylvère Lotringer wrote: "In 1974 we were in the last gasp of Marxism and I knew the terrorists were right, but I could not condone their actions. That is still the way I feel right now."[4] Godard's shocked voice in the voice-over states that, in the face of the outcome of the Palestinian resistance: "On a filmé les acteurs du film en danger de mort."[5] Sketching out the links between resistance, revolution, television, cinema and journalism, the film

---

[2] "You are completely irresponsible, our enemy is ferocious and unlike us, they take things very seriously. That makes three times that the reconnaissance units have made us cross the Jordan River at the exact same spot and three times that the enemy has been waiting for us there and that we have lost brothers." Ibid., p. 116.

[3] "We are certain that there was something else to do... we feel that dying for the sake of our image is foolish ... it makes us afraid."

[4] "Introduction: The History of Semiotext(e)," in *Hatred of Capitalism* (Los Angeles: Semiotext(e), 2001), p. 10.

[5] "We were filming the actors while they were in deadly danger."

ends with a plea to show the image of a refugee camp in Western television: "Passez cette image de temps en temps."[6]

As we have seen, Sonimage's ethical-political imperative becomes to take enunciative responsibility for *speaking* images (acknowledging authorship over them), to make images speak, and to restore the speech that has been taken away from them. In that regard, following Serge Daney, Godard's filmic project is a painful meditation on the topic of reparation, an effort of giving back images and sounds to those from whom they had been stolen.[7] For Daney, this restitution-reparation takes place, at least ideally, in *Ici et ailleurs*, where representation becomes a matter of restitution of the voice grounded in the task to transform "signs" into living presences.

By the mid-1970s, the media had become the privileged site for ethical-political intervention in the name of human rights, particularly in light of the Leftist belief in its emancipatory potential. Stripped of Leftist ideology, engaged intellectuals began speaking for others from the standpoint of a depoliticized universal "we" and an objective "it speaks" embedded in the non-discourse of rights from within a community of civilized nations. By the late 1970s, human rights had entitled everyone to equality and visibility as well as the right to be informed and the right to be heard and to bear witness: "the world thus began to see itself in the media, ready to hear and speak, discuss, protest, explain themselves, look at ourselves as humans fulfilling the duty of making rights prevail."[8] The discourse of human rights, however, is problematic because it claims to do unquestionable good and to have a prescriptive status that is independent of political interests. But this only proves that the wrongs of the unfit should be solved by those who are fittest, as Gayatri Chakravorty Spivak puts it, which is an agenda of a kind of Social Darwinism: it is the "white man's burden" to civilize and develop those who cannot constitute themselves politically.[9] In such a dynamic, images are used to validate humanitarian aid, and the human rights are alibis for economic, military and political

---

[6] "Display this image [of the Palestinians] from time to time [on Western television]."

[7] Serge Daney, "Le thérrorisé (pedagogie godardienne)" *Cahiers du Cinema* No. 262–263, Special Issue: Five essays on Jean-Luc Godard's *Numéro deux* (1976), 39.

[8] Jean-François Lyotard, "The General Line" (1990), in *Political Writings* (Minneapolis: University of Minnesota Press, 1997), pp. 110–111.

[9] Gayatri Chakravorty Spivak, "Righting Wrongs," *South Atlantic Quarterly* 103, nos. 2–3 (Spring/Summer 2004), pp. 524–525.

intervention.[10] The impulse to denounce and to bear witness to the abuses of human rights was fueled by the professional foreign correspondents, documentarists and agents who served the industrial production of witness-images for a consumer market.[11]

Over the past 50 years, witness-images have sought to address a disinterested and liberal viewer who would potentially act upon the events on the screen; moral shame and indignation were believed to be the catalysts prompting outrage in the observer as a potential agent for intervention. Paradoxically, the media render the viewer impotent, as they present events to a spectator who consumes information passively. In parallel, we have seen "the witness's narrative" proliferate as a new mode of aesthetic expression linked to experimentations with modes of archiving, alternative forms of writing histories and to the predominance of documentary film. This narrative does not necessarily imply the recounting of an event as an act of witness; it's more of a *there was* that goes beyond thought. In this form of ethical-aesthetic expression, images and their origin are unquestionably "true" to each other: the space between face and voice is also obliterated, amalgamating them. Rendering the viewer unable to act upon the events depicted by the images shown on the screen, witness-images produce a form of "consensual stupor."[12] Political theorist Anita Chari situates this problematic form of spectatorship as the central capitalist pathology of reification. In her reading of Adorno and Lukács, she describes reification as a position of spectacular spectatorship without engagement that individuals assume toward the world and in relationship to their own practices and habits.[13] For Chari, under this pathology the economy exists as an apparently independent habit of human activity; reified subjectivity hinders a vision of one's own involvement in capitalist processes, fomenting the incapacity to understand forms of domina-

---

[10] See Michael Ignatieff, *Empire Lite: Nation-Building in Bosnia, Kosovo and Afghanistan* (Toronto: Penguin, 2003), pp. 45–74.

[11] See Jonathan Benthall, *Disasters, Relief and the Media* (London & New York: I.B. Tauris, 1993). This industry (as well as that of war photojournalism) has a history over 100 years old, accounted for by Susan Sontag in *Regarding the Pain of Others* (New York: Farrar, Straus, and Giroux, 2003).

[12] Jacques Rancière, *The Future of the Image* (London and New York: Verso, 2006), p. 47.

[13] Anita Chari, *A Political Economy of the Senses: Neoliberalism, Reification, Critique* (New York: Columbia University Press, 2015).

tion in the context of social totality. Thus, when it comes to the issue of human rights violations, the same discourse obliterates capitalism's role in such violations. Moreover, because of an excess of visibility, images of tragedies and violence elsewhere have lost their potential to call for an ethical or political response, while at the same time justifying economic, political and relief interventions that aim at "breaking in" by developing "intractable" problematic communities and subsuming them within international economic interests.[14]

The proliferation of witness-images has therefore led to a devalued experience insofar as images documenting the real are less and less intelligible. Jean Genet wrote that when we contemplate a dead body, or look closely at a dead person, a curious phenomenon happens: the absence of life in a body is the equivalent of its total absence; the dead body's image is its uninterrupted receding. Even if we approach the body, according to Genet, we will never touch it.[15] Alarmingly, the contemplation of the images of dead bodies has become an ethical intervention in itself, while its exposure is the most profound desubjectification as victims reinforce their status as "precarious life."[16] The problem is that images of violence, voluntarily or not, systematically violate the gap between the image, its origin and its destination, and the distance between the viewer and the support of the image, creating a continuum where any kind of possibility of alterity is misled. Godard, as we will see, posits the issue of images that witness violence, death and war as a matter of the terms and the *place that is given to the viewer* with regards to the screen (or support) as a matter of regulating the distance to what is seen. Moreover, for Godard, an image depicting violence must allow us to identify the irrepresentable in the visible, and thus can only be sustained in dissimilitude, in the gap between the visible and the subject of the gaze, which is instituted by the voice.[17]

Evidently, the question of the image in Godard is inextricably bound to alterity and thus to politics. As we have seen, the Image (as opposed to

---

[14] Gayatri Chakravorty Spivak, "Righting Wrongs," pp. 524–525.
[15] Jean Genet, "Quatre Heures à Chatila," *Revue d'études palestiniennes* no. 6 (January 1983), p. 9.
[16] Judith Butler, *Precarious Life: The Power of Mourning and Violence* (London and New York: Verso, 2006), pp. 33–34.
[17] Marie-José Mondzain, *L'Image, peut-elle tuer?* (Paris: Bayard, 2002), p. 54.

a picture, or cliché)[18] is a third image delivered by montage and bears redemptory power. This kind of image inscribes itself in the visible but without being fully visible. The force of this Image comes from the desire to see, from the belief in seeing, from building a gap between that which is given to see and the viewer. In his short film, *Changer d'image* (1982) Godard states: "any contract accepted with visibilities opens up as a collaboration with the enemy. To defend the image is to resist all that eliminates the alterity of the gazes that build the invisibility of sense. The force of the image is the measure of the power of the voices that inhabit it." Thus for Godard the visibility of sense relies in precisely maintaining the gap inherent in the alterity of the exchanges of gazes embedded in the image. For Godard, as we have seen, an image is a gaze cast upon another gaze already addressed to a third: for an image to deliver visibilities, it needs to embody an ethical pact negotiated amongst the gazes—to find the "just" distance amongst them—instituted by the voice, by the text. Clearly, in Godard the issue of aesthetico-political representation persists in his work as he incessantly asks, through his experimentations with images: to make someone visible, is it to allow her voice to be heard, is it to incarnate, or is it to personify? Is it to give speech to flesh or is it to give body to a discourse?

As we have seen, in the early 1980s Godard experimented with forms to "show the invisible." In parallel, he began to explore the history of painting as a source for his films. Godard's shift from photography or photograms as the source of film to painting implies a shift from *resemblance* and *selection* of material vestiges of an "original" to *interpretation*. As he brought a relationship of interpretation as opposed to resemblance to the core of the Image, Godard began to experiment with the Christian concept of the image as incarnation. Most notably in *Je vous salue, Marie* (1985), Mary is the condition of possibility of the image because the Verb took form in her body and became visible. Like Godard's blank screen—which began to appear often in his films and in the *scénarios* for his films, as we have seen—Mary has the power to conduct what is invisible by giving flesh and body to an image. In Christian theology, the "image of the invisible" is the apparition of Christ which presents a possibility of vision

---

[18] See Serge Daney, "Before and After the Image," trans. Melissa McMahon, *Discourse*, Vol. 21, No. 1, Middle Eastern Films Before Thy Gaze Returns to Thee (Winter 1999), pp. 181–190 originally published in French "Avant et après l'image", *Revue d'études palestiniennes* no. 40 (Summer 1991).

purified of sensuous immediacy and thus represents the promise of spirit's victory over dead matter. In Godard, "dead matter" is the spectral image that haunts the living in the present as televisual, informational, advertising and brand images. In *On s'est tous défilé* (1988), the figures are stripped of flesh and lack form and content; therefore, they are a mere surface, projecting themselves onto the world and giving it appearance. In this regard, Godard posits representation in television as a simulacrum that replaces the original with its own appearance whose presentation fails to deliver presence. Following Michael Witt, Godard's critique of television includes a theorization of what might constitute a real image in the age of mass media.[19]

In that regard, the Catholic concept of the image as Verb offered Godard the possibility of conceptualizing different techniques to give images back their flesh; a restitutive, redemptive act. Another Christian element that becomes key in Godard is the notion of the icon: the image as the unmediated imprint of the sacred, which is recognized by the seer (Bernadette) who encounters it. As in Christianity, in Godard the voice is at work at the heart of the image. According to the Christian notion of the image, the image is not a sign amongst others, but it has the power to *make visible*, to offer to the gaze spaces and bodies because it has the power to embody. Within this logic of representation, the visible depends on speech. The essence of speech is to *make seen*, thus speech refers, summons the absent, reveals the hidden. This form of making visible, however, operates through the paradox of its own failure to represent the totality of that which is absent. Therefore, through montage, Godard seeks to restitute, on the one hand, the belief in the image and, on the other, to give images—and thus the vanquished of history, the victims whose images circulate in the mass media or in documentary film like specters of themselves—back their flesh.

Representation and the Shoah: Forbidden Images, Forbidden Montage, Forbidden Testimony

Le Dernier mot (1988) is an eight-minute-long video that was commissioned by *Figaro* magazine to draw a portrait of the French. For the first time, Godard explicitly expresses a concern about the relationship of cin-

---

[19] Michael Witt, *Jean-Luc Godard, Cinema Historian* (Bloomington: Indiana University Press, 2013), p. 178.

ema to the Shoah. In the video, he addresses the past of World War II in the French present: it is the end of the war, there is a man about to die at the hands of German soldiers, and a visitor from the future—the son of the executed prisoner—travels back through time to witness the event. The German occupation of France, the organized Resistance against it, and the Shoah would be recurrent themes in Godard from then on. Three years before *Le Dernier mot* appeared, Claude Lanzmann's film *Shoah* was released. The nine-hour film expresses mistrust of representation and ambivalence toward direct images of the past. These are the reasons why Lanzmann refused to use archival images in his film, which is entirely based on testimony of the past in the present. The aesthetico-political problem the Shoah poses is that the extermination of European Jews shattered the possibility of representation itself, insofar as, as a historical event, it implied dehumanization to the point of the destruction of the field of perceptible reality. With *Histoire(s) du cinéma* (begun in 1988 and released in 1998, but whose origins date back to Godard's seminar in Montréal on the history of cinema in 1978), Godard engaged in a debate with Lanzmann about the ethics, politics and aesthetics of the representation of the catastrophe. Taking up further the issue of restitution and reparation of the redemptive image potentially offered by cinematic montage, Godard explored the power of image to make contact with historical reality and be effective in it, emphasizing montage's redemptive power. Lanzmann's and Godard's different positions *vis-à-vis* the representation of the Shoah initiated a heated debate in France, in which thinkers such as Jacques Rancière, Gérard Wajcman, Jean-Luc Nancy, Georges-Didi Huberman, Marie-José Mondzain and Bernard-Henri Lévy, as well as film critics like Alain Fleischer, Maurice Darmon, Céline Scemama, Richard Brody, Antoine de Baecque, amongst others, have been taking part.

Within the poles of the debate, either it is impossible to represent the extermination because the event itself exceeds thought and any attempts to render it legible risk banalizing it, and/or in connection with the biblical prohibition of representation, it is forbidden to do so. Therefore, Godard's debate with Lanzmann is based on the interrogation of whether images have the duty or the capacity to bear witness. "It showed nothing at all," was Godard's indictment of Lanzmann's *Shoah*. Lanzmann's strategy to evoke the horror of the elimination of European Jews by the Nazis is to narrate the absent in order to see horror in the face but without delivering an image of it. For Lanzmann and others, the very existence of the camps implies forbidden representation. Moses' ban on representation via the Kantian sublime has moreover informed claims that the Holocaust or Shoah is beyond representation and that it should not be retrieved within images.

We must bear in mind that for many, the twentieth century was the "era of the witness."[20] The first phase of this era was marked by visual testimony of the concentration and extermination camps when they were liberated in 1945. This visual consciousness was evidently filtered journalistically, militarily and politically. This phase was followed by the Eichmann Trial (1961–62), which marks the legitimization and empowerment of the victims' discourse by their new roles, not as victims but, as Shoshana Felman stated, as prosecution witnesses within a trial.[21] Primo Levi conceived witnessing itself as "incommunicable," as the obligation to work through the enunciation of the unsayable, which is the description of death at work. Thus the speech of the witness, which is a first-person narrative of suffering trauma, contains silence, distortion, confusion and terror. These traits were understood as the indexes of the traumatic character of the event embedded in the testimonies.[22] The narrative and emotional force of the testimonials conceived the (Eichmann) trial as a historical and political pedagogical vehicle to reach the hearts of men with the injunction: "Never to forget, so as not to let it happen again."

In a commemoration of the 60th anniversary of the liberation of Auschwitz, however, historians Annette Wieviorka and Georges Didi-Huberman spoke about a current "saturation of memory." For Wieviorka this means: "a perverse fascination for horror, a deadly taste for the past and the political instrumentalization of the victims." For Didi-Huberman, Auschwitz had been rendered "unsayable": a historical event more and more disconnected from its history. The Shoah had become a "concept, an abstraction and absolute limit of the namable, thinkable, and imaginable."[23] In spite of the existence and legibility of documentary and spoken testimony, the saturation of memory has to do with a crisis of legibility prompted by the series of interdictions regarding images, montage and testimony operating at the crux of the debate launched around Godard's and Lanzmann's different stands around the representation of the Shoah. That

---

[20] Annette Wieviorka, *The Era of the Witness* (Ithaca, NY: Cornell University Press, 2006).
[21] Thomas Keenan and Eyal Weizman, *Mengele's Skull: The Advent of a Forensic Aesthetics* (Frankfurt and Berlin: Portikus/Sternberg Press, 2012), p. 11.
[22] Ibid., p. 12.
[23] Georges Didi-Huberman, "Ouvrir les camps, fermer les yeux" (2005) chapter from *Remontages du temps subi. Annales. Histoire, Sciences Sociales* 2006/5 61e année, pp. 1011–1049.

is to say, when Didi-Huberman states that Auschwitz had been rendered unimaginable, he is referring, amongst other things, to the polarity and polemic around the ethics and aesthetics of the representability of the Shoah.

The lesson drawn from post-structuralism is that of the internal impossibility of representation. As Jacques Rancière pointed out, representation carries with it the impossibility of bringing forth the essence of the thing represented. No image can bring an absence before our eyes, because an image is incommensurable with what it represents. Rather, an image is the interplay between presence and absence, the material and the intelligible, exhibition and signification. When it comes to the Shoah, it is the nature of the event itself that renders its representation impossible.[24] Jean-Luc Nancy takes the issue of the representation of the Shoah further: in his view, Auschwitz is the devastation of the possibility of representation. In that sense, it implies a forbidden representation.[25] If representation is a gesture placing before the eyes a *mise en scène* of the absence of a thing, the death camp constitutes the stage for the spectacle of annihilation of what is non-representation, in as far as it implies the total destruction of what was already considered to be "non-human."[26] Thus, at Auschwitz, the space of representation was shattered and reduced to the presence of a gaze appropriating death for itself by filling itself up with the dead gaze of the other. How to represent devastated representation? For Nancy, Auschwitz cannot be translated into an image, but only remembered by humans removing the blemish the event left on the world. In this sense, Lanzmann's *Shoah* incessantly questions the possibility of its own staging or its refusal to stage, thematizing the unrepresentability produced by the devastation of representation, seeking to inscribe the wound in the texture of representation, as the truth of truths.[27] This is the reason why Lanzmann rejects the archive in favor of testimony. In his film, through the interviews, and by visiting the places where the events took place, Lanzmann seeks to access the past directly, the life of the past in the present.

---

[24] Jacques Rancière, "Are Some Things Unrepresentable?" in *The Future of the Image*, trans. Gregory Elliott (London: Verso, 2007), p. 109.
[25] Jean-Luc Nancy, "Forbidden Representation," in *The Ground of Images*, trans. Jeff Fort (New York: Fordham University Press, 2005), p. 38.
[26] Ibid.
[27] Ibid., p. 47.

For Godard, representation is necessary and showing the images of the camps "would change something." Regarding archival images of the Shoah, he made the following statement:

> Les camps, ça a été filmé sûrement en long et en large par les Allemands, donc les archives doivent exister quelque part, ça a été filmé par les Américains, par les Français, mais ça n'est pas montré parce que si c'était montré, ça changerait quelque chose. Et il ne faut pas que ça change. On préfère dire: plus jamais ça.[28]

Although this statement has granted him accusations of demanding proof of the events and thus of being a Holocaust denier, for Godard, the representation of the Shoah implies *seeing* delivered through montage juxtaposing incommensurable elements, including archival images of the events. In his book *Images malgré tout*, Georges Didi-Huberman discusses the existence of the archival images of Auschwitz, those remaining after the Nazis burnt their archives toward the end of the war, and the prisoners in charge of carrying out the task hid as many as they could from destruction. There remain about 4000 images. For Didi-Huberman, these kinds of "image-archives" are a historical perversity. That is to say, they are fetishistic images that show the historical perversity as proof, attesting to the "truth" produced by the event. Didi-Huberman also discusses the history and ethical implications of the four images taken in August 1944 by members of the Sonderkommando of Crematorium V at Auschwitz. He concludes that archive-images are inadequate, but necessary; inexact, but true. Any such image is the gaze of history with the vocation for making things visible that needs, in order to bear witness, to include an act of memory to combine language and image. For Didi-Huberman all three regimes of legibility of the past are in solidarity, exchanging incessantly reciprocal lacunae: an image comes when words fail, a word comes when imagination fails, because the "truth" of Auschwitz is indeed no more or less unimaginable than it is unsayable. For Didi-Huberman, as for Godard, if the horror of the camps defies imagination, it is necessary to rip images away from such experience.[29]

---

[28] "The camps were surely extensively filmed by the Germans; the archives must exist somewhere. They were [also] filmed by the Americans, by the French. But the films were not shown, because if they had, something would have changed. And things should not change. We would rather say 'never again.'" Jean-Luc Godard, *L'Autre Journal* no. 2, January 1985.

[29] Georges Didi-Huberman, *Images malgré tout* (Paris: Éditions de Minuit, 2003).

Therefore, in his *Histoire(s) du cinéma*, Godard set himself a double task: first, to denounce cinema for not having filmed the extermination camps,[30] and second, by means of the juxtaposition of images from Western visual culture (including documentary images of the camps), to render temporarily visible the horrors of the Shoah.[31] Critiquing Godard for the statements he made about the existence of archival footage of the Shoah and about the possibility of filming the event,[32] French psychoanalyst Gérard Wajcman claimed that the Shoah is irrepresentable not as a matter of choice or interdiction, but because "it is *impossible* to see."[33] For filmmaker Claude Lanzmann, as for Jean-Luc Nancy, the very existence of the extermination camps implies a forbidden representation. The filmmaker claims that "there is nothing to see" because the Holocaust shows that "there is no image." These injunctions mean that the horror of the event exceeds any image seeking to transmit it. Any attempts to represent it would be grotesque, and images trying to con-

---

[30] As Godard famously stated: "[…] We didn't film the concentration camps. At that moment, cinema completely neglected its duty. Six million people, mainly Jews, were killed or gassed, and cinema was not there […] In not filming the concentration camps, cinema completely gave up." Quoted by Libby Saxton, "Anamnesis and Bearing Witness: Godard/Lanzmann," *For Ever Godard*, ed. Michael Temple (London: Tate, 2004), p. 48.

[31] There are many lengthy, rich discussions about *Histoire(s) du cinéma* that spell out Godard's juxtapositions seeking to deliver an image of the Shoah. See for instance: Richard I. Suchenski, *Projections of Memory: Romanticism, Modernism, and the Aesthetics of Film* (Oxford: Oxford University Press, 2016), James S. Williams, *Encounters With Godard: Ethics, Aesthetics, Politics* (Albany: State University of New York Press, 2016); Russell J.A. Kilbourn, "'The Obligations of Memory': Godard's Underworld Journeys" and Junji Hori, "Godard, Spielberg, the Muselmann, and the Concentration Camps" published in *The Legacies of Jean-Luc Godard*, ed. Douglas Morrey, Christina Stojanova, Nicole Côté (Waterloo: Wilfrid Laurier University Press, 2014); Daniel Morgan, *Late Godard and the Possibilities of Cinema* (Los Angeles: University of California Press, 2013). There are also Céline Scemama, *Histoire(s) du cinéma de Jean-Luc Godard: la force faible d'un art* (Paris: Harmattan, 2006), Georges Didi-Huberman, *Images malgré tout* and *Passés cités*, Libby Saxton, "Anamnesis and Bearing Witness," in Michael Temple, James S. Williams and Michael Witt (eds.), *For Ever Godard: The Work of Jean-Luc Godard 1950-2000* (London: Black Dog, 2004), Jacques Rancière's "A Fable Without a Moral: Godard, Cinema (Hi)stories," in *Film Fables*, trans. Emiliano Battista (Oxford, New York: Berg, 2006), Miriam Heywood, "Holocaust and the Image: Debates Surrounding Jean-Luc Godard's *Histoire(s) du cinéma* (1988-98)," *Studies in French Cinema* 9/3 (209).

[32] Gérard Wajcman, "'Saint Paul' Godard contre 'Moise' Lanzmann," *Le Monde*, December 3, 1998.

[33] Ibid.

vey the horror would domesticate the event, create a distance or provide consolation. This logic, which follows the Platonic denunciation of images via the Sublime and *Bilderverbot*, has conferred on the event a certain aura of sacredness. That "there is no image" of the Shoah refers to the fact that the Nazis eliminated traces of the extermination: the camps themselves thus imply the execution of representation, as the relationships between presence and absence, the material and the intelligible, were shattered by the event itself.

For Lanzmann, the image as archive is merely a fetish and he thus rejects it. In his view, these images lack imagination; they petrify thought and kill all the power of evocation. For him, representation of the Shoah implies rigorous work of elaboration, of the creation of the memory of the event. In that regard, he conceives his film as a "monument."[34] The problem with archival images, for Lanzmann, is that they are not made to render known something, but to prove the facts when there is no need to prove anything. Therefore, his monumental *Shoah* posits an ethics and aesthetics of cinema seeking to *see horror in the face* without images. Refusing fiction and the idea of the archive (including reconstruction, images, documents, reports),[35] Lanzmann bases his film on interviews with Jewish survivors, Polish gentile bystanders and Nazi perpetrators, all of whom we see and hear remembering the extermination against the backdrop of the sites where the events took place. Lanzmann parts from the principle that the past continues to live on in the present through memory and, in the movie, the witness, "like a psychoanalytic patient, finds himself re-living past experiences."[36] In *Shoah*, the distance between past and presence is erased by speech and bodily gestures. The calmness of the sites where the film is shot is incommensurable with the horror conveyed by the witnesses, which incarnates "truth in the present," bringing the past into presence. In this manner, Lanzmann stages the erasure of the extermination that implies the very ruin of representation as his film embodies the shattering of a stable relationship between what is perceptible and what is intelligible.[37] His film can be described as a presentation of representation,

---

[34] Claude Lanzmann, "Le monument contre l'archive? (Entretien avec Daniel Bougnoux, Régis Debray, Claude Mollard et al.)," *Les cahiers de médiologie* nr. 11, 2001, p. 274.
[35] Gérard Wajcman, "'Saint Paul' Godard."
[36] Dorian Stuber, "Seeing Nothing: Lanzmann, Godard and Sontag's Fantasies of Voluntarism" *Screenmachine*, August 2011.
[37] Rancière, *The Future of The Image*, p. 123.

as the documentation of the production of representation. Through "re-enactments" of the events by the witnesses, he breaches the gap between reality and recollection. Lanzmann's radical refusal of the visibility of archival and fictive images privileges legibility only in the speech of the survivors. In this sense he seeks to oppose the silence of horror with absolute, "pure" speech, underlining speech's opacity and thus the vagueness of what it makes visible.[38]

Godard's declaration about *Shoah*—"It showed nothing at all"—launched the polarity (and polemic) around the legibility of images of the extermination. If, for Lanzmann, no image is capable of telling the story and this is why he filmed the speech of the witnesses, for Godard, all images tell us about the Shoah and this is why he tirelessly revisits our visual culture. From Godard's point of view, the legibility of the Shoah can be articulated into a concrete, immanent and singular visibility. Images can be rendered legible through montage, seeking a point of view and the proper distance, and by being brought into a dialectic in Walter Benjamin's sense.[39] For Godard, as we have seen, images are only part of a process, images are relationships amongst images. The more distant the relationships, the more just and strong the image.[40] We could argue that in both *Histoire(s) du cinéma* and *Shoah* two different sensibilities, forms of montage and ethics to relate image and history are at work. Godard's composite, artificial, even baroque and irreverential images are opposed to Lanzmann's, a monumental effort not to communicate, but to encompass everything. By bringing together images, sounds and texts by juxtaposing or superimposing them, Godard both extends an invitation and exercises restraint. According to this logic of montage, two photographs of the different eras can show the same historical moment. And this is the grounds for a second polemic raised by Godard regarding the representation of the Shoah.

Godard has returned many times in his films and texts to the confrontation of photographs of deportees with the captions—in the voice-over or embedded as text—"Jew" and "Muslim." For Giorgio Agamben and

---

[38] Jacques Rancière, *The Future of The Image*, p. 121.

[39] Georges Didi-Huberman, "Ouvrir les camps, fermer les yeux" (2005), in *Remontages du temps subi. Annales. Histoire, Sciences Sociales* 2006/5 61e année, pp. 1011–1049.

[40] *Jean-Luc Godard par Jean-Luc Godard*, II, p. 430.

Primo Levi, the *Muselmann* is the witness who cannot bear witness, the threshold figure between the human and the inhuman.[41] For Agamben the *Muselmann* is naked life with a specific referent: an irrevocable juridical and moral status. Useless for fighting, crippled, fallen behind, weak and ill, the only thing that remains is the absence of death. The *Muselmann* is the living-dead that embodies radical otherness, the reduction of the human being to inhumanity. Gil Anidjar inquired into why Jews were called Muslims by the Nazis, and he argues that it is related to the way in which the Nazis used language, as the key to the operation "was never to utter the words that would be appropriate to the action." He cites Raul Hilberg who noted the use of *Häftlinge* (with its pejorative suffix) to refer to the prisoners, *Kapo* (a slang term meaning 'comrade policeman') to denote a prisoner functionary, *fressen* (rather than *essen*) to denote eating and *Figuren* for corpses. According to Anidjar, the "Muslim" is a theological figure of passivity and subjection, the "image" of absolute subjection and broken will. In his view, "[t]he 'Muslims' testify to the theological in that they are lacking in divinity, in that they mark the death of a divine (non)human... a paradoxical threshold that also inscribes itself into political meaning. As figures of absolute subjection, the Muslims can no doubt represent a degree zero of power, of someone who 'died a death that was social...'."[42]

The first time Godard drew this juxtaposition was in *Ici et ailleurs* (1976) and then in a letter Godard wrote to Elias Sanbar in 1977: "La guerre actuelle au Moyen Orient est née dans un camp de concentration le jour où un grand clochard juif avant de mourir s'est en plus fait traiter de musulman par un quelconque SS."[43] For Godard the link comes from the "genius of evil," the hatred of the Other that resulted in the Shoah, the deaths of six million Jews, and transferred it in turn to another outsider people *(un autre peuple juif)*, the Palestinians, following the logic that

---

[41] Giorgio Agamben, *Remnants of Auschwitz: The Witness and the Archive* (New York: Zone Books, 2002), p. 55.

[42] Gil Anidjar, *The Jew, The Arab: A History of the Enemy* (Stanford, CA: Stanford University Press, 2013), pp. 138–145.

[43] "The current war in the Middle East was born on the day when, in a concentration camp, a Jewish vagrant was, prior to execution, called a 'Muslim' by some functionary in the SS." Godard's letter to Elias Sanbar dated July 19, 1977 published in *Cahiers du Cinéma* No. 300 (Godard Special), 1979, p. 19.

intolerance and hatred create still more intolerance and hatred.[44] The Palestinians, in turn, have become both the non-politicizable, incessantly derealized "others"—because they are perceived as a threat to the Israeli state, and enemies, insofar as their sameness has been erased by the permanent state of exception under which they live. A people's status as "other" does not imply that their deaths cannot be sacrificial (Agamben's bare life),[45] but that their lives cannot be mourned insofar as the Other is *derealized*, negated and phantasmic. The ideas of "Europe and the Jews" and "Islam and the West," along with anti-Semitism and Orientalism, are categories which are the theological and political constitutive Others of Judeo-Christian Europe.[46] The enemy is the essential figure of hostility, exceeding the parameters of war and ethical life, and similar to Butler's concept of "precarious life," the enemy is "another life," an "alien to be negated."[47] In Anidjar's account, furthermore, the enemy is not the Other, but rather, once the distinction between inside and outside has solidified, the stranger becomes an enemy.[48] Arguably, Palestinians oscillate between the theological-political Other of Israel (as Arabs, Muslims and Christians—as Jews

---

[44] As the letter continues, alluding to Alain Resnais' documentary about the Shoah, *Nuit et brouillard* (1955): "Il fallait effectivement être le génie du mal pour pouvoir inoculer dans le souvenir de six millions de morts juifs le souvenir de la haine de l'autre, mais de l'autre juif cette fois, car dans trente ans le people juif allait rencontrer son semblable, un autre peuple juif, et sur un territoire bien précis, pas dans *la nuit et le brouillard*, mas un peu dans le soleil, et qui lui disait: je suis pareil a toi, je suis un Palestinien." Published in a special issue of *Cahiers du Cinéma* by Godard (No. 300, 1979). Žižek posits the problem in terms of corruption and persecution, quoting Arthur Koestler, the great anti-communist convert: "If power corrupts, the reverse is also true; persecution corrupts the victims, perhaps in subtler and more tragic ways." Slavoj Žižek, *Violence*, p. 123.

[45] "Bare life" is a term coined by Giorgio Agamben to describe the life that remains outside the walls of the city and of the law, the life that may be spared but not sacrificed. See his *Homo Sacer: Sovereign Power and Bare Life*, trans. Daniel Heller-Roazen (Stanford, CA: Stanford University Press, 2003).

[46] In his article, "Europe and the Muslims: The Permanent Crusade?" Tomaž Mastnak argued that Muslims became the enemies of Christianity in the Middle Ages and that this enmity came to constitute Christendom, "The Unified Christian society that found its realization in the crusade." Furthermore, he argues that "Europe emerged as a political community when Latin Christians set out to chase the Turks out of Europe," following the fall of Constantinople. In *The New Crusades: Constructing the Muslim Enemy*, edited by Emran Qureshi and Michael A. Sells (New York: Columbia University Press, 2003).

[47] Ibid., pp. 71, 72.
[48] Ibid., p. 79.

were the constitutive religious Other of Europe before) and enemies, and such nationalistic, ethnic and religious distinctions have further naturalized asymmetrical oppositions such as "Israelis and Muslims," the "West and Islam," "Palestinians and Jews." With George W. Bush's declaration of the "Axis of Evil" in his infamous 2002 speech, these oppositions have recently been naturalized as enmities.

In this context, Godard has been harshly criticized for his juxtaposition of the Shoah and the Nakba, especially after an interview with Stéphane Zagdanski (France Culture, November 18, 2004) where he raises the issue of sacrifice in relation to the term "Holocaust" and to the state of Israel, implying that the victims from the past are today's aggressors:

> Par rapport aux camps de la mort, même quelqu'un comme Hannah Arendt a pu dire 'Ils se sont laissé emmener comme des moutons.' Moi, je me suis mis à penser au contraire que c'est eux qui ont sauvé Israël. Au fond, il y a eu six millions de kamikazes. Les six millions se sont sauvés eux-mêmes en se sacrifiant. Les films à faire là-dessus n'ont jamais été faits...[49]

Here Godard implies that the Holocaust victims were the "saviors" of Israel, taking literally the meaning of "Holocaust" in Hebrew, which is "sacrifice." The polemic stems from the already mentioned juxtaposition in *Ici et ailleurs* from 1976 that comes back in *Histoire(s) du cinéma*, and for which Godard has been blamed for anti-Semitism and of amalgamating "l'état d'être juif" and "l'État juif,"[50] and thus positing history as merely having changed sets based on a form of simplistic reasoning. According to Didi-Huberman, Godard's judgment denies Israeli Jews their right to exist, while Jews in the diaspora are identified with a government position (as the Jewish State) and diagnoses them as having a general "hatred for the Other." In his

---

[49] "In regards to the death camps, even someone like Hannah Arendt was able to say: 'They let themselves be taken like sheep.' On the contrary, I started thinking that it was they who saved Israel. In essence, there were six million kamikazes. The six million saved themselves by sacrificing themselves. Films about this have never been made...." See also: Céline Scemama, *Histoire(s) du cinéma de Jean-Luc Godard: La force faible d'un art* (Paris: L'Harmattan, 2006), 18–30. Michèle Cohen-Halimi, Francis Cohen, "Juifs, martyrs, kamikazes: La monstrueuse capture; question à Jean-Luc Godard," *Les Temps Modernes* No. 629 (November 2004–February 2005), pp. 301–310.

[50] "Being Jewish" and "The Jewish State." See Georges Didi-Huberman, *Passés cités*, p. 100.

view, this is the reason why in Godard's montage, real Jews cease to exist and become "mere citations," whose history has been denied, by having offered the Shoah to the Palestinians "against all historical evidence of this memory." For Didi-Huberman, this evidences the "perversity of Godard's quoted pasts."[51] The French historian wrote his diatribe in a letter addressed to Godard, in which also he accuses the filmmaker of "amalgamating" Hitler and Golda Meir, Moshe Dayan and the Wehrmacht in *Ici et ailleurs*. As we will see below, however, Godard builds a series of juxtapositions that become a "palimpsest" of failed revolutions and in *Notre musique*, of wars of annihilation. Most of the critiques of Godard unfortunately fail to acknowledge the complex and fine polysemy of his films and his sensibility toward decolonial issues. Instead, Didi-Huberman posits Godard's juxtaposition of the Nazis and the Israeli Jews as merely unjust and a result of Godard playing with the possibility of orientation and disorientation of meaning created by montage. He therefore demands that he revisit these juxtapositions and give them a new meaning as, in these matters, Godard's politics of montage shows a banal radicalism that seeks to divide the present in an ambivalent taking of sides, delivering a politics of a clearly torn, unhappy consciousness showing a pathos of a generalized mourning. Finally, Didi-Huberman accuses Godard of being a radical Maoist "checking his right flank," who follows undialectical, unilateral thinking that results in a vicious circle of a politics that is tortured by internal divisions.[52]

Godard's perspective on the Israeli–Palestinian conflict and the Shoah is clearly a militant taking of a position by delivering a fertile provocation, summoning a historical analogy to invite a historical, ethical and political judgment of the suffering of Palestinians. After all, for Godard, the task of

---

[51] Georges Didi-Huberman, *Passés cités*, pp. 102–103. Other critics who have engaged in accusing Godard of anti-Semitism have been: Alain Fleischer, *Réponse du muet au parlant. En retour à Jean-Luc Godard* (Paris: Éditions du Seuil, 2011); Céline Scemama, *Histoire(s) du cinéma de Jean-Luc Godard*; Bernard-Henri Lévy, "Godard est-il anti-Semite? Pièces et documents inédits autour de quatre films inaboutis", *La règle du jeu*, no. 45, 2000; Richard Brody, *Everything is Cinema: The Working Life of Jean-Luc Godard* (New York: Picador, 2009); Antoine de Baecque, *Godard, Biographie* (Paris: Pluriel, 2010); Daniel Cohn-Bendit, "Mon Ami Godard", *Le Monde*, 3 December 2010 available online: http://www.lemonde.fr/idees/article/2010/12/25/mon-ami-godard_1457343_3232.html. Maurice Darmon, *La Question juive de Jean-Luc Godard: Filmer après Auschwitz* (Cognac: Éditions Le Temps qu'il fait, 2011).

[52] Didi-Huberman, *Passés cités*, pp. 113, 116–119.

cinema is to show invisible relationships.[53] The extent of the controversy arising from Godard's juxtaposition has prompted Israeli filmmaker Eyal Sivan to qualify it as "forbidden montage." Why is it forbidden? In the Jew/Muslim juxtaposition, the *Muselmann* stands for the radical Other insofar as it is derealized, negated and phantasmagoric. Before, the Jew and the Muslim were not opposite paradigms, but it was the most common (racist) analogy to make (Jews and Muslims were both expelled from Iberia following the reconquest of Granada in 1492, representing the first "epistemicide" constitutive of European modernity, as we will see below). Anti-Semitism and Islamophobia, however, persist in Europe and elsewhere, and yet Godard's bringing into a relation the Jew and the Muslim seems unacceptable and not understandable today: they are not supposed to be brought together.[54]

"Muslim" denotes the Middle East conflict as well, and in Godard's 2004 film, *Notre musique*, as I describe below, the images of the deportees and their captions appear to be confronted according to the logic of shot/reverse-shot. In the film Godard brings the Jews and Palestinians into a relationship as two communities of survivors and exiled peoples.[55] The Shoah and the Nakba are brought into an asymmetrical relationship: the Israelis found the "Other" in the Palestinians, but Israelis are not the Other of Palestinians.[56] "The truth has two faces," states Palestinian poet

---

[53] For a formidable and line-by-line rebuttal to Didi-Huberman's various accusations against Godard see: Saad Chakali, *Jean-Luc Godard dans la relève des archives du mal* (Paris: L'Harmattan, 2017), pp. 230–237, where he, amongst other things, contests Didi-Huberman's scandalous affirmation that Godard makes Jews disappear in his work, reminding us that Godard does know how to make principled distinctions and that he too has a constellation of Jewish friends, who include thinkers, filmmakers, philosophers, and writers, to whom he renders homage in his films.

[54] See Eyal Sivan's conference around his multimedia project "Montage Interdit," available online at: http://issuezero.org/mi.php?id=11

[55] The interview is available at http://parolesdesjours.free.fr/gozag.htm. See also the "morceaux choisis" of the interview published as "Le cinéma, est-il une imposture?", *Le Nouvel Observateur* No. 2009 (18–24 November, 2004), 24–26. See: Céline Scemama, *Histoire(s) du cinéma de Jean-Luc Godard: La force faible d'un art* (Paris: L'Harmattan, 2006), 18–30. Michèle Cohen-Halimi, Francis Cohen, "Juifs, martyrs, kamikazes: La monstrueuse capture; question à Jean-Luc Godard," *Les Temps modernes* No. 629 (November 2004–February 2005), pp. 301–310.

[56] Jean-Luc Godard with Michael Witt, "The Godard Interview; I a Man of the Image," *Sight and Sound* (June 2005), 28–32. Available at http://old.bfi.org.uk/sightandsound/feature/313

Mahmoud Darwish in the film. Godard has made it clear that for him the Shoah and the Nakba are not the same thing. Consensually, the Shoah is an incomparable crime in European history, which needs to be evoked to impose limitations on political acts that display hubris, not to justify them.[57] As I will suggest below, the infamous montages by Godard are embedded in more complex relationships of montage with an array of things, texts, images, historical moments, all of which, unfortunately, Didi-Huberman (and Godard's critics and those who accuse him of anti-Semitism) have refused to see.

Regarding the three prohibitions—forbidden images, forbidden montage, forbidden testimony—they posit the problem of the interdiction of representation, albeit presupposing an ideal of total intelligibility of the forms of human experience. Every appearance is, however, fragmentary and, in this regard, the "truth" of Auschwitz is neither unimaginable nor unsayable. Without a doubt, all images always fall short in representing the essence of what they show. The knowledge they provide is not intrinsic to single images, but visibility derives from drawing hiatuses, analogies, incommensurabilities, correspondences and constellations through montage, which for Godard is famously "a form that thinks." Montage is also a construction, the articulation of a historical narrative, the possibility of approaching elements that are thought to be separate in time and space. Unfortunately, Godard's bringing together of the Jewish Question in Europe, and Palestine, has provoked a blockage, the impossibility of thought, transforming it into forbidden montage. Each historical moment has evidently its own history and particularities, but that

---

[57] For Žižek when we judge Israeli politics toward Palestinians we should *abstract* from the Holocaust because the Holocaust was a graver crime and thus a line must be drawn in evoking it in defense of Israeli political acts against Palestinians. This, for him, "secretly implies that Israel is committing such horrible crimes that only the absolute trump card of the Holocaust can redeem." (Slavoj Žižek, *Violence: Six Sideways Reflections* (New York: Picador, 2008), p. 112) Further, according to Žižek, the misfortune of Israel is that it was established as a nation-state a century or two too late because in the global moralizing world, states are treated like moral agents to be punished for their crimes and thus Israel cannot demand from Palestinians that they erase or forget the violence that comes with the foundation of *every* state power. The current problem for Žižek is that the state of Israel, "though 'continually victorious,' still relies on the image of Jews as victims to legitimize its power politics as well as to denounce its critics as covert Holocaust sympathizers." Slavoj Žižek, *On Violence*, p. 118.

does not mean that the interdiction of the juxtaposition can be justified, as analogies between the two different historical moments can be drawn.

If testimony defines the cultural sensibility of the twentieth century, and we find ourselves before a saturated memory, it is because documentary images and oral testimony are currently facing a problem of illegibility. According to Israeli theorist Eyal Weizman, the voices of recent victims have been doomed to be indeterminate and fragile, as well as undermined by suspect political subjectivities. One means of compensating for this has been a turn away from a preoccupation with the subjective and linguistic aspects of trauma and memory, toward a concern with information saturated in the material world.[58] Scientists are nowadays called as expert witnesses to interpret and to speak on behalf of things with the purpose of constructing and understanding juridical facts in human rights violation cases.[59] Unlike the testimony of the victims, scientific evidence pronounced by expert witnesses is more difficult to contest, and thus "evidence speaks for itself."[60] This inaugurates what Weizman has called the era after testimony of "forensic aesthetics" (marked by the Mengele case, where bones were rendered eloquent by experts in order to solve the case). This new form of producing evidence about crimes against humanity implies a form of *seeing* as tautological vision, reassuring vision without a closed certitude or failure. With forensic aesthetics, "what you see is what you see": the traces form the irrefutable presence of proof. In this regard, to desaturate memory would imply to give back to archives and to spoken testimony their political value, going beyond the humanitarian and non-governmental ethics of recognition and restitution, opening up the possibility of political self-determination after peace and decolonization in a present of total war. Starting, as for Godard, with a "simple conversation" (*Notre musique*).

---

[58] Eyal Weizman, *The Least of All Possible Evils: Humanitarian Violence from Arendt to Gaza* (London and New York: Verso, 2011), p. 144.
[59] Thomas Keenan and Eyal Weizman, *Mengele's Skull*, p. 70.
[60] Eyal Weizman, *The Least of All Possible Evils*, p. 103.

The Wars of Annihilation/Memory and Resistance Against War and the Reign of Fear

In a short film that was commissioned by Cannes, *De l'origine du XXIème siècle* (2000) Godard paints the twenty-first century as beginning in the twentieth, leading to the twenty-first as a war of annihilation. The film revisits the last century in reverse, "à la recherche du temps disparu,"[61] with a historical sequence that begins and ends in Bosnia. The video echoes chapter 3A, "La Monnaie de l'absolu", of *Histoire(s) du cinéma*, which starts with Godard whispering in the voice-over a speech by Victor Hugo titled "Pour la Serbie" (1876). In this text, Hugo delivers a *plaidoyer* (plea) protesting against the impassivity of European governments in the face of the massacre of the inhabitants of the Bulgarian village Batak by the Ottomans. Hugo is also calling European governments to take action, and people to raise their voices in universal indignation. Simultaneously, we see footage of the Bosnian War between 1992 and 1995 followed by an image of the Mostar Bridge in Bosnia and Herzegovina before it was destroyed. With the juxtaposition of images, Godard echoes Hugo's double call to action. *De l'origine* is composed of a parade of images from the history of cinema and from the mass media, juxtaposing armies, refugees, prisoners, trains containing goods and piles of dead bodies, conquests and occupations, torture and general *avilissement* or degradation. The present appears as one of a total war of annihilation. This approach accords with the description by French philosopher Jean-Paul Curnier (who would appear five years later as one of the characters in *Notre musique*) of the present as being trapped in the first half of the twentieth century under a reign of fear:

> Comme si le XXème siècle n'avait jamais dépassé sa moitié et que nous en soyons au point où il faut encore *crier* pour faire entendre la limite atteinte, sinon dépassée, d'une *suffocation* générale où l'espèce humaine est plongée. [...] celle de l'homme gouverné au nom de la *peur*.[62]

---

[61] "In search of the time that disappeared." This Proustian sentence with a twist is used for the first time in the voice-over in *Pierrot le fou* (1965).

[62] "It's as if we were only halfway through the 20th century and still at the point at which it is necessary to *cry out* to assert that the limit that has been reached, if not surpassed, concerning the state of general *suffocation* in which humankind finds itself [...] the condition of man governed by *fear*." My italics. Jean-Paul Curnier, "Le noir du vivant, la cruauté, encore," declaration read in Rodez on June 10, 2000, at the Journées Poésie, published in

Evoking André Breton's *scream* (discussed in Chapter 2) and Victor Hugo's *plaidoyer*, Curnier describes the transformation of indignation into a general feeling of humanity suffocating, submerged in fear. In this regard, an appropriation in *De l'origine* that strikes us is the famous one from Kubrick's *The Shining* (1980) with the boy furiously pedaling his little tricycle, traversing the empty vast corridors of the hotel. Following Fredric Jameson, the film evokes the shift in the figuration of collective paranoia from the fantastic representations of fear during the Cold War period that ranged from the enemy as subhuman to the enemy as a global ethnic-religious threat. The enemy of Empire had ceased to be the communist world and thus a "new ideological genre of the occult realized in 'metaphysical' nostalgia for absolute Evil..."[63] was foregrounded. Hierarchy and domination are allegorized, in Jameson's view, in Jack Nicholson's "possession." Kubrick's film figures the passage of absolute evil within: invisible, unpredictable, thirsty and pitiless. An analogy could be made to Brian Massumi's understanding of the form of control post-9/11 as power propagating itself by breeding fear, addressing bodies' affectivities. The "state of pure alert" created by the US government's threat-level color code in 2002 reminds us of the figuration of the moment of absolute, unlocalizable fear as a contagious concatenation of intensities in *The Shining*. In the sequence, the camera's point of view follows the boy and we fear that the camera incarnates the father threatening the child—as viewers, we embody that threat as well: the enemy is within and virtual, in "a futurity that is made directly present, without ceasing to be a futurity."[64]

In *De l'origine* we see some recurring images that appear in Godard's short videos of the early 2000s and, in *Notre musique*, Ceauşescu's hanging, a woman made to drink urine coming out from a penis, and the scene from *À bout de souffle* (1960) in which Jean Seberg traces her lips with her pinky nail and asks, while staring deadpan at the camera, "Qu'est-ce que c'est 'dégueulasse'?"[65] In another short film, *Prière pour refuzniks 1* (2004), Godard describes war and violence in the twenty-first century at a standstill, and the short ends with the intertitle:

Lignes no. 3 (October 2000), http://journees-poesie-rodez.net/IMG/pdf/Revue_Arachnee_no_1.pdf

[63] Fredric Jameson, "Historicism in *The Shining*," (1981) in *Signatures of the Visible* (New York: Psychology Press, 1992).

[64] Brian Massumi, "Fear (The Spectrum Said)," *Positions: East Asia Cultures Critique* 13:1 (2005), 31–48.

[65] "What is it that is disgusting?"

Il n'y a pas de victoire, il n'y a que des drapeaux et des hommes qui tombent.[66]

This sentence could sum up Godard's conception of a worldly state of affairs at the turn of the century: the twenty-first century is marked as heir to the wars and the failed revolutions of the twentieth, transformed into an invincible permanent war of rights of "all against all." What aesthetic techniques, formalist devices, content and expression are appropriate to express the unending war of annihilation, to give voice to its victims? What forms of politicization are possible under this situation, beyond unending mourning? As we have seen, for Godard cinema not only has redemptive qualities but everything can be represented, and he has drawn distinctions between the "irrepresentable," the "invisible," and the "inexpressible." Godard, in *De l'origine*, claims his position regarding the quandary of the irrepresentability of catastrophe:

> J'ai essayé de couvrir le souvenir des terribles explosions et crimes en tout genre des hommes par le visage des enfants et les larmes et les sourires des femmes.[67]

Godard's task to cover memories of war and horror with beauty unburdens art from the mandate to bear witness, to produce (fragmented) information of trauma from memory and to unveil truths. In *De l'origine*, Godard takes further a stand against Claude Lanzmann by problematizing the subsumption of image to speech in testimonial accounts, which he equates in the voice-over to Hollywood's subsumption of literature to the consumer-image. As we will see below, Godard's critique of the massively industrialized cinematic representation of memory in Hollywood cinema, based on manufactured desires and identification, unfolds explicitly in *Éloge de l'amour* grounded on a contradiction Godard had laid out almost a decade earlier in *Je vous salue, Sarajevo* (1993) between "culture" and "art." In Godard's juxtaposition, culture stands for the colonization of memory by international capital, in a world in which history and the gaze are for sale, undermining any possibility of politicization which, in order to foresee a future and organize, is necessarily based on memory and history.

---

[66] "There is no victory, there are only flags and falling men."
[67] "I have tried to cover up the memories of the terrible explosions, and of all kinds of crimes committed by men, with the faces of children and the tears and the smiles of women."

Je vous salue, Sarajevo is a short video reminiscent of Godard's and Miéville's films from the 1970s in which they portrayed a number of images, mostly from the mass media, on each of which the camera would linger for several minutes. *Je vous salue, Sarajevo* is a microscopically detailed, forensic examination of a photograph taken by the freelance photojournalist Ron Haviv of Serbians rampaging through the houses of Bosnian Muslims in the town of Bijeljina in April 1992. In the photograph, victims and perpetrators appear in the same frame: a Serb soldier with glasses perched on his head, a cigarette between his fingers and his rifle in his hand, is about to kick the head of a woman who is lying on the ground, while two other soldiers pass by nonchalantly, their gazes directed outside of the picture frame.[68] The voice-over in *Je vous salue, Sarajevo* is centered on the analogy between culture/art and ethnocentric wars, the latter of which, for Godard, eliminate the exception and obstruct empathy due to difference. Godard states: "Il y a la culture qui c'est de la *règle*, il y a l'exception qui c'est l'art."[69] He goes on, "The exception is written (Dostoyevsky), composed (Mozart, Gershwin), painted (Vermeer, Cézanne), filmed (Antonioni, Vigo), or *lived*." Culture here is rendered as the agreement with the rule as the everyday, and as such, it is "de la *règle* de vouloir la mort de *l'exception*," thus "il sera donc de la *règle* de l'Europe de la *culture* d'organiser *la mort de l'art de vivre* qui fleurit encore."[70] The *exception* that is *lived* is "Srebrenica, Mostar, Sarajevo," and the art of living together, multicultural co-existence eliminated by the war. Godard's paradigm of "culture as the rule and art as the exception" is along the lines of Adorno's critique of the Culture Industry that opposes the absolute autonomy of art with the massification of culture through the democratization of art and its becoming a "cultural product."[71]

Godard brings up the opposition between culture (industry) and art in chapter 4B of *Histoire(s) du cinéma*, "Les Signes parmi nous", where culture and communication are posited as the foes of art. The opposition is reiterated in *Éloge de l'amour* (2001) in the context of Godard's reproach

---

[68] Joshua Lipton, "Ron Haviv: Shooting War," *Columbia Journalism Review* (July 2002).
[69] "It's culture that's the *rule*, art the exception."
[70] "It's the *rule* to desire the death of the *exception*....it will therefore be the *rule* in the Europe of *culture* to organise *the death of the art of living* which still thrives."
[71] In 1993, when the GATT (General Agreement on Tariffs and Trade) was under negotiation in Europe, the concept *exception culturelle* (cultural exception) was introduced to exclude "cultural products" from trade agreements. This policy designates "art" as a "cultural product" subject to protectionist measures and subventions. This designation of art directly undermines the European tradition of art's autonomy subsuming it within national "cultural policies."

to Steven Spielberg for having "rebuilt" Auschwitz in his film *Schindler's List* (1993) by having falsified the memory of the Shoah. Godard targets the film in *Éloge de l'amour*, positing it as an example of a big-budget Hollywood film borne out of the cultural-industrial matrix that is globally propagating a prosthetic memory through a seductive language. *Éloge de l'amour* seems to ask, "How can we maintain this link to the past, to history, in a world that seems to deny history, in the perpetual present of a corporate culture conforming to a model provided by America, that is to say, a country without a history?"[72] A poem by Godard included in a letter he addressed to Bernard-Henri Lévy in 1998 bears the same title of the movie and seems to describe it. The first and last strophes are:

> Une trinité d'histoires. Le début. L'accomplissement. La fin. Le renouveau. De l'amour. Modifications par l'âge. Les conditions sociales. De l'amour. Passe le temps. Ne bouge pas. Restent les humains.[73]

Bernard-Henri Lévy is a French intellectual and one of the leaders of the "Nouveaux Philosophes" movement, which was a target of critiques by Godard (as well as by Régis Debray and Gilles Deleuze) in the 1970s. They saw in the Nouveaux Philosophes' work in the mass media the "journalisation of the intellectual function," and thus the "mediatization of mediation." Lévy's intellectual work from the 1990s onwards has been highly critical of Islam, even bordering on Islamophobia, and his position regarding Israel is openly Zionist. In 1998, Godard initiated a series of conversations and letter exchanges around the topic of Israel-Palestine with Lanzmann and Lévy, geared at becoming a film. The exchanges eventually led to nothing, only the letters remain. The fragment of the poem Godard wrote in his letter to Lévy describes the plot of *Éloge de l'amour*, where Godard posits the problem of the massification of memory and thus of the co-optation of memory and resistance by the culture industry represented

---

[72] Russell J.A. Kilbourn, "The obligations of memory: Godard's Underworld Journeys," *The Legacies of Jean-Luc Godard*, ed. Douglas Morrey, Christina Stojanova, Nicole Côté (Waterloo: Wilfrid Laurier University Press, 2014), p. 83.

[73] "A trinity of histories. The beginning. Consummation. The end. Renewal. Love. Modifications by age. Social conditions. Love. Time passes. Do not move. Humans remain." Translated and reproduced in Bernard-Henry Lévy, "Is Jean-Luc Godard Antisemitic? Not a Gala Dinner (Third Episode, 1999)" *Huffington Post*, November 18, 2010, available online: http://www.huffingtonpost.com/bernardhenri-levy/post_1285_b_785058.html

by Hollywood. Godard seems to be addressing many fronts in the film: the massification of the memory of the Shoah *and* of the French Resistance by the culture industry, and the problem of their representation. As for Godard, cinema failed to film the camps; a second lacuna in the history of cinema is the lack of films about the French Resistance.

Overall, *Éloge de l'amour* is an attempt to show the invisible unfolding between love and memory intertwined in the passage of time and in the Rimbaudian transformation inherent in "Je e(s)t un autre" from "le moi précedent / n'existe plus."[74] Memory is posited as a task (*devoir*) in the film and as a right. The first part of the film is shot in black and white and shows the four moments of love—encounter, physical passion, separation, reconciliation—all lived through the three ages of humankind: youth, adulthood, old age. In order to counter conventional Hollywood storytelling, based on a character's story, in the film we learn that Godard is not telling "the story of Eglantine and Perceval" (the young lovers), but "the moment of history traversing" Eglantine. This narrative configuration has evidently historical materialist implications, insofar as Godard, instead of "personalizing" historical events, posits the story's characters as historical figures produced by the events. In other words, Godard's characters are Brechtian insofar as they are socio-historical figures that transcend individual and collective events. In general, Godard's characters are made out of tissues of citations, agglutinations of codes, complexified ready-made voices and discourses; they are something in between taxonomies of the socio-historical and "original" copies indexing the actual state of affairs. The adult lovers from *Éloge de l'amour* are a waitress and a Renault worker who meet exhausted after work; she is the granddaughter of an old member of the CGT (General Confederation of Labor) and both ponder on the status of the workers' movement 30 years after its demise. The old lovers are former heroes in the Resistance against the German occupation of France. Their story unfolds in the second part of the film, set in Brittany, two years previously, and shot in digital and in (highly manipulated) color. The aging couple is in need of money, so they sell the rights to their story between 1941 and 1944 to "Spielberg Associates" to produce a film starring Juliette Binoche. We learn that Mme Bayard was never paid. Godard thus attacks Spielberg and Hollywood for the appropriation and commercialization of the memories of others, accusing "America" of stealing the

---

[74] "The preceeding I / no longer exists." Which Godard uses to construct the temporalities at play in *Ici et ailleurs*, that of the "*mois qui passent.*"

stories of others because they have none of their own. The opposition between films that honor memory and those that do not, and between film as culture and film as art, is transposed in another scene in the film: outside of a movie theater, we see the posters of Robert Bresson's *Pickpocket* (1959) hanging next to the Wachowski Brothers' *The Matrix* (1999). The juxtaposition evokes two radically different forms of the representation of (a) reality: that of classical cinema, which opens a window into another world, allowing a story to unfold, and the introduction of virtual reality co-existing with the reality of the narrative of the film. The latter represents a radically different way to understand cinema, memory and the image based on the waning of memory, and memories of the past. *Éloge de l'amour* is a eulogy, a love letter to the death of memory; simultaneously, it is an attempt to revive it and, especially, the memory of the history of the French Resistance during World War II. Godard concludes in the film that the Resistance was mere youth, never reaching adulthood because it was never passed on. Thus, in Godard's historical materialist film, in our present of occupation by total war and fear, the possibility of Resistance would replace the Marxist imperative of the Revolution as the motor of history.

In *Notre musique* (2004), a key feature film, Godard takes further concerns raised in *Histoire(s)*, *De l'origine*, and *Éloge de l'amour*. He draws a historical landscape relating the failed revolutions of the twentieth century and the wars of annihilation of the twenty-first. If the second half of the twentieth century endured struggles for independence and revolutions that went wrong, and if "revolution" means that it is possible to begin *tabula rasa*, in retrospect, the potential new beginning was hindered by the failure of revolutions. In historical materialist terms, the violence inherited from the twentieth century has put the world at a standstill and thus, the twenty-first century is a sum of the ruins of the twentieth cemented in hyper-real repetition.[75] The remnants of depoliticized ethnic wars of bearers of rights are non-redemptive, culturalized ruins. For Godard the only chance of salvation is resistance by the vanquished. Along similar lines to previous films, Olga, one of the characters in *Notre Musique*, draws a series of links between culture, war, a general

---

[75] For Baudrillard, the hyper-real is that which it is possible to substitute with a reproduction. It is the fourth phase of the image, and it "bears no relation to any reality whatever," it is its own pure simulacrum. Jean Baudrillard, "The Evil Demon of Images and the Precession of Simulacra," in Thomas Docherty, ed., *Postmodernism: A Reader* (New York: Columbia Univ. Press, 1993).

state of poverty of expression, and the need to do away with culture for the sake of art (of the defeated):

> Le paysage est chargé de fils de fer, le ciel est rouge d'explosions. Puisque *cette ruine n'a pas épargné la notion même de culture, il faut d'abord avoir le courage de la jeter*. Il faut se débrouiller avec peu; quand la maison brûle déjà, il est absurde de vouloir sauver les meubles. S'il reste une chance à saisir, c'est celle des vaincus.[76]

Olga's line draws a specific link between the redemptive qualities of art, ruins, and culture: "Cette ruine n'a pas épargné la notion même de culture"[77] means that culture survives war, persisting as a ruin. Thus, in *Notre musique* Godard expresses a diatribe against culture, introducing the problem of the picture of the world as a war ruin, and interrogates the possibility of reconciliation in the aftermath of war. Echoing his ongoing inquiries on representativity, Godard questions the kind of intellectual intervention that this situation elicits. We must recall here the plot of his feature *For Ever Mozart* (1996), centered on the question of the representativity of the Balkans War. In the film, Vicky Vitalis (Vicky Messica) is an elderly film director who accompanies his daughter Camille (Madeleine Assas), a professor of philosophy, to stage *Le Jeu de l'amour et du hazard*, a romantic comedy from 1730 by Pierre de Marivaux, in war-torn Sarajevo. Unable to find a copy of the play, however, she settles for *On ne badine pas avec l'amour* (1834) by Alfred de Musset.[78] Camille's cousin, Jérôme (Frédéric Pierrot), choses to accompany them to Sarajevo along with Jamila (Ghalia Lacroix), the family's maid. On their way to Bosnia, Vicky abandons them and returns to make a black and white film about war, embodying the figure of the filmmaker who turns his/her back to the horrors of the Bosnian War. For their part, the younger idealist intellectuals are captured; Camille and Jérôme dig

---

[76] "The landscape is strewn with [barbed] wire, the sky is red with explosions; and *this ruin didn't spare the very notion of culture; we must boldly dismiss it.* We have to make do with very little. If the house is already on fire, it's mad to try to save the furniture. If there is still an opportunity to be seized, it belongs to the defeated." My italics.

[77] Olga's lines about the poverty of expression echo Jean-Paul Curnier, in the diatribe he wrote against cultural politics and culture as the form in which public power pacifies tensions. Culture for him has become a new mode of *persuasion de masse* and the apparatus of the moralization of art. Jean-Paul Curnier, "Le noir du vivant, la cruauté, encore" *Revue Lignes* No. 3, éditions Léo Scheer (Octobre 2000).

[78] The plot of the film is an obvious wink to the controversy raised by Susan Sontag's trip to Sarajevo to stage Beckett's *Waiting for Godot*, as we will see below.

their own graves and are murdered, and only Jamila survives. *Notre musique* takes place in the aftermath of the Balkans War in Sarajevo and draws a palimpsest of wars of annihilation: the Red Indians of North America, the Shoah, the Israeli–Palestinian conflict and the Balkans War.[79] Godard commented that he chose to film Sarajevo post-reconciliation, as opposed to filming in the Middle East, because he felt incapable of going there,[80] and because he was interested in the fact that the city "Permet encore de faire cohabiter dans un même espace des regards,"[81] meaning multicultural coexistence still seemed possible. Reconstructed Sarajevo—the war had ended in 1995 and once the city had been (partially) reconstructed and the parts "reconciled," Godard decided to go to film *Notre musique* there in 2002[82]—allowed him to try to see and to show that which is not visible or visualizable after a catastrophe. In Sarajevo, the reconstruction of the historical sites symbolizes reconciliation and recovery, but as Spanish writer Juan Goytisolo (who appears in the film) and journalist Marcus Tanner reported, the memory of the war had not been erased in order to move on. In their accounts, the commemoration of the common multicultural past in Sarajevo delivered reified tourist sites or fundraising photo opportunities, furthering collective amnesia and rendering reconciliation banal.

One of the key insights in *Notre musique* is that there is no alterity in war. French writer Jean-Paul Curnier states toward the beginning of the film that the survivor of war is not the other, but *someone else*. Following Gil Anidjar, war or the permanent possibility of war, suspends the law and it "does not manifest exteriority and the other as other," rather, "it destroys the identity of the same," and thus in the state of exception, "there are no others, only enemies."[83] Once war is over, the vanquished enemy becomes the survivor, "an other," as opposed to "the Other." This is because, for Curnier, violence cuts the line of life and renders irretrievable the trust in

---

[79] "The Godard Interview."

[80] "Godard, qui voulait initialement faire de *Notre Musique* une déclaration directe sur la Palestine, mais se sentait incapable de retourner filmer au Moyen-Orient." [Initially Godard wanted to make in *Notre Musique* a direct declaration about Palestine, but he felt that we was unable to go back to the Middle East to shoot.] James S. Williams, "Presentation," in *Jean-Luc Godard Documents*, 408.

[81] "This place still allows the coexistence of gazes in the same space." Godard in conversation with Jean-Michel Frodon, "Jean-Luc Godard et *Notre musique*, Juste une conversation," *Cahiers du cinéma* (May 2004), p. 21.

[82] Ibid., p. 22.

[83] Gil Anidjar, *The Jew, the Arab: A History of the Enemy* (Stanford: The University Press, 2003), p. 4.

the world because seeing our neighbor turn against the self engenders a feeling of horror that infuses under the skin. Thus, the survivor is not the Other, it is someone else ("un autre") who has undergone not only the destruction of her life-world, but also the annihilation of the bond that is "in between" humans, which is also the link to the world. The characters in *Notre musique* ponder this in different ways, grappling with the ethical and political questions that are raised in the aftermath of war. Is it a matter of acknowledging guilt and suffering, or asking for forgiveness? Is it a matter of judgment and trial, establishing a relationship of infinite debt? Can it be re-established with a promise, with forgiveness, or redress? How can the bond between men and the world, destroyed when the neighbor turns against the self, be restituted?

As we have seen, the ethical mandate to bear witness to the interminable catastrophe tends to put all the emphasis on effect for the sake of immediacy. Amalgamating voice and face, the witness-narrative can be described as an excess of presence obliterating the distance between the viewer and what is seen on the screen, rendering alterity ambiguous. In the film, moreover, French intellectuals Pierre Bergounioux and Jean-Paul Curnier express diatribes against the discourses of victimhood and witnessing. Curnier states: "Le monde est au présent clivé entre ceux qui se bousculent pour faire entendre leur malheur et ceux à qui cette défilée publique porte chaque jour sa dose de confort morale à leur domination."[84] Bergounioux responds: "Sans s'accorder autant de cynisme... il est devenu insupportable d'entendre des victimes sans colère et sans dégoût d'en être arrivé là; avec ou malgré soi; et c'est pour ça qu'on donne à entendre des victimes que tous sont invités à s'exprimer en tant que victimes."[85] Still, for Godard, "la seule chance de se sauver, c'est celle des vaincus."[86] With his statement, Godard enacts a rhetorical shift in the film from "victims" to "the vanquished," while making a plea for their "right to fiction," as well as for undoing the amalgam of voice and face inherent to the witness-image. Furthermore, Godard displaces the question of the "traces of the unthinkable" as the problem of

---

[84] "The world is today split in two, between those who line up to voice their misery and those for whom this public display provides a daily dose of moral comfort to their domination."

[85] "Without giving way to cynicism... it has become intolerable to hear victims [speaking out] without becoming angry or disgusted at their having being reduced to this status; and also with (or in spite of) oneself. That is why we give a platform to the victims, inviting them to express themselves in their capacity as victims."

[86] "The only chance for salvation is granted to the vanquished."

the relationship between image and text. Throughout the film he asks, what scheme of intelligibility is proper to account for the dead word? What is the textual function of intelligibility?

THE IMAGE HAS BEEN COVERED BY TEXT

Notre musique is a triptych structured after Dante Alighieri's *Divine Comedy* and like Dante, Godard in *Notre musique* engages with the Christian medieval vision of life after death, posited as an inquiry into contemporary situations of suffering, guilt, morality and redemption. The film encompasses two domains of visibility—light and darkness—and three registers of legibility: the real (as Godard's critique of the hyper-real), the symbolic (as the bridge between forgiveness and redemption, and ethics and knowledge), and the imaginary (as the only form that can encompass both horror and beauty). Godard refers to these three registers as "movements," as in a musical composition, and they mirror the three Dantesque realms of life, purgatory and death. Godard plays himself in the film, and more than Virgil, he is like Odysseus who was sent down to Hades by Homer "to visit the babbling, brainless wraiths of the heroic dead." The film begins in "Hell," with eight minutes of a parade of images of death, disaster, and devastation that unfold flickering and departing from "full" (black) screens. This section of the film shares many images with *De l'origine*, which perhaps we could think of as a prequel to *Notre musique*. One of Godard's manifest concerns is the uniformizing properties of the digitalization of images. In this parade of images, Godard thus manipulates slightly the images by rendering them blurry, slowing them down or tinting them. The first image is shaky with documentary immediacy and that is why we are uncertain of what it documents; what we recognize, however, is that it is a zone of conflict. "Hell" is further divided into four series. In the opening series, we see battles from everywhere with people killing each other, accompanied by a quote from Montesquieu in the voice-over (all spoken by Sarah Adler, in character as Judith Lerner):

> Ainsi, dans le temps des fables, après les inondations et les déluges, il sortit de la terre des hommes armés, qui s'exterminèrent.[87]

---

[87] "Thus, in the times of fables after the floods, armed men came out from the earth to exterminate each other." Charles Montesquieu, from *De l'esprit des lois*, Book XXIII, 334.

This series includes, first, scenes from Peter Brook's *Lord of the Flies* (1963), John Ford's Westerns, Eisenstein's abandoned project *¡Que Viva México!* (1930), footage of piles of corpses in German concentration camps and other scenes of violence, war and death. Second, accompanying images of the machinery of war and their effects (tanks, bombs, destruction, missiles and explosions), we hear a quote from Alice's thoughts commenting on the Queen of Hearts' court: "They are dreadfully fond of beheading people here; the great wonder is that there's anyone left alive!"[88] Third, we see images of victims, bodies being hanged and burned, shot at. Then, a sequence of clips from movies relating women to war: a group of women doing the Nazi salute, a Western reporter at the war front, and the scene from Robert Bresson's *Les Anges du péché* (1943) in which three nuns prostrate themselves on the floor, seeking forgiveness from the Mother Superior (the film was Bresson's only feature released during the German Occupation of France). During this sequence we hear the first sentence of the Christian prayer: "Pardonne-nous nos offenses, comme nous pardonnons aussi à ceux qui nous ont offensés."[89] Fourth, we see images of Sarajevo during the 1990s.[90] We then hear: "On peut comprendre la mort et la vie, l'une comme étant l'impossible du possible; l'autre, comme le possible de l'impossible. Or, je e(s)t un autre."[91] Then we see a clip in strident colors that shows the two tower blocks being shelled in central Sarajevo that Godard took from *Do You Remember Sarajevo?*, a documentary from 2002, which is a compilation of home movies when the bombing of the city in 2002 began.[92]

Godard's parade of images in "Hell" does not privilege documentary, fiction or journalistic images. The parade is an appeal to the imaginary that has been liquidated by the hyper-real. The sources are as varied as Godard's archive of images is immense. As a concentration of horrors,

---

[88] Lewis Carroll, *Alice in Wonderland*, chapter VIII available at https://ebooks.adelaide.edu.au/c/carroll/lewis/alice/chapter8.html

[89] "Forgive our trespasses as we forgive those who have trespassed against us."

[90] "The Godard Interview." Available at http://old.bfi.org.uk/sightandsound/feature/313

[91] "We could understand death and life as follows: the first, as being the impossibility of the possible; the second, as the possible of the impossible. And yet, I is/and an other."

[92] A textual resonance for "Hell" is a passage from Juan Goytisolo's *El Bosque de las Letras* (Madrid: Alfaguara, 1995). Both Goytisolo and Godard cite the image of a wounded child's face covered with flies.

"Hell" is comparable to Goya's *Disasters of War*, depicting the atrocities that occurred during the Peninsular War of 1808–1814. Godard's parade does not interpellate the viewer at the level of affect, nor does it present us with a hyper-real inexorable stream of disaster images. For Godard, the question of the autonomous migration of images is not a matter of critiquing the excess of violence and the voyeurism present in regimes of visibility—for him, when it comes to images of dead people, difference in terms of origin is absent because war undoes socio-historical determination. War further divides the world in two: enemies and friends, winners and survivors, torturers and victims. That is why this parade is not a collection of "archive-images" (Georges Didi-Huberman's term) or "brand" images (as in *Ici et ailleurs*), recording and attesting to historical perversity or appearing as emblems of historical events.[93] This parade tells us that war is hell:[94] suffering without consolation.

"Purgatory," the second section of the film, is set in the immediate past or recent present in Sarajevo. There, Godard restages his intervention at the European Literary Encounters conference at the Centre André Malraux, creating an intersection of imaginary (ambassador, translator, bridge-maker, journalist, filmmaker, host) and real characters. In his lecture, Godard discusses the relationship between image and text. When a student asks him if he thinks that the new digital video cameras will be able to save cinema, he sighs and remains silent. In the scene, the camera is framing Godard's face in a manner that recalls Rembrandt's late self-portraits (one of which appears in a sequence and in some of his other films). It is well known that death of cinema is a recurrent theme and Godardian predicament. Video will kill cinema in *Sauve qui peut (la vie)* of 1979, as cinema and video are like Cain and Abel. Many have read his *Histoire(s)* as an absolutization of cinema and as its End in the author. Arguably, it is not that for Godard "Cinema" begins and ends with his *Histoire(s)*, but that Cinema has been systematically killed by Capital and television, and Godard is trying to save it.

In the lecture, moreover, Godard explicates his theory of the image by telling the story of Bernadette, "the seer," the little shepherd girl who had a vision of the virgin of Fatima and who first appeared in Godard's film *Passion* (1982). Godard discusses further the relationship between text and

---

[93] Georges Didi-Huberman, *Images, malgré tout* (Paris: Éditions de Minuit, 2003); English edition (translation by Shane B. Lillis), *Images in Spite of All: Four Photographs from Auschwitz* (Chicago: University of Chicago Press, 2008).

[94] Susan Sontag, *Regarding the Pain of Others*, p. 90.

image, which he explains as analogous to the principle of montage upon which he has constructed *Notre musique*: the "shot/reverse-shot." In general, the shot/reverse-shot means to present two sides of a story, two faces of truth, two parts in a conversation; it is also "the same but in a different situation." In order to explain how this basic element in filmic grammar operates, Godard holds up two stills: one of Cary Grant and one of Rosalind Russell from Howard Hawks's *His Girl Friday* (1940). Godard problematizes that Hawkes is bringing to the two headshots a false unity or perfect symmetry by being unaware of the *differences* between man and woman.

Arguably, the relationships between images, characters, places and histories in *Notre musique* can be analyzed in terms of the shot/reverse-shot. The characters are dense with superimpositions, multiple stories and complex, multicultural identities. Moreover, they are what the "vanquished" are to Homeric historiography, what the "proletariat" is to historical materialism. The "vanquished" are the only chance of salvation, and they unfold into their reverse-shots. One of the characters is an Israeli journalist, Judith Lerner (Sarah Adler). "Judith" is the savior of her people in the Old Testament. "Lerner" in German means *she who learns*; her name is also a possible allusion to Yehuda Lerner, the Jewish man who led the heroic uprising in the concentration camp of Sobibor in 1943.[95] In *Notre musique*, Judith Lerner is a freelance reporter from the Israeli newspaper *Haaretz* on a multiple mission in Sarajevo: to arrange a conversation between her grandfather and the man who, resisting Nazi occupation and authority, refused collaboration and hid Judith's grandparents in his garret in 1943. This man is Naville, the French Ambassador to Sarajevo. Naville ponders on Judith's invitation to have a "simple conversation" with her grandfather as a "free man." He hesitates to accept her invitation because, he tells her, in order to do it, he might have to relinquish his job at the French Diplomatic Service. Perhaps quitting his job is necessary because such a conversation would raise uncomfortable questions about the responsibility of the Vichy government that collaborated with the Germans in prosecuting the Jews and the Resistance during World War II.

Later in the film, Judith interviews the Palestinian poet Mahmoud Darwish. The script of the interview is based on an interview between the poet and the Israeli writer Helit Yeshurun from 1996, conducted in Hebrew. The interview took place in the period of optimism following the

---

[95] This uprising is the subject of Claude Lanzmann's film *Sobibor, 14 octobre 1943, 16 heures*. (2001), in which Yehuda Lerner tells his own story.

Oslo Accords of 1993–1995, and they discuss the Palestinian and Israeli stories of victimhood. The tone of the interview is quite bitter and ironic on both their parts. Making a plea for equilibrium, Darwish asserts that Israelis have a monopoly on victimhood, and demands the right to cry as a victim.[96] In response, Yeshurun situates the Jewish people's status of the vanquished as an incomparable aesthetic enterprise: "La culture juive a crée de grandes oeuvres de peuple vaincu. Vous n'aimez pas entendre cela. Ne faites pas de nous des vainqueurs nés d'hier."[97] The interview becomes, in a sense, a combat of words of the vanquished. Darwish lays out further the paradox of the predicament of the Palestinians:

> J'ai appris à pardonner.
> Chaque Palestinien est un témoin de la déchirure.[98]

For his re-enactment of this interview in *Notre musique*, Godard renders the encounter asymmetric in the sense that he introduces a series of differences: it is a conversation between a young journalist and a poet of renown, as opposed to two poets, and this is how the dialogue's acerbity is toned down. The conversation begins with a question posed by Judith while Darwish's silhouette is facing the window against the Sarajevo cityscape, as seen from the Holiday Inn hotel. After Darwish asserts, "the truth has two faces," a frontal shot of the poet is seen, facing Judith. Difference is further asserted by language: Judith addresses Darwish in Hebrew while he responds in Arabic. The encounter between them raises some of the film's key issues: first, the question of the relationship between the defeated and the conquerors, their cyclical exchangeability and their potential trans-historical relationship; second, matters of alterity, ethical responsibility and atonement.

Judith embodies hope and enlightenment, striving for reconciliation and dialogue: the French Ambassador compares her to Hannah Arendt in that they are both as forceful as "12 Synagogues." Judith's answer, when Naville asks her, "Pourquoi Sarajevo?" is: "Parce que la Palestine et parce que j'habite à Tel Aviv; je souhaite voir un endroit où la réconciliation semblait

---

[96] First published in Tel Aviv in *Hadarim* No. 12 (Spring 1996), translated by Simone Bitton and reprinted in *La Palestine comme métaphore* (Paris: Actes Sud, 1996), p. 151.

[97] "Jewish culture has created great works as a vanquished people. You do not like hearing this. Do not consider us as a vanquished people that were born yesterday." Ibid., p. 155.

[98] "I have learned to forgive." "Every Palestinian is a witness to the rupture." Ibid. The sentences correspond to pages 115 and 122 respectively.

possible."[99] Godard referred to Judith in an interview as a "good Israeli", after the term "good German," to describe someone who was against Hitler.[100] In the original script, Godard "envisaged just one girl, a Jewish Israeli journalist who at the end commits suicide."[101] Godard, however, stated that he realized that it was excessive to have this character (Judith) go back to Jerusalem to blow something up. Also, the actress Sarah Adler wanted to play Judith but without doing the suicide part, because she had ethical qualms regarding the darker aspects of the character's choices.[102] Although some commentators have mistaken the two characters for one, they are not.[103] Olga Brodsky (Nade Dieu) is a Russian Jew accompanying her uncle Ramos García (Rony Kramer) to the Literary Encounters conference in Sarajevo. Ramos is a blind translator fluent in Russian, Spanish, French, Hebrew, Arabic and English. He signals the importance of language as the grounds for transcending into the other as expression (*Mitteilung*),[104] and its indissociability from translation. Furthermore, the languages Ramos speaks have been the languages of Empire at distinct historical junctures and further draw the geopolitical cartography of Europe's relationship to the Middle East, from Andalusia to the recent immigrants to Israel, the Russian Jews. When Godard asks Ramos García about his background, a parallel between his father's personal history and Henri Curiel's is drawn: each grew up in a well-to-do family in 1920s Cairo, getting an education in a Jesuit school and then moving to France to attend university. Henri Curiel became a political activist for nationalist struggles in the 1950s, and García's father migrated to Israel. Here personal identity is inextricable from history; by way of the two figures, García's father and Henri Curiel, Godard gives us an image of Egypt in relationship not only to Arab nationalism but also to the creation of Israel, evoking the Arab Jews' stories and their status as "a silent hyphen that fails to fuse," as Judeo-Christian

---

[99] "Why Sarajevo?" "Because of Palestine and because I live in Tel Aviv; I wanted to see a place where reconciliation seemed possible."

[100] Godard in an interview with Olivier Bombarda and Julien Welter for *Cahiers du Cinéma* on November 2007, http://www.cahiersducinema.com/article1424.html

[101] Godard, "The Godard Interview."

[102] Ibid.

[103] Ibid.

[104] Emmanuel Lévinas cited by Ernst Wolf, *De l'éthique à la justice* (Dordrecht: Springer, 2007), p. 211.

Europe's cultural-historical religious and political constitutive Other.[105] Through his own personal history, Ramos also lays out one of the literary questions in the film: "L'exode, ce n'est pas l'Exodus," he states, linking Greek tragedy and Biblical text. "Exode" (exit ode) in Greek drama follows the conclusion of a play, and is delivered as the chorus exits the scene. "Exodus" is the section in the Bible that tells how Moses leads the Israelites out from Egypt toward the Promised Land; and SS *Exodus* is the name of a ship carrying Shoah survivors from France to British Mandatory Palestine in July 1947. Another asymmetry is created: *L'Exode* (the end of the tragedy), *ce n'est pas l'exodus* (permanent condition of exile, expulsion), drawing a promise of return embedded in exile.

Olga has the same last name as the Nobel Prize-winning Russian Jewish writer, Joseph Brodsky. As an aspiring filmmaker, she gives Godard a DVD with video-work for him to see. She attends the filmmaker's lecture, where she learns that "Truth has two faces," and she closes her eyes to "see." Olga confronts us with the question of terrorism and martyrdom. Toward the end of the film, we learn from a phone conversation between Ramos García and Godard that presumably it was Olga who had entered a cinema in Jerusalem. Taking the public hostage, she stated that she would be happy if there was one Israeli who would go down with her for peace. After everyone ran out from the movie theater, the marksmen shot her only to find books in her bag. With her action, Olga invites death by drawing attention to her campaign for peace.[106] Olga takes Camus' problem of absolute freedom, the indistinction between life and death, into literal action: "La liberté sera totale quand il sera indifférent de vivre ou de mourir. Ça sera mon but."[107] She ponders the issue of suicide after Camus, for whom it is "le seul problème philosophique vraiment sérieux."[108] Because we are incapable of freeing ourselves, Olga's invitation to us to view suicide as a means of killing terror in the name of pacifism is a kind of post-ideological, atheist suicide. Because the means of death is beyond her control and her gesture is performed in the name of peace, the act is

---

[105] See Gil Anidjar's introduction to Jacques Derrida, *Acts of Religion* (London: Routledge, 2001), p. 10.

[106] As articulated by Michael Witt in "The Godard Interview."

[107] "Freedom will be total when there is no difference between living and dying. That will be my goal." This is a line from Dostoyevsky's Kirilov, in *The Possessed* (1872). Albert Camus' *Le Mythe de Sisyphe* (1942) (Paris: Gallimard, 1985) is a study of this character and the absurdity of his acts in relationship to God, the meaning of life and death, etc.

[108] "Suicide is the only philosophical problem that is truly serious" is the opening line of *Le Mythe de Sisyphe*.

distinguished from the radical action of suicide bombing as a means of achieving fundamentalist martyrdom, with its mystical and political connotations. With Olga, Godard poses the question of the void created by the failure of Leftism as revolutionary politics and the propagation of religious fundamentalism in monotheistic religions. Moreover, Olga's martyrdom mirrors Christ's own, who sacrificed himself—letting himself be killed—in the name of our sins, short-cutting penance by way of forgiveness and redemption. Later in the film, Olga utters Zosima's famous line to his mother on his deathbed from Dostoyevsky's *The Brothers Karamazov* (1880): "Each of us is guilty before the other for everything, and I am more (guilty) than any."[109] Olga explores in full measure the consequences of these words. Affirming this message of shared guilt and responsibility, she takes radical action, hoping that "Paradise arrives *now* in forbearance and forgiveness of one another."[110] Olga's suicide also highlights the parallel between Christian and Islamic theologies in which spiritual salvation and worldly justice are interrelated. Godard does this, without referring to the ethical scandal of the *passage à l'acte* killing innocent civilians, or without delving into elucidations about the causes and motivations of suicide bombers, because suicide is posited after Camus as an attempt to find answers in absurdity, pointing at the idea that the world is not only ruled by chance, but by absurdity.

Olga also embodies the question of the image in the film: struggling to remain a body, resisting becoming a figure, testing instances of the image as mimesis, becoming the symbolic, with her "suicide." In a scene at the Centre André Malraux, she enacts the relationship between image and text as mimesis when she sits, flipping over her lap pieces of card on which, like intertitles, her thoughts are written. Anticipating the narrative, she embodies the question of the image as the equation between thought and image (mimesis):

---

[109] Fyodor Dostoyevsky, *The Brothers Karamazov*, translated by David McDuff (London: Penguin 2003), 374. This line has also been quoted by Lévinas in *Ethics and Infinity*, translated by Richard Cohen (Pittsburgh: Duquesne University Press, 1985), 98. Lévinas further asserts that "I am responsible for the other but the other is not responsible for me," discussed by Slavoj Žižek in "Smashing the Neighbor's Face." Available at: http://www.lacan.com/zizsmash.htm

[110] Dostoyevsky, *The Brothers Karamazov*, 374. Godard stated that he identifies with Olga: "I thought if I were to commit suicide... I'd do it like Olga. I would achieve my suicide because I'd know the soldiers would shoot me three minutes later... And it would be done in the name of peace, with my friends the books. I am an image who has his friends, the books, in his pocket. And I said to myself, that I can do." Godard in "The Godard Interview."

Et la victoire?
Et la délivrance?
Ça sera mon martyre
Je serai ce soir au paradis[111]

As we will see below, Olga will again embody the question of the image as a matter of alterity and as the intensification of presence.

The question of the relationship between image and text as (in)memorial traces is evoked by Godard's crediting the Palestinian intellectual Elias Sanbar as the memory of the film. Sanbar in his work has drawn a link between the "Red Indians" in North America and the Palestinians. Godard borrows this idea—although let us also remember that the figure of the North American Red Indian appeared in Godard's work as early as *Weekend* and *One A.M.* and *Le Vent d'Est* representing the oppressed—and at the threshold of playing both themselves and fictional characters, three "Red Indians" (played by Georges Aguilar, Leticia Gutiérrez and Ferlyn Brass) appear at times in "ethnic" warrior attire or in "Western" clothes as imagined by Judith in a scene in which she makes photographs of the Mostar Bridge.[112] Before their appearance at the bridge, they haunt the Vijećnica Library, where they recite passages from Mahmoud Darwish's poem, "The Speech of the Red Indian,"[113] and are present as specters hovering around Judith's interview with the poet.

The characters in *Notre musique* that play themselves are authors like Godard: the writers Juan Goytisolo, Mahmoud Darwish, Pierre Bergounioux and Jean-Paul Curnier. Evidently there are echoes in their respective careers and works (e.g., in the late 1960s, Godard and Darwish asked questions about revolution and politics in their works; Curnier's most recent work parallels Godard's in problematizing the

---

[111] "And victory? And consolation? That will be my martyrdom. This evening I will be in paradise."

[112] A link could be drawn here to James Luna's photographic installation, *Apparitions* (2005). In this photographic superimposition, five Native Americans appear against the backdrop of contemporary consumerist life "armed with commodities" mirroring the ghostly image of their ancestors, proudly posing for the camera in warrior garb behind them. See also James S. Williams' discussion of the scene in his *Encounters With Godard: Ethics, Aesthetics, Politics* (Albany: State University of New York Press, 2016).

[113] Available at http://www.thecornerreport.com/index.php?title=speech_of_the_red_indian&more=1&c=1&tb=1&pb=1. It was first published in his collection *Eleven Planets* (1992), published in English as *The Adam of Two Edens*, translated by Munir Akash and Daniel Moore (Syracuse: Syracuse University Press, 2001).

links between culture, morality and war).[114] Gilles Péqueux, the French architect who worked on UNESCO's reconstruction of the Mostar Bridge, also plays himself in the film. Observing how the work on the bridge has become a metaphor for reconciliation in Sarajevo, Judith wonders: "Comment construire une visage avec des pierres?"[115]

The locations in the film have roles; like the characters, they contain palimpsests of meanings and histories. As a place where reconciliation between "East and West" seems possible, Sarajevo appears as a European city filled by the sound of the muezzins calling worshippers to prayer. In the movie also appear: the Centre André Malraux, which is the site for intellectual discussion and exchange; the French Embassy, a dislocated institution dedicated to transnational diplomatic dialogue; the airport, which is a liminal site of passage where connections are made with the rest of the world; the ruin of the Sarajevo Public Library, the Vijećnica, which was blown up by the Croats in 1992; and the Holiday Inn which, during the war, was a kind of Green Zone as the headquarters of international media agencies and the temporary home of their journalists and intellectuals.[116]

The film ends when Olga enters paradise, a beautiful forest guarded by American marines and populated by characters reading or playing, reminiscent of the paradise in Truffaut's *Fahrenheit 451* (1966). The inhabitants of this paradise communicate through body and facial gestures. Is heaven post- or pre-spoken language? Other silent signs appear; two characters mime playing with an invisible volleyball. Like Solomon in Dante's paradise, Godard's is one for contemplation. In heaven there is an oscillation between the question of the image posed by Olga in terms of the icon, as we will see below, and the proliferation of symbols (the apple, the American marine, the forest, the garden of delights). Heaven in *Notre musique* draws on its Judeo-Christian (and Islamic) ensemble of symbols, making connections between suicide and redemption, absurdity and salvation, martyrdom and joy, the earthly and divine world. This scene is as long as the first part of the triptych, and in it, inverting the Biblical story,

---

[114] For a detailed comparison of Godard's and Darwish's works and biographies see James S. Williams, "Presentation," in *Jean-Luc Godard Documents*.
[115] "How to build a face with stones?" (in Lévinas' sense of the face).
[116] Sontag and Goytisolo stayed there and often evoked it in their Sarajevo memoirs. Goytisolo, in his *Cuadernos de Sarajevo* (Madrid: Aguilar, 1993, pp. 63, 64) describes the hotel as a temple lacking its romantic aura, a kind of jail, a metaphor of the city under siege, a kind of exotic Polynesian cabin imported from Disneyland.

a young man offers Olga an apple upon her arrival in heaven. The apple is the Judeo-Christian symbol of knowledge, which is the desire to ask ethical questions in order to live freely. The film ends when Olga closes her eyes in paradise, where, we hear, "Il faisait beau et clair."[117]

From Speaking in the Name of Others to a Simple Conversation

Evidently questions of dissent, engagement, activism and responsibility regarding public intellectuals' intervention elsewhere arose during the Balkans War. Immersed in the actuality and the reality as the consciousness of the world, Juan Goytisolo's description of the destruction of the Vijećnica Library is an example and part of a longer document, his *Cuadernos de Sarajevo* (1993). The *Cuadernos* (notebooks) document "una larga lista de vilezas,"[118] recounting the horrors in the city under siege. The genocide was widely covered and it was the first televised event of its kind.[119] By "covered" I mean both in the journalistic sense and in the sense of "covering" horrors with mass-media images in Baudrillard's sense of the hyper-real. This war, moreover, for Susan Sontag and many others, symbolized the end of the belief that, if people around the world knew, they would do something about it.[120] Sontag and Goytisolo lamented the general apathy of intellectuals and artists, as their attempts to bring in renowned intellectuals to Sarajevo during the siege were futile. Goytisolo compared the conditions of intervention in Sarajevo with the engagement of the rest of the world during the Spanish Civil War in 1936, wondering, "¿Dónde están los Hemingway, Dos Passos, Koestler, Simone Weil, Auden, Spender, Paz, que no vacilaron en comprometerse e incluso a combatir, como Malraux y Orwell, al lado del pueblo agredido e inerme?"[121] Evoking the 1930s and the 1960s, Sontag condemned the

---

[117] "It was beautiful and clear."

[118] "A long list of despicable acts."

[119] Here we can draw a parallel to the Romanian revolution, and to the First Gulf War, the first of their kind to be televised. For a literary and critical reflection (with lots of humor) on the implications of the broadcasting of the Romanian revolution see Chris Kraus' novel, *Torpor* (New York: Semiotext(e), 2006). See also Jean Baudrillard, *The Gulf War Did Not Take Place*, translated by Paul Patton (Bloomington: Indiana University Press, 1995).

[120] Susan Sontag, "Here and There," p. 320.

[121] "Where are [today's counterparts to] Hemingway, Dos Passos, Koestler, Simone Weil, Auden, Spender, Paz, who did not hesitate to commit themselves or, like Malraux and

"morosely depoliticized intellectuals of today", lamenting the decay in international solidarity.[122] The reason for this, she elucidated, might have been the individual dedication to private life, which is perhaps the reason why the stretch between "here" and "there" has become too great to encourage solidarity. Other explanations for the lack of sympathy were, for Sontag and Goytisolo, a kind of "ideological confusion" and a "resigned stupor" in the face of ethnic cleansing. Sontag speculates that the reason why intellectuals worldwide took no position *vis-à-vis* the conflict was due to an aversion to Islam and to prevailing stereotypes about Muslims, a failure of identification and thus the inability to incite empathy.[123]

Susan Sontag was in and out of Sarajevo between 1993 and 1995. For her, the task at hand was no longer to bring the information home.[124] Drawing a distinction from her former revolutionary excursions, where she mainly visited, observed and wrote (in Vietnam, Cambodia, China, North Africa, and Mexico), *doing something* became crucial to her. Striving to actively engage with the besieged, she stated that her commitment was based on solidarity as a form of "endurance with," differently from being a passive observer:

> I made a commitment at the risk of my life, under a situation of extreme discomfort and mortal danger. Bombs went off, bullets flew past my head... There was no food, no electricity, no running water, no mail, no telephone day after day, week after week, month after month. This is not "symbolic." This is real.[125]

More than being a witness, she had a *reason* to be there: her commitment to stage a play in collaboration with local actors. They chose Samuel Beckett's *Waiting for Godot*. Jean Baudrillard wrote a diatribe against Sontag, accusing her of being "merely a societal instance of cultural soul-boosting," and of "adopting a condescending attitude toward an unequal

---

Orwell, fought alongside those who were under assault and defenceless?", *Cuadernos de Sarajevo*, p. 98.

[122] Susan Sontag, "Here and There," (1995), in *Where the Stress Falls* (New York: Farrar, Straus and Giroux, 2001), p. 328.

[123] Susan Sontag, "Waiting for Godot in Sarajevo," in *Where the Stress Falls*, p. 307.

[124] "Bringing the information home" a rearticulation of the Weather Underground's slogan: "To bring the war home," was appropriated by Martha Rosler and expressed in her 1969–72 collage series, *Bringing the War Home: House Beautiful*.

[125] Susan Sontag in Conversation with Evan Chan, "Against Postmodernism etcetera" (July 2000) available at: http://pmc.iath.virginia.edu/issue.901/12.1chan.html

exchange with the victims of the siege."[126] For Baudrillard, Sontag's intervention exemplified a general loss of confidence by intellectuals, a symptom of a larger intellectual crisis at stake. In sum, he blamed Sontag for coming to Sarajevo to convince the besieged of the "reality" of their suffering by doing something useful, cultural and theatrical that stemmed from Western values.[127] What kinds of engaged relations could be woven with peoples undergoing humanitarian crises? What are the limits of interested engagement as solidarity and endurance or in making known the catastrophe? Is "making known" a formal problem or an ethical imperative? Is there an equivalent in aesthetic practice to UNPROFOR's "right of humanitarian intrusion"? What are the cognitive models that would be capable of accounting for catastrophe in the age of hyper-reality? Is the effort to bring solace and consolation to the besieged a sign of narcissistic projection and of intellectual futility? How would we frame the intervention of the mujahideen, who came to fight in solidarity alongside the Bosnians?[128]

Godard's response to the debate raised by Sontag's intervention was to go to Sarajevo, not in the middle of the war like Sontag, Goytisolo and international journalists, but after it had ended, when the city had been (partially) reconstructed and the parts "reconciled," at a moment when, according to Godard, Sarajevo had become an empty Tower of Babel, "a place to which no one goes anymore."[129] In a statement he made about the need to film in Sarajevo, and drawing up the genealogy of *Tiersmondisme* along with the questions such interventions raise, Godard said:

> The film answered a sort of call. A little like when I was an active militant for peace in Vietnam or in Palestine, a process of which I'm an old veteran, nearly 30 years now, old enough to be an adult.[130]

---

[126] Jean Baudrillard, "No Reprieve for Sarajevo," translated by Patrice Riemens, initially published in *Libération* (January 8, 1994). Available at: http://www.egs.edu/faculty/baudrillard/baudrillard-no-reprieve-for-sarajevo.html

[127] Baudrillard, "No Reprieve for Sarajevo."

[128] See Jean-Arnault Dérens, "Islam in Bosnia," *Le Monde diplomatique* (September 2008). Available at: http://mondediplo.com/2008/09/10bosnia

[129] Ibid.

[130] Godard, "The Godard Interview."

In another interview, Godard addressed the issue of representativity at the core of politically engaged filmmaking *elsewhere*, in *Notre musique*:

> In this film, you hear voices from around the world, but they aren't Bosnian voices, because *I can't speak for them*. I haven't made a "nice" militant film. But I show people who want to be part of a conversation and who want the conversation to continue. And conversation is thought – it's not the chatter of the media, not what we're doing right now.[131]

The statement, "I can't speak for the Bosnian voices," evokes Godard's and Gorin's quandaries as "militants" and "filmmakers," which have the question of the possibility of representativity at their core. Godard further differentiates his work from mass media and posits his intervention as a *conversation*. A question that becomes central in *Notre musique* is that of the relationship between *praxis* and *poiesis*, political action and aesthetic representation, inherited from Marxist militantism in the twentieth century framed by the larger scope of History and the Homeric epic within the frame of the Balkans War. In a dialogue at the French Embassy in Sarajevo, Naville, the French Ambassador, asks Péqueux if intellectuals "know" what they are talking about. Evoking Homer, Péqueux answers that the poet neither saw nor was present at the battlefields, the massacres, or the moment of victory, that he is blind and bored and that he recounts the actions of others. Péqueux thus suggests a contradiction between acting and saying: "Ceux qui agissent n'ont jamais la capacité de dire ni de penser de façon adéquate ce qu'ils font. Inversement, ceux qui racontent des histoires, ils composent des vers, ne savent pas de quoi ils parlent."[132] He then adds with bitter humor: "Rappelles-toi Mao Tsé Tung."[133] Péqueux bestows the capacity to "speak" to poets, historians and the *powers of the false*. In Godard's statement above, and in the discussion between Naville and Péqueux, *poiesis* is valued as the potential to create a redistribution of the signs amongst us by eliminating the noise that can be created by passionate action. As Godard makes in *Notre musique* a plea on

---

[131] Jean-Luc Godard, "Occupational Hazards: JLG at Work, as told to Frédéric Bonnaud," in *Film Comment* (January–February 2005), p. 37.

[132] "Those who act never have the capacity to adequately think about what they are doing and describe it for us. Conversely, those who tell stories and compose verses have no real knowledge of what they are talking about."

[133] "Remember Mao-Tse Tung."

behalf of conversation, the right to speak (for which students and workers fought in May 1968) becomes the right to interlocution, to open up the possibility of merging into a community grounded in signs (which is the pre-political). Moreover, in *Notre musique*, *praxis* and *poiesis* relate like the shot/reverse-shot in a relationship that is established amongst the characters: the journalist (Judith) and suicidal filmmaker (Olga) take direct action in the world, and thus they belong to the realm of *praxis*, while the older writers relate to the world as *poiesis*.[134] Godard's plea for *poiesis* is for the right to fiction, for the text, for the imaginary as the only possible way to think of horror.

In another scene in the film, wandering through the Vijećnica Library, Goytisolo raises again the issue of the relationship between *poiesis* and *praxis* as a matter of the image and in terms of relationships between creation, voice and image: "Si nuestra época ha alcanzado una interminable fuerza de destrucción," he states, "hay que hacer la revolución que cree una indeterminable fuerza de creación, que fortalezca los recuerdos, que precise los sueños, *que corporice las imágenes*." (my italics)[135] For Goytisolo, the task at hand is to wage a revolution with a creative force that would strengthen memories, spell out dreams, and "render images corporeal" or "provide images with a body." Aside from his enthusiastic defense of creativity, he poses the question of images in terms of the dogma of incarnation—the problem of the body without a figure. This implies a notion of the image as an artificial image with a consubstantial relationship to the invisible and to our corporeal reality. Furthermore, this artificial image is an imaginary that is visible through its consubstantiality with the Word, which is the origin of the image as a sacred imprint.[136] Within this paradigm of the image, Goytisolo's appeal to render bodies corporeal implies, first, displacing the illusion of real presence,

---

[134] The distinction in the film between (female) *praxis* (Olga, Judith) and (male) *poiesis* (the parade of authors) brings to mind Godard's and Miéville's *Soft and Hard* (1985) in which both, playing themselves, provocatively enact the gendered roles of women as producers and men as creators.

[135] "If our epoch has arrived at an unending destructive force, we must wage a revolution by creating an unending force of creation that would strengthen our memories, concretize our dreams, and *corporealize images*" (my italics).

[136] Marie José Mondzain, *Image, icône, économie: Les Sources byzantines de l'imaginaire contemporain* (Paris: Seuil, 1998), translated by Rico Franses, *Image, Icon, Economy: The Byzantine Origins of the Contemporary Imaginary* (Stanford: Stanford University Press, 2004), p. 70.

and second, strengthening the "voice that comes from elsewhere to inhabit the visible."[137] The visible would then become the site for address and for listening, a kind of "voice-in" of the image, making the force of the image measurable in relation to the power of the voice inhabiting it.[138] Along similar lines, Godard stated:

> I as a man of the image was pleading on behalf of the other and in the name of the text, like the Bosnian who pleads on behalf of the Serb. I was pleading in the name of the text.[139]

Godard's plea in the name of the text stems from the problem he poses in *Notre musique*: "le champ du texte a été recouvert par le champ de la vision...les faits ne parlent plus pour eux-mêmes...."[140] This resonates with D.N. Rodowick's definition of the *figural*, a regime of visibility that disturbs the analogy between image and text. Image and text relate as two separate streams, the first characterized by simultaneity (repetition and resemblance between a thing and its figure) and the other by succession (differentiation and affirmation). In the figural, however, the world of things is penetrated by discourse welding the two streams together, as in branding.[141] In his lecture, Godard holds up a photograph of a ruin, asking the students to guess where it was taken. After a few failed attempts (Berlin, Sarajevo, Chechnya), we are all surprised to learn that it is an image of Richmond, Virginia, taken in 1865 after the conclusion of the American Civil War. Godard demonstrates here that, in spite of their indexical status, our exposure to the excess of images of debris has removed their particularity. In this manner, the field of the text (here, the caption) has been re-covered by the image. This implies that images offer themselves simultaneously to the gaze and to a discourse marking the disappearance of the invisible.[142] In other words, when a sensible reality

---

[137] Marie-José Mondzain, *L'image, peut-elle tuer?* (Paris: Bayard, 2002), p. 84.
[138] As Mondzain put it, incarnation is God's 'voice-in.' In *L'image, peut-elle tuer?* p. 89.
[139] Godard, "The Godard Interview."
[140] "The field of the text has been re-covered by the field of vision...The facts no longer speak for themselves." From Godard's lecture at the Centre André Malraux in *Notre musique*.
[141] D.N. Rodowick, *Reading the Figural, or, Philosophy After the New Media* (Durham, NC: Duke University Press, 2001), p. 8.
[142] As a way to explain the relationship between text, image, the imaginary and the real, in his lecture in *Notre musique* Godard gives us the following example: "En 1938, Heisenberg et Bohr se promènent dans la campagne et parlent de physique et ils arrivent devant le château d'Elsinore et l'allemand dit 'Oh lala il n'y a rien d'extraordinaire!' Oui, mais si vous

offers itself simultaneously to the gaze and to knowledge, it is because the relationship between text and image is considered as arbitrary or incomparable, which is different from ambivalent, or bearing a relationship of resemblance. For Godard, to make a plea in the name of the text is to intercede for the ambivalence between text and image. This would imply that meaning is invisible because the image is doing something more than the text, which, in turn, as we have seen, can never fully account for it.

Moreover, a plea is a form of speech as intercession, here on behalf of poetry and history. Aside from pleading, Godard has used other forms of speech on behalf of the other, like greeting and praying. For instance, he "hails Sarajevo" in his video-letter *Je vous salue, Sarajevo*, in which he addresses the inhabitants of the besieged city by summoning them up as interlocutors. Engaging with two famous cases of Israeli refuseniks who served prison sentences because of their self-claimed status as "conscientious objectors" (2002–04), Godard made two short films for them in the form of prayers: *Prière pour refuzniks 1 et 2*, a double gesture of support as a prayer and as a gift. Pleading, summoning and praying are corporeal events that concern an action in relationship to a bodies that are interpellated through intercession, summoning and a greeting. These are events of language that invoke the other and "by which the posing subject exposes herself."[143] Godard's repeated reference to such events of language implies that a social link is established by the event of language. For Lévinas, praying is prior to both common content and understanding. Evidently, interceding, summoning and invoking the other are different from bringing into presence, conveying chatter or transmitting a scream of indignation in the face of horrors committed by humanity (as Godard, influenced by Adorno, posited as the task of intellectuals, as we saw in Chapter 2). Moreover, praying, pleading and greeting are at the margins of determination: they are speech-acts invoking the other, thereby establishing a bond that is not reducible to

---

dites: 'Le château d'Hamlet,' alors il devient extraordinaire. 'Elsinore' est le réel, et 'Hamlet,' l'imaginaire: champ et contrechamp. Imaginaire: certitude. Réel: incertitude." In the interview with Michael Witt, he gives the example again: "A good example of a real shot/reverse-shot is one I took from a book by German physicist Werner Heisenberg who, on visiting his friend Niels Bohr before the war, arrived at Elsinore Castle. Here the shot is the castle, the reverse-shot the description "Hamlet's castle." In this case the image is created by the text. It's what poetry does – like two stars whose rapprochement produces a constellation." In "The Godard Interview."

[143] "Par la parole proférée, le sujet qui se pose s'expose et, en quelque manière, prie." Lévinas, *Hors sujet*, 203, cited by Ernst Wolf, *De l'éthique à la justice*, p. 213.

the representation of the other because "what is named is at the same time what is called."[144] Thus, for Godard, "speaking for others" in *Notre musique* implies summoning up interlocutors and filming them as part of a conversation. A conversation is "the creation of extraordinary words put to the most ordinary use, not to raise objections, but to use inexact words to designate something exactly, *pas une conversation juste, juste une conversation,*"[145] where two sides of a story, two versions of the truth are brought together face-to-face.

Shot/Reverse-Shot

Conventionally, the shot/reverse-shot technique of montage in classic cinema helps to depict dialogue by using close-ups of the characters that are having a conversation face-to-face. Creating an axis and alternating the images of the interlocutors, their gazes "meet" in the sequence, representing two points of view in a conversation. When we see the shot, the reverse-shot is the frontal out-of field of the shot. Godard stated that, for him, the reverse-shot is not the "other" of the shot, but "the same" in a different situation. Rather than impose a view that would orient us in the landscape presented to us,[146] the montage of "shot 1" and "shot 2" helps to interrogate the facts that are produced, but that we do not know how to bring into a relationship.[147] "Shot 1" and "shot 2" are unstable and thus exchangeable, the juxtapositions undo and unfold into others. Distinct from Godard's *in-between* method of montage, in which meaning is exchanged through a concatenation of series of images, in the shot/reverse-shot, two sides of a story are brought together face-to-face.

In the staged lecture at the Centre André Malraux shown in *Notre musique*, Godard juxtaposes two photographs from 1948, one of the future Israelis docking in Israel and one of Palestinians fleeing by sea, and states: "En 1948 les Israélites marchent dans l'eau dans la terre promise; les palestiniens marchent dans l'eau, dans la noyade: Champ et contre champ; le peuple juif rejoint la fiction, le palestinien, le documentaire."[148]

---

[144] Emmanuel Lévinas, *Entre nous (Essais sur le penser-à-l'autre)* (Paris: Poche, 1993), p. 7.
[145] Gilles Deleuze and Claire Parnet, *Dialogues*, translated by Hugh Tomlinson and Barbara Habberjam (New York: Columbia University Press, 1987), 3.
[146] Godard in "Jean-Luc Godard et *Notre musique*, Juste une conversation," p. 21.
[147] Ibid.
[148] "In 1948 the Israelites wade through water towards the Promised Land, while the Palestinians walk into it and are submerged [lit. drowned]. Shot and reverse-shot: the Jewish people enter fiction, the Palestinian people, documentary."

This statement has been very controversial and has gained Godard further accusations of anti-Semitism. In my view, Godard's pro-Palestinian position means that, after the history of Zionism, Israelis were finally established in their fictional land.[149] "Israeli fictions," following the reading by Gilles Deleuze, can be interpreted as Israel's "right" to negate the existence of Palestine and Palestinians. By having evacuated them geographically, Israeli apologists argue that theirs is not a colonial enterprise, since the Palestinians were not exploited but expelled from the land.[150] Furthermore, Israelis defend themselves from the charge of genocide because, for them, the elimination of a Palestinian presence is a means to ensure the Jewish identity of the Israeli state. The cost of the Jewish identity is physical expulsion of the "other", contingent upon geographical evacuation and ongoing erasure. This problematic equation of nation, religion and ethnic identity has not only transformed the Palestinians into the "others" of Israelis, but it has also allowed critiques of both Israel's exclusive origins and its enduring policies to be characterized as anti-Semitism.[151] Godard's assertion in *Notre musique* that Palestinians fell into documentary, therefore, refers to the fact that through documentary and documentation, Palestinians have presented themselves as a people with a history and as victims of Israeli expulsion and occupation, putting forth their cause as a liberation of the territory where their history was written. In *Notre musique*, as we will see, a plea is made for belief as the right to fiction of Palestinians, when Jean-Paul Curnier, citing Pascal, states: "moi je ne crois que dans les histoires où les témoins se font égorger."[152] This plea goes hand in hand with a plea in the name of the text (storytelling, poetry, the powers of the false).

Another element from *Notre musique* that has caused polemics is the example Godard gives us of the shot/reverse-shot in his lecture as an image of a face with the caption "Jew"[153] and the image of a Jew in a concentra-

---

[149] This corresponds to Godard as well to a phrase by Elias Sanbar (also quoted in the film): "When an Israeli dreams at night, he does not dream of Israel, but of Palestine, while when a Palestinian dreams at night, he absolutely does not dream of Israel, but of Palestine." From a public discussion between Godard and Sanbar on January 16, 2005 as recounted by Christoff Kantcheff. Available at http://www.politis.fr/article1213.html

[150] Gilles Deleuze, "Grandeur de Yasser Arafat," *Revue d'études Palestiniennes* No. 10, (Winter 1984), 41–43. Reprinted in *Two Regimes of Madness: Texts and Interviews 1975–1995*, translated by Ames Hodges and Mike Taormina (Cambridge, MA: MIT Press, 2007).

[151] Gilles Deleuze, "Grandeur de Yasser Arafat," pp. 41–43.

[152] "I only believe in stories in which the witnesses get their throats cut."

[153] We can read in the image that this is an anti-Semitic portrayal of a Jew.

tion camp at the threshold of death, captioned by the word "Musulman."[154] This juxtaposition is not new in Godard, and between the two images there is a third one, of an animated skull wearing the mask of a skull. Although Godard brings the Jews and Palestinians into a relationship as two communities of survivors and exiled peoples, and Palestinians as the same-others-enemies, as unmournable lives for Israelis, Godard relates the Shoah and the Nakba as the shot/reverse-shot, an asymmetrical relationship because he argues the Israelis found the "other" in the Palestinians, but Israelis are not the "other" of Palestinians.[155] Godard has made it clear that for him the Shoah and the Nakba are not the same thing. As he put it:

> I bring together two situations; it is not that I contend that the Shoah suffered by the Jews and the Nakba suffered by the Palestinians are the same thing. Of course not! The shot and the reverse-shot do not mean equivalence, they rather pose a question. When the Israelis found "the other" in the Palestinians…they had to encounter them face to face. Whereas for the Palestinians it is not the same thing, Israel is not the "other" of Palestinians. This dissymmetry constitutes a true shot/reverse-shot, a bringing into relation that poses questions rather than equating them.[156]

In *Notre musique*, moreover, juxtapositions are never equivalent or stable: "Le vrai contrechamp des palestiniens c'est sans doute moins Israël que les Indiens."[157] Thus in *Notre musique*, the "Red Indians," along with the Balkans War, as historical figures and references, are introduced as mediators: the four histories merge into one another and exchange places in terms of the shot/reverse-shot logic.

Annihilation, the "Pure Past" and Phaedra

Two sets of ruins from Sarajevo appear in the film: the numbered fragments of the bombed and then reconstructed Mostar Bridge, and the burnt remains of Vijećnica Library. *Shot*: The restored bridge uniting the

---

[154] The word "Muselmann" appeared as well in *Ici et ailleurs* as the caption for an image from Resnais' documentary footage of the concentration camps in *Nuit et Bruillard* (1955).
[155] Godard, "The Godard Interview."
[156] Ibid.
[157] "The true reverse-shot of Palestinians is, without a doubt, less Israel than the [Red] Indians." Godard, as reported by Christophe Kantcheff, in a public discussion between Godard and Sanbar on January 16, 2005.

Christian and Muslim communities in Mostar. "Mostar" means "Bridge-keeper." The bridge was commissioned by Suleiman the Magnificent and built in 1566 by the Ottoman architect Hayyedin, with 456 blocks of stone. In the film we see amateur video images documenting the collapse of the bridge as it was blown up in 1993 by the Croats. We also see a scene in which Judith watches the history of the bridge being taught to children who then sing a song about it. Rebuilt in 2003, for Judith the bridge is a sign of hope and reconciliation. Péqueux, who was put in charge of the UNESCO project of rebuilding the bridge along with the six others that spanned the Neretva River in 1995, states in the film: "Il ne s'agit pas de rétablir le tourisme. Il faut à la fois restaurer le passée pour rendre le futur possible. Marier la souffrance avec la culpabilité."[158] Michael Ignatieff has argued that the reconstruction of the bridge be seen as an imperialist effort of nation-building. For him, it is not by chance that Péqueux is French, and he points at the imperial implications in the fact that Péqueux was trained at the École des Ponts et des Chaussées, founded by Napoleon. Péqueux wanted to rebuild the bridge as close as possible to the original, reviving and teaching Muslim and Croat masons the Ottoman techniques. In the end, they did not rebuild the old bridge with the old stones, but a new old bridge.[159] The questions that arise here are: does restoring cultural symbols from the past entail the recognition of a wrong that has been done and constitute acknowledgement of guilt? Does the acknowledgment of responsibility and suffering have the redemptive power of actualizing a new, virtual past? The reconstruction of the bridge symbolizes the reunification of the ethnic-religious divide that the war created between the Muslim and Croat communities. In the film, we are led to believe that the bridge was meticulously reconstructed from the fragments that were recovered from the Neretva River and then numbered in order to put them back together. *Reverse-shot*: This was not the case, as Godard reveals in an interview:

> Gilles Péqueux was fired and replaced by a Croat who made a bridge like any other, constructed out of new stone clad to make it look authentic. It's what they do on DVDs: a restoration. All the stones I filmed, which were retrieved from the river and individually numbered, weren't used – though watching

---

[158] "The project is not about bringing back tourism. It is necessary to rehabilitate the past in order to make the future possible. Marrying suffering with guilt."
[159] Michael Ignatieff, *Empire Lite*, pp. 39–41.

the film the viewer thinks they're going to be. They're now in a spot the inhabitants of Mostar call "the cemetery of stones."[160]

"Authenticity" is a key word here, in the sense of the contemporary subjective conjunction of "tourism" and "experience." "Culture," in other words, is the main component of enlightened travel whose purpose is to create surplus value from tourism by gaining (cultural) knowledge of the elsewhere. The link Godard makes between the restoration of memory (as culture) and restoring classical films and selling them as DVDs in massive quantities, points at a false unity of the object delivered by the memory industry, as memorials are always fragmented and falling short in accounting for the past. Industrialized memorials represent reified memory, a form of remembrance that is politicized by claiming a historicity that is only legible at a certain moment in time. In short, the restoration of Mostar Bridge has become an instance and a metaphor for reconciliation that is capable of creating cultural surplus value. For Goytisolo and Marcus Tanner, a reporter for *The Independent*, "The bridge's symbolism has changed from a symbol of ethnic unity to a tourist trap."[161] Evidently, the restoration of the bridge was not enough to reunite the communities after the war. During the war the Bosnian Croats had allocated Mostar as the future capital of a Croatian mini-state that would be called Herzeg-Bosnia, but the city was full of Muslims who objected. The HOS (Croatian Defense Forces) failed to displace them and, instead of taking over Mostar, they concentrated on the western part of the city and locked up the Muslims in the eastern part by blowing up the bridge, dividing Mostar into two cities, like Belfast, Nicosia or Jerusalem. What used to be the Muslim homes were taken over by Croats who had fled the Muslim attacks in central Bosnia. Today the western part is richer than the eastern one and, according to Tanner, "a new generation of children born in the 1980s has no memory of the daily contact between Muslims and Serbs."[162] Rather than bringing the former organic community back together, the bridge has become a wall of separation, a substitute for reconciliation. According to Ignatieff, the links between physical and mental reconstruction, between rebuilding infrastructure and reconciling mentalities remain

---

[160] Godard, "The Godard Interview."
[161] From: "A symbol of hope is reborn in Mostar" by Marcus Tanner, *The Independent*, April 18, 2004. Available at https://www.independent.co.uk/news/world/europe/bridge-over-the-ethnic-divide-a-symbol-of-hope-is-reborn-in-mostar-5355111.html
[162] Ibid.

unclear.[163] Furthermore, Ignatieff tells us, leaders from both communities are aware that foreign funds for reconciliation in Mostar will dry up unless they show multi-ethnic efforts of co-operation and thus they meet for photo opportunities when necessary.[164] Architectural rehabilitation in *Notre musique* is problematized along with official commemoration and the management of the memory of the recent past as an industry, evidently lacking any redemptive potential beyond the scope of immediate consumption and echoing Godard's concern since *Je vous salue, Sarajevo* and especially in *Éloge de l'amour* with the reification of memory by the culture industry.

The second ruin from Sarajevo that *Notre musique* lingers on is the Vijećnica Library, which has only recently been considered for reconstruction and rehabilitation. It was bombed in 1992 by the Serb nationalists. The Vijećnica was the first victim of the war, and it symbolized the elimination of the "historical substance" of the former Yugoslavia, because, following Goytisolo, libraries are symbols of dialogue amongst peoples and active transmitters of knowledge of this dialogue. Goytisolo, echoing Tanner, states that the restored multi-religious architectural fabric of Sarajevo is only good for tourism and that, after the war, each community withdrew into itself: the loss of the myth of multicultural Sarajevo as the "European Jerusalem" is the reality of a deep wound incised by ethnic hatred.[165]

In *Notre musique*, Judith and Péqueux address pressing questions of memory and whether restitution, rehabilitation and reconciliation are the means to do justice, leading toward a peaceful future. The kind of ethics that they open up is not to "right wrongs" in the sense of demanding justice and restitution based upon responsibility for the other and accountability for oneself (because in ethical terms, after Dostoyevsky's quote, we are all guilty and thus responsible for the other). They strive for a retrospective judgment that allots to the involved parties a position in the conflict. This is the Homeric moment of the rewriting of history, considered here as a "pure past." A pure past entails an understanding that the past can be subjected to retroactive change in a new present. This is possible because the past is incomplete: therefore, we have the capacity to change it retroactively. In other words, we are determined by and dependent on the past, but we

---

[163] Ignatieff, *Empire Lite*, p. 36.
[164] Ibid., p. 38.
[165] Juan Goytisolo, "Polvo y Cenizas," *El País*, July 27, 2008, http://www.elpais.com/articulo/opinion/Polvo/cenizas/elpepiopi/20080727elpepiopi_5/Tes

have the freedom to define the scope of this determination, that is, to (over)determine the past which will determine us.[166]

In its bringing together of a series of historical moments, *Notre musique* recalls D. W. Griffith's 1916 film *Intolerance*. According to its opening expository intertitle, *Intolerance* is "an investigation into how hatred and intolerance through all ages have fought against love and charity." When Deleuze discusses the film in *Cinema 1*, he argues that the film raises the question of the pure past as the submission of the recent or ancient past that is brought to trial. The trial has the purpose of disclosing good and evil and asking what it is that produces decadence and what it is that produces new life. The trial thus calls for "a strong ethical judgment that must condemn the injustice of 'things,' and to bring compassion."[167] The histories told in *Intolerance* are individual stories: a peasant girl in the court of Babylon as it was destroyed by the Persians; a Pharisee observing the Calvary of Christ; a young Protestant girl during Catherine de Medici's and Philip II's persecution of the Huguenots in France; and a working-class girl in the modern United States. In terms of the narrative structure, Griffith explained that:

> The stories begin like four currents looked at from a hilltop. At first, the four currents flow apart, slowly and quietly, but as they flow, they grow nearer and nearer together, and faster and faster until the end. In the last act they mingle into one mighty river of expressed emotion.[168]

Deleuze calls the parallel editing of the stories from *Intolerance*, "organic montage," which he opposes to the Russians' dialectical montage. The stories meet at the narrative cusps and Griffith's montage creates a false continuity that is analogous to a linear conception of history. After Deleuze, the parallels that converge through the actions (i.e., the chariot race in Babylon, and the race between the car and the train in the modern United States), create a contracted present that presents (linear) monumental history as a *whole* that happens at the *interval* between the actions.

---

[166] Deleuze in *Difference and Repetition*, 181–183, quoted and commented on by Žižek, *In Defense of Lost Causes* (London: Verso, 2009), p. 313.

[167] Gilles Deleuze, *Movement-Image* (Minneapolis: University of Minesotta Press, 2002), p. 151.

[168] D.W. Griffith quoted in *Highlights* edited by Sarah Lucas (New York: The Museum of Modern Art, revised 2004), 96. For further reference, see the narrative scheme of the film published in *Cahiers du Cinéma* (Spring 1972).

The interval gets smaller and smaller in the accelerated montage, provoking the actions to converge throughout the centuries in a *superimposition of the different histories*.[169] By filming universal history as an immutable past and as a superimposition of injustices and horrors, Griffith's *Intolerance* accuses and pronounces verdict, condemning wrongs, reiterating the infinite debt owed to the victims by the oppressors. The establishment of the relationship of "creditor-debtor" acknowledges suffering by a judgment in the sense of Greek tragedy, a genre that is indissociable from a tribunal, merging obligation, defense and accusation.[170]

The superimposition of historical injustices in *Intolerance* is comparable to that in *Notre musique*, but rather than meeting at the narrative cusps via superimposition, *Notre musique* is a palimpsest of histories of wars of annihilation. The histories relate as the virtual and the actual of each other, insofar as the pure past is sedimented as the fundamental scission in time: "making the present pass, conserving the past."[171] The film's interweaving of temporalities and histories renders it endlessly evocative of the different presents and pasts of the victims of hubris. In *Intolerance* (and in Greek tragedy), the guilty are brought to trial in order to rearrange the past and to make the future possible, creating the infinite debt of restitution. In *Notre musique*, as we have seen, Godard postulates that *we are all guilty for everyone and for everything (and I am the guiltiest of us all)*, and thus to seek to establish relationships of restitutionary debt is beside the point. An attempt at a new beginning based on restitution and cultural rehabilitation as ways toward forgiveness was made in Sarajevo, but forgiveness is not a guarantee. Rehabilitation cannot rearrange the past, because it re-establishes the past as it previously existed and as novelty. In principle, rehabilitation does not readjust the past, accounting for the present *and* for the past.

Furthermore, forgiveness and making a promise are paradoxical modalities of judgment that happen intrasubjectively, in lived time, as opposed to being addressed to the act of hubris. Promise is a "supreme sovereignty by which man answers for himself as for the future,"[172] inheriting debts

---

[169] Gilles Deleuze, *Movement-Image*, pp. 31, 32.
[170] Gilles Deleuze, "To Have Done With Judgment," in *Essays Critical and Clinical*, translated by Dan Smith and Michel Greco (Minneapolis: University of Minnesota Press, 1997), p. 126, 128.
[171] Gilles Deleuze and Claire Parnet, *Dialogues* (Paris: Flammarion, 1996), 184.
[172] Julia Kristeva, *Hannah Arendt: Life is a Narrative* (Alexander Lectures) (Toronto: Toronto University Press, 2001), p. 78.

and a guilty conscience. Forgiveness is a way to break away from this infinite indebtedness and, along with making a promise, it is the possibility of new beginnings.[173] Rehabilitation, however, neither promises nor guarantees forgiveness but rather separates justice from its immediate realization in vengeance and from the possibility of intrasubjective judgment. In other words, the "promise of justice" embedded in rehabilitation is politicized "grace."[174]

Godard evokes Greek epic with Homer, and Greek tragedy (in its Christian version) via Racine's *Phèdre*, a figure that symbolizes the Jansenist belief that grace and the forgiveness of sins cannot be earned or bought, but are allotted by God as he sees fit. That is, the condition of grace is within man, but the cause of grace dwells outside.[175] Phaedra is neither fully guilty nor completely innocent. Her incestuous love for Hippolyte is impure, but as love, it is pure. Her line, cited in *Notre musique*, is spoken by Godard: "Quand tu sauras mon crime, et le sort qui m'accable, je n'en mourrai pas moins, mais j'en mourrai plus coupable."[176] This quote crystallizes Phaedra's conundrum: her guilt and her inability to utter her crime. According to Roland Barthes, *Phaedra*'s problem is nominal: to name her crime, which is her monstrous desire. "To name or not to name" is not the question of the meaning of language but its manifestation.[177] To surrender to logos would liberate Phaedra, but the creation by speech is definitive (because speech is action), and she thus avoids speech and therefore actions, shifting the responsibility to others.[178] In the end, Phaedra speaks three times: first narcissistically, then she represents her love and lastly she confesses. In the tragedy, language is recovered and charged with a positive function. According to Barthes, Phaedra dies having found

---

[173] Ibid., p. 85. The Israeli filmmaker Udi Aloni made a film in 2002, *Local Angel*, documenting his and his mother's visit to Yasser Arafat asking him for forgiveness.

[174] See Howard Caygill, "The Promise of Justice," *Radical Philosophy*, no. 143 (May–June 2007).

[175] Gustav Thibon, introduction to Simone Weil, *Gravity and Grace* (London: Routledge, 2002), p. xxxiii.

[176] "When you shall know my crime and heavy fate, I shall not die the less. I shall still die, but [be] blamed for ever." Jean Racine, *Phèdre*, translated by Margaret Rawlings (London and New York: Penguin Classics, 1992), pp. 46–47.

[177] Roland Barthes, "Phèdre" (1964) translated from the French by Richard Howard, reprinted in *The Questions of Tragedy*, edited by Arthur B. Coffin (New York: Edwin Mellen, 1992), p. 212.

[178] Barthes, "Phèdre," p. 215.

harmony amongst her speech-act, death and guilt.[179] The reference to *Phèdre* brings to *Notre musique* a dilated temporality, the languorous *meanwhile* of Phaedra's experience of guilt, which, according to Simon Critchley, injects fearful languor into Phaedra's limbs, linking it to the concept of the original sin.[180] Like Phaedra, Olga experiences absolute guilt. Eschewing Phaedra's melancholic torpor (or her descent to the vegetative level, when "God becomes bread," as Simone Weil understands Phaedra),[181] she takes radical redemptive action as I discussed above. The original sin is evoked once Olga is in paradise, when a young man offers her an apple. This takes into account the sketching out of a possible futurity of peace and reconciliation by Godard's analogy between the War of Troy, Europe, Israel, Palestine and the Balkans.

THE MEMORY OF THE FILM

As we have seen, Godard engages with the Palestinian image as the "others" of Israelis, an image that resonates with the European colonialist image of "Arabs,"[182] and via Elias Sanbar, with their Biblical image of Palestinians, based on the text. Godard further borrows Sanbar's analogy between the Palestinians and the "Red Indians," and engages with the Palestinian figure of absence as the *memory* of *Notre musique*. As the memory of the film, the Palestinian discourse of absence is a trace that is simultaneously erased and

---

[179] Ibid.

[180] Simon Critchley, "I want to Die, I Hate My Life – Phaedra's Malaise," *New Literary History*, vol. 35, no. 1 (Winter 2004), p. 17.

[181] Simone Weil, *Gravity and Grace*, p. 32.

[182] "Elias Sanbar montre très bien comment, de ne pouvoir exister que comme 'autres' des Israéliens, les Palestiniens ont dû se fabriquer une image. Une image d'autres, ces autres-là que les Européens appellent Arabes depuis l'époque de la colonisation... Sanbar a bien montré que les Palestiniens ont eu besoin de se faire photographier, pour que cette image existe, avant ils n'étaient que du texte. Moi, quand j'essaie de réfléchir à cela, je le fais forcément en cinéaste, il me semble que le champ/ contre-champ, le montage du champ 1 et du champ 2, reste la manière d'interroger des faits qui se produisent mais que nous ne savons pas mettre en relation."

[Elias Sanbar shows very well how, as Palestinians are unable to exist as the 'others' of Israelis, they were pushed to constructing an image of themselves. An image of others, those others that Europeans have called Arabs since the era of colonisation... Sanbar has shown very well that Palestinians needed to be photographed, for this image to exist, before they were only text. When I think about this, I necessarily do it as a filmmaker, it seems to me that the shot/reverse-shot, montage of shot 1 and shot 2 remains a way of interrogating the facts that are produced [by the Israeli–Palestinian conflict], which we do not know how to bring into a relation.] Godard in conversation with Jean-Michel Frodon, p. 21.

remembered, a simulacrum of presence that refers beyond itself. The status of Palestinian absence as a mnemonic trace is analogous to the presence of the "Red Indians" in the film as *revenants*.

In *Notre musique*, as we have seen, Goytisolo wanders through the library reciting passages from his book *El bosque de las letras*, translated by Ramos García into French. Meanwhile, people (a woman, a girl) approach a man behind a desk (a librarian?) with the apparent purpose of returning books to him. After the librarian has made a note of each book, it gets thrown in a deplorable pile in the corner. At the end of Goytisolo's recital, the "Red Indians" approach the librarian as if addressing a timeless tribunal of justice and state:

> Let Columbus scour the seas to find India,
> It is his right!
> He can call our ghosts the names of spices,
> He can call us Red Indians,
> He can fiddle with his compass to correct his course,
> Twist all the errors of the North wind,
> But outside the narrow world to his map,
> He cannot believe that all men are born equal
> The same as air and water,
> The same as people in Barcelona,
> Except that they happen to worship Nature's God in everything,
> And not gold.[183]

Their post-colonial *plainte* is beyond claiming restitution and recognition or singing a nostalgic elegy to what was lost. The words come from Mahmoud Darwish's poem, "The Speech of the Red Indian." In these lines, they confer on Columbus a list of "rights" that pertain to his particular way of mapping the world, which is a colonial cartography. Although they see that his map is already narrow, one thing that they do not grant him is the right to believe that all men are equal. Here the "Red Indians" convey their past-present not as their ghostly differential appearance (as they do in the scene with Judith and Darwish and at the Mostar Bridge), but as the inevitable outcome of a historical event that has perpetuated inequality and further humiliation in spite of the universal proclamation of the equality of all humans.[184]

---

[183] Mahmoud Darwish, "Speech of the Red Indian."

[184] I address this further below in terms of the historic-political quandary of the Fourth World peoples. For a brilliant re-make of the classic Western movie with post-colonial implications see Jim Jarmusch's *Dead Man* (1995).

The juxtaposition, in *Notre musique*, of Palestine with the Native North American ordeal is specific to the history and to the form of colonization both peoples have undergone. As the "Fourth World," they share more than the potential universalization of their specific suffering.[185] The disaster both peoples have undergone, as Chief Seattle put it, is "the end of life and the beginning of survival."[186] As in Latin American and African colonial and neo-colonial processes, Native North Americans and Palestinians have not only been exploited but expelled from their land, their histories erased, their cultures suppressed—what is known as epistemicide. In both cases, as Chief Seattle stated, the colonialists' appetite devoured the earth and left behind only a desert.[187] According to the decolonial thesis, moreover, colonization is not only based on epistemicide—by having eliminated originary peoples' knowledges and forms of life, parting from the premise that they are inferior and need to be "modernized"—but is a manifestation of the epistemic racism that is foundational to Western structures of knowledge. That is to say, colonization must be considered as the other constitutive side of modernity grounded on the four genocides and epistemicides that occurred in the long sixteenth century. The first took place against Jews and Muslims following the conquest of Granada in 1492; the second, against indigenous peoples during the conquest of America; the third, against Africans kidnapped and enslaved in the transatlantic slave trade; and lastly, the prosecution of women for witchcraft—which often resulted in them being burned—in medieval and early modern Europe. These four genocides/epistemicides are not only part of the logic of the current expansion of global capitalism but, following the decolonial thesis, are also supported by Enlightenment

---

[185] Ella Shohat and Robert Stam have provided a definition of the "Fourth Peoples": "Variously called 'indigenous,' 'tribal,' or 'First Nations'; the still-residing descendants of the original inhabitants of territories subsequently taken over or circumscribed by alien conquest settlement. As many as 3000 native nations, representing some 250 million people, according to some estimates, function within the 200 states that assert sovereignty over them. [...] As non nation-state communities, native peoples rarely 'scan' on the global screen and are often not even identified through their self-chosen names; rather, they are called 'rebels,' 'guerrillas,' or 'separatists,' involved in 'civil wars.'" In *Unthinking Eurocentrism* (New York and London: Routledge 2004), p. 32.

[186] "Chief Seattle's Thoughts," available at http://www.kyphilom.com/www/seattle.html

[187] Ibid.

reasoning and its focus on man as the measure of all things.[188] In juxtaposing the Palestinians and the Red Indians, Godard evidences how both peoples share not only the history of epistemic racism inherent to European colonial modernity, but also the contemporary predicaments of how to assert their historical presence following historical effacement and epistemicide. Their ordeals differ, however, in the historical stage of their colonization. I addressed above the Palestine Question. In North America, annihilation has moved toward the incorporation of the native peoples, prompting contradictions in their everyday existence analogous to the dichotomy of the global versus the local, as many parts of the world find themselves in between "local tradition" and "Western progress." As a people of the Fourth World, they are without political autonomy or self-determination. Today, they are forced to exist within a system that has been imposed on them, to which they have been forced to adapt. As imagined by Judith, both in "Western" clothes and in warrior "ethnic" garb, they are evoked as belonging to a specific historical register that is absent and yet remembered or reactivated in the present. Haunting her encounter with Darwish, they pertain to a different register in the narrative because they are never interpellated by other characters. They speak to the librarian at the Vijećnica—but they are not acknowledged or spoken back to by him. The "Red Indians" are specters demanding to be heard. Their injunction is to "meet the stranger at the tip of the abyss," a pending encounter of two peoples who are strangers to the same land:

> Isn't it about time, stranger, for us to meet face to face in the same age,
> both of us strangers to the same land,
> meeting at the tip of an abyss?[189]

In *Notre musique*, like the "Red Indians," the Palestinian discourse of absence and their image as the "others" of Israelis is a trace simultaneously evoked and effaced. For Darwish, writing gives power,[190] and thus the task

---

[188] See: Ramón Grosfoguel, "The Structure of Knowledge in Westernized Universities: Epistemic Racism/Sexism and the Four Genocides/Epistemicides of the Long 16th Century" *Human Architecture: Journal of the Sociology of Self-Knowledge* XI, Issue 1, Fall 2013, pp. 73–90.
[189] Mahmoud Darwish, "The Speech of the Red Indian."
[190] Interview with Helit Yeshurun, *La Palestine comme métaphore*, p. 140.

of the Palestinian poet is to turn the trace into writing, as the poet of the Trojans writing the great epic of the vanquished.

Apology of the Vanquished for their Loss

Mahmoud Darwish's allusion to the "Homeric pause" in this passage could be read as a suspended moment—the *meanwhile* between war and poetry. In this suspension, the possibility that the vanquished let their wounds heal by "living near memory," "mending the wounds with salt," and "waiting for resurrection." The impossibility of healing is imbued with the melancholy of the defeated and the nostalgia of the exiled, but attributed to the stupor and torpor of a lethargic, catatonic night that impedes writing. This lethargy has rendered a Trojan and a Greek woman indistinguishable, which means that the present is neither resolved nor finished, as the future of Palestine as Troy has been infinitely suspended, which is precisely what bestows on Darwish the possibility to write as "the poet of the Trojans":

> Myths come banging on
> The door whenever we need them.
> There's nothing Homeric found here.
> Only a general exhuming the rubble
> Of a state fast asleep
> Slumped in the ruins of a future Troy.[191]

Troy and Homer are constant references in Darwish's work and the ur-example (or the most ancient example) of a war of annihilation, embellished by the Greeks and the Romans. Through historical distance, poetical and historical recollection, Arendt argues, Homer undoes this annihilation with the impartiality that is at the beginning of historiography.[192] Arendt asserts via Homer that hostile encounters, once the suffering and the barbarity are over, give rise to something people have in common as the two sides of an event. This "means that the event itself has already been

---

[191] Mahmoud Darwish, verse from "A State of Siege" (2002), translated by Ramsis Amun. Available at https://www.arabworldbooks.com/Literature/poetry4.html. Published in *The Burden of the Butterfly*, translated by Faudy Joudah (Port Townsend, WA: Copper Canyon Press, 2006).
[192] Hannah Arendt, *The Promise of Politics* (New York: Schocken, 2007), p. 163.

transformed from conflict into something else that is first revealed to the remembering and celebrating eye of the poet or to the retrospective gaze of the historian."[193]

Arendt's reading of Homer may be a key to how the different stories of the vanquished interrelate in *Notre musique*. *Notre musique* is an encounter of sorts, of the Trojans of history as the survivors of the war of annihilation in their different historical moments: "reconstructed" Sarajevo, the Israeli descendants of some survivors of Hitler's genocide, the Native North Americans and the Palestinians as the people of the Fourth World. According to each specific historical moment, the film creates, invokes or foregrounds the moment for Homeric impartiality; this aspect can be linked to Godard's echoing Edward Said's plea for Palestinians' "right to fiction." To convoke the Homeric-Trojan poets implies further that their texts will be the grounding myths immortalizing the vanquished of a posthumous future. For example, in Virgil's account the Trojans' defeat prefigures their flight to Rome and subsequent ascent to power (Empire).

In Wolfgang Schivelbusch's study about the culture of the vanquished, Troy is the myth of the end and the new beginning that is inscribed in the cycle of victory and defeat: "What triumphs today will be defeated tomorrow." According to Schivelbusch, the myths written about the war attest to how little the Greeks gained from their conquest, and this conferred on the vanquished a higher moral ground. History apparently teaches that the vanquished will be enriched more than the victors and, in this account, being defeated appears a source of intellectual progress and humanity.[194] The historical immanence of Homer's account of the Trojan War relies on the fact that it is the interruption of the myth of a people, and the people's new beginning as its rewriting, and this is why Homer is the mythic hero writing the myth that is able to "speak to all epochs." The account of the War, however, was narrated by the victors and, differentiating his position from Homer's, Darwish has stated that he found hope in calling himself "the poet of the Trojans," at a historical moment in which the defeated were still challenging the victors. To proclaim oneself defeated, Schivelbusch discovered, gives consolation by finding cultural and moral

---

[193] Ibid., pp. 176–177.
[194] Wolfgang Schivelbusch, *The Culture of Defeat: On National Trauma, Mourning, And Recovery* translated by Jefferson Chase (New York: Metropolitan Books, 2003), p. 3.

superiority over the victor and faith in the idea that the position of victor and vanquished are in eternal rotation.[195] Darwish tells Judith:

> I wanted to speak in the name of the absentee, in the name of the Trojan poet. There is more poetic inspiration and humanity in defeat than there is in victory. Even in defeat there is deep poetry, and probably deeper poetry. If I belonged to the victors' camp, I would participate in demonstrations in support for the victims.[196]

In Mahmoud Darwish's poetry, Andalusia represents the myth of the loss of the multiconfessional, multicultural era under Arab rule and the Arab expulsion from Spain. Referencing Andalusia evokes the cycle of the position of winners and losers. Elias Sanbar in a public conversation with Godard points at a nuance in Darwish regarding the position of the defeated in *Notre musique*: "Il ne fait pas l'apologie de la défaite, mais l'apologie de la perte. Ce n'est pas du tout la même chose. [...] D'une certaine façon, nous sommes, parmi les Arabes, les Troyens. Ce n'est pas du tout pour valoriser la défaite, mais pour dire que dans la perte il y a infiniment plus d'humanité que dans l'accumulation des victoires."[197] In this sense, the elegy of the defeated is an apology of loss, recalling the pre-Islamic poetry of the *Jâhiliya*, a nostalgic *qasida* (ode) that evokes the ruins (or *atlal*) of the home that is no longer.[198]

The Trojans' political existence was presupposed by a defeat; theirs is "a community of interrupted myth,"[199] to borrow Jean-Luc Nancy's term. In *Notre musique*, the defeated and the exiled gather in Sarajevo and in Cinema, which are, for the filmmaker, places of exile with which he aligns himself.[200]

---

[195] Ibid., p. 19.

[196] Transcribed from the film and retranslated by Kiffah Al Fanni.

[197] "(Darwish's work) is not an apology of defeat, but an apology of loss. It is not the same thing at all. [...] In a way, we are, amongst the Arabs, the Trojans. It is not a matter of valorizing defeat, but to say that in loss, there is infinitely more humanity than in the accumulation of victories." Godard in a public conversation with Elias Sanbar at the Volcan au Havre, as reported by Christophe Kantcheff in "Jean-Luc Godard – Elias Sanbar," *Politis*, Sunday January 16, 2005.

[198] As told to me by Palestinian poet Kiffah Al Fanni. For further reference see Suzanne Pinckney Stetkevych, "Structuralist Interpretations of Pre-Islamic Poetry: Critique and New Directions," *Journal of Near Eastern Studies*, Vol. 42, No. 2 (April 1983), pp. 85–107.

[199] Not to be confounded with "the interruption of the myth of the writer," which is not the same thing as the "disappearance of the last writer." Jean-Luc Nancy, "Literary Communism" *Inoperative Community* (Minneapolis: University of Minnesota Press, 1991), pp. 70, 71. Nancy here, like the Godardian gathering of poets, vouches for storytellers.

[200] As the "Jew of cinema." He stated: "Places like Sarajevo, Bosnia, or Palestine are also a little bit of a metaphor for what the cinema has become for me, French cinema at least: a

Notre musique's convocation of the vanquished to speak powerful words in "simple conversations" perhaps could be considered as evoking a prepolitical space. In Ancient Greek democracy, the poets "were left to concern themselves with the fate of the vanquished and the defeated, and their poetic, artistic and historical accounts also became part of the *polis* and politics."[201] As we have seen, the sites for action and speech in *Notre musique* are liminal spaces where different worlds meet. These encounters are kinds of manifestations that characterize our contemporary transnational exchanges: the airport, the French Embassy, the Centre André Malraux and the Holiday Inn. Such places are not the *polis*, but they acquire the potentiality for becoming spaces for the political, similar to the Greek political space "where people assemble, a space which is common to all where things can be first recognized in their many-sidedness, where people can understand how to assume the many possible perspectives provided by the real world."[202] In the film, the poets meet to exchange powerful words, but not to proclaim or to persuade others of their status as victims; rather than expressing their opinion of how the world appears to them, they converse face-to-face by way of the resonances in every author's thought and writing. The possibility of the articulation of poetic speech implies making truth accessible to mythical thought. The poets and their voices here are not the originary figures of their histories, but storytellers accounting for the interruption of their founding myth, and this brings consolation to them.

As the gathering of exiles in *Notre musique*, Israeli Jews and Palestinians are comparable as two communities that demand their rights to the world; Godard thereby undoes the idea of Palestinians as the "others" of Israelis, by positing them as "the same" but in a different situation. Judith tells Darwish: "You say there's no more room for Homer and you are the Trojans' bard and you love the vanquished. You're talking like a Jew!" She further states: "In *La Palestine comme métaphore*, you write: If they defeat us in poetry, then it is the end." Darwish's answer is linked to the idea that Homeric impartiality shows that "all things with two

---

country still heavily dependent on subsidies, that can't survive by itself, that is under attack by the various forms of organized crime, that is drifting into prostitution. Cinema is an occupied country with a governor, like the Roman governor of Palestine. Palestine, Sarajevo, the current cinema, these are all places of exile which is good for me because I've always felt profoundly exiled, because of family wars and *cultural wars*." Godard as told to Frédéric Bonnaud, "Occupational Hazards," p. 37.

[201] Hannah Arendt, *The Promise of Politics*, p. 177.
[202] Ibid., p. 167.

sides make their real appearance only in struggle, and that such appearance is possible through great words."[203] The struggle is to be gauged in writing, bringing Palestinians and Israelis together into a kind of combat of words. To confront both sides implies demanding and obtaining redress, establishing temporal finite relations as opposed to demanding restitution, because the latter establishes an infinite debt. In a way, Israeli negotiations with Palestinians have suspended restitutionary matters at the political level (the right of return, the status of Jerusalem, the 1948 "transfer"), perpetuating an asymmetric relation that was never symmetric or political in the first place. When a war of annihilation occurs, Arendt wrote, a portion of our common world is destroyed. What is destroyed is considerably more than the world of the vanquished enemy; it is the in-between space that formerly lay between the people in combat. The reconstruction of this "in-between" world needs human action, and it cannot be reproduced by human hands.[204] Arendt and Godard point at the fact that the victims and the oppressors cannot meet in between. In *Notre musique*, poetic speech has the potential to open up new reserves of common signs, thereby creating a new distribution of the sensible.

Our Music

As we have seen, the characters in *Notre musique* who enter into conversation are the vanquished, those who are denied a legitimate and stable place in their life-territory. The vanquished can be seen as survivors trying to bring out hope, or to signal that there is still hope, despite the situation. Arguably, in the film, there is a concern with the vanquished as poets and historians calling for the Homeric moment of writing history and poetry, seeking to bring great words into simple conversations. This concern goes somewhat against the grain that tends to show a plural world filled with singular voices of the dispossessed who demand restitution. There is also an evident concern with laying out a kind of immediacy that is different from transparency or difference. One of the issues raised by the Homeric epic is that it is considered a work capable of transcending historical context and speaking to all epochs. Perhaps Godard avoids such notions of abstract universality by putting forth the vanquished as historically concrete

[203] Ibid., p. 165.
[204] Ibid., p. 190.

subjects who express a real predicament through language, not only as a way to express relationships between things, but by way of non-communicative language, language without speech,[205] something that is neither the divine word nor what we call language, a brushstroke of universality,[206] a conversation. The Latin noun *conversatio* comes from the verb *conversari*, which means "to keep company with, *to live together*."[207] Furthermore, the reference to Homer in the film is a textual historical layer that relates to the other histories like the actual and the virtual, making the present pass by conserving the past.[208] The film renders a polyphonic world. The polyphony is made by us, and this aspect is highlighted by the film's title, *Notre musique*, the "*entre nous*." "In the film, writers read from their works and along with actors and artists they have made *our little music*," Godard stated.[209] Further:

> *Notre musique* is theirs, ours, everybody's. It's what makes us live, or makes us hope. One could say "our philosophy" or "our life," but "our music" is nicer and has a different effect. And then there's also the question of *what aspect of our music was destroyed at Sarajevo? And what remains of our music that was there?*[210]

In this manner, what is evoked is a particular instance—a spatio-temporal one, of the "in-between" which is more of a *parmi nous* (amongst us) than an *entre nous* (between us). The "in between-amongst us" is a cosmic space for connections and relations, string theory, what is amongst us is that which is proper to us all, tuned in, vibrating, being together. Moreover, the "in-between" is not a multicultural differential

---

[205] Language without speech is creation in the Old Testament, Psalm 18, where God speaks without speech before the prophets, before Israel. God speaks in creation and creation is nature. This question is addressed by Paul Virilio and Sylvère Lotringer in a conversation published in *The Accident of Art* (New York: Semiotext(e), 2005), p. 35.
[206] John Berger cited by Kiffah Al Fanni in a conversation.
[207] Cesare Casarino, "Surplus Common: A Preface," *In Praise of the Common: A Conversation on Philosophy and Politics*, with Antonio Negri (Minneapolis: University of Minnesota Press, 2008), p. 2.
[208] Gilles Deleuze with Claire Parnet, *Dialogues* (Paris: Flammarion, 1996), p. 184.
[209] Godard as told to Frédéric Bonnaud, "Occupational Hazards," p. 37.
[210] Interview with Michael Witt (italics mine).

space of co-existence, but *living together*. For Arendt the in-between (*inter-esse*) is a bond created amongst men that allows for the political, for dialogue: something that is man-made, a space for laying out "a who," which is destroyed by brutality and violence. The in-between is the event of language between two people. Along similar lines, Godard's *plea in the name of the text* is a call for a relationship with the other as different from comprehension or understanding. Here Godard privileges language, neither as speech, which is action (the political proper), nor as the divine Word. Rather, different forms of language are evoked by the reference to Dante's apology for vernacular language,[211] to language as a matter of naming, through Phaedra's conundrum, evidently to poetry (with the parade of poets reciting), and to the issue of translation, which comes up with Ramos García, the blind translator. In poetry, language has a particular form of behaving, as it allows for proximity because it goes toward the other, corresponding with what Lévinas calls *le dire*. "Saying" is transcending or passing toward the other. "Saying" is *parole* addressed to the other as disclosure of the self, saying is to un-say the said without presupposing the representation of the other. "Saying" is the "inspired word" that says the unsaid within the said.[212]

Finally, Godard ponders in the film the matter of the text as having been re-covered by the image. As we know, for Godard the image has redemptive powers, and in *Notre musique* Olga incarnates the question of the image, once as mimesis at the Centre André Malraux, and another time in the voice-over. We hear the voice-over the first time she appears in the film (in "Paradise"), while she advances toward the camera from outside the depth of field. Her image is initially blurry, coming gradually into focus. Somewhat translating the pictorial technique of perspective, the scene recalls Godard's *défilés* of bodies that acknowledge the cinematic translation of plastic space into time as the becoming image of a body. We hear Olga say:

---

[211] For a brief discussion of Dante's *De vulgari eloquentia*, and his praise for the vernacular, see Cesare Casarino, "Surplus Common: A Preface."

[212] Ernst Wolf, *De l'éthique à la justice*, pp. 295–296. We could make a link to Lyotard's claim for the right to speak only to announce something: *le dire* as opposed to *le dit*. Jean-François Lyotard, "The Other's Rights," *The Politics of Human Rights,* ed. The Belgrade Circle (London: Verso, 2002), pp. 135–147.

> C'est comme une image, mais qui viendrait de loin. Ils sont deux, côte à côte. À côté d'elle, c'est moi. Elle, je ne l'ai jamais vue, moi je m'y reconnais. Mais de tout cela je ne me souviens pas. Cela doit se passer loin d'ici, ou plus tard.[213]

As faraway semblance, rendered side by side, the imaged is no one or nothing other than resemblance by way of the intensification of presence. The image is in essence distinct from the thing, but consubstantial, interdependent with the thing. The thing is distinct from the being-here of the image, and that is why the image is far away. The image is the other, and the other is the opposite of near. That which is not close can be drawn apart in two ways: separated by distance or separated by identity. The other is different according to these two manners: it does not touch, and it is dissimilar. The image needs to be detached, brought outside and in front of our eyes to save the real. Yet, it is inseparable from a hidden face that cannot be detached, an "under-face."[214] The detachment happens far away, or later, in a different spatio-temporality than my here and now. Never to have seen it, and yet to recognize myself in it, appeals to Godard's subscription to the Paulist redemptive notion of the image that emerges at the junction of two: redemptive individuation by recognition.[215] It also takes two to look at a third: the third gaze is necessary to bring the visible and the invisible together. For this another is convoked as an indispensable partner. The image is born from faith in forgetting: "Qui veut se souvenir doit se confier à l'oubli."[216] Resemblance resembles in its force of identification, and it resembles like the force of the same. I know very well who I am, I am beyond what I am for you. With the image, we touch the intensity of this retreat or this excess.[217] Building a gap between that which is given to see and the object of desire, the power of the image comes from the desire to see.

---

[213] "It is like an image, but one coming from afar. They are two, side by side. That's me, beside her. I have never seen her before, yet I recognize myself in her. But I do not remember any of this. It must be happening far from here, or at some later time."

[214] Jean-Luc Nancy, *Au fond des images* (Paris: Gallimard 2004), pp. 12–13.

[215] As I discussed in the introduction, in Godard Paulism presupposes *individuated salvation* through an interpellation. The individuation takes place *seeing*, and the paradigm of the seer is Bernadette, the little shepherd girl who sighted the Virgin of Fatima, who, in recognizing the sacred imprint, confirms both the Image's divine origin and herself as a seer.

[216] "Who wants to remember must have faith in forgetting." Jacques Aumont attributes this sentence (quoted by Godard in *Histoire(s)*) to Charles Peguy's *Clio* in *Amnésies: Fictions du cinéma d'après Jean-Luc Godard* (Paris: P.O.L., 1999), p. 253.

[217] Jean-Luc Nancy, *Au fond des images*, p. 24.

Bibliography

Agamben, Giorgio. *Homo Sacer: Sovereign Power and Bare Life*, trans. Daniel Heller-Roazen (Stanford: The University Press, 2003)

Agamben, Giorgio. *Remnants of Auschwitz: The Witness and the Archive* (New York: Zone Books, 2002)

Anidjar, Gil. *The Jew, the Arab: A History of the Enemy* (Stanford: The University Press, 2003)

Arendt, Hannah. *The Promise of Politics* (New York: Schocken, 2007)

Aumont, Jacques. *Amnésies: Fictions du cinéma d'après Jean-Luc Godard* (Paris: P.O.L., 1999)

Barthes, Roland. "Phèdre" (1964) trans. Richard Howard, reprinted in *The Questions of Tragedy*, edited by Arthur B. Coffin (New York: Edwin Mellen, 1992)

Baudrillard, Jean. "No Reprieve for Sarajevo," translated by Patrice Riemens, initially published in *Libération* (January 8, 1994)

Baudrillard, Jean. "The Evil Demon of Images and the Precession of Simulacra," in Thomas Docherty, ed., *Postmodernism: A Reader* (New York: Columbia Univ. Press, 1993)

Baudrillard, Jean. *The Gulf War Did Not Take Place*, translated by Paul Patton, (Bloomington: Indiana University Press, 1995)

Benthall, Jonathan. *Disasters, Relief and the Media* (London and New York: I. B. Tauris, 1993)

Brody, Richard. *Everything is Cinema: The Working Life of Jean-Luc Godard* (New York: Picador, 2009)

Butler, Judith. *Precarious Life: The Power of Mourning and Violence* (London and New York: Verso, 2006)

Camus, Albert. *Le Mythe de Sisyphe* (1942) (Paris: Gallimard, 1985)

Carroll, Lewis. *Alice in Wonderland*, Chapter VIII. Available at: https://ebooks.adelaide.edu.au/c/carroll/lewis/alice/chapter8.html

Casarino, Cesare. "Surplus Common: A Preface," *In Praise of the Common: A Conversation on Philosophy and Politics*, with Antonio Negri, (Minneapolis: University of Minnesota Press, 2008)

Caygill, Howard. "The Promise of Justice," *Radical Philosophy*, no. 143, (May–June 2007)

Chari, Anita. *A Political Economy of the Senses: Neoliberalism, Reification, Critique,* (New York: Columbia University Press, 2015)

Chief Seattle, "Chief Seattle's Thoughts." Available at: http://www.kyphilom.com/www/seattle.html

Cohen-Halimi, Michèle and Cohen, Francis. "Juifs, martyrs, kamikazes: La monstreuse capture; question à Jean-Luc Godard," *Les Temps Modernes* No. 629, (November 2004–February 2005)

Cohn-Bendit, Daniel. "Mon Ami Godard", *Le Monde*, 3 December 2010. Available at: http://www.lemonde.fr/idees/article/2010/12/25/mon-ami-godard_1 457343_3232.html.
Critchley, Simon. "I want to Die, I Hate My Life – Phaedra's Malaise," *New Literary History*, vol. 35, no. 1 (Winter 2004)
Curnier, Jean-Paul. "Le noir du vivant, la cruauté, encore," *Lignes* no. 3 (October 2000). Available at: https://www.cairn.info/revue-lignes1-2000-3-p-53.htm
Daney, Serge. "Le thérrorisé (pedagogie godardienne)" *Cahiers du Cinema* No. 262–263, Special Issue: Five essays on Jean-Luc Godard's *Numéro Deux*, (1976)
Darmon, Maurice. *La Question juive de Jean-Luc Godard: Filmer après Auschwitz* (Cognac: Le Temps qu'il fait, 2011)
Darwish, Mahmoud and Yeshurun, Helit. "Interview," *Hadarim* No. 12 (Spring 1996), translated by Simone Bitton and reprinted in *La Palestine comme métaphore*, (Paris: Actes Sud, 1996), p. 151
Darwish, Mahmoud. "Speech of the Red Indian." Available at: https://www.poemhunter.com/poem/speech-of-the-red-indian/comments/
Darwish, Mahmoud. *The Adam of Two Edens*, translated by Munir Akash and Daniel Moore (Syracuse: The University Press, 2001)
Darwish, Mahmoud. *The Burden of the Butterfly*, translated by Faudy Joudah (Townsend: Cooper Canyon Press, 2006)
De Baecque, Antoine. *Godard, Biographie* (Paris: Pluriel, 2010)
Deleuze, Gilles. *Cinema 1: The Movement-Image* (Minneapolis: University of Minnesota Press, 2002)
Deleuze, Gilles and Parnet, Claire. *Dialogues*, translated by Hugh Tomlinson and Barbara Habberjam (New York: Columbia University Press, 1987)
Deleuze, Gilles. "Grandeur de Yasser Arafat," *Revue d'études Palestiniennes* No. 10 (Winter 1984), reprinted in *Two Regimes of Madness: Texts and Interviews 1975–1995*, translated by Ames Hodges and Mike Taormina (Cambridge, MA: MIT Press, 2007)
Deleuze, Gilles. "To Have Done With Judgment," in *Essays Critical and Clinical*, translated by Dan Smith and Michel Greco (Minneapolis: The University of Minnesota Press, 1997)
Deleuze, Gilles. *Difference and Repetition*, trans. Paul R. Patton (New York: Columbia University Press, 1994)
Dérens, Jean-Arnault. "Islam in Bosnia," *Le Monde diplomatique* (September 2008). Available at: http://mondediplo.com/2008/09/10bosnia
Derrida, Jacques. *Acts of Religion* (London: Routledge, 2001)
Didi-Huberman, Georges. "Ouvrir les camps, fermer les yeux" (2005) in *Remontages du temps subi. Annales. Histoire, sciences Sociales* 2006/5 61e année, pp. 1011–1049.
Didi-Huberman, Georges. *Images malgré tout* (Paris: Éditions de Minuit, 2003)

Dostoyevsky, Fyodor. *The Brothers Karamazov*, translated by David McDuff (London: Penguin 2003)
Fleischer, Alain. *Réponse du muet au parlant: En retour à Jean-Luc Godard* (Paris: Éditions du Seuil, 2011)
Genet, Jean. "Quatre Heures à Chatila," *Revue d'études palestiniennes* no. 6 (January 1983)
Frodon, Jean-Michel. "Jean-Luc Godard et *Notre musique*, Juste une conversation," *Cahiers du Cinéma* (May 2004)
Godard, Jean-Luc. "Occupational Hazards: JLG at Work, as told to Frédéric Bonnaud," *Film Comment* (January–February 2005), pp. 37–41
Godard, Jean-Luc. Interview with Michael Witt, "The Godard Interview: I a Man of the Image," *Sight and Sound* (June 2005), 28–32. Available at: http://old.bfi.org.uk/sightandsound/feature/313
Godard, Jean-Luc. Interview with Olivier Bombarda and Julien Welter, *Cahiers du Cinéma* on November 2007. Available in three parts at: https://www.youtube.com/watch?v=yFpLgvMSefY; https://www.youtube.com/watch?v=FhiMqh2UqQY; https://www.youtube.com/watch?v=G6kLg0Ryb_U
Godard, Jean-Luc. *L'Autre Journal* no. 2, January 1985
Goytisolo, Juan. "Polvo y Cenizas," *El País*, July 27 2008. Available at: https://elpais.com/diario/2008/07/27/opinion/1217109605_850215.html
Goytisolo, Juan. *Cuadernos de Sarajevo* (Madrid: Aguilar, 1993)
Goytisolo, Juan. *El bosque de las letras* (Madrid: Alfaguara, 1995)
Grosfoguel, Ramón. "The Structure of Knowledge in Westernized Universities: Epistemic Racism/Sexism and the Four Genocides/Epistemicides of the Long 16th Century," *Human Architecture: Journal of the Sociology of Self-Knowledge* XI, Issue 1, Fall 2013, pp. 73–90
Heywood, Miriam. "Holocaust and the Image: Debates Surrounding Jean-Luc Godard's *Histoire(s) du cinéma* (1988–98)," *Studies in French Cinema* 9/3 (209)
Hori, Junji. "Godard, Spielberg, the Muselmann, and the Concentration Camps" *The Legacies of Jean-Luc Godard*, ed. Douglas Morrey, Christina Stojanova, Nicole Côté (Waterloo: Wilfrid Laurier University Press, 2014)
Ignatieff, Michael. *Empire Lite: Nation-Building in Bosnia, Kosovo and Afghanistan* (Toronto: Penguin, 2003)
Jameson, Fredric. "Historicism in *The Shining*," (1981) in *Signatures of the Visible* (New York: Psychology Press, 1992)
Kantcheff, Christophe. Discussion between Jean-Luc Godard and Elias Sanbar on January 16, 2005. Available at: http://www.france-palestine.org/Jean-Luc-Godard-Elias-Sanbar
Keenan, Thomas and Weizman, Eyal. *Mengele's Skull: The Advent of a Forensic Aesthetics* (Frankfurt and Berlin: Portikus/Sternberg Press, 2012)
Kilbourn, Russell J.A. "The obligations of memory: Godard's Underworld Journeys," in *The Legacies of Jean-Luc Godard*, ed. Douglas Morrey, Christina Stojanova, Nicole Côté (Waterloo: Wilfried Laurier University Press, 2014)

Kristeva, Julia. *Hannah Arendt: Life is a Narrative* (Alexander Lectures) (Toronto: The University Press, 2001)
Lanzmann, Claude. "Le monument contre l'archive? (Entretien avec Daniel Bougnoux, Régis Debray, Claude Mollard et al.)." *Les cahiers de médiologie* nr. 11, 2001
Lévinas, Emmanuel. *Entre nous (Essais sur le penser-à-l'autre)* (Paris: Poche, 1993)
Lévinas, Emmanuel. *Ethics and Infinity*, translated by Richard Cohen (Pittsburgh: Duquesne University Press, 1985)
Lévy, Bernard-Henri. "Godard est-il anti-Semite? Pièces et documents inédits autour de quatre films inaboutis", *La règle du jeu*, no. 45, 2000
Lévy, Bernard-Henri. "Is Jean-Luc Godard Antisemitic? Not a Gala Dinner (Third Episode, 1999)." *Huffington Post*, November 18, 2010. Available at: http://www.huffingtonpost.com/bernardhenri-levy/post_1285_b_785058.html
Lipton, Joshua. "Ron Haviv: Shooting War," *Columbia Journalism Review* (July 2002)
Lotringer, Sylvère and Virilio, Paul. *The Accident of Art* (New York: Semiotext(e), 2005)
Lotringer, Sylvère. "Introduction: The History of Semiotext(e)," in *Hatred of Capitalism* (Los Angeles: Semiotext(e), 2001), p. 10
Lyotard, Jean-François. "The General Line" (1990), in *Political Writings* (Minneapolis: University of Minnesota Press, 1997)
Lyotard, Jean-François. "The Other's Rights," in *The Politics of Human Rights*, ed. The Belgrade Circle (London: Verso, 2002)
Massumi, Brian. "Fear (The Spectrum Said)," *Positions: East Asia Cultures Critique* 13:1 (2005), 31–48. Available at: www.16beavergroup.org/mtarchive/archives/001927.php
Mastnak, Tomaž. "Europe and the Muslims: The Permanent Crusade?" in *The New Crusades: Constructing the Muslim Enemy*, edited by Emran Qureshi and Michael A. Sells (New York: Columbia University Press, 2003)
Mondzain, Marie-José. *Image, icône, économie: Les Sources byzantines de l'imaginaire contemporain* (Paris: Seuil, 1998), translated by Rico Franses, *Image, Icon, Economy: The Byzantine Origins of the Contemporary Imaginary* (Stanford: The University Press, 2004)
Mondzain, Marie José. *L'image, peut-elle tuer?* (Paris; Bayard, 2002)
Montesquieu, Charles. *De l'esprit des lois*, Book XXIII, 334. Available at: https://www.ecole-alsacienne.org/CDI/pdf/1400/14055_MONT.pdf
Nancy, Jean-Luc. "Forbidden Representation," in *The Ground of Images*, trans. Jeff Fort (New York: Fordham University Press, 2005)
Nancy, Jean-Luc. "Literary Communism," in *Inoperative Community* (Minneapolis: University of Minnesota Press, 1991)
Nancy, Jean-Luc. *Au fond des images* (Paris: Gallimard 2004)
Racine, Jean. *Phèdre*, translated by Margaret Rawlings (London and New York: Penguin Classics, 1992)

Rancière, Jacques. "A Fable Without a Moral: Godard, Cinema (Hi)stories," in *Film Fables*, trans. Emiliano Battista (Oxford, New York: Berg, 2006)
Rancière, Jacques. "Are Some Things Unrepresentable?" in *The Future of the Image* trans. Gregory Elliott (London: Verso, 2007)
Rancière, Jacques. *The Future of the Image* (London and New York: Verso, 2006)
Rodowick, D.N. *Reading the Figural, or, Philosophy After the New Media* (North Carolina: Duke University Press, 2001)
Sanbar, Elias. "Vingt et un ans après," *Traffic* no. 1 (1991)
Saxton, Libby. "Anamnesis and Bearing Witness," in Michael Temple, James S. Williams and Michael Witt (eds.), *For Ever Godard: The Work of Jean-Luc Godard 1950–2000* (London: Black Dog, 2004)
Scemama, Céline. *Histoire(s) du cinéma de Jean-Luc Godard: la force faible d'un art* (Paris: Harmattan, 2006)
Schivelbusch, Wolfgang. *The Culture of Defeat: On National Trauma, Mourning, And Recovery*, trans. Jefferson Chase (New York: Metropolitan Books, 2003)
Shohat, Ella and Stam, Robert. *Unthinking Eurocentrism* (New York and London: Routledge 2004)
Sivan, Eyal. "Montage Interdit," (2012). Available at: https://anti-utopias.com/editorial/montage-interdit-a-conversation-with-eyal-sivan/
Sontag, Susan. *Regarding the Pain of Others* (New York: Farrar, Straus, and Giroux, 2003)
Sontag, Susan. *Where the Stress Falls* (New York: Farrar, Straus and Giroux, 2001)
Spivak, Gayatri Chakravorty. "Righting Wrongs," *South Atlantic Quarterly* 103, nos. 2–3 (Spring/Summer 2004), pp. 524–525
Stetkevych, Suzanne Pinckney. "Structuralist Interpretations of Pre-Islamic Poetry: Critique and New Directions," *Journal of Near Eastern Studies*, Vol. 42, No. 2 (April 1983), pp. 85–107
Stuber, Dorian. "Seeing Nothing: Lanzmann, Godard and Sontag's Fantasies of Voluntarism" *Screenmachine* (August 2011)
Suchenski, Richard I. *Projections of Memory: Romanticism, Modernism, and the Aesthetics of Film* (Oxford: The University Press, 2016)
Tanner, Marcus. "A symbol of hope is reborn in Mostar," *The Independent*, April 18, 2004. Available at: https://www.independent.co.uk/news/world/europe/bridge-over-the-ethnic-divide-a-symbol-of-hope-is-reborn-in-mostar-5355111.html
Thibon, Gustav. "Introduction to Weil, Simone," in G. P. Putnam's Sons (eds.), *Gravity and Grace*, (London, 1st edition 1952).
Wajcman, Gérard. "'Saint Paul' Godard contre 'Moïse' Lanzmann," *Le Monde*, Jeudi 3 Décembre 1998
Weizman, Eyal. *The Least of All Possible Evils: Humanitarian Violence from Arendt to Gaza* (London and New York: Verso, 2011)
Wieviorka, Annette. *The Era of the Witness* (Ithaca, NY: Cornell University Press, 2006)

Williams, S. James, *Encounters With Godard: Ethics, Aesthetics, Politics* (Albany: State University of New York Press, 2016)
Witt, Michael. *Jean-Luc Godard, Cinema Historian* (Bloomington: Indiana University Press, 2013)
Wolf, Ernst. *De l'éthique à la justice* (Dordrecht: Springer, 2007)
Žižek, Slavoj. "Smashing the Neighbor's Face" (2005). Available at: http://www.lacan.com/zizsmash.htm
Žižek, Slavoj. *In Defense of Lost Causes* (London: Verso, 2009)
Žižek, Slavoj. *Violence: Six Sideways Reflections* (New York: Picador, 2008)

CHAPTER 6

Conditions of Visuality and Materialist Film at the Turn of the Twenty-First Century

As we have seen, Jean-Luc Godard's cinema operates between the registers of the real, the imaginary, art and visual culture. For the filmmaker, only cinema is capable of delivering images as opposed to imagery (or the "visual"). He therefore, as I will argue in this chapter, seeks to convey not subjects that can be reduced to signs or communication, but rather, his cinema is a ceaseless search to convey the supposition of the subject of the aura, or in Christian terms, of the verb (or substance).[1] For Godard, alterity is absolutely necessary for the image: the *image* is an *intensification of presence*—this is why an *image* is able to hold out against all experiences of vision.[2] In this light, Godard's cinematic project can be interpreted as a conception of the image as a promise of corporealization. Furthermore, for Godard, the image is incertitude, "trying to see" and the possibility of "giving voices back to their bodies." In Godard, *images do not show*; rather, they are a matter of belief and a *desire to see* (which is different from the desire *to know* or *to possess*). This is why, in the background of Godard's search for an image, there is always a paradigm of the visual against which his own work is dialectically opposed in order to deliver potential *images* from within the

[1] Georges Didi-Huberman, "The Supposition of the Aura: The Now, the Then, and Modernity," in *Walter Benjamin and History*, ed. Andrew Benjamin (New York: Continuum, 2006), 8.
[2] Serge Daney, "Before and After the Image," trans. Melissa McMahon, *Discourse*, Vol. 21, No. 1, Middle Eastern Films Before Thy Gaze Returns to Thee (Winter 1999), pp. 181–190; originally published in French "Avant et après l'image", *Revue d'études palestiniennes* no. 40 (Summer 1991), para. 2.

© The Author(s) 2019
I. Emmelhainz, *Jean-Luc Godard's Political Filmmaking*,
https://doi.org/10.1007/978-3-319-72095-1_6

realm of imagery: Spectacle (1960s), the economy of information (1970s), the culture industry (1980s and 1990s), the explosion of witness accounts in the mass media, film, arts and literature and semiocapitalism (1990s and 2000s). In parallel, Godard's work registers the shifts in the history of media technology, linked to changes in the conditions of visuality. This is related to the fact that every historical moment is accompanied by a particular sensible regime: a hegemonic form of imagining the real. Our current era is characterized by images of simplifying transparency, evidencing the failure of imaginative power and the obliteration of memory, and by an unprecedented explosion in the circulation of visibilities. In the regime of the visual, aside from having become shields against reality, imagery is not only a substitute for first-hand experience, but has also become a certifier of reality. Forty years after Susan Sontag's injunction that images have extraordinary powers to determine our demands on reality,[3] posing for, taking, sharing, liking, forwarding and looking at images are actions that are not only integral to tourism, they actually *give shape* to contemporary experience. As a consequence, representation has ceased to exist in plain view and manifests itself as experience, event or as the appropriation and sharing of a mediatic space. Representation has been further supplanted by media objects (e.g., a twitterbot), which purport to provide vague, participatory, representational events that ground our cultural and social experience.

The companion film to Godard's 2006 exhibition *Voyage(s) en utopie, JLG 1946–2006, À la recherche d'un théorème perdu*, at the Centre Georges Pompidou in Paris is titled *Vrai faux passeport pour le réel*. This film is comparable to *Le Gai savoir* (1969) in the sense that Godard exposes pedagogically his filmmaking program. In *Vrai faux* he shows his method for choosing images to counter problematic regimes of visuality. The film presents itself with the intertitle: "Fiction documentaire sur des occasions de porter un jugement à propos de la façon de faire des films."[4] The opposition between true/false image(s) announced in the title, is quickly undone in the voice-over with which the film begins: "Depuis Saint Augustin, la vérité est tellement aimée que même les menteurs veulent que ce qu'ils disent soit la vérité."[5] *Vrai faux* comprises 29 summonses of images to appear for judgment that are qualified by Godard not as true or

---

[3] Susan Sontag, *On Photography* (New York: Farrar, Straus and Giroux, 1977), p. 80.

[4] "Documentary fiction about instances of making a judgment on the way of making films."

[5] "Since St. Augustine, the truth has been so much loved that even liars want what they say to be considered as true."

false, but as "Bonus" or "Malus"; each summons encompasses a representational category or signifier: history, torture, freedom, beauty, childhood, existence, eros, etc. and many of the "Bonus" scenes are counterposed to examples of "Malus". "Bonus" scenes are from Cocteau, Mankiewicz, Dreyer, Bresson, Fellini, Hitchcock and Watkins. Instances of "Malus" are scenes of violence from Tarantino and Amos Gitai, André Malraux's discourse of an official burial in the Panthéon in Paris, a display of state militia (Nazi and French) and images of official celebrations of the French Revolution. In almost every instance, fiction, fantasy and illusion triumph over the "reality" of objective journalism or realistic images of violence and war. A sequence from *True Romance* in which an Elvis impersonator tortures a man is "Malus" and counterposed to the testimony of a Frenchman who was a torturer during the war in Algeria, who breaks down in tears as he declares that he is unable to forget that he had been a torturer. The shot in which we see a dart bearing the crescent moon from Elias Suleiman's *Divine Intervention* (2004), in the scene in which a woman belonging to the fedayeen defends herself from Israeli soldiers with weapons made up of Palestinian national symbols is qualified as "Malus," while the scene from *Ici et ailleurs* (1976) in which we see a little Palestinian girl reciting Mahmoud Darwish's poem "I Shall Resist," standing in the ruins of Karameh, that is being commented on by Anne-Marie Miéville in the voice-over, contextualizing the image within the history of revolutionary theatrics, is marked as "Bonus." Both scenes appear under the category of "Freedom." One of the traveling shots from Chantal Akerman's *D'Est* (1992) is qualified as "Malus," while the blind beggars family scene in Artur Aristakisian's *Palms* (1998) is praised as "Bonus;" both sequences appear under the category of "Poverty." Under the category "Terror," we see a sequence of an Israeli journalist who is trying to document the damage caused by a terrorist attack in a flea market; this "Malus" sequence is counterposed against the scene from *Notre musique* (2004) in which Ramos García, the translator, calls Godard at his home to tell him that he has seen in the news that a woman has killed herself in the name of peace in a Jerusalem cinema with a bag full of books. While we hear the conversation, we see images of blooming flowers in Godard's garden. Another important contraposition is that of an interview with Magnum photojournalist Luc Delahaye explaining his *métier*, with that of a woman who tells her story of finding herself seriously wounded, trying to turn around to see her father whom she hears breathe, while realizing that she is being photographed by a man who fails to come to her aid (who turns out to be Delahaye). For Godard, the "Bonus" scenes respond correctly to their category; similar to aesthetic judgments, Godard summons the viewer to agree or disagree with his choices. At some point, the sequences or images cease to be qualified with seals, and several "Bonus" scenes are succeeded without negative counterpoints. Many of the "Malus" instances can be qualified as imagery, or the "visual." Passing for representations of "truth," showing naked reality, for Godard they are images that do not offer us the world in the "right" way. *Vrai faux* is a clear exposition of Godard's montage method in which he summons images to appear before the viewers; in this manner, Godard returns to his blackboard filmic pedagogy, addressing the viewer as a potential judge of imagery searching for images in our current visual regime.

In our contemporary world, the opposition between reality-based and image-based modes of representation breaks down, and the most intense and vivid reality is precisely the reality of images.[6] In other words, imagery has in itself become opaque, with cognitive and empirical experiences dissociated from human vision and directly tied to power and capital—best exemplified by publicity, photojournalism, Hollywood films and even counter-information documentary. Against this background, Godard experiments ceaselessly with the possibilities of representation and its undoing, and *Vrai faux* constitutes an example of this practice. Insofar as the image is no longer sacred (due to mechanical reproduction) and vision is no longer tied to the human (as we will see below), we currently lack a unified basis for understanding both the world and the potentially catastrophic events affecting humanity worldwide. Thus, in *Vrai faux*, Godard expounds the logic behind specific techniques he has chosen not to convey as "truth," but to show/say something about the reality of a "truth" that could deliver an *image* that could potentially restore the links between man and the world and amongst humans themselves.

The Old Place (2001) is an essay-film in which Godard and Miéville address the current groundlessness of vision and the lack of *images* of the world and of humanity from a classical humanistic point of view. While we see images from outer space, Miéville and Godard discuss a microsatellite sent into outer space in 2001, with the mission of returning to Earth in 5000 years to inform its future inhabitants about the past. Aside from carrying traditional forms of human knowledge, the satellite will deliver messages written by the current inhabitants of the globe. Miéville and Godard ponder whether humanist messages such as "Love each other," or

---

[6] Steven Shaviro, "Post-Cinematic Affect: On Grace Jones, *Boarding Gate* and *Southland Tales*," *Film Philosophy*, Vol. 14, No. 1 (2010), p. 12.

"Eliminate discrimination against women," will be included in the messages (they doubt it). Later on, they conclude:

> We are all lost in the immensity of the universe and in the depth of our own spirit. There is no way back home, there is no home. The human species has blown up and dispersed in the stars. We can neither deal with the past nor with the present, and the future takes us more and more away from the concept of home. We are not free, as we like to think, but lost.

Here Godard and Miéville paint the termination of a world, its exhaustion and estrangement from its conditions of possibility. As they underscore the lack of a home for the spirit, they highlight the loss of a sense of origin and destination, implying that the active principle of the world has ceased to function.[7] The last line is spoken while we see the image of a mother polar bear staring at her dead cub, followed by an image of Alberto Giacometti's sculpture *L'Homme qui marche* (Walking Man, 1961): life persists irrationally, not given form by imagination, ceasing to cohere with a higher truth.[8] In *The Old Place*, Godard and Miéville explore the image of humanity throughout the Western history of art, underscoring the fact that for 2000 Eurocentric, Christian years, the image was sacred. We also see images of violence, torture, and death juxtaposed with beautiful sculpted and painted figures and faces created throughout all the ages of humanity: people by turns smiling, screaming or crying.

In *The Old Place*, the image is posited as something related to "the origin" that reveals itself as the new but that had been there all along: an originary landscape always present and inextricable from history. Marking the passage to the current regime of communicative capitalism, where images are permeated by discourse and tautological truths about reality, they declare: "The image today is not what we see, but what the caption states."[9] This is also the definition of publicity, which they further link to the transformation of art into market and marketing represented by Andy Warhol and by the fact that "The latest Citroën [in 2001] will be named *Picasso*," the consequence of which is that "[t]he spaces of publicity now

---
[7] Dominic Fox, *Cold World: The Aesthetics of Dejection and the Politics of Militant Dysphoria* (London: Zero Books, 2009), p. 7.
[8] Ibid., p. 70.
[9] This idea will be explored further in *Notre musique* as the proposition: "the image has been covered by text."

occupy the spaces of hope." And yet, in spite of the ubiquity of communicative capitalism, for them there is something that resists, something that remains in art and in the image. Meanwhile, we see a blank canvas held by four mechanical legs moving furiously, an installation by Christophe Cardoen and Patrick Bokanowski included in the *Projections, les Transports de l'Image* exhibition that took place at Le Fresnoy, Studio National des Arts Contemporains from November 1997 to January 1998. Godard visited the exhibition and filmed the installation there.[10]

Portraying the fiercely moving blank canvas from this installation, Godard evokes the resisting image to come; this resisting image is a question of (sensible, un-automated) purity and, in the post-Christian secular sense, of sacredness and redemption, of an ambivalent relationship between image and text, foreign to knowledge and intrinsically tied to belief. At the end of *The Old Place*, the filmmakers posit the Malay legend of A Bao A Qu as the paradigm of the image of these times in which "we are lost without a home," as they state: "The text of A Bao A Qu is the illustration of this film."[11] A Bao A Qu is an inhuman being activated by the passage of humans wishing to see the most beautiful landscape in the world. The act of vision is a unique event, and what delivers the vision of the landscape and of the creature is the purity and desire of the viewer. A Bao A Qu is an image of alterity; it stares back with all of its body. An antidote to the lack of imagination in our times, it is an inhuman vision that undermines the narrative that holds the human as the central figure of its ultimate form of vision and destruction. In *The Old Place*, Godard and Miéville explore the imprint of the quest of what it means to be human throughout the history of images. Humanity transpires as a mark that is perpetually reinscribed in the form of an address. In the film they address modernity's (semiocapitalism's) spectacular crisis of visuality, which causes a lack of imagination, or even blindness. They also posit alternatives: an inhuman vision beyond a humanist-centered view, a post-anthropocentric "other" embodied in the A Bao A Qu. In contrast to post-humanism, the filmic camera and technology are not what enable vision in these films. Rather, vision is enabled by a mythical being: A Bao A Qu.[12]

---

[10] I am indebted to Michael Witt for this reference.
[11] The legend is reinterpreted by Jorge Luis Borges in his *Book of Imaginary Beings*, trans. Andrew Hurley (New York: Viking, 1967), p. 2.
[12] In *Adieu au langage* the being enabling vision is Roxy the dog, as we will see below.

Dialectical Materialist Film-making in *Film Socialisme*

A set of tools that Godard has recently re-employed to open up possibilities of representation, includes those offered by militant filmmaking. In the "*Hier*" room in the *Voyage(s) en utopie* exhibition held at the Centre Pompidou in 2006, tiny plasma screens showing sequences from *Le Vent d'Est*, *One Parallel Movie* and *Weekend* were embedded in a wall next to a screen showing the last scene from *One Plus One (Sympathy for the Devil)*. In it, Anne Wiazemsky, dressed in a white robe and carrying a gun, runs across a beach toward a film crane. The young "militant filmmaker" lies down to be lifted by the crane alongside the red and black flags denoting strike action. The scene in this context stands for both a celebration and a recuperation of militant filmmaking in Godard's most recent work.

As we saw in Chapter 2, in the debates around militant filmmaking, film was considered to be an ideological state apparatus for two reasons. First, because the logic of representation that is inherent to film is embedded in the optical model based in an artificial renaissance perspective, a code in which the impressions of reality of a film are instrumentalized to offer a "spectacular image" of the world. As the code gives it form, this image is seen as real, as true. Second, as an ideological state apparatus, the film ends up covering up for the real conditions of the existence of individuals. The role of radical filmmakers is therefore to "undo" the representation of ideology through reflection, visibilization, blockage, at the level of the relationship between the signifiers and the signified. In other words, the task of militant filmmaking is to become a revolutionary theoretical instrument by bringing language and other bourgeois values such as unity of sense, communicative clarity and the identity of the subject-author into crisis. In this regard, as we have seen, the most effective militant film or "dialectical materialist film" does the work of theory, not of ideology.[13]

Godard's *Film Socialisme* (2010) takes up directly the heritage of militant filmmaking to create a dialectical materialist film for the twenty-first century. This does not mean that in the movie or with the movie Godard seeks or vouches for rescuing a "socialist politics," as the word and image "socialism" do not operate in the movie like predicates and neither are they referents of political action. Digital imagery and communication,

---

[13] Introduction by Emiliano Jelicié to Jean-Louis Comolli et al. *Mayo Francés. La cámara opaca. El debate cine e ideología,* in E. Jelicié comp. (Buenos Aires: El Cuenco de Plata, 2016), pp. 28–29.

which constitute the current visual regime and determine the relationships amongst humans and their world, become the equivalent of "ideology" in the 1960s, in the sense that representations provided by the digital are materialized in concrete practices that determine intrasubjective relationships, bringing language into crisis and thus destroying these relationships.

The title of the film evokes the four categories devised by Jean-Paul Fargier in 1969 to classify films according to their historical-ideological function: social films (which vindicate socialist realism), socialist films (which represent the visible reality of the working class and co-operate with the socialist state), militant films (which engage directly in class struggle) and dialectical materialist films.[14] Godard's title is a wink to this classification while the ambitions of *Film Socialisme* inscribe Godard in the category of "dialectical materialist filmmaker" (a category which his work inspired in Fargier's taxonomy). If films are ideological because they represent a ready-made world following Renaissance perspective visual conventions, "materialist films" cut through this form of representation (which was created by the camera obscura). Apparently, the title of the movie emerged out of Jean-Paul Curnier's confusion in a letter to Godard, where he links film and socialism when pointing to their exhaustion at the beginning of the twenty-first century. For Curnier, this exhaustion is due to the poverty of ambitions and vulgarity in the recent use of both terms.[15]

When asked about the title of the film in an interview, Godard declared that if we speak about "association" we can say "socialism" and that if we say "socialism" we can talk politics.[16] Here "association" stands for new kinds of relationships based on "dissonant resonances" amongst images, sounds, histories and characters that resonate amongst each other and deliver an image of the past that could afford actualization in the present. Therefore, in Godard's assemblage, the temporality of *Film Socialisme* is that of the revolutionary possibility of the reinvention of the past (of resistance, occupation, revolution) in the present. Arguably, by evoking the image and word "socialism," an operation of intellectual subjectivation takes place. That is, the symbolic narratives invoked by "socialism" are

---

[14] Ibid., p. 23.

[15] The letter is reproduced in a booklet containing the script and portraits of those who participated in the film. Godard, J.L. *Film Socialisme: Dialogues avec visages auteurs* (Paris: P.O.L. 2010)

[16] Statement by Godard in an interview with Mediapart filmed in Rolle on April 27, 2010. Accessed: 01/08/2013 http://www.dailymotion.com/video/xd8tiy_jlg-1-10-entretien-avec-godard-medi_news

situated like symbols to affirm the possibility of a flight from the actual state of things; these narratives point also toward the uninterrupted existential sequence of socialism (as association, as politics) circulating at the latent, imperceptible level. The ideological illusion of socialism becomes a symbolic fiction charged with the possibility of inserting itself in reality in order to form part of our singular experience of matter. Furthermore, by dissociating "socialism" from its historical representation and its totalitarian connotations, its social function is rescued in the face of the imminent dismantling and disintegration of the social. Denis de Rougemont's phrase that Godard cites in the movie and evokes elsewhere in an interview about it, sketches out this movement of ideological illusion toward singular experience: "Socialisme: un sourire qui congédie l'univers".[17] "Socialism" also implies the possibility of elaborating a sensibility, to share it, and to show the existence of the common and of the construction of a force in common.

For the film, Godard gathers images that, resonating amongst themselves, evoke the actual moment of crisis in Europe (as a communitary project) passing through the shattering of global financial capitalism: "l'argent est un bien publique, comme l'eau" are the first lines in the voice-over we hear in the movie, and allude to the "Greek debt" and to the European states' rescue of the financial sector with social spending. The implications are, here, the current violation of the social values of equality and justice by the imminent and gradual dismantling of the social pact of the welfare state in many European countries and the repression of dissident voices of citizens in Greece, France, Ireland and Spain. Moreover, *Film Socialisme* makes explicit reference (while it is also a *hommage*) to the 1963 experimental film *Méditerranée* by Jean-Daniel Pollet and Volker Schlöndorff (with a text for the voice-over by Philippe Sollers). *Méditerranée* was pivotal for Godard as well as for French critics and theorists in the 1960s in defining a non-ideological and theoretical method for filmmaking. Together with Godard's body of work from that era, *Méditerranée* was placed at the center of a debate about engaged cinema that took place between *Tel Quel* and *Cinéthique* in 1969.[18] Along

---

[17] "Socialism: a smile that dismisses the universe." Godard quotes the sentence in the "Interview with Dany Le Rouge (Daniel Cohn-Bendit)," *Telerama*, available online: http://www.telerama.fr/cinema/jean-luc-godard-a-daniel-cohn-bendit-qu-est-ce-qui-t-interesse-dans-mon-film,55846.php

[18] *Cahiers du Cinéma* dedicated an entire issue to the movie (No. 187, February 1967), which included "Impressions anciennes," Godard's own review of the film.

similar lines to *Méditerranée*, *Film Socialisme* could be described as a search for images of the real parting from the poetic imaginary and memory. An assemblage of images, texts and sounds, the film forces spectators to work with the film's signifiers in order to add referents and find meaning.

Film Socialisme is structured as a triptych. The first section, "Des choses comme ça" (Things such as these), is set on board a luxury cruise ship, the *Costa Concordia*, sailing around the Mediterranean with European tourists enjoying a variety of hedonist pleasures, a metaphor for Europe and Western society. The ship later sank off the Italian coast in 2012.[19] In the film, the passengers are far away from the world woven around them by Godard, who stages one of his characteristically mosaic narratives in a plot that involves a former Nazi spy, a French investigator, a Russian officer, a Mossad agent, a Palestinian couple, and three thinkers: an intellectual, a philosopher and an economist.

Aside from the narrative, Godard includes an assemblage of images, histories, memories and sensible regimes from the Mediterranean, passing through three countries (Egypt, Palestine, and Greece) and three cities (Odessa, Naples and Barcelona) that have been fundamental for the filmmaker.[20] The second part of the movie, "Quo Vadis Europa" is about the Martin family, who manage a gas station in the east of France. The mother is planning to run for office in the local elections. A news crew hangs around the gas station hoping to get some images of her. Children play a key role in the narrative design that divides them into two groups: Alissa and Ludo, who roam about the cruise ship looking and listening, while the Martin kids, Florine and Lucien, interrogate and discuss, while their parents sign an agreement to hold a debate with them every year.[21] This section of the film makes a reference to the "Famille Martin," a resistance group during World War II whose credo was: "To liberate and to federate." The last part of the film, "Nos humanités," is film essay and collage that revisits the sites that the cruise

---

[19] Jean-Luc Godard, "Entretien avec Jean-Luc Godard," FranceInter Radio, 21 May 2014 available online: http://www.franceinter.fr/emission-le-79-jean-luc-godard-invite-du-79

[20] Jean-Luc Godard, "Interview with Dany le Rouge (Daniel Cohn Bendit)."

[21] Artur Mas and Martial Pisani, "Film Socialisme" *Independencia* (June 1, 2010) Available online: http://www.movingimagesource.us/articles/film-socialisme-annotated-20110607

ship passed through in the first part of the movie. The sites draw a historico-political geography that evokes memories of revolt, occupation, annihilation, civil war (or fraternal combat) and resistance and mobilization: Spain in 1937, especially Barcelona, evoking the fratricidal combat amongst the Republicans, and Greece after the war and the repression of civilians in Odessa in 1905. Stories of resistance are recalled by the reference to Youssef Chahine's film of 1985, *Adieu Bonaparte* (*Farewell, Bonaparte*), about an Egyptian family resisting during Napoleon's occupation; to *Quattro giornate di Napoli* (*The Four Days of Naples*), by Nanni Loy (1962), which narrates the history of the resistance of the Neapolitans against the Nazis; there is also André Malraux's anti-fascist film *Espoir* (*Hope*, completed in 1939 but not released until 1945) about the Spanish Civil War. Godard invokes the "Réseau du musée de l'Homme" and the "Famille Martin,"[22] which are names of French resistance groups operating during the German occupation. The detour to Odessa is necessary: this is for Godard the only moment in which cinema was at the same level as History.[23] In this regard, the images assembled in the movie contain the potential for the "spontaneous liberation of the people." The question of the search for the image of Palestine is at the center in "Nos humanités," as we will see below.

A constant feature of Godard's work, at least since *Ici et ailleurs* (1970–74), and which is the generative principle of *Histoire(s) du cinéma* (1988–98) is Godard's subscription to Walter Benjamin's notion of revolutionary redemption by way of repetition of the past. A recurrent aphorism in Godard's movies is worth recalling: *L'image viendra au temps de la résurrection* (The image will come at the time of resurrection). This aphorism attests to Godard's faith in the redemptive potential of the Image that will come by invoking images that persist in the collective imaginary like historical specters, haunting memory, demanding their divulgation and insisting on becoming alternative visions of the past in the present. This Marxist historiography has the task in *Film Socialisme*, not of describing or imagining events as they happened, nor of explaining how they generated the ideological illusions that accompanied them, but of opening a breach

---

[22] "Network of the Museum of Mankind" and "The Martin Family," respectively.
[23] Jean Douchet and Fernando Ganzo, "Jean-Luc Movimiento Godard" *Lumière Internacional* (October 2010), p. 10.

between socialism and its totalitarian outcome. Also, to unearth the emancipatory utopian potential that was precisely betrayed in the actuality of revolution.[24]

Like much of Godard's work, *Film Socialisme* inquires about the destiny of Europe: what it is, and what it will become. On the one hand, the film alludes to a post-political Europe operating according to world market interests. Bearing in mind that Europe is, as a communitarian project, falling apart in Athens, the filmmaker argues that for many reasons Europe is indebted to Greece, and not the other way around: such is the idea of democracy seen in HELLAS, which includes the echo of HELL in HÉLAS [Hellas, Hell, Hel(a)las]. In this regard, the film alludes to the current historical era, marked by the progressive disintegration of syndicates, Leftist parties and welfare states. This is also a moment in which militant apathy is limited to expressing an ambiguous position before what could be a response to the economic crisis and fiscal austerity measures taken up by European governments. On the other hand, *Film Socialisme* calls for a repoliticized Europe with a shared emancipation project, the Europe of Greek democracy and of the French and Russian revolutions. It is perhaps that when thinking of the first scenario that utopia can emerge at the moment of the suspension of the political.[25] Bearing this in mind, the forms of historical events evoked by the movie are strata in the image of the present.

THE EXHAUSTION OF THE IMAGINARY

In "Des choses comme ça" Godard interweaves the sensible regimes of tourism, capitalism and historical memory in order to fashion a voyage into the imaginary that neither describes the real nor strives toward becoming real. Rather, the immanence of the imaginary in the real is revealed during the voyage, allowing the viewer to see what is heading toward the imaginary. The unconscious associations, the strata of signification, the aphorisms and citations are based on a scrutiny of a simplified

---

[24] Slavoj Žižek, *Living in the End Times* (London: Verso 2010), p. 97. Regarding Benjamin's materialist historiography and Godard see: Junji Hori, "Godard's Two Historiographies" in *For Ever Godard*, ed. Michael Temple (London: Black Dog, 2004) and Youssef Ishaghpour's interview with Godard, *Cinema: The Archeology of Film and the Memory of a Century* (London: Berg, 2005).

[25] Fredric Jameson, "The Politics of Utopia," *New Left Review* no. 25 (January–February 2004).

and generic image of a Mediterranean Sea placed under the gaze of the tourist industry and the world of the retired European baby boomers hedonistically entertaining and pleasing themselves. The images of the ship itself constitute an assemblage of high-definition and shiny images that create blocks of color; this assemblage includes low-quality material made up of surveillance images and cell phone photographs or videos degraded and edited with psychedelic visual interference. All the images have optimized color and a strident palette that affirms the persisting effects of digital technology.[26] The sharpness of the external shots of the impeccably clean boat defy its corrosion by seawater, denoting in this manner the Calvinist triumph of capitalism and industry over the primitive action of the sea against the degradation of matter.[27] The cruise ship becomes a metaphor of the capitalist fantasy of the conquest of decay and entropy. As such, the boat, which is in itself a metaphor (a mode of transport), conveys the myth of betterment on which the industry of sensorial anesthetization, simulation and self-complacency thrives.

Godard's emphasis on the omnipresence of both photographers and photographed on board ship posits the digital image as the predominant mediator between subjects and reality. Reality becomes a series of events to be documented, removing both travel and the image from the work of imagination and memory. When seeing the movie, we are reminded of Susan Sontag's classic analysis of photography and tourism.[28] For the writer, the tourists' compulsion to photograph is due to the fact that it may assuage the feelings of disorientation they may experience when traveling; in this way, experience becomes a way of seeing, which in turn, is identical to taking photographs.

Godard is said to have launched a war against digital media, when, already with the appearance of video in the 1970s, he announced the death of cinema. Why? I believe it has to do with the indexical nature of cinema, which

---

[26] This taxonomy of images in the "Des choses comme ça" section is provided by Andréa Picard in her review of *Film Socialisme* for the Canadian magazine *Cinema Scope* No. 43 (June 2010), Available online: http://cinema-scope.com/spotlight/spotlight-film-socialisme-jean-luc-godard-switzerlandfrance/

[27] David Foster Wallace, "A Supposedly Fun Thing I'll Never do Again," in *A Supposedly Fun Thing I'll Never Do Again* (New York. Back Bay Books, 1997), p. 263.

[28] She argues that: "Cameras make real what one is experiencing [...] [a] way to certify experience, taking photographs is also a way of refusing it – by limiting experience to a search for the photogenic, by converting experience into an image, a souvenir." Susan Sontag, *On Photography* (New York: Farrar, Straus and Giroux, 1977), p. 18.

according to Mary Ann Doane, attests to existence and thus bears the potentiality of the cinematic image to become an icon. As a source of indexical images, cinema stakes a claim to authenticity by the privilege of contact, touch and physical connection to its referent. In contrast, digital is a medium without materiality. It is comprised of pure abstraction, made up of zeroes and ones because it is a code. It is the presence of absence and thus the dematerialization and annihilation of the medium.[29] If the digital outlasts its material support, "what is perceived as lost in the move to the digital is the imprint of time, the visible degradation of the image."[30] Analogue cinema, in contrast, depends upon a photochemical epistemology and ontology that signify the utopia of the certitude of the imprint or trace on a concrete medium. It is not a matter of realistic representation of objects or people; rather, analogue media verify an existence and thus reveal more than the digital. Moreover, analogue media are the index fossils of historical reality, meaning that the history of photography and cinema is the history of perception as it is historically encoded.[31] Finally, like the impeccable cruise ship, the digital survives in spite of the decay of its support, contrary to the politics of cinema as medium, which, as Doane points out, in its promise to touch the real, attempts to grasp and retain embodiment and corporeality—which are conditions for the possibility of signifying as a form of historical labor.[32] The transparency of the digital image is analogous to the transparency that a historical city may acquire when it gets "branded," as its identity gets over-simplified, its singularity obliterated by making its generic characteristics stand out. Cities and sites are rendered transparent like logos that become the currency of tourism.

As I have argued, every historical moment is accompanied by a particular sensible regime, that is, a historical and hegemonic form of *imagining* the real. Images, in other words, materialize conceptions of reality at a given time. Our contemporary epoch is distinguished by images of simplifying transparency, and this evidences the current failure of imaginative power and the obliteration of memory, which Godard precisely gives himself the task of making operative (as opposed to rescuing or preserving) in

---

[29] Mary Ann Doane, "Indexicality and the Concept of Medium Specificity," in *The Meaning of Photography*, edited by Robin Kelsey and Blake Stimson (Williamstown, MA: Sterling and Francine Clark Institute, 2008), p. 10.

[30] Ibid.

[31] Bernard Stiegler, "Photography as the Medium of Reflection," in *The Meaning of Photography*, p. 195.

[32] Doane, p. 12.

the movie. In the montage, the images resonate and are thereby transformed into emblems, descriptions, allegories, fetishes, symbols, clichés, signals, ideograms, and cultural citations (a shot of the Owl of Minerva superimposed on the Odessa Steps from *Battleship Potemkin*).[33] Much like memory, the sensorium of the past, locked in the Mediterranean, remains secret, indescribable and indecipherable, in the form of tangible yet blurry strata.

The notion of "the real" in *Film Socialisme* could be explained by recalling Gaston Bachelard's "poetic imaginary," which implies an external gaze entering and exiting the "materiality" of things. Bachelard was somewhat inspired by what Merleau-Ponty called the "visual field": "the world hidden from us beneath all the sediment of knowledge and social living [...] a vision of things themselves, the presence of the world of lived experience, where objects *hold our gaze* and ask questions of it."[34] Along similar lines, for Bachelard "the real" are material forms moving toward becoming a poetic image. The poetic image stems from pure imagination and emerges in language, and that *is reality*.[35] For Godard, however, "dire ne suffit pas jamais,"[36] and thus by way of montage, the movie opens up a gap between things, their image and the name that we have imposed on them. Thus the pertinence of the question the film poses early on: "Comment mettre de la réalité dans la réalité?".[37]

Evidently, the kind of realism evoked here has nothing to do with truth, immediacy or the transparency of the image. It is also absolutely foreign to the genre of realism that prevails in the contemporary audio-visual field characterized by an aesthetics of demise that has given itself the task of documenting the horrors of capitalism and war. The realism that Godard appeals to could be said to be that of literary or spoken imagination translated into a cinematographic image.[38] For Bachelard, moreover, the phenomenology of the poetic image is based on the principle that poetic images emerge at the intermediate zone between the unconscious and rational consciousness, at the limit of rational thought, that is, at the limit of objective knowledge we have of the world. For Bachelard, the poetic

---

[33] Nicole Brenez, "Liberté, Égalité, Prodigalité," *Cahiers du Cinéma* No. 657 (June 2010), pp. 26–27.
[34] Maurice Merleau-Ponty, *The World of Perception* (London: Routledge, 2004), pp. 92, 93.
[35] Gaston Bachelard, *The Poetics of Space* (Boston: Beacon, 1964), p. xxvii.
[36] "Saying is never enough."
[37] "How to insert reality within reality?"
[38] Bachelard, p. 32.

image has the potential of changing the perception and habitual experience of matter surrounding us, considering not the reality of the object, but the object as a conductor of the real:

> We always want imagination to be the faculty of *forming* images. But in reality, it is the faculty of *deforming* images, those images given by perception and above all, the faculty of freeing us from the first images, to *change* images.[39]

Bearing in mind that matter is what directs our imagination, even our own being, aspiring to the poetic image implies that we aspire to new images, *prompting images to move with imagination*, charging them with "spiritual mobility." In "Des choses comme ça", Godard establishes a tension between "static images" (digital, surveillance, capitalism, the Mediterranean under the gaze of tourism and "culture") and "poetic images." Therefore, Godard bets on the transformation of images by charging them with "spiritual mobility," parting from the projection of intimate impressions on the external world (gaze and touch): consider, for example, Antonioni's *Lo sguardo di Michelangelo* (*Michelangelo's Gaze*, 2004). Bachelard's notions of "poetic image" and "spiritual mobility" could be linked to Henri Bergson's phenomenology of duration, which Godard evokes with the following quote in many of his movies: "L'esprit emprunte à la matière les perceptions d'où il tire sa nourriture, et les lui rend sous forme de mouvement, où il a imprimé sa liberté."[40] Bergson's phenomenology of duration could definitely work as a metaphor for cinema, and this is precisely what interests Godard: the idea that spirit feeds itself from perceptions of matter, giving back, imprinting on them their freedom by way of movement. Bergson drew an analogy between consciousness and the process of appearance of the photographic image facilitated by chemicals, positing consciousness as a revelation, an analogy that Godard evokes in *Film Socialisme* with: "clarum per obscurius."[41] We could interpret this phrase and link it to Bergson's quote, arguing that both allude to the apparatus of the daguerreotype in which the image "reveals itself" from darkness. Going

---

[39] Ibid.

[40] "Spirit borrows from matter the perceptions on which it feeds, and restores them to matter in the form of movement which it has imprinted with its own freedom." Henri Bergson, *Matière et mémoire: Essai sur la relation du corps à l'esprit* (Paris: Presses Universitaires de France, 1964), p. 378.

[41] "Clarity perceived through darkness."

back to the notion of duration in relationship to consciousness, the idea of explaining change through movement in terms of becoming instead of "being" is crucial.

In Godard, the real is in the movement of becoming, and images are "relationships" (*rapports*) or associations amongst things established by way of montage. The montage of *Film Socialisme* is based on a logic that Godard calls "dissonant resonances," which could be interpreted as a montage striving to become an organizing force that finds its way toward dissonant things, images and words that change their vibrational pattern and allow for the energy within and around them to flow effortlessly. Dissonant resonances amongst things, images and words depart from the search not only for a realist poetic image but also for an image based on the material experience of sensible memory that is embedded the materiality of things, in place of "the truth of things." Montage in *Film Socialisme* becomes thus "dissonances announced by a note in common,"[42] made up of asymmetrical analogies and unexpected associations that come up between image, text and meaning, in a search toward another way of imagining the real. The principle of resonances, as opposed to analogy or similitude, implies dissonance (differential equivalence) and contagion: what is constituted in this manner propagates like a shock wave, and what resonates is a singular body dispersing itself in time and space.

Sensible Memory in *Film Socialisme*

In *Film Socialisme*, Godard not only renders homage to Pollet's and Schlondorff's *Méditerranée*, but also to Michelangelo Antonioni's penultimate film, a short titled *Lo sguardo di Michelangelo* and deconstructs Manoel de Oliveira's *Um filme falado* (*A Spoken Film*, 2003). The latter narrates the story of the visit of a mother (a history professor) and her daughter to the main sites of Mediterranean civilization. In the narrative, political discussions are interwoven with ancient and contemporary history. In Oliveira's film, moreover, East and West are confronted from a Western point of view, as the film ends with the boat being blown up by a bomb from Aden. Antonioni's movie depicts the filmmaker's visit to Michelangelo's *Moses* sculpture in the San Pietro in Vincoli church in Rome. Godard chose to reproduce in *Film Socialisme* a shot in which we

---

[42] From the voice-over in *Film Socialisme*.

see the filmmaker caressing the sculpture with his gaze. We are reminded of instances in which Godard is "seeing with his hands" in other films such as *Numéro deux* (1976) and *Scénario du film Passion* (1982). Godard is known to have said many times that, as a filmmaker, he would prefer to lose his sight as opposed to the use of his hands. Bearing in mind these key references, *Film Socialisme* could be described as a search for the poetic imaginary of the reality of the present based in the sensible experience of matter, from which memory is inseparable.

Méditerranée is a film that transforms a tourist trip into a mythological journey, recreating a legendary Mediterranean with documentary images, awakening the sensible memory of specific sites in a similar way to that of *Film Socialisme*. What is more, in his movie, Godard resurrects many of the images that appear in *Méditerranée*: a young girl buttoning down her dress (similar to the one Florine wears in the second part of the film), the Egyptian god Horus, a statue with her mouth closed, a shot of a *corrida* (to signify Spain), and the sea seen through barbed wire (to signify Palestine). According to Jean-Paul Fargier, *Méditerranée* owes its relevance to its repetitive shots, its associations and oppositions, and to the incessant flux of images and text that breaks with the logic of cinematographic writing. Fargier posited the film's multiplying repetitions to be more akin to music and poetry than filmic writing. *Méditerranée* was thus understood as the cinematic equivalent of procedures used in vanguardist modern literature; hence it was conceived as a materialist and thus a revolutionary film in the sense that it escapes ideology. The logic that governs the succession of shots in the movie was understood as a deconstruction of the "idealist system of Representation" as well as of filmic narrative. The film was thought to be revolutionary because, like *Film Socialisme*, it forces the spectator to work with the film's signifiers and to look for external signifieds in order to add referents and find meaning. For these reasons, *Méditerranée* announced a new mode of film production and signification based on the destruction of representation and subjectivity, and thus of ideology. In addition, the film presents raw matter (pre-signifying images) as thought process. This is because the sequences repeat themselves, returning unexpectedly as they are chained according to the logic of the unconscious. Therefore, they undo the "logic of the signifier" and transgress the fundamental illusion of the cinematic apparatus as codifying machine, as images respond infinitely to one another, opening up meaning.[43] For Fargier, the fact that in the film the machine of signification is broken liberates the viewer's consciousness, enabling him/her to see the trap of representation. This is the reason why *Méditerranée* became both the paradigm and the epitome of revolutionary materialist film.[44]

Evidently, the work of memory is pivotal to the experience of watching both films. The assemblage of images in *Méditerranée* is accompanied by a voice-over based on a non-descriptive and poetic text by Philippe Sollers.[45] Arguably, Pollet established in *Méditerranée* a model of montage leading to a material and sensible imaginary, based in duration and unconscious memory, in a melancholic search for, contemplation of and sensible gaze toward the past:

> Sommeil par effacement, région des passages et des doubles et des choses vues sans vision [...] Que le point de vue se situe également partout. Tableaux [...] L'accumulation de mémoire se poursuit, monotone. Tandis qu'une clarté, un réveil aveuglant, déborde et recouvre tout en silence, où l'on n'est plus qu'un point de plus en plus perdu et lointain [...].[46]

Differently from *Méditerranée* and Oliveira's *Um filme falado*, Godard converts the passage through the "Cradle of civilization" into a search for the traces of the sensible in which the geographical distinction between East and West becomes blurred: figurative language (Egypt), European painting (Naples), tragedy and the epic recounting of war (Greece), revolutionary film (Odessa), and the problem of aesthetico-political representation (Palestine). Finally, the search extends to the production of texts and images of solidarity with allusions to resistance texts by Ernest Hemingway and

---

[43] Jean-Paul Fargier, "Jean-Paul Fargier vs. *Tel Quel*," *VH 101* Nr. 9 (1972), p. 16.
[44] Jean-Paul Fargier, "Hacia el relato rojo: Notas sobre un nuevo modo de producción del cine" in Jean-Louis Comolli, et al. *Mayo Francés*, p. 286.
[45] Ibid.
[46] "Sleep by erasure, a region of passages and doubles, and of things seen without seeing [...] A point of view that is identical everywhere. Tableaux [...] The continuous and monotonous accumulation of memory. Meanwhile, a clarity, a blinding awakening, transcending and spreading in total silence, where one is nothing more than a dot, increasingly distant and lost to view." From the voice-over in *Méditerranée*, written by Philippe Sollers. Available online: http://www.pileface.com/sollers/article.php3?id_article=268

Simone Weil,[47] and to the images of Robert Capa and Roman Karmen taken in Spain during the Civil War (Barcelona).

Nos Humanités

"Nos Humanités" is a collage of returns to the places the cruise ship visited in "Des choses comme ça." It includes images quoted from *Méditerranée* and others that return phantasmagorically from the first section of the film. In the second stop in Odessa, the filmmaker alludes to the repression of civil resistance and revolutionary cinema, juxtaposing scenes from Eisenstein's *Battleship Potemkin* (1925)—which appeared in "Des choses comme ça"—with images of a group of teenagers on a guided visit to the Odessa Steps. In general, the films quoted in "Nos humanités" take up politics as a subject, and sometimes they address East/West relations. Examples are Claude Lanzmann's *Tsahal* (1994), Pier Paolo Pasolini's *Il fiore delle mille e una notte* (*Arabian Nights*, 1974), Udi Aloni's documentary about the Israeli-Palestinian conflict *Local Angel* (2002) and Karin Albou's *Le Chant des mariées* (*The Song of the Brides*, 2008). In part, *Film Socialisme* originated in a series of letters Godard exchanged with Bernard-Henry Lévy between 2001 and 2006 after a meeting in December 2001 when they discussed Israel, Islam and Palestine. Lévy proposed making a trip to Israel, meeting up in Haifa and that their conversations culminate in a film about their points of view. The exchange initially included Claude Lanzmann and a debate on the relations between image and text. The exchange, however, ceased when Godard was unable to accept Lévy's refusal of his proposal to include Tariq Ramadan in the project, because Lévy considered him to be an Islamofascist.[48] Traces of this dialogue appear in *Film Socialisme*, and at the center of "Nos humanités" there is an investigation about the image and the imaging of Palestine and the Palestinians. This investigation is announced by an image of young veiled Muslim women eating ice cream while they contemplate the Mediterranean, accompanied by a quote in the voice-over from Jean Genet's *Un captif amoureux* (*Prisoner of Love*, 1986), his book about Palestine and the

---

[47] Simone Weil, *Écrits historiques et politiques* (Paris: Gallimard, 1960), and Ernest Hemingway, *For Whom the Bell Tolls* (New York: Scribner, 1995).
[48] The letters have been published in "Terre promise" (quatrième et dernier épisode, 2001) Bernard-Henry Lévy, available online: http://laregledujeu.org/2010/11/18/3426/%C2%AB-terre-promise-%C2%BB-quatrieme-et-dernier-episode-2001/

Palestinians: "Mettre à l'abri toutes les images du langage et se servir d'elles, car elles sont dans le désert où il faut aller les chercher."[49]

Palestinians are the figure of territorial dispossession and Palestine is the emblem of geographic invisibility. The aesthetico-political dilemma for Palestinians has been how to inscribe their historical presence in view of their geographic, discursive and figurative absence. According to Zionist discourse, Palestinians were never there and thus they are absent from their land. For Palestinian writer Elias Sanbar, to date, Palestine is the emblematic figure of the problem of her own imaging. This predicament is an aspect of Palestinians' powerlessness to appear as a nation due to the dissolution of territorial frontiers, and the physical expulsion accompanied by the discursive and visual programming of their absence. Looking at the history of the modern figure of Palestine, Sanbar argues that it was obliterated from the beginning by the figure of the Holy Land. The origins of the modern image of Palestine and Palestinians coincided with the proliferation of travel accounts that romantically depicted the trip to the Orient. The pilgrimage to the Holy Land was imbued by a colonial vision in the spirit of a "peaceful crusade." In such accounts and images, the land was made familiar by making it correspond to the texts from the Old Scriptures. Inductively, Palestinians were captured in poses and gestures that reinforced Western perceptions of images and attitudes identical to those described in the Bible. Their images would then be distributed in the West, accompanied with quotations from the Bible, as if the land had not changed in 1800 years.[50] In accord with nineteenth-century traditions of typecasting and classifying, such images tended to obliterate their subjects. Once portrayed according to stereotypes, they had their individuality removed, becoming representatives of "types" of people living in the Holy Land.[51] For Sanbar, however, the era that was pivotal to the narrative for-

---

[49] "Stock up on all of language's images and help yourself to them, because they're in the desert where you must find them."

[50] Elias Sanbar, *Les Palestiniens: La Photographie d'une terre et de son peuple de 1839 à nos jours*, (Paris: Hazan, 2004), pp. 7–13.

[51] Issam Nassar, "Familial Snapshots, Representing Palestine in the Work of the First Local Photographers," *History & Memory* 12 no. 2 (Fall/Winter 2000), p. 9. In the early 1960s, the Italian filmmaker Pier Paolo Pasolini traveled to the Holy Land searching for stereotypical figures in his notebook-film of 1963 *Sopralluoghi in Palestina*. Guided by a Catholic priest, he traveled throughout the land looking for locations for his film *Il vangelo secondo Matteo (The Gospel According to St. Matthew*, 1964). From the beginning he was on a quest for an ancestral, "pure" and remote archaic biblical world. However, to his disappointment

mation of the Palestinian figure of the absent was the five-year period between 1917 and 1922.[52] The nineteenth-century figure of the Holy Land coincided with the Zionist discourse of the Promised Land, and in the twentieth, it became "a land without a people for a people without a land," a clichéd sentence (often attributed to Zionist discourses) that disassociates and renders Palestinians absent from the territory. During the post-Nakba period, according to Edward Said, the figure of "the Arab" had become in Palestine a non-person, and the "Zionist" had become the *only* person in the land because of his/her perceived prejudice of the Arab's negative personality as Oriental, decadent and inferior.[53] Mahmoud Darwish illustrated the ordeal of Palestinian absence in the title of his poem "Who am I, Without Exile?"[54] By raising the question in this manner, Darwish described the material and political realities of the Palestinian disappearance from the landscape and at the representational level. There has been evidently a shift in the *imaging* of Palestine, as embedded in a quotation from Jean Genet, who wrote that with the Palestinian Revolution, "Absence was in their hands as it was under their feet."[55] This formulation implies agency for self-determination. The nature of this form of agency, however, has waned and has been transformed into the insistent inscription of absence and in the reiteration of the ongoing dispossession as speaking truth to power. The problem is the constant derealization of Palestine as a politically constituted entity.

In dialogue with Sanbar, Godard takes up these issues in *Film Socialisme*. In the "Des choses comme ça" section, a photograph is shown both as a *mise-en-scène* and as inserted through montage.[56] As a *mise-en-scène*, the

---

he found a land that was less remote and displaced by a modern industrialized Israel. He ended up filming *Il vangelo* in the Italian city of Matera, in the region of Basilicata.

[52] Elias Sanbar, *Figures du Palestinien: Identité des origines, identité du devenir* (Paris: Gallimard, 2004), p. 97.

[53] Edward Said, *The Question of Palestine* (New York: Vintage Books, 1991), p. 54.

[54] This is a title of one of his poems from the collection *Unfortunately, It was Paradise*, ed. and trans. Munir Akash and Carolyn Forché with Sinan Antoon and Amira El-Zein (Berkeley and Los Angeles: University of California Press, 2003).

[55] Jean Genet, *Prisoner of Love* (New York: Wesleyan, 1992), p. 125.

[56] Roland-François Lack, "Una fotografía y una cámara: dos objetos *Film Socialisme*" *Lumière Internacional* (October 2010) The version in English appeared in *Vertigo Magazine* (Spring 2012) available online: http://www.closeupfilmcentre.com/vertigo_magazine/issue-30-spring-2012-godard-is/a-photograph-and-a-camera-two-objects-in-film-socialisme/

photograph appears in the hands of Sanbar who shows it and passes it on to someone else outside of the frame, while we hear in the voice-over:

> Après la réception de Daguerre par Arago à L'Académie des Sciences, une armada de majorité britannique – donc bien avant la déclaration de Lord Balfour – se précipitait en Palestine. Voici l'une des premières photographies de la baie d'Haïfa.[57]

Until that moment, we have only seen the photograph from the back, now held by a woman who passes it on, again out of the frame, to take a photograph with a digital camera (we do not see what she records with her camera's lens).[58] She states:

> **Ayna Anti al Aan? Ayyatuja Al Ard Al 7abiba.**
> أين أنتِ الآن؟ أيتها الأرض الحبيبة.

"Where are you, oh my beloved land?" Two images later, we see the photograph she had been observing. According to Roland-François Lack, the way Godard treats this image is strongly connoted. The image could be associated with the army of photographers that invaded Palestine at the time of the invention of photography mentioned in the movie. As Lack argues, however, the photograph was taken by Felix Bonfils, a Frenchman living in Beirut, who took the picture around 1880. Lack discusses how the photograph was hand-colored by a Swiss workshop that also effaced the photographer's signature—in that sense, the "Swiss" appear as manipulators of images and the Palestinian woman, by taking the photograph, becomes the maker of (searching for) her own image. The view of Haifa is followed a few frames later by an explicitly political image of an olive tree taken by French photographer and author Joss Dray in 1989. The source of both images is Sanbar's book *Les Palestiniens: la photographie d'une terre et de son peuple de*

---

[57] After Arago formally received Daguerre at the Academy of Sciences (in 1839), an army of visitors, British for the most part (and thus long before the Balfour Declaration in 1917), descended on Palestine. Here is one of the first photographs of the Bay of Haifa.

[58] The action of the characters "passing" images is reminiscent of Godard's emblematic and well-known scene of the staging of the filmic apparatus in *Ici et ailleurs* (1970–74) in which we see people parading themselves holding still images in front of a movie camera. This action emulates the passage of the photogram through the film projector I discussed in Chapter 3.

1839 à nos jours (2004, English edition published in 2015), an illustrated history of the representation of Palestine and Palestinians. The premise of the book is precisely that the lack of representation has been due to their absence as nation and as a people. Sanbar underlines this point in his brief appearance in "Des choses comme ça," stating that Palestinians, in order to exist, have had to use what we commonly call "image," in spite of the fact that from the beginning they have been absent from it: the negative and Orientalist figure of the Arab as decadent or inferior,[59] or as victims demanding recognition and restitution, bearing witness, denouncing the violation of their rights, as fundamentalists or terrorists. In an evocative passage in *Memory for Forgetfulness: August, Beirut, 1982*, Mahmoud Darwish writes that the image that Palestinians have created for themselves is a problematic foothold of vision.[60] Setting the political reality against its own materiality, such an image invokes, in his view, a specific kind of representation that becomes reality itself by way of its becoming image—something like a "speech act" in Deleuze's sense: what is spoken (or imaged) creates a state of affairs.[61] These forms of imagining Palestine and Palestinians are not unproblematic and have been specific to historical junctures.

The question of the "mise en image" of Palestine has been key in Godard's work since the 1970s. In the movies in which the filmmaker has taken up the Palestine question, he has explored new ways of imagining the conflict. As I discussed earlier, in *Ici et ailleurs* (1970–74), Godard and Miéville juxtaposed images and sounds of the Palestinian resistance movement next to images and sounds of the political situation in France after May 1968. The movie is a reflection of the circulation of images from "elsewhere" in the mass media "here." The Palestinian Revolution appears embedded in the histories of revolutions and their failure. As we have seen, in *Notre musique* (2004) Godard alludes to the actual circulation of images of war and disaster in the sensible regime that reflect the global permanent state of war. The narrative in the movie problematizes the complicity between NATO's self-proclaimed right to interfere, the organizations of humanitarian help and ethnic wars waged in the name of the defense of human rights. In *Notre musique*, Godard approaches the conflict making a stopover in post-war Sarajevo. Palestine appears like one of the strata that integrate a palimpsest of histories of wars of annihilation

---

[59] Edward Said, *The Question of Palestine* (New York: Vintage Books, 1991), p. 54.

[60] Mahmoud Darwish, *Memory for Forgetfulness: August, Beirut, 1982*, translated by I Muhawi (Berkeley: University of California Press, 1995), pp. 45–46.

[61] Jean Baudrillard, "No Reprieve for Sarajevo," trans. P. Riemens, *Libération*, January 8, 1994. Available online: http://www.egs.edu/faculty/baudrillard/baudrillard-no-reprieve-for-sarajevo.html

cemented onto the Homeric recounting of the Trojan War. As I mentioned in the previous chapter, Godard borrows in *Notre musique* Elias Sanbar's comparison of the forced resettlement and ethnic cleansing[62] of the Palestinians to that of the "Red Indians" in North America.[63] In the film, Godard engages with the Palestinian image as the "others" of Israelis, one that resonates with the European colonialist image of "Arabs," and with their Biblical image based on text. From the point of view of militant filmmaking, as we have seen, he articulates the question via the shot/reverse-shot method with the purpose of interrogating given facts by bringing things into relationships.[64] In *Notre musique*, the Palestinian figure of absence incarnates the *memory* of the film and, as such, Palestinian absence is a trace that is simultaneously erased and remembered, a simulacrum of presence that refers beyond itself. The status of Palestinian absence as a mnemonic trace is analogous to the "Red Indians'" presence in the film as *revenants*.

As in *Notre musique*, in *Film Socialisme* the form and content of the expression of struggle and of political violence are at stake. In "Nos humanités" we see the cover of Racine's *Principles of Tragedy* and during the stopover in Greece, where Godard declares that civil war is the daughter of democracy and of tragedy: "Démocratie et tragédie ont été mariées à Athènes, sous Périclès et Sophocle. Un seul enfant: La guerre civile."[65]

---

[62] See Ilan Pappé, *The Ethnic Cleansing of Palestine* (New York: Oneworld Publications, 2007).

[63] This hypothesis, which was further developed in his book *Figures du Palestinien* (2004), was first evoked in an interview with Gilles Deleuze, "Les Indiens de Palestine," published in *Libération*, May 8–9 1989, reprinted in *Deux régimes de fous et autres textes* (Paris: Éditions de Minuit, 1995), 179–184. It is also evoked in Deleuze's "Grandeur de Yasser Arafat" in *Revue d'études Palestiniennes* 10 (1984), also reprinted in *Deux régimes de fous*.

[64] "Elias Sanbar montre très bien comment, de ne pouvoir exister que comme 'autres' des Israéliens, les Palestiniens ont dû se fabriquer une image. Une image d'autres, ces autres-là que les Européens appellent Arabes depuis l'époque de la colonisation… Sanbar a bien montré que les Palestiniens ont eu besoin de se faire photographier, pour que cette image existe, avant ils n'étaient que du texte. Moi, quand j'essaie de réfléchir à cela, je le fais forcément en cinéaste, il me semble que le champ/contre-champ, le montage du champ 1 et du champ 2, reste la manière d'interroger des faits qui se produisent mais que nous ne savons pas mettre en relation." [Elias Sanbar shows very well how, being unable to exist as something other than the "others" of Israelis, Palestinians had to fabricate their own image. An image of others, those others which Europeans had been calling Arabs since the era of colonization… Sanbar shows very well how Palestinians needed to be photographed, so that their image could exist. Before that, they were only text. When I try to reflect upon this, I necessarily do it as a filmmaker, and it seems to me that the shot/reverse-shot, the editing of shot 1 and shot 2, remains the way in which we can interrogate the facts that are being produced but that we are unable to bring into a relationship]. Godard in conversation with Jean-Michel Frodon, p. 21.

[65] "Tragedy and civil war wed in Athens under Pericles and Sophocles. They had a single child: Civil war."

The Greek philosopher Solon's definition of democracy applies here: the right to politics and thus civil rights is bestowed upon taking a stand. According to him: "Whoever fails to take a stand in a civil war is an infamous coward and has lost the right to be active in politics."[66] Civil war demands the equation of action and thought, and Godard situates civil war at the terrain of language, indicating how actions, ideas, words, gestures and life are intrinsically linked. The stop in Barcelona evokes, as I mentioned above, the texts, literature and images produced about and during the Civil War in 1936, an epoch when, as we hear in the voice-over, "Les spectateurs sont partis à la guerre."[67] The allusion to the Spanish Civil War implies an active call to join the struggle against the passivity of spectators and intellectuals, an issue raised by Susan Sontag and Juan Goytisolo in Sarajevo in 1993, evidently at stake in *Notre musique*.[68] In that sense, the assemblage of images, sounds and texts in *Film Socialisme* goes against the grain of the current reduction of war to empty forms and images that lack the work of the imagination and that paralyze the viewer. It also counters the degradation of political engagement to the liberal ethics of the defense of human rights, which Jean-Paul Curnier so harshly criticizes in *Notre musique*.

In "Nos humanités," the third section of *Film Socialisme*, we see the inscription on the screen—"ACCESS DENIED"—followed by an image of the sea seen through barbed wire that Godard gleaned from *Méditerranée*. According to Nicole Brenez, this shot signifies the impossibility of filming Palestine;[69] however, this take, along with Godard's allusion to the denial of access to Palestine, evokes more the apartheid state in which Palestinians live and their status as forced exiles rather than refugees, simply because they are increasingly farther away from the possibility of return and thus have no access to their territory or history.

When she is asked where she is heading to, the Palestinian woman in the cruise ship says, "Palestine," adding that: "Il s'agit d'un aller pour l'instant, pas d'un retour."[70] When the same character states: "Where are you, oh my beloved land?" while she examines Bonfils' photograph of the Bay

---

[66] *Aristotle's Constitution of Athens*, trans. Dymes, T.J. (1891) (London: Seeley and Co) available online: http://oll.libertyfund.org/?option=com_staticxt&staticfile=show.php%3Ftitle=580&chapter=64588&layout=html&Itemid=27

[67] "The spectators went to war."

[68] See my essay: "From Thirdworldism to Empire: Jean-Luc Godard and the Palestine Question," *Third Text*, Vol. 23, Issue 5 (September 2009), pp. 649–656.

[69] Brenez, "Liberté, Egalité, Prodigalité".

[70] "For the moment, it is a question of going, not of returning."

of Haifa, Godard situates the problem of the figuration and self-determination of Palestine and the Palestinians directly in the terrain not of the image, but of language. In an intertitle, Godard superimposes "Falestine" (the French version of "Filastin") over *Dawlat Filastin* ("Palestinian state" in Arabic).[71] In Hebrew it is pronounced "Palestina". We should take into account the fact that the word "Filastin" is not accepted in Israel, except by the radical left, while one of the preconditions of Israeli parties of both the right and center-left for negotiating a final peace settlement is that both Palestinians and the Arab countries recognize Israel as a Jewish state.[72] Thus the issue of the obliteration of Palestine becomes a textual reinscription. The problem is that, if Palestinians and Arab countries accept Israel as a Jewish-only state, Israel could expel the Palestinians living in Israel and eliminate the right of return of the Palestinian refugees. As a result, the only current option for Palestinians is to focus their efforts on improving their conditions, albeit within the context of subjection to the occupation. With the intertitle, moreover, Godard indicates the 'Hebrewization' of Palestine by way of the inclusion of its territory and the exclusion of its population. Paradoxically, conferring on the Palestinian state its name in Hebrew would imply recognition by Israel, along with the possibility of a binational state. Godard thus seeks to confer territorial status on Palestine at the level of language, underscoring the asymmetry between the status of the land and the unacknowledged people and their obliterated state. At the same time, he posits the following question (to which the answer is obvious according to the point of view one has of the conflict): which one of them is a fact—the juridical status of the "state" or of the physical territory?

In a collage in "Nos humanités," we see an image of Palestinians rendered prisoners wearing the iconic eye-cover used by the Israel Defense Forces (IDF); that of a young Israeli-Jewish soldier praying on the battlefield; the shot of the marble angel from Udi Aloni's 2002 film *Local Angel* that evokes Walter Benjamin's Messianic Angel while it recalls Aloni's mix of hope and skepticism in the movie before the possibility of forgiveness and reconciliation explored in his documentary. References are also made

---

[71] Although in the intertitle it is not written properly, it is: دولة فلسطيني as opposed to: دولة فلسطينية

[72] These reflections emerged from the comments and a conversation with Mexican visual artist Silvia Gruner about the implications of the intertitle in the movie.

to Isaac and Abraham, to the Holocaust (as the catastrophe in the Bible and the Shoah), to images of war and destruction, to blood-stained hands, to a statue of the Virgin Mary and to a crocodile devouring a goose while we hear "Palestine." Godard inserts a further three elements that become key to reimagining peace in the Middle East. They are lodged in a sequence that the filmmaker borrowed from Agnès Varda's autobiographical movie *Les plages d'Agnès* (2008). The sequence consists of three circus artists doing acrobatics on a trapeze before the ocean while we hear the voice of a young woman singing the first line of the Talmud and the voice of another one singing the Koran. The voices come from the Tunisian movie *Le Chant des mariées* (2008), a narrative about the friendship between a Jewish girl and her Muslim neighbor and how their friendship survives in spite of the separation of their communities by the oppression of Jews and the political pressure exerted on Muslims during the Nazi occupation of Tunisia. In the meantime, we see the trapeze artists balancing out and exchanging places with one another. Immediately after, we hear another sound with a heavy symbolic charge: Marlene Dietrich's voice singing "Sag mir wo die Blumen sind,"[73] a pacifist song very well known in the 1960s. Dietrich sang this song during a tour she made in Israel in 1966; by singing in German, she broke the taboo that until then had prevailed in Israel of speaking German in public. In an interview in which Godard speaks about *Film Socialisme*, he made an analogy between socialism, resistance, the trapeze artists and peace in the Middle East: "If Israelis and Palestinians opened a circus and performed together a trapeze number, things would be different in the Middle East, it would be a perfect accord."[74] When the theme of Israel-Palestine is brought up in *Film Socialisme*, a dissonant ensemble of notes played on a piano is heard. In a way, the "conversation" that Godard calls for in *Notre musique* is not enough to bring peace to Palestine, but something more: the trapeze number. This is because the trapeze artists "se renversent, s'en donnent en silence,"[75] at a moment in which singular bodies resonate, diffusing in time and space. For Godard, both socialism and the trapeze artist have the capacity to "announce the dissonances

---

[73] Originally: "Where have all the flowers gone?"

[74] Statement by Godard in the Mediapart interview (May 2010) Available online: January 24, 2013 http://www.dailymotion.com/video/xd8tiy_jlg-1-10-entretien-avec-godard-medi_news

[75] "They turn around and give themselves to each other in silence."

by a note in common."[76] If in *Notre musique* Godard makes a plea in the name of what is in between us, in *Film Socialisme* he vouches for what we have in common in a dissonant resonance, which is the possibility of living together announced by poetry and by the power of poetic imagination. For Bachelard, the poetic image is reverberation, it has a sonority of being, resonances dispersed on the different planes of our life in the world; repercussions are what invite us to give greater depth to our existence: "In the resonance we hear the poem, in the reverberations [created while] we speak it, it is our own. The reverberations bring about a change in being. The multiplicity of resonances then issues from the reverberations' unity of being."[77] The latter is posited as both superior to rational epistemology and scientific, potentially able to negotiate a utopian reconception and reorganization of human life. Evidently, the call for peace in *Film Socialisme*, emerging as it does from the principle of "turning around to face the other and change places," is much more ambitious than the plea Godard makes in *Notre musique* for the redistribution of the signs in common, the aware amongst us—and perhaps we will say: utopian. But also the situation is much more urgent than it was not so very long ago.

Adieu au Langage or Film as Metaphor

Godard has spent six decades exploring language: cinematographic, spoken, written, visual, sonorous and the relationship between text and image. In his most recent film at the time of writing (*Le Livre d'image* (2018) has appeared subsequently), for Godard "il n'y a plus de langage" and images have become "the murder of the present." The title of the film has been interpreted as a fatalist omen of the filmmaker's last words saying melancholically farewell, as the "testament of a misanthrope."[78] The contradiction that implies that Godard rejuvenates himself with this movie, however, applies also to the title: "*Adieu*" in Francophone Switzerland also denotes a greeting. *Adieu au langage* is radically experimental: it was filmed breaking the rules of three-dimensional (3D) imaging in an exploration of relief in digital imaging and with forms of structuring and filming images and then superimposing or overimposing them. The film begins with allusions to the Chicahua cosmogony and to Gustave Courbet's 1866 *L'Origine du*

---

[76] From the voice-over in *Film Socialisme*.
[77] Bachelard, p. xxii.
[78] James Quandt, "Last Harrumph," *Artforum International*, Vol. 53, No. 1 (September 2014).

monde, and this "Essay on literary investigation," is centered on the forest as a metaphor to describe the world. In the road from nature to metaphor, a confrontation with the visible takes place. At the center of the film there is a dialogue with painting translated to a saturated color palette evoking abstract, Fauvist, Cubist and even Impressionist painting. A striking visual analogy drawn in a sequence concatenating a fragment from a Pierre Soulages painting, a muddy patch in the forest, and Roxy the dog's fur, is an example of the film's construction as a whole oscillating between the representational and the figurative, the concrete and the abstract. An aphorism attributed to Monet, based on a quote by Proust, frames Godard's experimental research: "Il ne s'agit pas de peindre ce qu'on voit, parce qu'on ne voit rien, mais de peindre ce qu'on ne voit pas."[79] The aesthetic aporia attributed to Manet is at the core of Godard's filmmaking: the failure of the eye and the confrontation with the visible at the heart of Impressionist painting transposed to cinema, invariably includes a dialogue with literature. This is inscribed in Godard's interest in forms of visual thinking that can attack the presumptions of Western logocentrism and the possibility of conveying a pre-linguistic imaginary.[80]

Other kinds of images and sounds that appear in the film are derived from archival footage about the War and include a paddleboat ferry, *Le Savoie*, crossing Lac Léman (Lake Geneva). Threatening images of war and of memories of war appear to surround the apparent quietness of life in the West. As many writers have pointed out, a number of Godard's films revolve around bringing together two people, often placed in conversation within the broader historical and political world, and this is the case in *Adieu au langage*. The narrative is simple: a man and a woman fall in love; the woman leaves the man (briefly) for another man (who gets murdered), their love story goes awry, and in order to find a new form of communication and re-establish harmony, the couple acquires a dog (Roxy Miéville).[81] Scenes are repeated at least once, and the story unfolds twice with different couples (played by Héloïse Godet and Kamel Abdeli, Richard Chevallier and Zoé Bruneau).

---

[79] "It is not about painting what we see, but about painting what we do not see."

[80] Michael Witt, "On and Under Communication," *A Companion to Jean-Luc Godard*, Tom Conley and T. Jefferson Kline, eds. (London: Wiley Blackwell, 2015), p. 337.

[81] Jean-Luc Godard, "Jean-Luc Godard. Exclusive Interview with the Legend Cannes 2014 - Canon" available online: https://www.youtube.com/watch?v=Bou1w4LaqMo&no redirect=1

A better way to understand how repetition works in the movie is to think that the images included in the two categories in which the film divides itself—Nature and Metaphor—unfold in their reversed reflection as they are structured by an internal doubling, like *Nouvelle vague*, *Hélas pour moi* and *Notre musique*:[82] a defecation scene evoking *Le Penseur* by Rodin, the ferry in Lac Léman, the gunshot, the woman behind the bar (May 1968, Flins) to whom the man says, "I am at your service," the appropriated war scenes (from *Apocalypse Now*), the superposition of a knife with blood and oranges (perhaps an allegory of the Israeli–Palestinian conflict), the bathtub covered in blood (Hitchcock), Roxy playing by the lake, the wild poppies growing by the highway, and the naked couple separating in a single plane that divides into two, creating a visual hallucination by breaking the rules of 3D film technology.[83]

With regards to technique, Godard declared two reasons for wanting to experiment with 3D: first, to "escape from himself" (from his collages of appropriated images and sounds); second, Godard saw in 3D a new technology with almost infinite potential.[84] *Adieu au langage* expands some of Godard's previous experiments with 3D in *Les Trois désastres* (2013), a 17-minute video that Godard contributed to *3x3D*, the anthology that includes work by Godard, Peter Greenaway and Edgar Pêra. Each "*désastre*" begins with a Mallarméan roll of the dice and comprises images of twentieth-century disasters and film history, seen through the lens of 3D film technology. For Godard, one of the implications of digital technologies is the "loss of depth" in inverse proportion to historical consciousness; Godard therefore seeks, through technique, a method to superimpose bidimensional images, to imbue them with plastic materiality and to open up both planes to restore to them their depth. Furthermore, in *Les Trois désastres*, Godard reflexively shows the apparatus of 3D technology in a sequence: we see a 3D camera made of two digital, single-lens

---

[82] For a discussion on the duplex construction of *Adieu au langage* see James S. Williams, "European Culture and Artistic Resistance in *Histoire(s)* Chapter 3A, *La monnaie de l'absolu*," in *The Cinema Alone: Essays on the Work of Jean-Luc Godard 1985–2000*, ed. Michael Temple and James S. Williams (Amsterdam: The University Press, 2000), pp. 249–250.

[83] Fabrice Aragno in "Autour de: Adieu au langage de Jean-Luc Godard. Entretien avec Fabrice Aragno, chef opérateur" (1ere partie) http://vimeo.com/97407055

[84] Jean-Luc Godard, "Jean-Luc Godard. Exclusive Interview with the Legend Cannes 2014 - Canon."

reflex cameras attached to each other, one the right-side up and the other upside down, mounted facing a large mirror. In mainstream films, the technique does not change the content; in Godard it does. In *Adieu au langage*, there are instances in which Godard plays with the lenses, distorting our perception to emphasize spatial relations reflecting the lack of understanding between the lovers in the film. The layers of the sound are as complex as the imaging techniques: sometimes dialogue is muffled by other sounds; the music starts and gets cut off, sound bounces from one speaker to the other.

Scenes of a fragmented narrative alternate with domestic passages in a bourgeois interior and the streets of the city of Nyon, Swizerland, before the cultural center bearing the sign "USINE À GAZ." The way in which the sign is filmed and its role in the narrative delivers a word play: in French, *usine à gaz* means something huge, complicated and useless that evokes the *usine à rêves* or "dream factory" which is Hollywood. The use of the sign *usine à gaz* in the film is a clear example of Godardian polysemy, which operates at another level when the couple fights and she announces, "They are dying…" and he answers, "Let them die!" evoking the Nazi extermination of European Jews. In the following sequence, we see a car passing by in such a way that the name of the cultural center reads "AGAZ," inevitably evoking the extreme situation in Gaza caused by the Israeli siege and thus the Godardian analogy between the Shoah and the Nakba.

Emblematic fragments of Hollywood films appear in a flatscreen in the couple's home, at times functioning like a false mirror before which the couple makes statements, pronouncements, philosophical reflections, recite aphorisms and fight. The juxtapositions created by the images on the screen—amongst which we see extracts from Jean-Pierre Melville's *Les Enfants terribles* (1950), Howard Hawks' *Only Angels Have Wings* (1939), Artur Aristakisyan's *Palms* (1993), Henry King's *The Snows of Kilimanjaro* (1952), Boris Barnet's *By the Bluest of Seas* (1936), Fritz Lang's *Metropolis* (1927), Rouben Mamoulian's *Dr. Jekyll and Mr. Hyde* (1931) and Robert Siodmak's *Menschen am Sonntag* (1929), or static broadcast—are sometimes mirrored by the actions of the characters from the film.

The "absence of language" and the "murder of the present" are Godard's central preoccupations in the film. The sources of both problems are the dictatorship of the digital media and the destruction of language by mediatized communication. Godard declared that "SMS" means "Save My Soul," which denotes our current situation of extreme alienation: "Faites en sorte que je puisse vous parler // Persuadez-moi que vous m'entendez."[85] In light of this, Godard posits that what we consider "man" to be—at the crossroads of complex epistemological knowledges and practices, the category of human (language, practices, points of view)—is no longer useful to define what is human. On the one hand, *Adieu au langage* takes up Godard's concern with communication that can be traced back to *Le Gai savoir* (1969) and to the television series *Six fois deux: Sur et sous la communication* (1976) and *France tour détour deux enfants* (1978), made in collaboration with Miéville.[86] On the other hand, the reference to Mary Shelley's *Frankenstein* unveils another of the themes of the film, which is the current failure of the humanities to define "the human." It has been argued that humanism has become the default ideology of capitalism. Under the current capitalistic regime, the possibility of emancipation proclaimed by the humanities is little more than freedom of choice in the market; thus, by default, subjects are "free agents," although their condition as "free market machines" serves to dehumanize them.[87] This form of dehumanization is coupled by Godard with the internal default of Western culture that led to the extermination camps or was unable to prevent them. As Daniel Morgan has pointed out, the promise of enlightened humanism is constantly shown by Godard as being bankrupted by the Shoah (and the Israeli–Palestinian conflict), along the lines of Theodor Adorno's paradoxical injunction that "Poetry after Auschwitz is barbaric."[88] Therefore, Godard asks, what kind of subjectivity is possible in the era of digital technology and communications in the light of the bankruptcy of the humanities evidenced by global total war? And what kind of self could emerge at a time in which objects and bodies are disfigurable and refigurable virtually and in reality?[89] For Godard, these issues are the cause of the disintegration of the possibility of the "face-to-face" encounter, a basic kind of human relation that is based on language. Devoted to maximum efficiency—especially of language—technology has

---

[85] "Make it so I can speak to you. Persuade me that you hear me." Maurice Blanchot, *L'Attente, l'oubli* (Paris: Gallimard, 1962).

[86] See Michael Witt, "On and Under Communication," in *A Companion to Jean-Luc Godard*, Tom Conley and T. Jefferson Kline, eds. (London: Wiley Blackwell, 2015), p. 322.

[87] See Benjamin Noys, *Malign Velocities, Accelerationism and Capitalism* (London: Zero Books 2014), p. 11.

[88] Daniel Morgan, *Late Godard and the Possibilities of Cinema* (Los Angeles: University of California Press, 2013), p. 67.

[89] See James S. Williams, *Encounters With Godard: Ethics, Aesthetics, Politics* (Albany: State University of New York Press, 2016), p. 83.

infiltrated every aspect of our existence, eliminating the margin of error between the sending and reception of a message. For Godard, the denial of the force of the word by digital communication and the failure of the humanities to define the human has come to inhabit interior experience, eliminating redundancy, misunderstandings, the possibility of reading between the lines and the elision of alterity as the beginning of ethics.[90] Quoting Philippe Sollers, Godard posits the origins of current totalitarianism in the interdiction of interior experience caused by Spectacle, which incessantly projects a subject beyond itself, cutting it from its interior life—a program that is paradoxically, highly seductive.[91] Furthermore, for Godard, the substitution of language by digital communication creates a new form of isolated solitude without ties to others, which imprisons us. That is to say, the *mise en abîme* of language by technology—which is not an extension of man, as McLuhan predicted, but which has become an autonomous realm, because digital media can communicate amongst themselves without human mediation—is a new form of totalitarianism akin to the totalitarianism described by Jacques Ellul and Solzhenitsyn, whom Godard quotes in the movie.

In a way, Godard's "farewell" to language implies giving life to metaphor. Metaphor means "transference" in Greek, and has a connotation of translation, transportation and movement. The appearance of Roxy Miéville is a metaphor of the possibility of an "other" post-anthropocentric language that moves "in between" humans and restores the possibility of language between the couple. In the film, the dog's

---

[90] Jean-Luc Godard, "Jean-Luc Godard. Exclusive Interview with the Legend Cannes 2014 - Canon."

[91] "Commençons par le commencement: L'expérience intérieure est désormais interdite. D'une façon drastique, totalitaire par la société en général et par le spectacle en particulier qui avale tout cela pour projeter sans arrêt le sujet dehors et le couper de sa vie intérieure. C'est un programme qui est en cours de façon tout à fait saisissante." [Let's begin at the beginning: inner experience is henceforth forbidden. In a drastic manner, totalitarian when adopted by society in general and by Spectacle in particular, all of this is swallowed in order to ceaselessly portray the subject from the outside while cutting him off from his inner life. It's a program that is happening in a very gripping manner.] From Philippe Sollers, "La Mutation du sujet (Entretien avec Philippe Forest)," *L'Infini* 117 (Décembre 2011) Source: Ted Fendt, "*Adieu au langage* – Goodbye to Language: A Works Cited," (An in-progress catalogue and translation of the various texts, films and music used in Jean-Luc Godard's *Adieu au langage*), October 12, 2014, available online: https://mubi.com/notebook/posts/adieu-au-langage-goodbye-to-language-a-works-cited

discourse is articulated by the questions posed also by dogs in Clifford Simak's science fiction novel *City* (1952, which subsequently appeared in France under the title *Demain les chiens*): "What is man? What is a city? Or even, What is a war?". Not only Roxy is endowed with speech but she converses with other elements of nature, and with man:

> L'eau lui parlait d'une voix profonde et grave. Alors Roxy se mit à penser. Elle essaie de me parler. Comme elle a toujours essayé de parler aux gens à travers les âges. Dialoguant avec elle-même quand il n'y a personne pour écouter. Mais qui essaie. Qui essaie toujours de communiquer aux gens les nouvelles qu'elle a à leur donner. Quelques uns d'entre eux ont tiré de la rivière une certaine vérité.[92]

For Godard, film's alliance between word and image is akin to the dog's particular form of communication, which Godard compares to *communion*[93]—a form of communication that involves sharing intimate thoughts and feelings, an exchange that can also be on a mental or spiritual level. Moreover, in the film, Roxy represents a new form of communication, an "other" language that Godard compares to the lost language of the poor, the excluded, animals, plants, the disabled—those who are out of the field of the image.[94]

In an interview, Godard declared that what interests him in 3D technology is finding what there is on the sides of the image, the out of field. While the camera may register many "languages," there is a lost "language" residing in animals, the poor, the homeless, and this language is out of frame: "à côté de la plaque."[95] And this out of field

---

[92] "The water spoke to him in a deep and serious voice. Roxy began to think. It's trying to talk to me. As it has always tried to talk to people through the ages. Dialoguing with itself when there is no one to listen. But trying. Trying always to communicate to people the news that it has to give them. Some of them have taken from the river a certain truth." An appropriated and rewritten note from Clifford D. Simak's *Time and Again* as noted by Ted Fendt, "*Adieu au langage* – Goodbye to Language: A Works Cited."

[93] Jean-Luc Godard, "Entretien avec Jean-Luc Godard," FranceInter Radio, 21 May 2014 available online: http://www.franceinter.fr/emission-le-79-jean-luc-godard-invite-du-79

[94] Artur Mas, Martial Pisani, "1 # La forme de l'entretien (Revers, doubles, reflets, ombres)" *Independencia*, May 31 2014, available online: http://www.independencia.fr/revue/spip.php?article941

[95] "Beside the point."

is the "out of place," the form of language that interests Godard.[96] With this declaration, Godard makes a political statement, while he marks a shift from seeking to film the space in between people created by the shot/reverse-shot, the space for a possible conversation between two parties, to searching what is next to the field of the image: an other language.

This is where 3D technology comes in again, which Godard also transforms into a metaphor. For the filmmaker, 3D results from a desire grounded in lack of imagination that causes obsession with "putting reality inside reality,"[97] delivering absence of thought and of reality. The illusion that 3D technology offers is that cinema is not flat, that it creates an autonomous reality with no out of field. Also, the technique is based on emulating human stereoscopic vision, with two cameras filming the same image from slightly different angles; when projected, the two images are superimposed on the screen and the brain assumes the task of assembling them to create a 3D image. In that regard, the 3D image imitates human frontal stereoscopic vision. And yet, it is not that we can *see more* with two cameras; cameras, like the human eye, have limitations. This is why Godard's camera is not satisfied with merely contemplating the characters; it is rather, an active, experimental eye in the tradition of early experimental films such as Joris Ivens' *Rain* (1929), quoted in the film. Godard thus posits film as a cognitive and psychological experiment that reveals the central processes of the nervous system. In parallel, Godard's references to romantic poetry in the film reawaken the romantic poet's desire to "describe" immediate reality by hallucinating signification created in the juxtaposition between letters, images, texts, colors, dimensions (in relief), the visible, the audible and what cannot be seen. He thereby seeks to startle the spectator with electroshocks, making a real visible and audible world emerge from language that is different from everyday perception and from the mainstream contemporary visual regime.

3D technology takes up a further task: in conventional Hollywood cinema, the classical technique to re-enact a "face-to-face" conversation is the shot/reverse-shot, where two points of view meet in alternating sequences.

---

[96] Jean-Luc Godard, "Jean-Luc Godard. Exclusive Interview with the Legend Cannes 2014 - Canon."
[97] Ibid.

As we know from the previous chapter, this form of montage is the conceptual node of *Notre musique*, which Godard posits as problematic because the two parties—in this case, victims and torturers in wars of annihilation—are always asymmetrical and the shot/reverse-shot gives them a false homogeneity and sense of equivalence. As in *Film Socialisme*, Godard eliminated the shot/reverse-shot in *Adieu au langage*. The eyes of the man and the woman never meet and they do not see each other face-to-face; they are always on the same plane, but looking in different directions. Godard, moreover, constructs the images as if he were unfolding them in their own mirror reflection in a way that when a character sees him/herself in the mirror, and the camera frames the subject and his/her reflection, the shot and the reverse-shot appear simultaneously. At the same time, the image appears unfolded in reverse, enabling the character to see his/her *semblable* (fellow man/woman) face-to-face.[98] As I mentioned, 3D technique becomes the content of the film: as the first couple separates in a scene that takes place on the same plane, one of the viewer's eyes stays with one of the characters while the second appears blurry, because the cameras are not aligned. In order to be able to stay with either one of the characters (or take his/her side), the viewer is forced to open and close each eye alternately. Moreover, the sequence invites us to shut our eyes so we can create a shot/reverse-shot on the same plane, reminding us that *we see* with our eyes.

In sum, the film is a giant mirror that reflects a grammar of thought that no longer resides in enunciation (and thus a farewell to language). Marking the absence of relation between the human characters, Roxy takes the place of a third, post-anthropocentric, "other" that enables communication between the couple, signifying the possibility of the re-establishment of their relationship. Insofar as Roxy is "outside of the frame," her "thirdness" alludes to a general condition in humanity: exclusion in/through language. In *Adieu*, Roxy substitutes the "human" of man, evoking the nineteenth-century debate about defining humanity. In a scene from the film, we hear Percy Shelley reading from his poem "Hell" about revolution and the threat of despotism, while Mary Shelley, his wife, appears in the act of completing *Frankenstein*, both at the shores of Lac Léman. For Mary's father, William Godwin, literature is an important line to demarcate the animal and human kingdoms. *Frankenstein* can be read as a critique of this belief: the monster can learn

---

[98] Fabrice Aragno in "Autour de: Adieu au langage de Jean-Luc Godard. Entretien avec Fabrice Aragno, chef opérateur" (1ere partie) http://vimeo.com/97407055

to master the art of language, culture and literature, but this does not mean that these achievements secure him a position in the human kingdom. According to Godwin's theory, literary education is crucial for human perfectibility; yet Shelley and Godard point out the failure of the promise of the humanities and letters to humanize man.[99] Roxy is the metaphor for a point of view *other* than human that can enable humanity to restore itself by re-establishing the link between the I and the Other. For Godard, the notion of "indivi*dual*" includes *duality*. We are always two and the forms of *communion* enabled by animals and plants can potentially restore the logic of the three, after Léon Brunschvicg: "L'un est dans l'autre et l'autre est dans l'un et ce sont les trois personnes."[100] The condition to be able to be foreign to each other is exemplified by quote by Lévinas in the film: "Seuls les êtres libres peuvent être étrangers les uns aux autres. Ils ont une liberté commune, mais précisément cela les sépare."[101]

Adieu au langage is not a film in the traditional sense of the word, based on cutting or making cuts in the real to create an imaginary reflection, but an experimental film in the most radical sense of the word: it is a cognitive and psychological experiment that reveals the central processes of the nervous system, creating a mechanism of possible deceptions of the real. The film begins and ends with the classic 1968 protest song "La violenza/la caccia alle streghe" (Violence/witch-hunting), by Alfredo Bandelli; the verse is repeated at the beginning and end:

> La violenza, la violenza,
> la violenza, la rivolta;
> chi ha esitato questa volta
> lotterà con noi domani![102]

As with *Film Socialisme*, *Adieu au langage* is a call to arms; if the former foresaw massive mobilizations in 2011 and 2012 at the global level (the

---

[99] Maureen N. McLane, "Literate species: populations, 'humanities,' and the specific failure of literature in *Frankenstein*," in *Romanticism and the Human Sciences: Poetry, Population, and the Discourse of the Species* (Cambridge: Cambridge University Press, 2000).

[100] "The one is in the other and the other is in the one and that is the three." Quoted by Jean-Luc Godard, "Entretien avec Jean-Luc Godard," FranceInter Radio, May 21, 2014 available online: http://www.franceinter.fr/emission-le-79-jean-luc-godard-invite-du-79

[101] "Only free beings can be strangers to each other. They have a shared freedom but that is precisely what separates them." Emmanuel Lévinas, *Totalité et infini: Essai sur l'extériorité* (La Haye: Nijhoff, 1961).

[102] "Violence, violence / violence, revolt / who has hesitated this time / will fight with us tomorrow!"

Arab Spring, Occupy, the Indignados in Spain) while resuscitating an impression of presence that is not given by ordinary imagery, *Adieu* is the novelty announced by the newborn's cry (which for Hannah Arendt represents the introduction into the world of the absolutely new, also referred to by Émile, in *Le Gai savoir*) and Roxy's bark that we hear at the end of the movie: what is to come is yet to be invented.

Bibliography

Aragno, Fabrice. "Autour de: Adieu au langage de Jean-Luc Godard. Entretien avec Fabrice Aragno, chef opérateur" (1ere partie). Available at: http://vimeo.com/97407055

Aristotle's Constitution of Athens, trans. Dymes, T.J. (1891) (London. Seeley and Co). Available at: http://oll.libertyfund.org/?option=com_staticxt&staticfile=show.php%3Ftitle=580&chapter=64588&layout=html&Itemid=27

Bachelard, Gaston. *The Poetics of Space* (Boston: Beacon, 1964)

Baudrillard, Jean. "No Reprieve for Sarajevo," trans. P. Riemens, *Libération*, January 8, 1994. Available at: http://www.egs.edu/faculty/baudrillard/baudrillard-no-reprieve-for-sarajevo.html

Bergson, Henri. *Matière et mémoire: Essai sur la relation du corps à l'esprit* (Paris: Presses Universitaires de France, 1964)

Blanchot, Maurice. *L'attente, l'oubli* (Paris: Gallimard, 1962)

Borges, Jorge Luis. *Book of Imaginary Beings*, trans. Andrew Hurley (New York: Viking, 1967)

Brenez, Nicole. "Liberté, Égalité, Prodigalité," *Cahiers du Cinéma* No. 657 (Juin 2010)

Daney, Serge. "Avant et après l'image", *Revue d'études palestiniennes* no. 40 (Été 1991)

Darwish, Mahmoud. *Memory for Forgetfulness: August, Beirut, 1982*, trans. I Muhawi (Berkeley: University of California Press, 1995)

Darwish, Mahmoud. *Unfortunately, It was Paradise*, ed. and trans. Munir Akash and Carolyn Forché with Sinan Antoon and Amira El-Zein (Berkeley and Los Angeles: University of California Press, 2003)

Deleuze, Gilles. "Grandeur de Yasser Arafat," *Revue d'études palestiniennes* no. 10 (1984), reprinted in *Deux régimes de fous et autres textes* (Paris: Éditions de Minuit, 1995)

Deleuze, Gilles. "Les Indiens de la Palestine," *Libération*, May 8–9 1989, reprinted in *Deux régimes de fous et autres textes* (Paris: Éditions de Minuit, 1995)

Didi-Huberman, Georges. "The Supposition of the Aura: The Now, the Then, and Modernity," *Walter Benjamin and History*, ed. Andrew Benjamin (New York: Continuum, 2006)

Doane, Mary-Ann. "Indexicality and the Concept of Medium Specificity," in *The Meaning of Photography*, edited by Robin Kelsey and Blake Stimson (Williamstown, MA, Sterling and Francine Clark Institute, 2008)

Douchet, Jean and Ganzo, Fernando. "Jean-Luc Movimiento Godard" *Lumière Internacional* (October 2010)

Fargier, Jean-Paul. "Hacia el relato rojo: Notas sobre un nuevo modo de producción del cine," in Jean-Louis Comolli, et al. *Mayo Francés: La cámara opaca: El debate cine e ideología*, comp. Emiliano Jelicié (Buenos Aires: El Cuenco de Plata, 2016)

Fargier, Jean-Paul. "Jean-Paul Fargier vs. *Tel Quel*" *VH 101* Nr. 9 (1972)

Fendt, Ted. "*Adieu au langage*—Goodbye to Language: A Works Cited," (An in-progress catalogue and translation of the various texts, films and music used in Jean-Luc Godard's *Adieu au langage*), October 12, 2014. Available at: https://mubi.com/notebook/posts/adieu-au-langage-goodbye-to-language-a-works-cited

Fox, Dominic. *Cold World: The Aesthetics of Dejection and the Politics of Militant Dysphoria* (London: Zero Books, 2009)

Genet, Jean. *Prisoner of Love* (New York: Wesleyan, 1992)

Godard, Jean-Luc. "Entretien avec Jean-Luc Godard," FranceInter Radio, 21 May 2014. Available at: http://www.franceinter.fr/emission-le-79-jean-luc-godard-invite-du-79

Godard, Jean-Luc. "Interview with Dany Le Rouge (Daniel Cohen-Bendit)," *Telerama*. Available at: http://www.telerama.fr/cinema/jean-luc-godard-a-daniel-cohn-bendit-qu-est-ce-qui-t-interesse-dans-mon-film,55846.php

Godard, Jean-Luc. "Jean-Luc Godard. Exclusive Interview with the Legend Cannes 2014 - Canon." Available at: https://www.youtube.com/watch?v=Bo u1w4LaqMo&noredirect=1

Godard, Jean-Luc. "Mediapart Interview," Rolle, April 27, 2010a. Available at: http://www.dailymotion.com/video/xd8tiy_jlg-1-10-entretien-avec-godard-medi_news

Godard, Jean-Luc. *Film Socialisme: Dialogues avec visages auteurs* (Paris: P.O.L., 2010)

Godard, Jean-Luc and Ishaghpour, Youssef. *Cinema: The Archeology of Film and the Memory of a Century* (London: Berg, 2005)

Hemingway, Ernest. *For Whom the Bell Tolls* (New York: Scribner, 1995)

Hori, Junji. "Godard's Two Historiographies," in *For Ever Godard*, ed. Michael Temple (London: Black Dog, 2004)

Jameson, Fredric. "The Politics of Utopia," *New Left Review* no. 25 (January–February 2004)

Jelicié, Emiliano. Introduction to *Mayo Francés: La cámara opaca: El debate cine e ideología*, comp. Emiliano Jelicié (Buenos Aires: El Cuenco de Plata, 2016)

Lack, Roland-François. "Una fotografía y una cámara: dos objetos *Film Socialisme*" *Lumière Internacional* (October 2010)

Lévinas, Emmanuel. *Totalité et infini: Essai sur l'extériorité* (La Haye: Nijhoff, 1961)
Lévy, Bernard-Henri. "Terre promise" (quatrieme et dernier episode, 2001). Available at: http://laregledujeu.org/2010/11/18/3426/%C2%AB-terre-promise-%C2%BB-quatrieme-et-dernier-episode-2001/
Mas, Artur and Pisani, Martial. "1 # La forme de l'entretien (Revers, doubles, reflets, ombres" *Independencia*, May 31 2014. Available at: http://www.independencia.fr/revue/spip.php?article941
Mas, Artur and Pisani, Martial. "Film Socialisme," *Independencia* (June 1, 2010). Available at: www.independencia.fr/indp/10_FILM_SOCIALISME_JLG.html
McLane, Maureen N. "Literate species: populations, 'humanities,' and the specific failure of literature in *Frankenstein*," in *Romanticism and the Human Sciences: Poetry, Population, and the Discourse of the Species* (Cambridge: Cambridge University Press, 2000)
Merleau-Ponty, Maurice. *The World of Perception* (London: Routledge, 2004)
Morgan, Daniel. *Late Godard and the Possibilities of Cinema* (Los Angeles: University of California Press, 2013)
Nassar, Issam. "Familial Snapshots, Representing Palestine in the Work of the First Local Photographers," *History & Memory* 12 no. 2 (Winter-Fall 2000)
Noys, Benjamin. *Malign Velocities, Accelerationism and Capitalism* (London: Zero Books 2014)
Pappé, Ilan. *The Ethnic Cleansing of Palestine* (New York: Oneworld Publications, 2007)
Picard, Andréa. "*Film Socialisme*," *Cinema Scope* No. 43 (June 2010). Available at: http://cinema-scope.com/wordpress/web
Quandt, James. "Last Harrumph," *Artforum International*, Vol. 53 No. 1 (September 2014)
Said, Edward. *The Question of Palestine* (New York: Vintage Books, 1991)
Sanbar, Elias. *Les Palestiniens: La Photographie d'une terre et de son peuple de 1839 à nos jours* (Paris: Hazan, 2004)
Shaviro, Steven. "Post-Cinematic Affect: On Grace Jones, *Boarding Gate* and *Southland Tales*," *Film Philosophy*, Vol. 14 No. 1 (2010)
Sollers, Philippe. "La Mutation du sujet (Entretien avec Philippe Forest)," *L'Infini* 117 (Décembre 2011)
Sollers, Philippe. "Méditerranée," (voice-over). Available at:: http://www.pileface.com/sollers/article.php3?id_article=268
Sontag, Susan. *On Photography* (New York: Farrar, Straus and Giroux, 1977)
Stiegler, Bernard. "Photography as the Medium of Reflection," in *The Meaning of Photography* (Williamstown, MA: Sterling and Francine Clark Institute, 2008)
Wallace, David Foster. "A Supposedly Fun Thing I'll Never do Again," in *A Supposedly Fun Thing I'll Never Do Again* (New York: Back Bay Books, 1992)

Weil, Simone. *Écrits historiques et politiques* (Paris: Gallimard, 1960)
Williams, James S. "European Culture and Artistic Resistance in *Histoire(s)* Chapter 3A, *La monnaie de l'absolu*," in *The Cinema Alone: Essays on the Work of Jean-Luc Godard 1985–2000*, ed. Michael Temple and James S. Williams (Amsterdam: The University Press, 2000)
Witt, Michael. "On and Under Communication," in *A Companion to Jean-Luc Godard*, Tom Conley and T. Jefferson Kline, eds. (London: Wiley Blackwell, 2015)
Žižek, Slavoj. *Living in the End Times* (London: Verso 2010)

CHAPTER 7

Conclusion: The Legacy of Militant Filmmaking or How to Rise Above Everything That Is Dying?

In the past few years and in the context of the impending need to make visible the intolerable wrongs brought about by capitalist absolutism, globalization and permanent war everywhere, films and art projects have revisited militant filmmaking from the 1960s and 1970s. Looking for frames of militancy and revolt that could offer an alternative to the melancholia inherited from the outcome of yesteryear's revolutionary struggles, artists, filmmakers and cultural producers have started to look for alternatives for political subjectivation and emancipation, situating culture and visual culture as key in political struggles. As we have seen, in the 1960s, militant cinema sought to share and disseminate strategies and tools to support political struggles across the globe. As Jean-Luc Godard put it: "A [militant] film is a flying carpet that can travel anywhere. There is no magic. It is a political work."[1] *Ici et ailleurs* (1976) is not only key in Godard's *oeuvre* but a main example of vanguardist political filmmaking and has been a recent topic of many discussions around the politicization of filmmaking and artistic production. As we have seen, the film is also a self-reflexive account of the outcome of revolutions *here and elsewhere* and of militant cinema and its effective disappearance by the mid-1970s. By self-reflexive I mean that aside from positing cinema as a politicized space, it is an interrogation on the *conditions of possibility of representation*—in the sense of speaking in the name of others through art or literature in relation to political

[1] Jean-Luc Godard "Manifeste", in *Jean-Luc Godard Documents*, edited by David Faroult, Centre Georges Pompidou, Paris 2006, pp. 138–140.

© The Author(s) 2019
I. Emmelhainz, *Jean-Luc Godard's Political Filmmaking*,
https://doi.org/10.1007/978-3-319-72095-1_7

struggles. As I have argued in the previous chapters, in the 1970s Godard's materialist filmmaking manifested as a *politics of the image*, laid out pedagogically in *Ici et ailleurs* within the context of the advent of the transhumance of images of the mass media. The becoming information of the image had become the prevailing framework to politicize the image, inaugurated by Godard and Gorin in the last film they made together in 1972, *Letter to Jane: An Investigation about a Still* (glimpses of which we see in *Le Gai savoir* and in the Dziga Vertov Group (DVG) films). During the 1970s, Godard and Anne-Marie Miéville continued in the Sonimage videos with this politics of the image, naming it "journalism of the audiovisual." One of the key elements of the Sonimage practice is their critique of the "mediatization of mediation," which is, as we have seen, the form of activism that ensued from the fall of Marxism-Leninism, based on the presupposition that counter-information and the visibilization of urgent problems would bring emancipation as betterment or reform.

It is often argued that after the Sonimage period, Godard's films and videos turned to the history of classical European painting, music and literature, and that the filmmaker withdrew from the political world toward the private realm. In this regard, his work has been read as deploying a conservative retreat from politics and a turn toward the aesthetic; it has been stated that the filmmaker, submerged in melancholia and repentance for his "Maoist excesses," began to focus on the idealist and romantic European aesthetic tradition. And yet, as Daniel Morgan sought to contest in his recent book on Godard, the contrary is the case, as his films from the 1980s onwards would continue to interweave several intellectual concerns that involve cinema history, politics and the arts, and as I have argued throughout this book, a sustained and coherent practice of reinventing materialist filmmaking based on a series of sustained preoccupations.[2] From my point of view, the issue of the possibility and outreach of intellectuals' political engagement *elsewhere* was an early concern in Godard; it is evident in *Le Petit soldat* and is consistently present throughout his *oeuvre*. His relentless inquiry into issues of representation and representativity, as we have seen, led Godard to construct and deconstruct his figure and position as filmmaker: the Maoist militant filmmaker becomes the "poor revolutionary idiot, millionaire in images from elsewhere;"[3] the pedagogue (DVG films, *Notre musique*); the self-absorbed neurotic director (*Passion*); the idiot (*Soigne*

---

[2] See Daniel Morgan, *Late Godard and the Possibilities of Cinema* (Los Angeles: University of California Press, 2013).

[3] From the voice-over in *Ici et ailleurs*.

ta droite); the artist drawing his self-portrait (*JLG-JLG*); the old filmmaker turning his back on world problems (*For Ever Mozart, Notre musique*); historian, philosopher, etc. In this regard, we should interpret Godard's ongoing dialogue and collaboration with Miéville as yet another effort to experiment with representativity. Moreover, his/their concern with constructing a position and a figure "which speaks" in film about an "Other" (or about deconstructing this Other) to an addressee, is inextricable from Godard's efforts to explore and undermine the many ways in which power crystalizes and orients historical sensible regimes (in Althusser's terms, in ideology and ideological state apparatuses). In other words, Godard's materialist filmmaking became early on a form of theoretical practice of filmmaking in the sense of conceiving cinema as self-knowledge by "rendering visible" not only the physical, economic and social materiality of cinema, but by showing the ideological, political and economical functions proper to cinema. "Rendering visible," in this sense, is a double act that consists of unveiling cinema's ideological nature while visibilizing human relationships as determined by social, economic, political and ethical givens in certain historical moments. It is within this context that we should interpret Godard's return to the Palestine question in *Notre musique* as revisiting the conditions of possibility of engagement and visibility of the Palestinians' struggle, 30 years later. In *Notre musique* the Palestinians are no longer "failed revolutionaries" and "dead bodies demanding restitution," but strata in the palimpsest of histories of "vanquished peoples," writing about their defeat in Homeric terms. In this regard, Godard's materialist filmmaking encompasses a concern with conditions of visuality and communication and the materiality of vision and language, without forgetting that the materialist categories of social class and class differences never disappear in his work, from *La Chinoise* to *Passion, Nouvelle vague, Éloge de l'amour* and *Notre musique*.[4] It could be argued, on the one hand, that Godard in his work posits "reality" as something to be unveiled, discovered

---

[4] James S. Williams has accused Godard of Euro-centeredness and even of racism in his perceived ambivalence in the way in which he represents alterity. Examples include Omar Diop in *La Chinoise*; the Black Panthers as sexual predators in *Sympathy for the Devil*, or the black young man in *Éloge de l'amour*. In this regard, it could be argued that Godard was uninterested in the cultural turn of Marxism, and that the way in which he addresses gender and ethnic difference in his work is strictly from a self-acknowledged Eurocentric and masculine point of view. His attempt to confront the viewer with his/her racial and gender prejudices are an attempt to confront his own, rather than to account for alterity through the mandates of multicultural political correctness. In my view, Godard is interested in *alterity* as it is figured by specific historical conjunctures, not as a universal category. See James S. Williams, *Encounters With Godard: Ethics, Aesthetics, Politics* (Albany: State University of New York Press, 2016).

by the medium-poet-filmmaker and, on the other, as something to be constructed. Akin to music, Godard is a composer who rewrites reality by quoting historical pasts that are embedded in the sensible regime determining how we see the past, the present and the future. In a modernist vein, Godard seeks to construct new visibilities that could bring about emancipation.

Arguably, the legacy of Godard's political filmmaking is very far removed from his post-1970s materialist filmmaking and manifests today in a niche in cultural production termed *sensible politics*.[5] As images have become forms of power and governance by carrying information without meaning and automating thought and will, *sensible politics* implies that political action has migrated to the mediascape and to the culture industry, manifesting in political action in the realm of signs, putting into action Jacques Rancière's definition of politics as an intervention within the sphere of the visible and the sayable.[6] This form of political intervention differs from an earlier critical tradition based on a relationship between appearance and reality and consciousness and illusion, a dialectic very much still at play in Godard's materialist filmmaking. For Rancière, the reconfiguration of the dominant landscape of perception and its conditions of possibility is called "dissensus" and seeks to displace what is thinkable and possible, in order to open up toward new arrangements of the sensible. While Rancière's dissensus bears the task of incessantly reconfiguring "alterity" and its agonistic place in the sensible regime with the political goal of achieving democracy, Godard's materialist filmmaking, as we have seen, is, among other things, a constant search for figures, images, characters that bear a concrete relationship to history and to possibilities for resistance and emancipation by way of revealing historical consciousness. In a way, Godard's plea in the name of (historical) fiction in general in his work, and specifically in *Notre musique*, is intrinsically tied to the *devenirs* of figures of resistance of the twentieth century, which were necessarily figures of alterity.

According to Serge Daney, Western universalism conceived an "abstract Other."[7] For Daney the image is always a slot where, paraphrasing Lacan, "there is some other"[8] to whom we are getting close by *imaging her*

---

[5] See Meg McLagan and Yates McKee, *Sensible Politics: The Visual Culture of Nongovernmental Activism* (Cambridge, MA: Zone Books, 2013).

[6] "Ten Theses on Politics," in Jacques Rancière, Davide Panagia, Rachel Bowlby, *Theory & Event*, Vol. 5, Issue 3, 2001.

[7] Serge Daney, "Before and After the Image," trans. Melissa McMahon, *Discourse*, Vol. 21, No. 1, Middle Eastern Films *Before Thy Gaze Returns to Thee* (Winter 1999), pp. 181–190 originally published in French "Avant et après l'image", *Revue d'études palestiniennes*, no. 40 (Été 1991).

[8] Serge Daney, "Before and After the Image".

through an interplay of presence and absence, distance and proximity, and a series of operations to render the sayable visible and vice versa. In the dominant imaginary of the twentieth century, images of this abstract other materialized in the "ethnographic," "witness" and "militant" image. Ethnographic images were mostly registers of non-Western peoples who were disappearing or on the brink of extinction. Infused with documentary or indexical pretension, ethnographic images are based on a divide instituted by representational technology itself. That is to say, ethnographic images always involve people with different levels of access to the means of reproduction. The "witness" image, in turn, is ethical, and came to prevail in the aftermath of the Shoah, when oral testimony, documents and documentary images were summoned not to prove facts, but as forms of memory to sustain the ethical imperative of collective remembering. Later on, witness images acquired a documentary function, proving injustices to demand restitution of rights. These images put on the table debates on the (im)possibility of representing trauma or catastrophe, including whether attempts to represent the catastrophes end up banalizing them. For their part, "militant" images are political and intended to announce and to bring forth the revolution to fight colonialism and imperialism. The need for the militant image gave intellectuals, artists and filmmakers the task of accompanying peasants, workers, colonized peoples, oppressed minorities and individuals in revolt. Following Nicole Brenez, these images embodied critique and followed the activist model of Eisenstein's *Strike* (1925).[9] The two main debates that militant images have brought forth relate to: (1) their capacity to raise consciousness, and mobilize the masses concerning the condition of the people, and (2) whether their autonomy as aesthetic creations is secondary to their propagandistic function. In other words, they posit the question: how should film function as an emancipatory response to injustice while responding to a politics intrinsic to cinematic and aesthetic production practices?

In the late 1980s Gilles Deleuze noted that unlike classical cinema, political cinema was no longer constituted on the basis of the possibility of revolution but on portraying the intolerable. The intolerable had become *the unknown*: what the media and hegemonic narratives were obscuring. This is why, in various texts, Deleuze wrote: "the people are missing," meaning that the proletariat or a unified people would no longer be on a quest to conquer power, and thus

---

[9] Nicole Brenez, "Contre-attaques. Soubresauts d'images dans l'histoire de la lutte des classes," in *Soulèvements* (Paris: Gallimard, Jeu de Paume, 2016), p. 72.

counter-information had come to prevail in the sensible regime as a way to give visibility to the unknown intolerable.[10] Along with the Third World *guerrillero*, the working class and other main protagonists of political struggle and of the militant image of the twentieth century had disappeared. As I have argued in the previous chapters, a new form of emancipation of the peoples of the Third World had been foregrounded in the 1970s, leading to the substitution of politics by a new ethics of intervention. Third Worldism or Internationalism had been a universal cause, giving a name to a political wrong. For the first time, the "wretched of the earth" emerged during a specific historic period as a new figuration of "the people" in the political sense: the colonized were discursively transformed into political figures.[11] Yet a new ethical humanism (or humanitarianism) substituted revolutionary enthusiasm and political sympathy with pity and moral indignation, transforming them into political emotions within the discourse of emergency and a universal battle for the defense and restitution of human rights. This led to new figures of alterity in the 1980s and 1990s, the "suffering other" that needs to be rescued, and to the post-colonial "subaltern" demanding restitution, presupposing that visibility within a multicultural social fabric would follow emancipation.

In the 1990s, the panorama of resistance opposed neoliberal reforms and fought for fair trade, sustainable development, human rights and corporate accountability; the anti-globalization movement conceived itself as a social base to criticize corporate capitalism and globalization, and the fact that multinational corporations had acquired more and more unregulated political power exercised through trade agreements and deregulated financial markets. Anti-capitalist politics, in this context, was characterized by interdisciplinarity, the adoption of an array of counter-cultural positions and provisional political associations with the goal of creating autonomous zones, albeit symbolically. Didactic and symbolic interventions or actions against capitalism in the public sphere prevailed. In parallel, minorities continued to claim visibility and accountability within the depoliticized frame of human rights as well as demanding inclusion and agonistic recognition within a globalized democracy.[12] In this context, counter-information came

---

[10] Gilles Deleuze, *The Time-Image: Cinema 2* (Minneapolis: The University of Minnesota Press, 2003), pp. 219–222.

[11] Kristin Ross, *May '68 and its Afterlives* (Chicago: The University of Chicago Press, 2002)

[12] See Irmgard Emmelhainz, "Geopolitics and Contemporary Art, Part I: From Representation's Ruin to Salvaging the Real" *e-flux Journal* # 69 (January 2016) available online:http://www.e-flux.com/journal/69/60620/geopolitics-and-contemporary-art-part-i-from-representation-s-ruin-to-salvaging-the-real/

to prevail as an aesthetico-political task and culture as the frame to channel antagonistic and agonizing voices. But once the outcome of neoliberal policies of deregulation, austerity, free markets and privatization manifested in the decline of living standards, people losing jobs, pensions and the safety net that both the state and society used to provide, Social Darwinism became the rule. One of the implications of this is that the colonial division between the First and Third Worlds as well as the global—"post-colonial"— distinction between North/South and East/West has become irrelevant, as a new arrangement of the world is now visible: modernized pockets of privilege and cultural sophistication thrive and coexist with enclaves inhabited by "redundant populations." This sector of the population has no or differential access to education, health services, loans and jobs, and is governed by various forms of state control traduced by differential degrees of exclusion, dispossession and coercion. These are communities whose commons and sustainable autonomous forms of life are being destroyed in the name of their wellbeing and development; yet, their destruction is *de facto* sustaining the lives of people living in modernized privileged enclaves. I am thinking about the destruction of entire communities and their lands in the State of Michoacán since the 1960s to provide Mexico City with very much needed water; or by shale gas extraction in Québec in order to provide gas for heating; or the status of non-citizens of Palestine governed by an apartheid Israeli state, with a different set of rights than the Israelis. It has now has become clear that under capitalist absolutism it is more profitable to destroy the lives and forms of lives and lands, rendering sectors of the population redundant, than to incorporate them into the system as consumers or exploited workers. In this panorama, the only categories that remain beyond class struggle are winners and losers, exploiters and exploited, citizens and non-citizens, included and excluded. Neoliberal commonsense preaches that either you are strong and smart, or that you deserve your misery.[13] What image of insurrection and what political praxis can be brought forth in the current context of capitalist absolutism?

As we have seen, the "ethnographic," "militant" and "witness" images are intrinsically linked to an ethical and politicized notion of alterity linked to Western universalism. But what kinds of discourses could underlie images of Western alterity in the aftermath of the post-colonial critique of the ethnographic image, the demise of the Third Worldist militant image, and now that the limits of the witness image have become evident, perpetuating the

---

[13] See Franco Berardi, *Heroes: Mass Murder and Suicide* (London and New York: Verso, 2015).

ineffective figure of the "victim"? Moreover, at the beginning of the twenty-first century, while the Other has been rendered transparent due to a series of discursive mutations, global connectedness has rendered the "elsewhere" immediate. In this regard, the extreme transparency of the Other implies a loss of an ethico-political link to it. Facilitated by the democratization of tourism, culture and information, encounters with the Other have been substituted by encounters with *different forms of life* that are different in the qualitative sense: that is, more or less different and now mediated by the mass media, tourism, aesthetic or humanitarian interventions and non-governmental politics. Godard and Miéville provide a visionary declaration of this at the end of *Ici et ailleurs*: "L'autre c'est l'ailleurs de notre ici."[14] Could we consider the possibility of a militant image—in the sense of an image of an Other that could threaten Western imperialism, under the current regime of capitalist absolutism, a system which is consensually driven by desire and for the need for visibility, and that is legitimating Social Darwinism with racism and misogynous speech in the public sphere?

We must bear in mind that the *image* is not a given, and that is why Daney draws a distinction between "image" and what he calls the "visual" or "imagery." Daney posits, in opposition to the image, "the visual," which is the optical verification of a procedure of power. It is composed of clichés and stereotypes. In Rancière's terms, "the visual" is a reality incessantly representing itself to itself.[15] For Daney, the visual is the tautology of discourse that does not amount to an image but is simply a series of eyeless faces of the Other. By eyeless faces, Daney implies anonymous faces with whom it is impossible to empathize. Taking up Daney's distinction, Jacques Rancière in "The Future of the Image" ties the notion of image to an aesthetic operation that produces a material presence by way of dissemblance. Following Godard's famous aphorism and modernist montage credo—"The image will come at the time of Resurrection"—Rancière links the image to Christian theology as a promise of the spirit made flesh. To distinguish a "genuine image" from its simulacrum, moreover, for Rancière it is necessary to separate the operations of art from the technique of reproduction. In his account, there is a taxonomy of three forms of "imageness" that borrow from each other and that come to occupy different places in the regime of the sensible. The *naked*—or documentary—image is not art because it functions as proof or witness of historical events. The *ostensive* image is sheer presence without signification,

---

[14] "The other is the elsewhere of our here".
[15] Jacques Rancière, "The Future of the Image," in *The Future of the Image* (London: Verso, 2007).

that is, the presentation of the presence as art as a form of *facingness*, an address to the viewer. Finally, the *metaphorical* image is a singular rearrangement of the images circulating in the mass media that displaces and critiques these representations of imagery.[16] Clearly, the "ethnographic," "militant" and "witness" visibilities have become the "visual" in Daney's sense.

One of the problems is that in our post-political era, as communication and speech (the grounds for political action, in Hannah Arendt's terms) have been transformed into codes, as we have seen, the main objective of many contemporary politicized images is to achieve the visibility of struggles or injustices being perpetrated here and elsewhere. Premised on the idea that moving images can provide a "common language" or a new form of literacy as political tools, art and culture have become inseparable from social movements. In this context, sensible politics represents politics in an abstract, vague and disinterested way, while it disseminates political practices without previous theoretical analysis that have fallen short in understanding the complexity of contemporary environmental and political problems that we are facing at the global level. Therefore, as opposed to creating a political space (like militant films used to do), confounding *artivism* with micro-politics, sensible politics promulgates forms of politicization that are unwilling to pay the real price of political struggle. Gilles Deleuze noted in his conference address at La Fémis film school in 1987 that counter-information only becomes effective when it is, by nature, an act of resistance. In our current historical moment, a real act of resistance is not to "counter-inform" but to resist against the destruction of forms of life and common experiences; it means to defend the right to protect something that already exists, or to protest against something that is already lost or about to be lost. In this regard, we should consider Serge Daney's definition of *true democracy*, which for him means to look into the collective mirror drawn up by images and to make a distinction between what can be done, what we know what to do, and what does not come cheap.[17] It is not *what we see*, produced by the culture industry, but what *cannot be shown*, which is intolerable. And what is it that tends not to be shown by contemporary images of struggle in the old formats of post-ethnography, militantism and witnessing? What is difficult for us to see is the abjection in which redundant populations are surviving across the world in areas disconnected from the flows of global exchange and their relentless destruction.

[16] Jacques Rancière, "The Future of the Image".
[17] Serge Daney, "Before and After the Image".

Early on, Godard expressed skepticism *vis-à-vis* the European policies in the 1980s and 1990s that supported cultural production. In the 1990s he began a war against the culture industry akin to his incessant critique of Hollywood from the 1960s onwards. Godard was critiquing the fact that state actors and corporations use culture as a tool as they search for economic and sociopolitical betterment—for instance, in peacefully resolving violence and crime, reconstructing the social fabric, transforming society, creating jobs, increasing civic participation and so forth. In the case of the aftermath of the war in the Balkans, as we have seen, Godard denounced how cultural production was deployed as a form of politicized grace to bring reconciliation about, through a false rehabilitation of the past that made it effectively a niche of cultural tourism. So, culture became a resource and a compensatory device for the ravages caused to the social fabric by wars of annihilation and capitalist destruction, alleging to give meaning and symbolic representation, and to provide mechanisms of solace, as well as tools for reinvention and amelioration. Insofar as museums, biennials, exhibitions and film festivals are part of the global military industrial complex, however, modernism is evidently a *pharmakon* that offers both the poisons of destitution and colonization along with the "cures" of democracy, development, human rights, social responsibility and support of cultural and academic production. In this context, Hamid Dabashi's statement: "We are no longer postcolonial," is a mandate to acknowledge that the *modus operandi* of modernism is colonial destruction—the constituent bankruptcy of modernism as evidenced in Godard's juxtaposition of the Shoah and the Nakba—and that a neoliberal global cartography beyond socialist internationalism has been established based on the competition of everybody against everybody toward "market success." In this regard, the demise of tolerance, inclusivity and the new identitarian essentialisms are operating as a public justification of Social Darwinism on a global scale.

Furthermore, Godard's expressed concern in *Ici et ailleurs* to "restitute images back to their bodies," is an attempt to contest the hollowing out of images by their simulacral transhumance in the mass media. Seeking to resacralize the image, restitution is a promise of justice. According to Saad Chakali, the political task of Godard's work after *Ici et ailleurs* becomes the poetic relief of the collapse of the bodies that have been brutalized by history, in as far as the brutality has been consigned to the archives. The relief, for Chakali, results from a singular dialectic according to which the image of the broken body will be redeemed.[18] In this narrative, therefore, the vanquished are waiting for us to relieve, to resurrect them, although this is not enough to deal with the trauma of defeat (of the failed revolution) and of the war of annihilation. And this is the reason why reality must be constructed anew (*De l'origine du XXIème siècle*, *Adieu au langage*): first, by questioning the legacy of modernity as expressed in the definition of the "human" by the humanities and of "alterity" by Western universalism; second, Godard shows that the promise of an enlightened, liberal humanism is bankrupt, as exemplified by SS guards who listen to Beethoven while they perform their duties; third, he makes a plea in the name of fiction in an attempt to restore the link between man and the world, in as far as the rupture of the link also represents the fracture of the link between perception and action because what is now seen—the intolerable—can no longer be recognized as something to act upon. The link between man and the world has been broken by the ongoing devastation of forms of life and ways of making a living for the populations made redundant through wars, genocide, environmental catastrophe, resource extraction, slow violence and other neo-colonizing practices. To describe these situations, Lebanese theorist and visual artist Jalal Toufic has coined the concept "the withdrawal of tradition in the aftermath of a surpassing disaster." In his view, the long-term effects of material and social destruction remain in the depths of the body and psyche as latent traumatic effects that become codified in the genes.[19] According to Toufic, the collateral damage of the surpassing (or ongoing) disaster implies the withdrawal of tradition. Therefore, it requires the work of resurrection. Paradoxically, modernism either willfully rejects tradition or is indifferent to it, while only those who fully discern the withdrawal of tradition following a surpassing disaster have tried to resurrect it and failed, because their history is now written by someone else as they are not victorious.

Before the historical landscape of the aftermath of the fall of the revolutionary ideals and of the ubiquity of wars of annihilation at the turn of the twenty-first century, Godard has repeatedly vouched for adopting

---

[18] Saad Chakali, *Jean-Luc Godard dans la relève des archives du mal* (Paris: L'Harmattan, 2017), p. 45.

[19] Jalal Toufic, "The Withdrawal of Tradition Past a Surpassing Disaster" (2009) available online: http://www.jalaltoufic.com/downloads/Jalal_Toufic_The_Withdrawal_of_Tradition_Past_a_Surpassing_Disaster.pdf

the *maquis* or the French Resistance to German Occupation during World War II as a model for a political framework to resist in the present. To adopt the *maquis* as a form of resistance would imply acknowledging occupation in various forms: by the culture industry, by neoliberal globalization, by capitalist absolutism (Empire), by neo-fascism and by the threat and reality of the ongoing elimination of entire populations rendered redundant by capitalism. To restore the obscured history of the *maquis* would imply considering it as a national insurrection in part in the name of Communism, a side that has been obscured by the Shoah as the main lens through which the history of World War II has been viewed, marginalizing the memory of Jewish resistance. It would also mean returning to the values of freedom and dignity as the basis of political action. And although the history of the French Resistance is contradictory and mythical, military, nationalistic and male,[20] the politics of resistance brought about by the *maquis* would supersede both the frame of the revolution as a horizon of emancipation and the myth of the universal struggle for the rights of man, while situating all of those who are not resisting, as collaborators. For Godard, one of the main problems of the present is the loss of depth in inverse proportion to historical consciousness. For Godard, as we have seen, the denial of the force of the word by digital communication and the failure of the humanities to define what is human, has come to inhabit interior experience eliminating redundancy, misunderstandings, the possibility of reading between the lines and the erasure of alterity as the beginning of ethics. This is why in *Adieu au langage* he vouches for the language of those who are out of the frame, the redundant populations "à côté de la plaque" (beside the point). And this out of field is the "out of place" where images that elicit belief and a *desire* not to possess, but *to see*, can be offered, embedded in a promise to incessantly recreate a mythical link to the world.

Bibliography

Berardi, Franco. *Heroes: Mass Murder and Suicide* (London and New York: Verso, 2015)

Brenez, Nicole. "Contre-attaques. Soubresauts d'images dans l'histoire de la lutte des classes," in *Soulèvements* (Paris: Gallimard, Jeu de Paume, 2016)

Chakali, Saad. *Jean-Luc Godard dans la relève des archives du mal* (Paris: L'Harmattan, 2017)

---

[20] See Robert Gildea, *Fighters in the Shadows: A New History of the French Resistance* (New York: Faber & Faber, 2015).

Daney, Serge. "Avant et après l'image", *Revue d'études palestiniennes* no. 40 (Été 1991)

Deleuze, Gilles. *The Time-Image: Cinema 2* (Minneapolis: The University of Minnesota Press, 2003)

Gildea, Robert. *Fighters in the Shadows: A New History of the French Resistance* (New York: Faber & Faber, 2015)

Godard, Jean-Luc. "Manifeste," in *Jean-Luc Godard: Documents*, ed. David Faroult (Paris: Centre Georges Pompidou, 2006)

McKee, Yates and McLagan, Meg. *Sensible Politics: The Visual Culture of Nongovernmental Activism* (Cambridge, MA: Zone Books, 2013)

Morgan, Daniel. *Late Godard and the Possibilities of Cinema* (Los Angeles: University of California Press, 2013)

Rancière, Jacques. *The Future of the Image* (London: Verso, 2007)

Ross, Kristin. *May '68 and its Afterlives* (Chicago: The University Press, 2002)

Touffic, Jalal. "The Withdrawal of Tradition Past a Surpassing Disaster" (2009). Available at: http://www.jalaltoufic.com/downloads/Jalal_Toufic_The_Withdrawal_of_Tradition_Past_a_Surpassing_Disaster.pdf

Williams, James S. *Encounters With Godard: Ethics, Aesthetics, Politics* (Albany: State University of New York Press, 2016)

Index[1]

A
A Bao A Qu (Malay legend), 258
Absence, 14, 17, 60, 109, 136, 162, 181, 186, 189, 191, 234, 235, 237, 266, 273, 274, 276, 277, 284, 288, 289, 299
Absolute evil, 199
Accusation, 2, 110, 187, 195n53, 226, 232
Active engagement, 45
Actuality, 5, 22, 36, 46, 47n36, 52–54, 65, 74, 75, 87, 102, 143, 144, 146, 148, 149, 151, 218, 264
Adachi, Masao, 101, 101n41
Aden Arabie (Nizan, 1960), 88
Adieu au langage (2014), 7, 21, 27, 28, 122, 151, 258n12, 281–291, 305, 306
Adler, Sarah, 208, 211, 213
Adorno, Theodor W., 7, 7n13, 32, 40, 78n113, 80, 80n117, 180, 201, 285

Affective labor, 25, 172
After-image, 13
Agamben, Giorgio, 145n48, 151n66, 190–192, 191n41, 192n45
Agarrando Pueblo (Ospina & Mayolo, 1978), 91
Akerman, Chantal, 255
Albou, Karin, 272
Algerian independence, 15
Algérie en flammes (Vautier, 1958), 89
Alighieri, Dante, 208
Allegory, 28, 145, 161, 283
Allégret, Marc, 89
Allemagne 90 Neuf Zéro (1991), 6, 53
Allende, Salvador, 101
Aloni, Udi, 233n173, 272, 279
  Local Angel (2002), 233n173, 272, 279
Alterity, 20, 22, 28, 122, 181, 182, 206, 207, 212, 216, 253, 258, 286, 297n4, 298, 300, 301, 305, 306

---

[1] Note: Page numbers followed by 'n' refer to notes.

© The Author(s) 2019
I. Emmelhainz, *Jean-Luc Godard's Political Filmmaking*,
https://doi.org/10.1007/978-3-319-72095-1

309

Althusser, Louis, 3, 33, 37, 46, 50, 52n53, 62, 80n118, 135, 297
Álvarez, Santiago, 94
Analogue film, 140
Anidjar, Gil, 191, 192, 206, 206n83, 214n105
Antenne 2 Midi, 118, 119, 168
Anthology of Negro and Malagasy Poetry (Senghor, 1949), 88
Anti-capitalism, 7
Anti-semitism, 26, 192, 193, 194n51, 195, 196, 226
Antonioni, Michelangelo, 24, 104, 104n50, 105n52, 107, 110, 165, 201, 268, 269
Anxiety of blindness, 15, 24, 91, 96, 103–111, 140
Appearances, 3, 10, 17, 18, 25, 32, 48, 55, 63, 68, 91, 107, 116, 118, 127, 128, 169, 183, 196, 216, 235, 242, 265, 268, 276, 286, 298
Appropriation, 15, 18, 135n20, 152, 158, 161–168, 199, 203, 254
Aragon, Louis, 33, 37–40
Archival images, 184, 187
Archive, 27, 69n91, 91n10, 118n89, 177–245, 305
Arendt, Hannah, 2, 2n2, 6, 193, 193n49, 212, 238, 238n192, 239, 241n201, 242, 244, 291, 303
Aristotle, 138, 138n28, 278n67
Armide (1987), 164
Artistic enunciation, 17, 32, 44, 45, 106
Art of the defeated, 205
Assujettissement, 104n49, 131, 136
Audiovisual journalism, 6, 93
Auschwitz, 26, 153, 185–187, 196, 202
Auteur theory, 45

Authenticity, 20, 128, 159, 229, 266
Authorship, 15–20, 45, 110, 169, 179
Avant-garde, 31–37, 39, 40, 45, 46, 49, 60, 74, 75, 97
Axis of Evil, 193

B
Bachelard, Gaston, 267, 268, 281, 281n77
Badiou, Alain, 50, 149, 149n61, 150
Balfour Declaration, 149
Balkans War, 26, 205, 206, 218, 227
Barthes, Roland, 3, 17, 17n36, 18, 62, 62n74, 153n73, 233, 233n177, 233n178
Battle/ruins of Karameh, 255
Battleship Potemkin (Eisenstein, 1925), 87, 272
Baudrillard, Jean, 20, 127, 127n1, 204n75, 218–220, 218n119, 220n126, 220n127, 276n61
Bazin, André, 60, 62, 63, 152, 169
Beckett, Samuel, 205n78, 219
Belief in the image, 10, 183
Bellour, Raymond, 31n1, 102n46, 109n61
Benjamin, Walter, 9, 34, 35, 35n7, 63, 79n115, 142, 144, 151, 151n65, 153, 190, 263, 264n24, 279
Berardi, Franco (Bifo), 172, 301n13
Berger, John, 148, 148n58, 152, 152n69, 243n206
Bergounioux, Pierre, 207, 216
Bergson, Henri, 1, 1n1, 147, 268, 268n40
Besançon, Julien, 38n13, 38n16, 76, 76n107
Bilderverbot, 26, 189
Black Panthers – Huey! (1968), 88
Black September (massacre), 75, 100, 145, 159, 178

Black September (terrorist group), 75, 100, 178
Black struggle/Black Panthers, 12, 53, 96, 297n4
Blank screen, 16, 18, 19, 48, 119, 133, 141, 168–170, 182
Blindness, 258
Blum, Léon, 145, 150
Blümlinger, Christa, 25, 102n46
Bolshevik Revolution, 150
Borges, Jorge Luis, 146, 146n52, 154, 258n11
Bosnia, 198, 205, 229, 240n200
Bourdieu, Pierre, 44n29
À bout de souffle (1960), 199
Brecht, Bertolt, 2, 13, 32, 55, 56, 64, 65, 88, 88n2, 135
Brenez, Nicole, 101n41, 111, 111n69, 267n33, 278, 299, 299n9
Bresson, Robert, 204, 209, 255
Breton, André, 32, 33, 33n4, 40–49, 63, 74, 144, 153, 199
British Sounds (1969), 45, 47n36, 48, 51, 75, 76, 96
Broadcaster, 136, 137
Brodsky, Joseph, 214
Brody, Richard, 184, 194n51
Brook, Peter, 209
The Brothers Karamazov (Dostoyevsky, 1880), 215, 215n109, 215n110
Bush, George W., 193
Butler, Judith, 181n16, 192

C
Cahiers du Cinéma, 8n14, 18n39, 37, 59n66, 60, 60n68, 61n69, 61n71, 72n100, 81, 81n120, 111n67, 112n72
Camera Eye (1967), 32, 40–42, 92, 93

Camus, Albert, 214, 214n107, 214n108, 215
Capa, Robert, 87, 150n63
Capitalism, 6, 7, 20, 37, 39, 75, 87, 121, 127–129, 131, 171, 172, 236, 257, 258, 261, 264, 265, 267, 268, 285, 300, 306
Capture of speech, 11, 67–74
Carnation Revolution, 111–115
Cartier-Bresson, Henri, 76n107, 88n3
Centre André Malraux, 210, 215, 217, 225, 241, 244
CGT, *see* Confédération génerale du travail
Chakali, Saad, 195n53, 304, 305, 305n18
Changer d'image (1982), 116–122, 133, 182
Chant des mariées (Albou, 2008), 272, 280
Chief Seattle, 236, 236n186
Children of Men (Cuarón, 2006), 146
Christianity, 183, 192n46
Chung kuo - Cina (Antonioni, 1972), 104
Cinéastes révolutionnaires prolétariens, 57
Cinélutte, 57, 72n100
Cinéma Libre, 57
Cinematic apparatus, 13, 25, 56, 103
Cinematic ontology, 60, 118, 141n36, 169
Cinematic reflexivity, 12, 60, 61
Cinéthique, 37, 58, 60–62, 60n68, 62n73, 261
Citroën, 168, 257
Civil resistance, 272
Class antagonism, 5
Cleaver, Eldridge, 12, 79, 80, 96
Clio, 171, 172

Closed Jeans (advertisement, 1988), 164, 167
Cohn-Bendit, Daniel, 46, 69, 70n93, 73, 73n102, 194n51
Cold War, 89, 121, 199
Collage, 81, 158, 169, 272, 279, 283
Colonization, 89, 115, 200, 236, 237, 304
Comment ça va? (1975), 93, 97n27, 108, 111, 112, 131–133, 135, 140, 161
Communication, 21, 25, 28, 50, 67, 91, 109, 121n96, 129, 136, 138, 139, 143, 158, 159n93, 161, 167, 172, 201, 253, 259, 282, 284–287, 289, 297, 303, 306
Conditions of visuality, 20–28, 254, 297
Confédération génerale du travail (CGT, General Workers Confederation), 49
Conflict zone, 208
Consciousness, 3, 11, 28, 33, 37, 44, 55, 64, 69, 96, 141–144, 147, 148, 156, 157, 185, 194, 218, 267–269, 271, 283, 298, 299, 306
Constellation, 19, 32, 135, 195n53, 196, 224n142
Contradiction, 2, 5, 16, 18, 24, 32, 35–37, 36n9, 43, 45, 45n30, 49, 51–53, 55, 58, 63, 65, 73–75, 90, 98, 100, 104–107, 109, 110, 110n64, 155, 156n85, 161, 200, 221, 237, 281
Contradiction (Maoist), 36, 51
Conversation, 27, 107, 138n28, 177, 197, 202, 211, 212, 214, 218–225, 240–243, 243n205, 255, 272, 277n64, 279n72, 280, 282, 288
Costa Concordia, 262

Counter-information, 2, 6, 37, 133, 135, 256, 296, 300, 303
Counter-memory, 22
Coup pour coup (1972), 58
Courbet, Gustave, 281
Crary, Jonathan, 127n1, 128, 128n4, 145n49, 146n51, 160n95
Crisis of representation/representativity, 4, 24, 36–38
Critique, 3, 6, 13, 17, 20, 23, 27, 34, 36, 37, 40, 48, 55, 59n66, 60, 61, 68, 74, 75, 88, 101, 108, 108n58, 117, 119, 128, 136, 139n30, 183, 194, 200–202, 208, 226, 289, 296, 299, 301, 303, 304
Cuadernos de Sarajevo (Goytisolo, 1993), 217n116, 218
Cuarón, Alfonso, 146, 148
Cuba, Cuban Revolution, 22, 87, 88, 93, 150, 153
Cultural producer, 21, 295
Cultural Revolution, 34, 49, 150
Culture, 2, 6, 18, 20, 26, 39, 42, 49, 115, 121n96, 122, 131, 134n19, 153n73, 188, 190, 200–202, 204, 205, 205n77, 217, 229, 236, 239, 253, 268, 285, 290, 295, 301–304
Culture industry, 7, 201–203, 230, 254, 298, 303, 304, 306
Curiel, Henri, 213
Curnier, Jean-Paul, 198, 198n62, 199, 205n77, 206, 207, 216, 226, 260, 278

D
Dabashi, Hamid, 304
Daney, Serge, 18, 18n38, 18n39, 27, 31n1, 81, 102n46, 117n85, 130n10, 130n11, 135, 135n20,

142, 142n39, 162, 168,
  169n109, 179, 179n7, 182n18,
  253n2, 298, 298n7, 298n8, 302,
  303, 303n17
Dantesque, 6, 26, 208
Darmon, Maurice, 184, 194n51
Darwish, Mahmoud, 27, 103, 196,
  211, 212, 216, 217n114, 235,
  235n183, 237–241, 237n189,
  238n191, 240n197, 255, 274,
  276, 276n60
De Baecque, Antoine, 45n32, 46,
  46n33, 47n36, 48n39, 184,
  194n51
Debord, Guy, 2, 20, 32, 37–40, 74,
  94, 127–129, 127n2, 129n7,
  145, 145n48, 146, 146n51, 148,
  152, 155
Debray, Régis, 91n10, 93, 189n34,
  202
Decolonization, 21, 88, 197
Deconstruction, 62, 270
Dehumanization, 184, 285
Deictics, 158
Delacroix, Eugène, 38, 169
Delahaye, Luc, 255
Delegacija, 87, 107
Deleuze, Gilles, 23, 23n48, 32, 32n2,
  34n5, 37n11, 90, 90n8, 91n10,
  93, 99n35, 101n42, 104n48,
  104n49, 107, 110, 117, 117n85,
  130n11, 144, 147, 147n57,
  152n71, 152n72, 153n73,
  154n78, 155, 156n85, 157–159,
  158n89, 158n90, 159n91,
  159n92, 160n93, 160n96, 164,
  202, 225n145, 226, 226n150,
  226n151, 231, 231n166,
  231n167, 232n169, 232n170,
  232n171, 243n208, 276,
  277n63, 299, 300n10, 303
*De l'origine du XXIème siècle/The
  Origin of the 21st Century
  (2000)*, 198, 305

Democracy, 11, 68, 73, 121, 150,
  241, 264, 277, 278, 298, 300,
  304
Derrida, Jacques, 3, 111n66, 154n79,
  155n81, 214n105
de Rougemont, Denis, 261
D'Est (Akerman, 1992), 255
Détournement, 39, 152
Dialectical materialist films, 2,
  259–264
Dialectical montage, 142, 231
Diderot, Denis, 140, 141n34
Didi-Huberman, Georges, 4, 19, 20,
  26, 36n9, 53, 53n54, 184–187,
  185n23, 187n29, 188n31,
  190n39, 193, 193n50, 194,
  194n51, 194n52, 195n53, 196,
  210, 210n93, 253n1
Diegesis, 40, 70, 135, 137
Dietrich, Marlene, 280
Digital image, 265, 266, 281
Direct action, 2, 11, 222
Direct address, 129, 136, 136n22,
  137, 139
Disaster, 75, 146, 210, 236, 276, 283,
  305
Disasters of War (Goya), 210
Discourse, 2, 7, 16, 18, 22, 33–35,
  37, 53, 54, 56, 58, 60–62,
  64–66, 69n91, 70, 71, 74, 75,
  78, 80, 81, 89, 91, 93, 101–103,
  118, 131, 134–137, 135n20,
  143, 145, 148, 158, 164, 166,
  179, 181, 182, 185, 203, 207,
  223, 234, 237, 255, 257, 273,
  274, 287, 300–302
Disinterestedness, 21, 34, 180,
  303
Dispossession, 22, 121, 274, 301
Dissonance, 269, 280
Dissonant resonance, 260, 269, 281
Divine Comedy, 208
Divine Intervention (Suleiman, 2004),
  255

D'où venons-nous? Qui sommes-nous? Où allons-nous?, 171, 172
Do You Remember Sarajevo? (2002), 209
Doane, Mary Ann, 266, 266n29, 266n32
Documentary, 12, 22, 47n36, 59, 79, 87–89, 89n5, 99, 100, 103, 104, 107, 110, 136, 144, 158, 159, 180, 183, 185, 208, 209, 225n148, 226, 227n154, 256, 272, 279, 299
Documentary image, 26, 59n66, 154, 155, 159, 160, 188, 197, 270, 299, 302
Dostoyevsky, Fyodor, 201, 214n107, 215, 215n110, 230
Duras, Marguerite, 89
Duration, 79n113, 146, 147, 268, 269, 271
Dynadia, 57

E
École des Ponts et des Chaussées, 228
Economy of information, 93, 112, 145
Écriture (Barthes), 16, 17, 100, 111
Eichmann Trial (1961–1962), 185
Eisenstein, Sergei, 46, 87, 138, 209, 272, 299
El Fatah (Palestinian journal published in France), 96n26, 97
El Greco, 167, 169
Éloge de l'amour (2001), 6, 16, 92, 200–204, 230, 297, 297n4
"Elsewhere" 87–122, 146, 149, 221, 276, 296, 302
Emancipation, 2, 11, 22, 34, 42, 43, 67, 74, 114, 134, 170, 264, 285, 295, 296, 298, 300, 306
Engaged activism, 17, 44, 78
Enlightenment, 23, 212, 236

Enquête, 59, 68, 69, 132, 171
Entry of the Crusaders into Constantinople (Delacroix, 1840), 169
Enunciation, 17, 18, 28, 34, 41, 68, 70, 74, 75, 81, 91, 106, 108, 109, 109n62, 129, 131, 135–140, 158, 159–160n93, 185, 289
Enzensberger, Hans Magnus, 90, 90n7
Epic, 159, 221, 233, 238, 242
Epistemicide, 195, 236, 237
Epistemology of seeing (video), 108, 140–142
Esquenazi, Jean-Pierre, 155n82
Établissement, 50, 50n46
Ethics, 2, 6, 22, 26, 33, 80, 106, 108, 109, 114, 137, 184, 186, 189, 190, 197, 208, 230, 286, 300
Ethics of restitution, 6
Ethnic cleansing, 219, 277
Ethnographic image, 299, 301
Eurocentrism, 2
European Literary Encounters (Centre André Malraux), 210
Execution of the Defenders of Madrid, 3rd May, 1808 (Goya, 1814), 169
Exile, 195, 214, 227, 238, 240, 241, 241n200, 278
Existentialism, 171, 261
Exodus, 214
Experimental film making, 261, 288, 290
Extermination camps, 8, 26, 185, 188, 189, 285
External observer, 22, 91

F
Face-to-face encounter/conversation, 225, 241, 285, 288
Factography, 2, 47, 99, 100

Fahrenheit 451 (Truffaut, 1966), 217
False appearances, 63, 146
Fanon, Frantz, 88, 121n96
Fargier, Jean-Paul, 3, 61n70, 140n33, 260, 270, 271, 271n43, 271n44
Faroult, David, 47n36, 48n38, 51–52n51, 52n52, 52n53, 70n93, 75n106, 96n25, 98n30, 99n32, 295n1
Fascism, 12, 69, 69n91
Faulkner, William, 165, 166
Fedayeen, 96–98, 97n27, 100, 154, 177, 178
Fellow travelers, 32, 33, 44, 68, 68n87
Felman, Shoshana, 185
Fiction, 28, 46, 47n36, 53–67, 74, 87, 103n47, 106, 147, 189, 207, 209, 222, 225, 225n148, 226, 239, 254, 254n4, 255, 261, 298, 305
Film Socialisme (2010), 6, 7, 27, 28, 53, 92, 259, 265n26, 267, 269, 269n42, 272, 274, 274n56, 277, 278, 280, 281, 281n76, 289, 290
Filmstrip, 60, 162
First World, 131, 146
Fleischer, Alain, 184
Flins, 51, 283
The Fold (Deleuze), 157
Ford, John, 209
For Ever Mozart (1996), 6, 205, 297
Forgiveness, 207, 208, 215, 232, 233, 233n173, 279
Foucault, Michel, 3, 17, 18, 18n37, 32, 34n5, 37n12, 51, 73n103, 110, 136, 154, 160
400 Million, The (Ivens, 1939), 87
Fourth World, 235n184, 236, 239
France Tour Détour Deux Enfants (1978–1979), 5, 116, 285
Frankenstein (Shelley), 285, 289
Freedom, 1n1, 15, 20, 36, 42–44, 73, 76, 134, 214, 214n107, 231, 255, 268, 268n40, 285, 306
French Communist Party, 11, 32
French resistance against the Nazi occupation (*Maquis*), 6, 306
French Revolution (1789), 89, 150, 153n74, 255
Frente de Libertação de Moçambique (FRELIMO), 113
"Funes el memorioso" (Borges), 146

G
Gauguin, Paul, 171, 172
General Assembly, 51, 67, 67n85, 70, 72, 72n100, 73, 78
Genet, Jean, 97n27, 181, 181n15, 272, 274, 274n55
Germania Anno Zero (Rossellini, 1946), 27
Giacometti, Alberto, 257
Gide, André, 88, 89
Globalization, 121, 295, 300, 306
Glucksmann, André, 50
Gorin, Jean-Pierre, 4, 24, 46, 47n36, 50, 68n88, 70n93, 100n39, 149, 149n60
Goya, 167, 169, 210
Goytisolo, Juan, 206, 209n92, 216, 217n116, 218–220, 222, 229, 230, 230n165, 235, 278
Grandeur et décadence d'un petit commerce de cinéma (1986), 164
Greek tragedy, 214, 232, 233
Green Zone, 217
Grenoble, 77, 103, 116, 140n33, 149
Grierson, John, 99
Griffith, David W., 231, 231n168, 232
A Grin Without a Cat (Marker, 1977), 89
Groupuscules (Maoist), 11, 46, 52

Guattari, Félix, 32n2, 34n5, 131, 131n12, 133n16, 166n105, 170, 171, 171n112
Guernica (Picasso), 32, 40, 40n21, 41, 44, 74–81
Guerra, Ruy, 113
Guevara, Che, 88, 121n96
Guilt, 80, 207, 208, 215, 228, 228n158, 233, 234
Gulag Archipelago (Solzhenitsyn, 1974), 101
Gulf War, 119

H

Hasta la victoria siempre (Álvarez, 1967), 94
Haviv, Ron, 201
Hawks, Howard, 211
Heidegger, Martin, 10, 90n9
Heude, Rémi-Pierre, 149n59
His Girl Friday (Hawks, 1940), 211
Histoire du cul, 132, 135
Histoire(s) du cinéma (1988–1998), 4n7, 6–9, 14n29, 15n32, 26, 92, 143, 148, 184, 188, 188n31, 190, 193, 194n51, 195n55, 198, 201, 263
History, 2, 4–6, 8, 8n14, 9, 15, 16, 19, 20, 23, 25, 27, 28, 33, 36, 45n32, 47n36, 53, 55, 58, 65, 87, 94n19, 95, 100, 103, 108n58, 127, 130, 132, 142–161, 164, 165, 167–169, 171, 182, 183, 185, 187, 190, 193, 194, 196, 200, 202, 204, 213, 214, 221, 224, 226, 228, 230–232, 236, 237, 239, 242, 254, 255, 257, 258, 263, 266, 269, 273, 276, 278, 283, 296, 298, 304–306
History of cinema, 8, 8n14, 19, 46–48, 61, 143, 144, 163n100, 184, 198, 203, 296

Hitler, Adolf, 145, 145n47, 148, 151, 154, 194, 213, 239
Hollywood, 92, 94, 95, 121n96, 122, 172, 200, 202, 203, 256, 284, 288, 304
Holocaust, 26, 185, 187, 188, 193, 196n57, 280
Holy Land, 273, 274
Homer, 6, 208, 233, 238, 239, 241, 243
Hope, 61, 138, 172, 212, 228, 239, 242, 243, 279
How Yukon Moved the Mountains (Ivens, 1976), 87
Hubris, 196, 232
Hugo, Victor, 198, 199
Humanitarianism, 6, 22, 26, 27, 122, 130, 179, 197, 220, 276, 300, 302
Humanities, 23, 28, 33, 34, 41–43, 138, 166, 169, 172, 197, 199, 239, 240, 240n197, 256–258, 285, 286, 289, 290, 290n99, 305, 306
Human rights, 102, 121, 179–181, 276, 278, 300, 304
Huppert, Isabelle, 169
Hyper-real, 2, 204, 204n75, 208–210, 218

I

Ici et ailleurs (1976), 4, 5, 7, 21n44, 21n45, 23–25, 32, 40, 41, 47n36, 65, 66, 74, 93n13, 96, 100–104, 107, 109–111, 114, 115, 120, 129, 131, 136, 137, 140, 142, 144, 145, 148, 150, 151, 153–156, 153n74, 155n83, 158, 160–163, 165, 170, 177–179, 191, 193, 194, 203n74, 210, 227n154, 255, 263, 295, 296, 296n3, 302, 304

Icon, 6n9, 14, 15, 27, 40, 76, 164, 183, 217, 266
Iconoclasm, 2, 38
Iconophile, 40
Ideological state apparatus, 37, 52, 62, 259, 297
Ideology, 3, 13, 22, 33, 35n8, 37, 54n56, 56, 58, 61–63, 74, 78, 88, 107, 135, 179, 259, 260, 270, 285, 297
Ignatieff, Michael, 180n10, 228–230, 228n159, 230n163
Il fiore delle mille e una notte (Pasolini, 1974), 272
Illusion, 13, 102n46, 170, 222, 255, 261, 263, 288, 298
Image, 2, 5, 7, 9, 21, 23, 28, 32, 63–66, 70, 71, 74, 77–79, 81, 87, 92, 93, 127, 177–183, 253, 296, 302, 304
Imagination, 187, 189, 257, 258, 265, 267, 268, 278, 281, 288
Imperialism, 37, 88, 95n22, 115, 299, 302
Impossibility of representation, 186
Incarnation, 14, 118, 182, 222, 223n138
Independence movements, 15
Indexicality, 60, 156, 159
India, 89, 235
India Song (Duras, 1975), 89
India, Matri Bhumi (Rossellini, 1959), 89
Individual, 10, 16, 18, 53, 54, 65, 97, 116, 133, 138, 156n85, 159n93, 180, 203, 219, 231, 259, 290, 299
Infinite debt, 207, 232, 233, 242
Information, 23, 37, 58, 62, 90, 91, 93, 103–104, 107, 111, 112, 118, 119, 122, 127–130, 133, 136, 143, 145, 146, 159, 159n93, 161, 168, 180, 197, 200, 219, 219n124, 296, 298, 302
Intellectual function, 43–45, 91n10, 202
Interpellation/address, 6, 10n19, 12, 15, 26, 28, 43, 52, 53, 56, 57, 73, 74, 81, 107, 109, 112, 129, 136, 145n47, 180, 184, 212, 223, 224, 235n184, 245n215, 256, 258, 272, 297n4, 303
Interpretation, 13, 153n73, 182
Interval, 120, 120n94, 155, 156, 231, 232
Intolerable, the, 23, 28, 207n85, 295, 299, 300, 303, 305
Intolerance (Griffith, 1916), 231, 232
Invisible, 14, 15, 47, 127–172, 182, 195, 199, 200, 203, 217, 222–224, 245
¡Qué viva México! (Eisenstein, 1931), 87, 209
Irrepresentable, the, 2, 181, 188, 200
Islamophobia, 195, 202
Israel, 100, 192, 193, 193n49, 196n57, 202, 213, 225, 226n149, 227, 227n157, 234, 241, 243n205, 272, 279, 280
Israeli–Palestinian conflict, 5, 27, 194, 206, 272, 283, 285
Ivens, Joris, 87, 88, 288

J

J'accuse (Maoist journal), 43n26, 45
Jameson, Fredric, 10, 10n21, 34n6, 36n10, 56n61, 117n86, 147, 147n56, 199, 199n63, 264n25
Je e(s)t un autre, 139, 139n31, 203, 209
Je vous salue, Marie (1983), 133, 168n107, 182

Je vous salue, Sarajevo (1993), 6, 7, 26, 200, 201, 224
Jews, 184, 188n30, 190–195, 195n53, 196n57, 211, 213, 226, 226n153, 227, 236, 280, 284
JLG par JLG (1993), 13n26, 21
Jourdan, Charles, 167
Journalism, 6, 32, 48, 92, 93, 103, 106, 122, 136, 178, 255, 296
Journalist, 21, 59, 77, 88, 91, 97, 98, 105–107, 110, 112, 132, 206, 210–213, 217, 220, 222, 255
Jusqu'à la victoire (1970), 24, 96–104, 115, 149
Justice, 81, 81n120, 115, 115n81, 215, 230, 233, 235, 261, 304
Juxtaposition, 7, 9, 14, 24–26, 48, 63, 66, 103, 104, 133, 142, 144n45, 145n47, 151, 152, 155, 157, 170, 188, 188n31, 191, 193–195, 197, 198, 200, 204, 225, 227, 236, 284, 288, 304

K

Kant, Immanuel, 89
Karmitz, Marin, 58, 59, 68n87, 74
Khaled, Khaled Abu, 103
Kino-eye, 15, 47, 141, 142, 156
Kissinger, Henry, 100, 145
Klein, William, 88
Kristeva, Julia, 3, 32, 153n73, 156n85, 232n172
Kubrick, Stanley, 199
Kuntzel, Thierry, 162, 162n98

L

La Bataille d'Alger (Pontecorvo, 1965), 89
Labro, Philippe, 168
La Cause du peuple (journal), 43, 45, 50, 59, 68n87

La Chinoise (1967), 6n9, 13n25, 32, 52, 63, 297
Lack, Roland-François, 156n85, 274n56, 275
Lac Léman (Lake Geneva), 283, 289
La Grande illusion (Renoir, 1937), 165
La Hora de los Hornos (Solanas, 1968), 96
Language, 7, 11–14, 19, 21, 22, 27, 43, 44, 52, 55, 67, 69, 70, 71n96, 71n98, 72, 79, 99, 129, 136, 137, 139, 153n73, 159, 159n93, 171, 178, 187, 191, 202, 212, 213, 217, 224, 233, 243, 243n205, 244, 259, 260, 267, 271, 278, 279, 281, 284–290, 297, 306
Lanzmann, Claude, 25, 26, 184–186, 188–190, 188n30, 189n34, 200, 202, 272
L'Avventura (Antonioni, 1960), 165
Léaud, Jean-Pierre, 62, 165
Le Dernier mot (1988), 183
Le Gai savoir (1969), 3, 4, 12, 12n23, 21, 62, 62n72, 62n73, 66, 66n80, 171, 254, 285, 291, 296
Le Goff, Jean-Pierre, 67n84, 77, 77n109
Lelouch, Claude, 88
Lenin, Vladimir, 2, 64, 155
Le Petit soldat (1963), 15
Le Pont des soupirs (2014), 27
Le Rapport Darty (1989), 6, 25, 171
Le Vent d'Est (1970), 4, 46, 52n52, 69, 70n93, 73, 94, 96
Les Anges du péché (Bresson, 1943), 209
Les Carabiniers (1963), 161
Les Groupes Médvedkine, 57
Les Trois désastres (2013), 7, 27, 92, 283

Lesage, Julia, 48n36, 51n51, 52n52, 64, 64n79
Letter to Jane: An Investigation About a Still (1972), 92, 140, 161, 296
Levi, Primo, 185
Lévinas, Emmanuel, 213n104, 215n109, 217n115, 224, 224n143, 225n144, 244
Lévy, Bernard-Henri, 50n45, 184, 194n51, 202, 202n73, 272, 272n48
L'Express, 50, 143n40, 151, 161
L'Homme qui marche (Giacometti, 1961), 257
Libération, 15, 44n29, 45, 65, 77, 92, 111, 133, 220n126, 277n63
Ligne Rouge, 57
L'Inde fantôme (Malle, 1969), 89
LIP (watch company), 76, 76n107, 76n108, 153, 154
Logocracy, 35, 79, 79n115
Loin du Vietnam (1967), 41, 88
Lord of the Flies (Brook, 1963), 209
L'Origine du monde (Courbet, 1866), 281–282
Lo sguardo di Michelangelo (Antonioni, 2004), 268
Lukács, Georg, 13, 16n35, 55, 56n60
Luttes en Italie/Lotte in Italia (1970), 48, 51–53, 96
Lyotard, Jean-François, 118, 118n87, 118n88, 137, 137n24, 179n8, 244n212

M
MacCabe, Colin, 31n1, 48n37, 49n41, 52n52
Macherey, Pierre, 80, 80n118
Machinic epistemology, 10
Mallarmé, Stéphane, 43, 166
Malle, Louis, 89

Malraux, André, 16, 161, 210, 215, 217, 218, 218n121, 223n140, 225, 241, 244, 255, 263
Malvinas (Falklands) War, 119
Man with a Movie Camera (Vertov, 1924), 162
Manet, Édouard, 167, 282
Maoism, 34, 35, 37, 49–55, 65, 74
Marithé-François Girbaud videos (1987), 6, 25, 165–167
Marivaux, Pierre de, 205
Marker, Chris, 74, 88, 89
Marxism, 5, 33, 36n10, 37, 89, 135, 150, 178, 297n4
Marxism-Leninism, 4, 24, 34, 74, 135, 296
Marxist historiography, 263
Mass media, 7, 20, 21, 25, 27, 91n10, 92, 93, 110–113, 116, 122, 127–131, 133, 136, 138, 142–144, 149, 159–161, 164, 165, 167, 169, 183, 198, 201, 202, 221, 276, 296, 302–304
Massumi, Brian, 34n5, 159, 199, 199n64
Materialism, 2, 3, 5n9, 6, 13, 47, 51, 55, 211
Materialist aesthetics, 2
Materialist cinema, 58, 61, 95, 95n23
Materialist fictions, 46, 54–67, 74
Materialist filmmaking, 3, 27, 28, 35, 55–67, 74, 120, 127–131, 168–172, 296–298
The Matrix (Wachowski brothers, 1999), 204
May 1968, 4, 11, 23, 24, 35, 37, 38, 40, 49, 52, 57, 57n62, 67, 70, 72, 75, 77, 111, 132, 135, 149, 150, 222, 276, 283
Mayolo, Carlos, 91
Mechanical reproduction, 127, 128, 146–149, 161, 256

Media technology, 254
Mediatization of mediation, 296
Mediterranean, 262, 265, 267–270, 272
Méditerranée (Pollet and Schlöndorff, 1963), 261–262, 269–272, 278
Meir, Golda, 145, 145n47, 151, 194
Melville, Jean-Pierre, 284
Memory, 6, 9, 13, 16, 20, 114n77, 127, 128, 143, 145–148, 145n48, 177–245, 254, 262–267, 269–272, 277, 282, 299, 306
Memory for Forgetfulness: August, Beirut, 1982 (Darwish), 276
Memory industry, 229
Merchandise, 165
Merleau-Ponty, Maurice, 5, 5n8, 32n2, 267
Messianism, 145n48, 151
Metaphor, 170, 172, 217, 217n116, 229, 240n200, 262, 265, 268, 281–283, 286, 288, 290
Me-Ti (Brecht), 64
Miéville, Anne-Marie, 4, 5, 7, 14, 21, 25, 32, 41, 69n91, 74, 75, 77–79, 81, 93, 97n27, 100, 101, 101n40, 103, 104, 107, 109–117, 116n82, 119, 128–133, 135, 136, 138–140, 149, 153, 161, 166, 168, 169, 171, 172, 178, 201, 222n134, 255–258, 276, 285, 296, 297, 302
Miéville, Roxy, 282, 286
Militancy, 121n96, 295
Militant film, 2, 46, 57–59, 92, 221, 259, 260, 295, 303
Militant filmmaker, 45, 60, 65, 74, 94, 95, 259, 296
Mistranslation (*traduttore, traditore*), 70, 72, 132

Modernity, 10, 28, 195, 236, 237, 305
Moi, je (1973), 137, 138
Mondzain, Marie-José, 14n28, 181n17, 184, 222n136, 223n137, 223n138
Montage, 6n9, 54, 99, 120, 127–172
Montesquieu, 208, 208n87
Morgan, Daniel, 134n19, 169, 169n111, 188n31, 285, 285n88, 296, 296n2
Mostar Bridge, 27, 198, 216, 217, 227, 235
Mozambique, 22, 111–115, 119, 133
Mujahideen, 220
Munich (terrorist attack 1972), 178
Musée imaginaire (Malraux, 1947), 161
Muselmann, 188n31, 191, 195
Music, 15, 242–245, 270, 284, 286n91, 296, 298
Muslim, 190, 191, 191n43, 195, 228, 229, 272, 280
Musset, Alfred de, 205
Myth of objectivity, 103, 104, 107, 108, 128

N

Nakba, 7, 26, 193, 195, 196, 227, 284, 304
Nancy, Jean-Luc, 184, 186, 186n25, 188, 240, 240n199, 245n214, 245n217
National liberation movements, 21
Native Americans, 12, 216n112
  See also "Red Indians"
NATO, 276
Nazis, Nazism, 6, 9n17, 20, 80n117, 151, 154, 184, 187, 189, 191, 194, 209, 211, 255, 262, 263, 284

Night Watch (Rembrandt, 1642), 169
Nixon, Richard, 145, 153
Nizan, Paul, 88
Notre musique (2004), 6, 21, 115, 204, 255, 276
Nouveaux Philosophes, 202
Nouvelle vague (1990), 5, 21, 283, 297
Now (Álvarez, 1965), 94
Nuit et brouillard (Resnais, 1955), 151, 227n154
Numéro Deux (1976), 5, 131, 179n7, 270

O

Objective denunciation, 32, 42–45
Objectivity, 43, 56, 58, 60, 90, 91, 93, 104, 106–110, 118, 128, 136, 137, 164
Occupation, Nazi (of France), 6, 20, 76, 96, 120, 158n91, 184, 203, 204, 209, 211, 226, 260, 263, 279, 280, 306
Odysseus, 208
"Oedipus in the Colonies" (Deleuze), 90, 107
The Old Place (2001), 7, 256
Oliveira, Manoel de, 269
On s'est tous défilé (1988), 25, 166
One American Movie or One A.M. (1968), 4, 12, 12n24, 55, 79, 96, 216
The Order of Things (Foucault), 154
Orientalism, 192
The Origin of the Milky Way (Tintoretto, 1575), 165, 169
Ospina, Luis, 91
Out of field, 106, 107, 130, 152, 163, 287, 288, 306
Outside, 17, 34, 49, 70, 90, 96, 97, 122, 131, 138, 153n73, 153n74, 156n85, 158, 158n89, 161, 166, 192, 192n45, 201, 204, 233, 235, 245, 275, 289
Overney, Pierre, 51, 60, 162

P

Palestine, 22, 47n36, 51, 77, 77n111, 88, 93, 98, 100, 103, 107, 111, 137, 149, 151, 154, 158, 159, 196, 206n80, 220, 226, 226n149, 234, 236, 238, 240–241n200, 241, 263, 270–276, 278–280, 301
Palestine Liberation Organization (PLO), 97, 100
Palestine question, 237, 276, 297
Palestinian revolution, 78, 92, 96–103, 145, 149, 162, 274, 276
Palimpsest, 194, 206, 217, 232, 276, 297
Paris Commune, 150
Pasolini, Pier Paolo, 89, 272
The Passenger (Antonioni, 1975), 24, 104–107, 105n52
Passion (1982), 5, 25, 109, 118, 133, 134, 164, 165, 168–172, 210, 296
Peace, 94, 197, 214, 215n110, 220, 234, 255, 280, 281
Pedagogy, 2, 58, 74, 81, 97, 103, 109, 136, 158
Péguy, Charles, 144n45, 147, 147n54
Pennebaker, D.N., 4, 12n24, 79
Péqueux, Gilles, 217, 221, 228, 230
PFLP, *see* Popular Front for the Liberation of Palestine (PFLP)
Phaedra, 227–234, 244
Phenomenology, 267, 268
Photo et Cie (1976), 112
Photograms, 13, 162, 163, 182, 275n58

Photojournalism, 88, 108n58, 159, 256
Picasso, Pablo, 32, 40, 44, 75, 79n113, 80, 257
Pickpocket (Bresson, 1959), 204
Pliny the Elder, 146, 146n53
Poète maudit, 107
Poetic image, 267–269, 281
Poiesis, 2, 19, 169, 221, 222, 222n134
Point of view, 10, 11, 19, 59n66, 65, 76n108, 90, 92, 95, 99, 101, 103, 106, 112, 118, 121n96, 135, 137, 157, 159, 190, 199, 256, 277, 279, 290, 296, 297n4
Political engagement, 5, 10, 15, 17, 21, 31–33, 37n11, 102, 105, 278, 296
Political film, 3, 58, 74, 131, 132
Political tourism, 54, 77, 96
Politics of representation, 6, 90
Politics of the image, 104, 296
Politics of visibility, 6
Pollet, Jean-Daniel, 261, 269, 271, 272
Polyphony, 243
Polysemy, 194, 284
Pontecorvo, Gillo, 89
Popular Front for the Liberation of Palestine (PFLP), 92, 101
Pornomiseria, 90–91, 94
Post-anthropocentric, 258, 286, 289
Post-humanism, 258
Post-structuralism, 11, 62, 186
Poverty of expression, 205, 205n77
Power relations, 130, 161, 170, 172
Pravda (1969), 48, 96
Praxis, 31, 35, 46, 58, 98, 99, 221, 222, 222n134, 301
Prayer, 112, 209, 217, 224
Precarious life, 181, 192, 227
Prehension, 144, 157, 158, 160
Presence, 2, 22, 40, 63, 80, 111, 117, 135, 162, 169, 179, 183, 186, 189, 197, 207, 216, 222, 224, 226, 235, 237, 245, 253, 266, 267, 273, 277, 291, 299, 302, 303
Prière pour refuzniks 1 (2006), 199, 224
Proletarian Left Party (*Gauche Prolétarienne*), 45
Proletariat, 5, 11, 33, 39, 44, 56, 60, 88, 132, 150, 170, 211, 299
Propaganda, 90, 98, 99, 107, 113
Psychogeography, 39
Publicity, 143, 256, 257
Pure past, 227–234

Q
Quotation, 19, 273, 274

R
Racine, Jean, 233, 233n176, 277
Racism, 77, 89, 236, 237, 297n4, 302
Rancière, Jacques, 9n18, 10n20, 50, 180n12, 184, 186, 186n24, 188n31, 189n37, 190n38, 298, 302, 302n15, 303n16
Reactionary, 33, 48n39, 101, 130
Real, the, 9, 13, 31, 39, 56, 104, 151, 169, 181, 223n142, 241, 245, 253, 254, 259, 262, 264, 266–269, 290, 303
Realism, 13, 33, 36–40, 55–57, 60, 62–67, 260, 267
Realist films, 38n15
Reality, 5, 11, 13, 16, 20, 31, 35, 47, 55–60, 62, 63, 65–67, 74, 81, 87, 90–92, 99, 100, 141, 142, 148, 163, 170, 184, 190, 204, 204n75, 218, 220, 222, 223, 230, 254–257, 259–261, 265–268, 270, 276, 285, 288, 297, 298, 302, 305, 306

Reconciliation, 27, 36, 53, 203, 205, 206, 212, 213n99, 217, 228–230, 234, 279, 304
Reconstruction, 27, 42, 189, 206, 228–230, 242
"Red Indians," 71, 206, 216, 227, 234, 235, 237, 277
Redemption/messianic image, 145n48, 151, 208, 215, 217, 258, 263
Redundant populations, 301, 303, 306
Referent, 2, 33, 36, 66, 137, 157, 191, 259, 262, 266, 270
Reflexivity, 10, 12, 36, 60, 61
Refuseniks, 224
  See also Prière pour refuzniks 1 (2006)
Rehabilitation, 217, 230, 232, 233, 304
Relationships of production, 3, 6, 48, 55, 130
Religious fundamentalism, 215
Rembrandt, 165, 169, 210
Remembrance, 147, 229
Renoir, Jean, 165, 167
Repetition, 47, 103, 135n20, 141, 143, 145n48, 157, 158, 158n89, 204, 223, 270, 283
Representation, 2–5, 10–15, 20, 23, 24, 26, 27, 34–36, 39–41, 39n18, 54, 58, 61, 62, 65, 67n82, 72, 73, 90, 91, 93, 95, 95n23, 102, 107, 115, 127, 128, 135, 139, 139n30, 145, 157, 169, 179, 182–197, 254–256, 259–261, 266, 270, 271, 276, 295, 299, 303, 304
Representativity, 15–20, 34, 35, 37, 38, 166, 170, 205, 221, 296, 297
Resemblances, 64, 154, 182, 223, 224, 245
Resistance, 6, 16, 28, 35n8, 37, 76, 96, 100, 109, 110, 120n94, 145, 156n85, 158n91, 178, 184, 198–208, 211, 260, 262, 263, 271, 280, 298, 300, 303, 306
Resnais, Alain, 88, 151, 192n44, 227n154
Restitution, 6, 8, 22, 145, 177–245, 276, 297, 299, 300, 304
Retour de l'URSS (Gide, 1936), 88
Reverdy, Pierre, 63
Revolt, 28, 132, 295, 299
Revolution, 2, 6, 20, 22, 28, 33, 34, 36, 38, 41, 42, 46, 46n34, 47n36, 57, 62, 64, 68, 78, 87–92, 90n7, 96–104, 111–115, 119, 121n96, 135, 145, 148–151, 155, 158, 161, 162, 178, 194, 200, 204, 216, 222, 222n135, 255, 260, 264, 274, 276, 289, 295, 299, 305, 306
Revolutionary cinema, 95, 272
Revolutionary failure, 78, 101, 107
Revolutionary subjects, 21
"Right to fiction" (Said), 207, 222, 226, 239
Rimbaud, Arthur, 23, 105, 105n51, 110, 110n63, 139, 139n31
Rocha, Glauber, 90, 94–96, 121n96
Rodowick, D.N., 14n30, 137n25, 143, 143n42, 155n83, 223, 223n141
Romanian revolution, 218n119
Rossellini, Roberto, 27, 89
Rouch, Jean, 89
Roussopoulos, Carole, 59, 59n66, 74, 107n57
Ruins, 6, 27, 189, 204, 205, 217, 223, 227, 230, 238, 240, 255
Russian avant-gardes, 46, 97

S
Sacred, 14, 109, 164, 183, 222, 245n215, 256, 257
The sacred of the image, 2

Said, Edward, 239, 274, 274n53, 276n59
Sanbar, Elias, 10n19, 27, 111, 112n72, 177, 177n1, 178, 191, 191n43, 216, 226n149, 227n157, 234, 234n182, 240, 240n197, 273–277, 273n50, 274n52, 277n64
Sarajevo, 26, 27, 53, 205, 205n78, 206, 209–213, 217–221, 217n116, 219n123, 220n126, 220n127, 223, 227, 230, 232, 239, 240, 240–241n200, 276, 278
Sartre, Jean-Paul, 2, 15, 32, 33, 37n11, 40, 51, 68n87, 69n90, 76n108, 78–81, 78n113, 79n114, 88, 88n3, 138n28
Scemama, Céline, 184, 188n31, 193n49, 194n51, 195n55
Scénario du film Passion (1982), 165, 168, 169, 270
Schindler's List (Spielberg, 1993), 202
Schlöndorff, Volker, 261, 269
Schygulla, Hanna, 164, 169, 170
Scientific/theoretical filmmaking, 5, 62
Seikun-PFLP: Sekai Senso Sengen (The Red Army/PFLP Declaration of World War, 1971), 101
Self-determination, 21, 22, 100–102, 197, 237, 274, 279
Self-knowledge, 56–58, 61, 297
Self-reflexivity, 9–10, 12, 58, 103, 135
Self-representation, 2, 6, 121
Semiocapitalism, 172, 254, 258
Senghor, Leopold Sedar, 88
Sensory memory, 269–272
Sensible politics, 28, 298, 303
Sensible regimes, 7, 254, 262, 264, 266, 276, 297, 298, 300
Sensorial anesthetization, 265

"Sepulchre South: Gaslight" (Faulkner, 1940), 165
Shelley, Mary, 285, 289, 290
Shoah (Lanzmann, 1985), 5, 7, 26, 151, 153, 183–197, 202, 203, 206, 214, 227, 280, 284, 285, 299, 304, 306
Shot/reverse-shot (champ/contre-champ), 9, 21, 26, 28, 115, 195, 211, 222, 224n142, 225–228, 227n157, 277, 288, 289
Signals, 161, 213, 242, 267
Signifiance, 153n73, 156, 156n85, 158, 159n93
Signifier, 11, 17, 33, 34, 36, 62, 65, 66, 102, 103, 128, 142, 152, 153n73, 155–159, 255, 259, 262, 270
Signs, 14, 18, 20, 39, 54, 94, 127, 129, 146, 153n73, 156, 159, 161, 166, 179, 183, 217, 220–222, 228, 242, 253, 281, 284, 298
Silverman, Kaja, 3n6, 19, 19n40, 62n72, 66n81, 168, 169, 169n110
Sino-Soviet split, 34, 49, 73
Situationism, 35–36, 152
Sivan, Eyal, 195, 195n54
Six Fois Deux: Sur et sous la communication (1976), 5, 69n91, 112, 116, 131
Social Darwinism, 179, 301, 302, 304
Socialism, 28, 88, 90, 102, 104, 145, 259–261, 264, 280
Socialist politics, 259
Social responsibility, 121, 304
Societé pour le lancement des oeuvres nouvelles (SLON), 57, 58, 72n100
Society of the Spectacle (Debord, 1973), 32, 129

Soft and Hard (1985), 14, 21, 133, 136, 222n134
Soigne ta droite (1987), 151, 297
Solanas, Fernando, 96, 121n96
Sollers, Philippe, 261, 271, 271n46, 286, 286n91
Solzhenitsyn, A., 95, 101, 286
Sonimage, 4, 6, 21, 32, 92–93, 100, 102, 104–117, 120, 128–131, 133, 135, 136, 136n22, 138, 140, 140n33, 151, 169, 179, 296
Sontag, Susan, 104n50, 108n58, 119n90, 145n50, 180n11, 189n36, 205n78, 210n94, 217n116, 218–220, 218n120, 219n122, 219n123, 219n125, 254, 254n3, 265, 265n28, 278
Soubirous, Bernadette de, 109, 167
Soulages, Pierre, 282
Sovereignty, 232, 236n185
Soviet Union, 53, 87, 88
Spanish Civil War, 16, 87, 88, 218, 263, 278
Spanish Earth (Ivens, 1937), 87
Spatio-temporalization, 137
Spectacle, 7, 20, 24, 37–40, 40n21, 110, 116, 127–131, 145, 146, 186, 254, 286, 286n91
Speech, 10–12, 14, 17, 19, 22, 50, 50n45, 62, 67–75, 77, 79, 80, 110, 111, 119, 132, 133, 134n18, 135–138, 145, 170, 172, 179, 182, 183, 185, 189, 190, 193, 198, 200, 224, 233, 241–244, 243n205, 287, 302, 303
Speech acts, 80, 109, 109n62, 136, 137, 139, 142, 159, 224, 234, 276
"Speech of the Red Indian" (Darwish, 1993), 216, 235, 237n189
Spielberg, Steven, 188n31, 202, 203

Spiritual mobility, 268
Stammering, 11, 67, 70, 71, 73, 109, 134, 170
State of exception, 22, 192, 206
Stoppage, 161–168
Stratigraphy, 15, 104n48
Strike (Eisenstein, 1925), 299
Subjectivation, 6, 37, 104, 110, 136, 260, 295
Suleiman, Elias, 228, 255
Superimposition, 172, 211, 216n112, 232
Surrealism, 39
Survivors, 26, 147, 189, 190, 195, 206, 207, 210, 214, 227, 239, 242
Syncategoreme, 154, 155

T
Tel Quel, 17n36, 261
Television (as social technique), 3, 5, 12n24, 21, 48, 69n91, 97, 103, 109, 112, 113, 116, 117, 119, 119n91, 120, 128, 129, 132, 136, 136n23, 148, 149, 159, 165, 178, 179, 179n6, 183, 210, 285
Territorial dispossession, 273
Terrorism, 31, 75, 95n22, 100, 145, 153, 178, 214
Theoretical practice, 3, 36n10, 56, 61, 62, 297
Third Cinema, 94, 96n24, 121, 121n96
Third image, 93, 182
Third World, 21, 22, 24, 65, 87–122, 95n22, 95n23, 96n24, 121n96, 131, 300, 301
Third Worldism, 4, 21, 22, 77, 89, 101, 102, 120, 121, 145, 300
See also Tiermondisme

3D technology, 7, 28, 283, 287, 288
Three Songs about Lenin (Vertov, 1933), 155
Tiermondisme, 21
  See also Third Worldism
Tintoretto, Jacopo, 165, 169, 170
Totalitarianism, 2, 101, 106, 286
Toufic, Jalaal, 305, 305n19
Tourism, 54, 77, 96–100, 122, 228n158, 229, 230, 254, 264–266, 268, 302, 304
Tout va bien (1972), 4, 21, 42, 49, 51n51, 52, 59, 60, 65, 92, 135, 157, 162
Trademark images, 24, 130, 142–151, 161, 165, 183, 210
Transparency, 56, 63, 242, 254, 266, 267, 302
Trauma, 26, 185, 197, 200, 299, 305
Trojan poet, 239, 240
Trojan War, 234, 239
Truffaut, François, 217
Truth, 6, 9, 20, 22, 34, 37, 39, 43, 44, 47, 56, 58, 62, 63, 67, 72, 73, 100, 102n46, 112n71, 128, 144, 178, 186, 187, 189, 196, 200, 211, 225, 241, 256, 257, 267, 269, 274
Tsahal (Lanzmann, 1993), 272
Tse-Tung, Mao, 53

U

Um filme falado (Oliveira, 2003), 269, 271
Un captif amoureux (Genet, 1986), 272
Unemployment, 76, 131, 134
UNESCO, 217, 228
Uninterrupted montage, 99
Union de Jeunes Communistes Marxistes-Léninistes (UJC), 50
Unitary urbanism, 39
Universalism, 28, 298, 301, 305
UNPROFOR, 220
Unrepresentable, 14, 26, 134n19, 177–245
Unthought, 9, 142, 153, 153n73, 157, 158
Utopia, 5n9, 20, 27, 67, 87, 120, 128, 264, 266

V

Vanquished, 6, 27, 183, 204, 206, 207, 211, 212, 212n97, 238–242, 297, 305
Varda, Agnès, 68n87, 74, 88, 280
Vautier, René, 89
Velázquez, Diego, 167
Vérité, 87, 287
  See also Truth
Veronica's veil, 19, 169
Vertov, Dziga, 2, 10, 32, 35, 46, 47, 47n35, 49n42, 52n52, 94, 98, 99, 99n32, 108, 120, 138, 141, 142, 142n38, 155, 156, 162
Victims, 22, 25, 26, 102, 130, 181, 183, 185, 192n44, 193, 196n57, 197, 200, 201, 207, 207n85, 209, 210, 212, 220, 226, 230, 232, 240–242, 276, 289, 302
Victor, Pierre, 50n45, 69n90, 76n108
Videographic machinic expression, 24, 129, 140
Video-mélange, 25, 167
Vijećnica Library, 27, 216, 218, 222, 227, 230
Virgil, 208, 239
Virtuality, 144, 144n45, 147
Virtual reality, 204
Visual regime, 3, 256, 260, 288
Vivre sa vie (1962), 42

Vladimir et Rosa (1971), 47n36, 48, 52, 65
Voice-over, 15, 18, 25, 41, 72, 74, 77, 79, 79n116, 93n13, 94, 95, 103, 110, 128, 135, 136, 153, 154, 161, 163, 167, 171, 178, 190, 198, 201, 208, 244, 254, 255, 261, 269n42, 271, 271n46, 272, 275, 278, 281n76, 296n3
Voyage au Congo (Gide and Allégret, 1925), 89
Voyage(s) en utopie (2006 exhibition), 27, 254, 259
Vrai faux passeport (2006), 7, 27, 168

W

Wachowski brothers, 204
Wajcman, Gérard, 26, 184
Waiting for Godot (Beckett), 205n78, 219, 219n123
Wakamatsu, Koji, 101
War of position, 35, 35n8, 37, 74, 75
Wars of annihilation, 194, 198–208, 232, 276, 305
Weekend (1967), 19, 216, 259
Weil, Simone, 50n46, 88, 88n4, 218, 218n121, 233n174, 234, 234n181, 272, 272n47
Weizman, Eyal, 185n21, 197, 197n58, 197n59, 197n60
Weltanschauung, 37, 55, 60
"What is there to be done?" 11, 33, 33n3, 50, 116
"Who speaks and acts? For whom and how?" 11, 24, 34, 41, 135
Wiazemsky, Anne, 65, 71, 72, 96, 259
Wieviorka, Annette, 185, 185n20
Williams, James S., 4, 188n31, 206n80, 217n114, 283n82, 285n89, 297n4

Witness images, 177–183, 207, 299, 301
Witnessing/testimony, 2, 22, 25, 91, 130, 146, 147, 179–181, 183–197, 200, 207, 212n98, 219, 226n152, 254, 276, 299, 302, 303
Witt, Michael, 4, 19n41, 45n31, 116, 116n82, 143, 144n43, 183, 183n19, 188n31, 214n106, 224n142, 243n210, 258n10, 282n80, 285n86
Wollen, Peter, 31n1, 51n51, 52n52, 64n78, 70n94, 104, 105n52
Workers, 11, 16, 22, 24, 25, 34, 35, 37, 44, 46, 49–51, 53, 57, 59, 65, 66–67n82, 68–71, 71n96, 71n98, 72n100, 75, 75n106, 76, 102, 103n47, 132–134, 134n18, 150, 151, 155, 163, 163n100, 164n103, 168–172, 203, 222, 299, 301
Working class, 21, 25, 37, 40, 41, 50, 57, 68, 75, 114, 130, 134, 134n18, 150, 154, 166, 260, 300
World War II, 8, 8n17, 16, 33, 184, 204, 211, 306
The Wretched of the Earth (Fanon, 1961), 88

Y

Yeshurun, Helit, 211, 212, 237n190

Z

Zagdanski, Stéphane, 193
Zionism, 226, 273, 274
Zoller, Pierre-Henri, 44n27

CPSIA information can be obtained
at www.ICGtesting.com
Printed in the USA
LVHW081828300419
616115LV00002B/3/P